DECISION ESTIMATION AND CLASSIFICATION

An Introduction to Pattern Recognition and Related Topics

DECISION ESTIMATION AND CLASSIFICATION

An Introduction to Pattern Recognition and Related Topics

CHARLES W. THERRIEN

Naval Postgraduate School

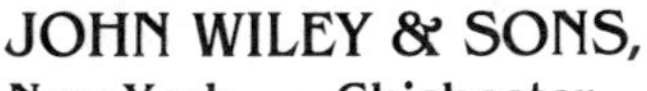

JOHN WILEY & SONS,

New York Chichester Brisbane Toronto Singapore

Library of Congress Cataloging in Publication Data:

Therrien, Charles W.

Decision, estimation, and classification : an introduction to pattern recognition and related topics / Charles W. Therrien.

p. cm.

Bibliography: p.

Includes index.

ISBN 0-471-83102-6 (pbk.)

1. Pattern recognition systems. I. Title.

TK7882.P3T47 1989 88-22340

006.4—dc19 CIP

Printed in the United States of America

10 9 8 7 6 5 4 3 2 1

To my Mom,
and the memory of my grandparents

CONTENTS

CHAPTER 1 INTRODUCTION

CHAPTER 2 PROBABILITY THEORY FOR RANDOM VECTORS

CHAPTER 3 SIMPLE STATISTICAL DECISION PROCEDURES

CHAPTER 4 OPERATIONS UPON RANDOM VECTORS

CHAPTER 5 FEATURE EXTRACTION AND NONLINEAR MAPPING

CHAPTER 6 QUADRATIC AND LINEAR CLASSIFIERS

CHAPTER 7 PARAMETER ESTIMATION

CHAPTER 8 NONPARAMETRIC ESTIMATION AND CLASSIFICATION

CHAPTER 9 ESTIMATING AND BOUNDING THE PROBABILITY OF ERROR

CHAPTER 10 CLASSIFICATION OF STATIONARY TIME SERIES

CHAPTER 11 CONTEXT-DEPENDENT METHODS

PREFACE

The statistical theory of decision, estimation, and classification is fundamental to many of the automated electronic systems that are in existence today. Its applications range from military defense and reconnaissance to medical monitoring and diagnosis, to home entertainment. Statistical pattern recognition addresses these problem areas through a common framework of analysis that allows the design of algorithms for automated systems to be developed in a reliable and practical way.

Pattern recognition was an area of intense activity in the 1960s and 1970s when the foundations of the methodology were being laid, and its applications have continued to flourish in the last decade. Furthermore, new results have evolved that enhance the earlier work and allow treatment of a broader class of problems. Advances in digital signal processing, computer systems, and integrated circuit technology have all spurred the development of military, commercial, and consumer-based systems that provide for automated decision, recognition, or related functions.

This book arose from a desire to present fundamentals of decision-making systems in general, and pattern recognition systems in particular, to readers in a relatively short, informative, and easy-to-grasp manner. The reader is assumed to have a general background in engineering, mathematics, or the physical sciences, but is not assumed to be knowledgeable in decision and estimation theory. Those who have had experience in a related area such as statistical communication theory, however, should find it easy to extend their knowledge to the special topics treated in this book and will hopefully find many of the more advanced topics of interest. Portions of these chapters were taught as a one-semester graduate level course at Northeastern University and at the Naval Postgraduate School. Since then the work has been expanded and revised considerably to bring in more material and examples. In its present form the book is suitable both for individual study by the practicing professional who wants to learn about pattern recognition, and for classroom use in a formal graduate program of study in engineering or computer science.

The book covers a wide range of topics starting from fundamental ideas in the early chapters and proceeding to advanced research topics in the later chapters. Consequently, it should be of interest to a wide spectrum of readers. After an introduction and definition of some basic ideas in Chapter 1, the reader is provided with a review of probability theory for random vectors in Chapter 2. The treatment is informal rather than axiomatic, with an emphasis on developing intuition and concepts in a form that can be used later. Chapter 3 is devoted to classical hypothesis testing and develops the theory on which most classification algorithms are based.

This chapter develops Bayes, Neyman–Pearson, and the Wald sequential methods of hypothesis testing. Chapter 4 is a combined review of linear algebra and an exposition of further ideas that relate to the statistical description of random vectors. Second moment statistics and the multivariate Gaussian density function are introduced here.

Chapter 5 deals with two traditional topics in pattern recognition that are usually treated separately. These are the topics of feature extraction and nonlinear mapping. Feature extraction is motivated from the point of view of sufficient statistics, and linear methods based on eigenvector analysis are discussed. Nonlinear mapping is developed as another type of transformation applied to random vectors. An example of a nonlinear mapping algorithm that can be used as a feature extraction procedure is given.

Quadratic and linear classifiers are introduced in Chapter 6. The quadratic classifier is developed as an optimal decision rule for Gaussian random vectors. The linear classifier is derived first as a special case of the quadratic, and then separately in a form that maximizes the Fisher criterion.

Chapter 7 begins the treatment of estimation theory and describes classical methods of estimation for both vector (i.e., multiple) parameters and random vectors. Chapter 8 deals with nonparametric methods. Parzen density estimation and the nearest-neighbor algorithm are developed as methods leading to nonparametric forms of classifiers. A brief introduction to nonparametric statistical methods is also given here, and some resulting forms of classification algorithms are considered. Chapter 9 focuses on methods of performance evaluation including Bhattacharayya and Chernoff bounds, bounds related to the nearest neighbor classifier, and methods of testing a classifier.

The last three chapters are for the most part devoted to newer and more advanced topics. Chapter 10 deals with the classification of stationary time series. This chapter uses ideas that will be familiar to those who are trained in statistical signal processing or detection and estimation theory for communications systems. However, the ideas are explained here without assuming any of this specialized background in electrical engineering. A form of classifier is developed that is particularly well suited to sequential testing.

Chapter 11 deals with methods of classification for interrelated objects. Most of the methodology has been developed or applied only in the last decade. The chapter begins with a description of the procedures that have come to be known as "relaxation methods." It goes on to examine a number of problems based on Markov models including some applications in image processing based on Markov random fields. It then describes a more general theory of classification in context and attempts to relate this to the methods discussed earlier in this chapter and in Chapter 3.

Chapter 12 is the last chapter and deals with three topics that are not treated elsewhere in the book. The first of these is unsupervised learning or clustering. Although clustering is not an advanced topic, it has a flavor of its own. A basic development of the ideas is followed by a description of the ISODATA algorithm. Clustering is then related to the application area of vector quantization coding (of signals and images for transmission and storage). The chapter then moves on to the topic of classification by significance testing. Fundamental ideas in statistical significance testing are developed and applied to classification problems where a statistical description of one class is available but statistical descriptions for other classes are not. The method is illustrated with an image processing problem. Finally, the rather new area of distributed classification is introduced. In distributed classification problems many observers view a common phenomenon and must work together under the constraint of limited communication to perform classification. The theoretical and practical problems of classification in this type of scenario are formidable; a few very recent results are discussed to provide a brief introduction to this fascinating area.

These opening remarks would not be complete without an acknowledgment of the many people who contributed both directly and indirectly to my experience in this area and to the writing of this book. In particular, I express appreciation to the people in former Group 92 of Lincoln Laboratory, and especially to W. H. Schoendorf and A. A. Grometstein, who were willing to take a chance on a novice engineer and let him learn about pattern recognition along with them. I also want to express my appreciation to Ken Fukunaga of Purdue, our great mentor and friend who taught me many things including that it is all right at times to be a "10% engineer." In addition, I want to thank Art Baggeroer of M.I.T., whose well-founded skepticism then, as well as now, continues to keep us honest with ourselves. Thanks are also due to Marty Kalisky of California Polytechnic State University, who encouraged me to publish what was originally only a small set of notes and who introduced me to the people at John Wiley. Finally, I wish to acknowledge Barbara Potkay, who did an excellent job in typing essentially all of the manuscript, and Roberto Cristy and Paul Moose of the Naval Postgraduate School for their review of some of the later chapters.

CHARLES W. THERRIEN
Monterey, California

CHAPTER 1

Introduction

Decision-making problems occur in numerous scientific and engineering applications ranging from basic measurements of the environment to machine-intelligent operations such as vision and speech recognition. Systems that perform some sort of pattern recognition or decision making surround us daily. Examples of these systems are the burglar alarms that protect homes, offices, and automobiles; remote control devices that control home entertainment systems, readers of UPC bar codes that expedite pricing and inventory of retail merchandise; and readers of magnetic-strip codes on credit cards that identify the user and determine if a purchase is authorized [1]. Often the information available to make a decision is less than precise and frequently the decision procedures are statistical in nature. The field of pattern recognition has evolved as a setting for studying general statistical-based decision methods particularly as they relate to implementation as digital information-processing algorithms. Algorithms similar to those employed in pattern recognition have been developed in other areas: particularly communication, signal processing, and control. Our purpose here is to study classes of decision algorithms primarily from the point of view of pattern recognition but more broadly to include decision-making procedures that could occur in any number of scientific and engineering applications.

1.1 DEFINITION OF PATTERN RECOGNITION

The goal of pattern recognition is to classify objects of interest into one of a number of categories or *classes*. The objects of interest are generically called *patterns* and may be printed letters or characters, biological cells, electronic waveforms or signals, "states" of a system or any number of other things that one may desire to classify. The algorithms are generally to be implemented on a digital computer or on a special piece of hardware to provide automatic recognition of the patterns without human intervention.

If there exists some set of patterns, the individual classes of which are already known, then one has a problem in *supervised pattern recognition*. The basic procedure followed in design of a supervised pattern recognition system is illustrated

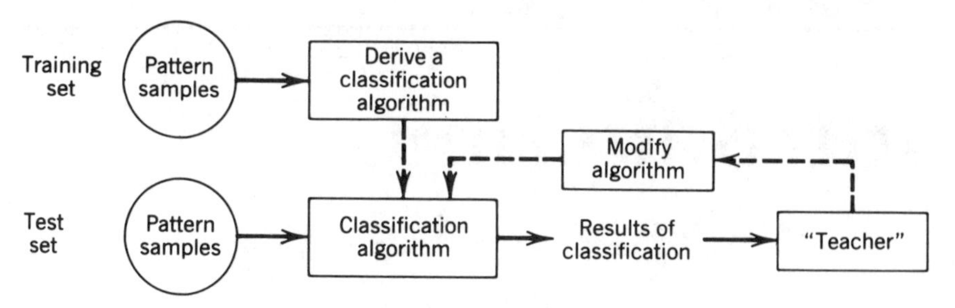

FIGURE 1.1 **The design procedure in supervised pattern recognition.**

in Fig. 1.1. A portion of the set of labeled patterns is extracted and used to derive a classification algorithm. These patterns comprise the *training set*. The remaining patterns are then used to test the classification algorithm; these patterns are collectively referred to as the *test set*. Since the correct classes of the individual patterns in the test set are also known, one can evaluate the performance of the algorithm. In pattern recognition problems of this sort, one often thinks of the results as being evaluated by a teacher or supervisor whose output dictates suitable modifications to the algorithm—hence the term *supervised pattern recognition*. Once a desired level of performance is achieved (which is measured in terms of the misclassification rate), the algorithm can be used on initially unlabeled patterns. Although now the feedback loop involving the teacher is formally broken, it is usually advisable to have some spot-checking of results. Such checks can be accommodated either by providing an alternative classification algorithm (such as a human observer) or in some situations by waiting a sufficient length of time until the correct classification is known. The latter form of checking procedure may be possible for example in the analysis of seismographic data for the detection of earthquakes.

If the classes of all of the available patterns are unknown, and perhaps even the number of these classes is unknown, then one has a problem in *unsupervised pattern recognition* or *clustering*. In clustering problems, one attempts to find classes of patterns with similar properties where sometimes even these properties may be undefined. Clustering problems occur in many chemical and medical applications where, for example, one may be attempting to categorize types of compounds or cells. Clustering problems may also occur in psychological, social, or economic studies as well, but they are not limited to these fields. Needless to say, the unsupervised pattern recognition or clustering problem is a much more difficult one than the supervised pattern recognition problem. Nevertheless, useful algorithms have been developed in this area and success depends to a large extent on the ability to learn the structure of pattern measurement data in high-dimensional spaces.

1.2 EXAMPLES OF PATTERN RECOGNITION PROBLEMS

Three examples of pattern recognition are presented in this section to illustrate the approach of pattern recognition and to define some relevant concepts.

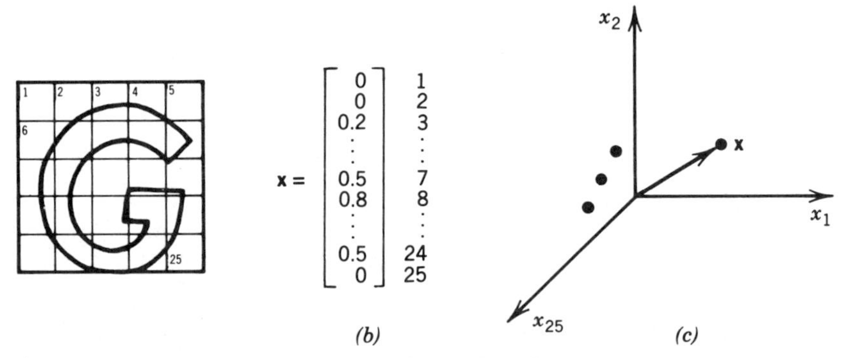

FIGURE 1.2 An observation vector for a printed character.

■ EXAMPLE 1.1

Character Recognition

Let the objects to be classified be various printed characters such as letters of the English alphabet and numerals. The classes in a pattern recognition problem are usually identified by the lowercase Greek letter ω with a numerical subscript. Thus the classes in this example could be denoted by $\omega_1, \omega_2, \ldots$ with ω_1 corresponding to "A", ω_2 corresponding to "B", and so on. In an optical character reader, the character can be thought of as projected onto a grid of cells as shown in Fig. 1.2 (*a*). Suppose, hypothetically for this example, that the grid has 25 cells and that thc electrical output of each cell increases as more of the character appears in the cell. Then one can define a 25-dimensional vector **x** comprised of the cell outputs; the ith component of **x** is proportional to the fraction of the ith cell covered by the character (see Fig. 1.2). The vector **x** is called the *observation vector* and the multidimensional space X in which it resides is called the *observation space*. Both are depicted in Fig. 1.2. Figure 1.3 shows the basic scheme for pattern recognition. A printed character is observed by some measurement device that produces the observation vector **x.** The observation vector is fed into a pattern recognition system whose output is a classification of the vector as one of the classes ω_i. Our concern here will be solely with the pattern recognition system, that is, with that part of the problem to the right of the dotted line. We shall not be concerned at all with the problem of making measurements on the patterns and producing observation vectors. Since the pattern recognition system always starts with an observation

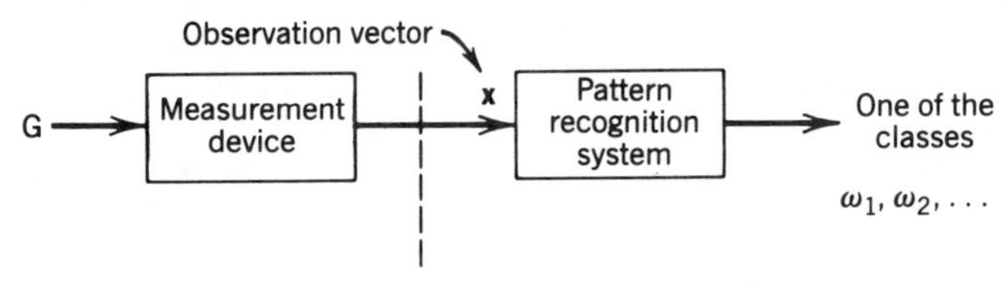

FIGURE 1.3 The basic scheme for pattern recognition.

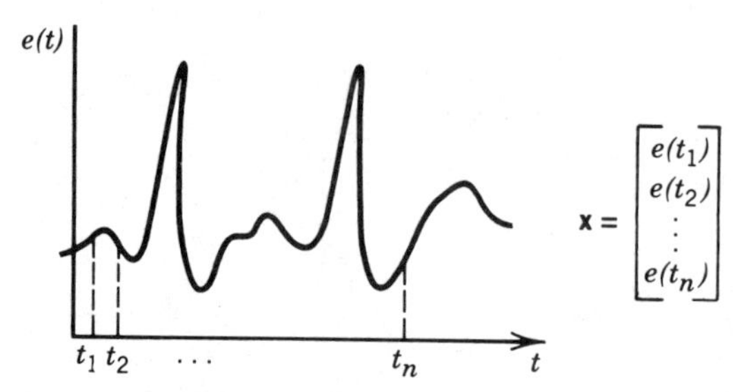

FIGURE 1.4 The formation of an observation vector for medical (EKG) diagnosis.

vector instead of the physical object to be classified, pattern recognition algorithms can often be developed without reference to a specific application. ■

■ EXAMPLE 1.2

Medical Diagnosis

Suppose that one is trying to distinguish normal hearts from hearts with ventricular defects by analysis of the electrocardiogram (EKG). This is a two-class pattern recognition problem in which the patterns to be classified are the various EKGs. One can form an observation vector whose i^{th} component is a sample of the EKG at the time t_i (see Fig. 1.4). The observation vector **x** is passed as in the previous example to a pattern recognition algorithm, which classifies it as being derived from either a normal heart (ω_1) or a heart with a ventricular defect (ω_2). ■

■ EXAMPLE 1.3

Psychology Experiment

Let the objects of interest be the members of the incoming freshman class at the Monterey Institute of Technology (M.I.T.). It is desired, to classify these potential geniuses or lunkheads into categories for future correlation with their scholastic achievement. But what are the categories and what students go into which ones? This is a problem in clustering! Dr. Byrdwhisker, who is conducting the experiment, decides to have each entering freshman fill out a questionnaire of some 200 items he thinks may be related to scholastic ability. The score on each question, which is on a scale of 1 to 10, becomes the component of a 200-dimensional observation vector in an observation space of the same dimensionality. Dr. Byrdwhisker enters this data into his Super-novel PDQ-8 computer, applies a triple inversion and an over-the-valley and next-to-your-neighbor clustering algorithm, followed by a non-linear mapping into three dimensions, to derive the classes or *clusters* and their members. We shall have to wait another four years to see if Dr. Byrdwhisker's clusters bear any relation to the scholastic achievement of the students. ■

These examples, and in fact every problem in pattern recognition, have at least two things in common. First the patterns are represented by vectors in a multidimensional space. This implies that in order to solve such pattern recognition problems, one must be able to deal with these vectors and linear transformations (represented by matrices) or sometimes even nonlinear transformations of these vectors. Thus the study of pattern recognition requires some knowledge of results from the fields of vector spaces and linear algebra. Secondly, one does not have an exact description of the various classes of objects—at least not in a deterministic sense. (Even if it were possible to describe each class deterministically, for most problems of interest that would be highly impractical.) Thus the pattern recognition problem, as we shall treat it, is inherently a probabilistic topic. The observation vectors for patterns to be classified are multidimensional random variables or *random vectors* and must be described in a statistical sense, that is by probability distributions, densities, moments, spectra, or other statistical functions. Similarly, the performance of the algorithm must be measured in a statistical sense, for example, by the probability of misclassification or *probability of error*. Thus an adequate background in probability and statistics is also important for these problems. Both concepts from probability and statistics and concepts from linear algebra, relevant to our treatment of pattern recognition, are reviewed and developed in the next few chapters.

1.3 THE PATTERN RECOGNITION APPROACH

Figure 1.5 represents a more detailed view of the box in Fig. 1.3 that we labeled a "pattern recognition system." The observation vector $\mathbf{x}$ is first transformed into another vector $\mathbf{y}$ whose components are called *features*. The features are intended to be fewer in number than the observations but should collectively contain most of the information needed for classification of the patterns. By reducing the observations to a smaller number of features, one hopes to design a decision rule that is more reliable. When the number of variables is large, it is difficult to obtain good estimates for the parameters of the decision rule. The feature vector $\mathbf{y}$ can be represented in a feature space Y similar to the way that observation vectors are represented in the observation space. The dimension of the feature space, however, is usually much lower than the dimension of the observation space.

Procedures that analyze data in an attempt to define appropriate features are called *feature extraction procedures*. Feature extraction procedures may be based

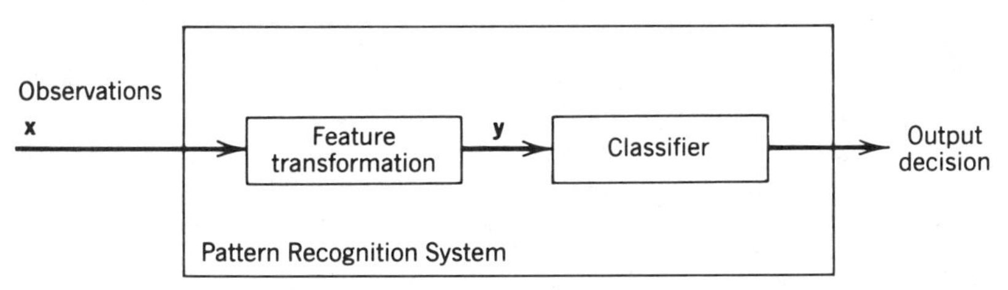

FIGURE 1.5 The basic approach to pattern recognition.

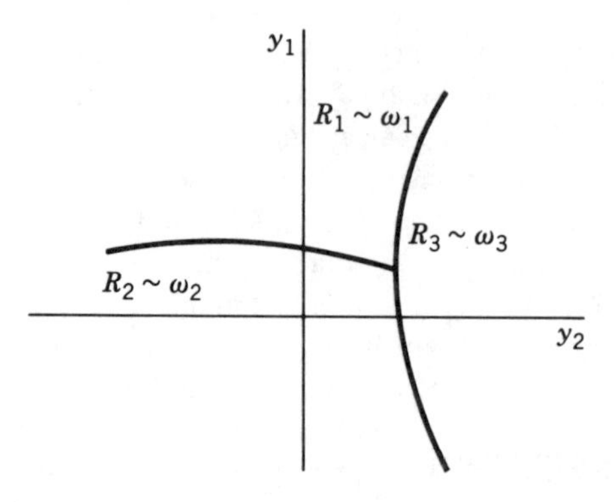

FIGURE 1.6 Partitioning of feature space induced by a classifier.

on intuition or physical considerations of the problem or they may be purely mathematical techniques that seek to reduce the dimensionality of the observation space in a prescribed way. Some of the latter types of feature extraction techniques will be discussed in Chapter 5.

The feature vector $\mathbf{y}$ is passed to a *classifier* whose purpose is to make a decision about the pattern. The classifier essentially induces a partitioning of the feature space into a number of disjoint regions as shown in Fig. 1.6. If the feature vector corresponding to a pattern falls into region R_i, the pattern is assigned to class ω_i.

A word about notation is probably worthwhile here. In general, the symbol $\mathbf{x}$ will be used to represent observation vectors and $\mathbf{y}$ will be used to represent feature vectors. However, in some applications the idea of a feature transformation may not really be relevant or one may wish to design a classifier directly in the observation space. Thus in the discussion of classifiers, we may refer to the vector input to the classifier generically as a *measurement vector* (i.e., an observation *or* a feature vector) and will use the symbol $\mathbf{y}$.

To illustrate the concepts just discussed, let us continue with the example of character recognition.

■ EXAMPLE 1.4

Two-Class Character Recognition

Assume for simplicity that the only characters desired to be recognized are 1's and 0's. A typical sample from each class is shown in Fig 1.7. Since the 0's generally cover a larger total area of the grid than do the 1's, one might decide on an intuitive basis that the total area covered by the character is a suitable feature y_1 for this problem. The value of the feature for any sample can, of course, be found by summing the components of the observation vector. A classifier for this problem might be derived as follows. One could compute the value of the feature for all patterns in the training set and plot a histogram of their values as shown in Fig. 1.8. In order to plot this histogram, one simply draws bars proportional in height

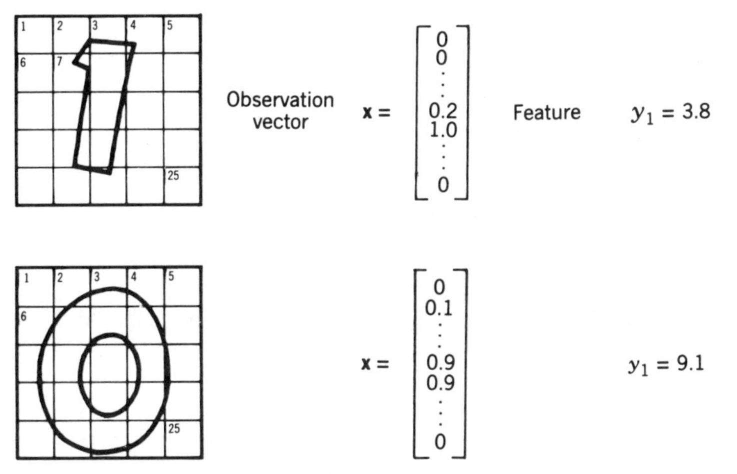

FIGURE 1.7 The construction of features for a two-class character recognition problem.

to the number of features lying in the intervals [0,1), [1,2), [2,3), and so on.[1] Separate histograms are plotted for each class on the same line (the feature space). As shown in Fig. 1.8, most of the features derived from 1's fall below 5 while most features derived from 0's fall above 6. If one were therefore to set a threshold or *decision boundary* at a point between 5 and 6, say at 5.5, and call everything at or below this point a 1 and everything above it a 0, then one would have defined a classifier. The decision regions induced by this classifier are the two intervals of the real line $(-\infty, 5.5]$ and $(5.5, \infty)$. This decision rule does not provide perfect classification of the training samples, and the errors made in classification of the

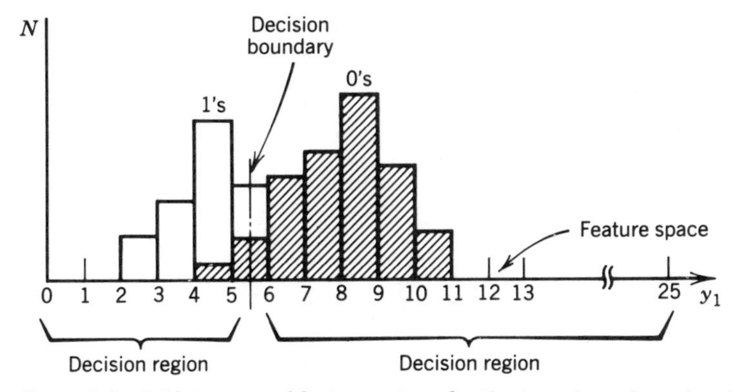

FIGURE 1.8 A histogram of feature values for the two-class character recognition problem.

[1]A square bracket indicates that the end point is included in the interval; a parenthesis indicates that end point is not included.

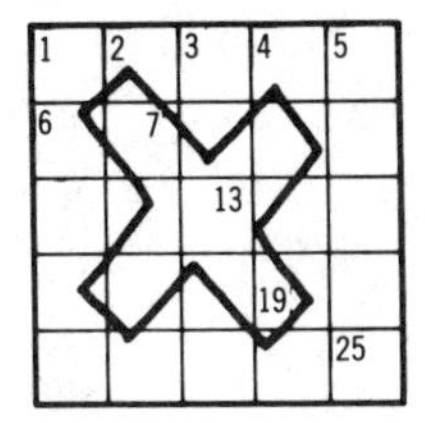

FIGURE 1.9 A sample of character 'x' to be recognized.

training set are represented by the portions of the 0 histogram to the left of the decision boundary and the portions of the 1 histogram to the right of the decision boundary. ■

The pattern recognition problem becomes slightly more complex if a third character is introduced. However, the basic approach is the same. This is illustrated in the following example.

■ EXAMPLE 1.5

Three-Class Character Recognition

Assume that in addition to the 1's and 0's, it is desired to recognize the character x. A sample of this character is shown in Fig. 1.9. It is obvious that the single feature y_1 defined in Example 1.4 is insufficient to recognize all three characters, since the x's and the 0's seem to cover very nearly the same total grid area. However, if another feature y_2 is defined as the sum of the areas of the character on the diagonal grid cells, numbers 1, 7, 13, 19, and 25, then the two combined features will probably serve to identify all three characters. Figure 1.10 shows the location of points corresponding to the training samples in the two-dimensional feature space. For this example, the two straight lines shown in Fig. 1.10 partition the space into regions that can be readily associated with the classes. The shaded area in Fig. 1.10 is a kind of "don't care" region, and it does not really matter how one assigns

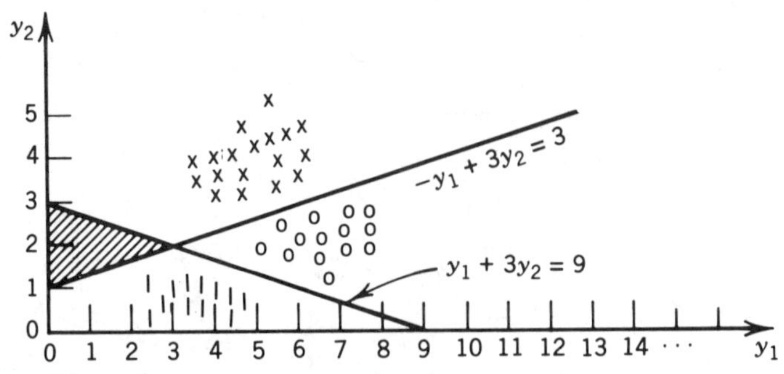

FIGURE 1.10 Decision regions for a three-class character recognition problem.

points falling in this region. Let ω_1 be the class of 1's, ω_2 the class of 0's and ω_3 the class of x's. A suitable decision rule is therefore

$$\begin{array}{llll} \text{if} & y_1 + 3y_2 < 9 & \text{say } \omega_1 & \text{class of (1's)} \\ \text{else if} & -y_1 + 3y_2 > 3 & \text{say } \omega_2 & \text{class of } (x\text{'s}) \\ \text{else} & & \text{say } \omega_3 & \text{class of (0's).} \end{array} \tag{1.1}$$

This particular decision rule can be put in a more convenient canonic form if one defines the functions

$$g_1(\mathbf{y}) = -y_1 - 3y_2 + 9 \tag{1.2a}$$

$$g_2(\mathbf{y}) = -y_1 + 3y_2 - 3 \tag{1.2b}$$

$$g_3(\mathbf{y}) = g_1(\mathbf{y}) \cdot g_2(\mathbf{y}). \tag{1.2c}$$

Note that g_1 is positive and g_2 and g_3 are both negative in the region where we wish to choose ω_1. Similarly, g_2 is positive while g_1 and g_3 are negative in the region where we wish to choose ω_2, and g_3 is positive while g_1 and g_2 are both negative in the region where we wish to choose ω_3. As a result, the decision rule can be expressed as:

$$\text{choose } \omega_i \text{ where } g_i(\mathbf{y}) = \max_j \, [g_j(\mathbf{y})]. \tag{1.3}$$

When the decision rule is expressed in this form, the functions $g_j(\mathbf{y})$ are called *discriminant functions*. Discriminant functions provide a particularly convenient way to implement a decision rule computationally: the computer has only to evaluate each discriminant function and choose the class corresponding to the function with the largest value. The decision regions R_i corresponding to the decision rule (1.3) are defined by the set

$$R_i = \{\mathbf{y} : g_i(\mathbf{y}) = \max_j [g_j(\mathbf{y})]\} \tag{1.4}$$

The decision boundaries are defined by the relations

$$g_i(\mathbf{y}) = g_j(\mathbf{y}) \tag{1.5}$$

for all pairs of nonidentical indices i and j. ■

Before concluding this section, we should note in passing that both Examples

1.4 and 1.5 could probably have been presented as problems in unsupervised pattern recognition as well. For instance, if one had been presented with just the feature vectors for samples from all three classes of characters in Example 1.5, but had not been told of their class identities, one could have deduced from the structure of the data in Fig. 1.10 that there were three classes represented and could have identified which samples belonged to which class. Thereupon one could have deduced the same classification rules as above without ever having known that the samples were derived from 1's, 0's, and x's or even that there were three classes.

1.4 OUTLINE OF TOPICS

With the introduction of the concepts provided by this chapter, the reader is probably in a better position to appreciate the contents of the remainder of this book. Chapter 2 provides a review of necessary concepts in probability needed for the study of pattern recognition. Chapter 3 describes the basic statistical decision procedures on which many of the classifiers are based. Chapter 4 then gives a review of the concepts from linear algebra and multivariate statistics that form a basis for the rest of the chapters.

Chapter 5 deals with feature extraction and nonlinear mapping of data to lower dimensional spaces. This chapter may be skipped without loss of continuity by the reader interested primarily in the design of classifiers.

Chapters 6, 7, and 8 focus on the *design* of classifiers, estimation of their parameters, and what to do when the problem does not have a clearly defined set of parameters. Chapter 9 deals primarily with the *performance* of classifiers by establishing bounds on the probability of error and outlining methods of testing.

Chapters 10 through 12 are devoted to a number of more advanced and mostly newer topics, which the author feels are important in a modern introduction to decision. Chapter 10 describes a set of procedures specific to the classification of signals and waveforms. Chapter 11 discusses methods that are applicable when the decisions made on patterns are interrelated. This represents a large class of practical problems. Chapter 12 then provides a brief introduction to clustering, significance testing, and to the new area of distributed classification.

1.5 SUMMARY

This chapter describes the essense of pattern recognition problems in simplified form. The reader has been introduced to the concepts of supervised and unsupervised pattern recognition (clustering), training and test sets, observation vectors and observation space, feature vectors and feature space, classifiers, decision boundaries and decision regions, and discriminant functions. Several examples are given to specifically illustrate these ideas.

REFERENCES

1. H. E. Burke. *Handbook of Bar Coding Systems*. New York: Van Nostrand Reinhold, 1984.

PROBLEMS

1.1 For the character recognition problem of Example 1.5, can the feature transformation be represented by the following linear transformation?

$$\mathbf{y} = \begin{bmatrix} y_1 \\ y_2 \end{bmatrix} = \mathbf{Ax}$$

If so, what is the matrix **A**?

1.2 Draw a histogram for the following data points:

$y_1 =$			
1.21	3.11	3.97	6.21
1.32	3.12	4.12	6.58
1.40	3.21	4.30	7.00
1.56	3.31	4.70	
2.07	3.37	4.86	
2.21	3.45	4.92	
2.22	3.50	4.97	
2.73	3.78	5.10	
3.00	3.90	5.70	

Let these points correspond to a class ω_1. Draw another histogram for the following data points:

$y_1 =$				
6.89	10.03	11.23	11.71	12.37
8.01	10.31	11.25	11.82	13.01
8.76	10.45	11.34	11.99	13.50
9.25	10.56	11.37	12.22	13.57
9.33	10.72	11.45	12.32	14.60
9.76	10.80	11.60	12.33	

which correspond to the class ω_2. If a decision boundary similar to the one in Fig. 1.8 is used to classify these two sets of points, where should it be drawn to minimize the total number of points of class 1 and class 2 that are misclassified?

1.3 Determine and sketch the decision regions and decision boundaries for the decision rule given by Eq. 1.4 as applied to Example 1.5.

CHAPTER 2

Probability Theory for Random Vectors

This chapter reviews concepts from probability theory that are fundamental to the material in the remaining chapters. The treatment is rather informal and although the chapter begins with fundamentals, it rapidly proceeds to the analysis of vector-valued random variables or random vectors. The reader who feels a need to review probability of events and concepts for single random variables may want to consult a basic text on probability such as [1] or [2].

2.1 PROBABILITY OF EVENTS

Let A, B, C, . . . , and so on, denote *events*. The *probability* of these events is a real number between 0 and 1 denoted by Pr[A], Pr[B], Pr[C], . . . , and so on. The notation of Pr with square brackets will always be used to denote probabilities of events. The probability of the universal event, that is, an event that is certain to occur, is 1 and the probability of the null event, that is, an event that cannot occur, is 0. If two events are complementary in the sense that one of them must always occur but the occurrence of one precludes the occurrence of the other, then their probabilities must add to 1. If A is one such event, its complement is denoted by "*not* A" and it follows that

$$\Pr[\textit{not}\ \mathrm{A}] = 1 - \Pr[\mathrm{A}]. \tag{2.1}$$

The joint probability of events A and B, denoted by either Pr[AB] or Pr[A *and* B] is the probability that both events A and B occur simultaneously. The probability that one or the other or *both* of A and B occur is denoted by Pr[A *or* B].[1] If events A and B do not occur simultaneously, then one has the relations

[1]The informal terms *and* and *or* will be used for what in a formal mathematical setting would be called intersection and union of events.

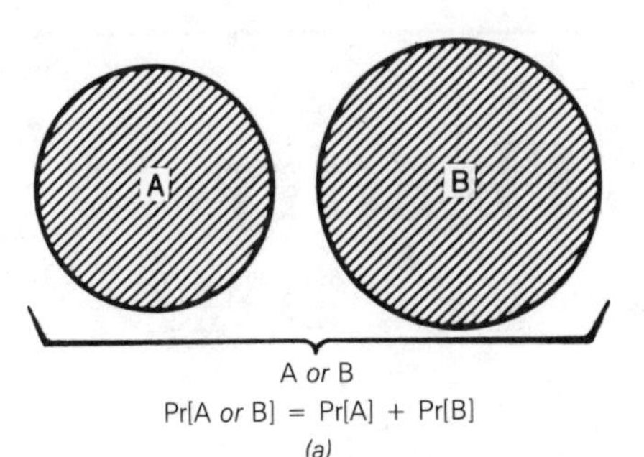

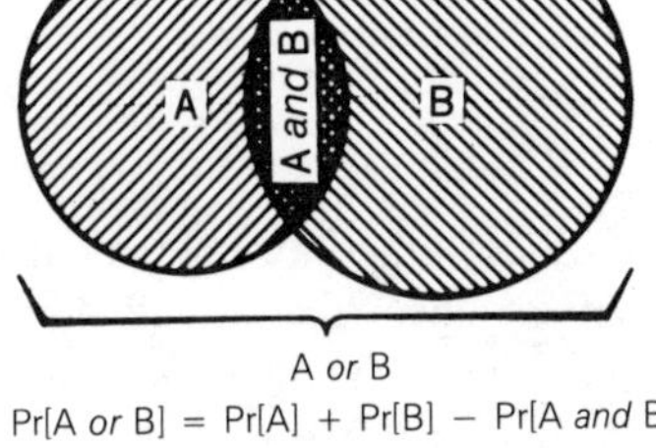

FIGURE 2.1 Venn diagrams for probability of events. (*a*) Nonoverlapping events. (*b*) Overlapping events.

$$\Pr[\text{A } or \text{ B}] = \Pr[\text{A}] + \Pr[\text{B}] \tag{2.2a}$$

$$\Pr[\text{A } and \text{ B}] = 0 \tag{2.2b}$$

This is illustrated by the Venn diagram of Fig. 2.1(*a*). If events A and B may occur simultaneously, then one has the more general relation

$$\Pr[\text{A } or \text{ B}] = \Pr[\text{A}] + \Pr[\text{B}] - \Pr[\text{A } and \text{ B}] \tag{2.3}$$

This is intuitively justified on the grounds that in summing the probabilities of the event A and the event B, one has counted the overlapping event "A *and* B" twice [see Fig. 2.1(*b*)]. Thus the probability of the event "A *and* B" must be subtracted to obtain the probability of the event "A *or* B."

Finally, let $A_1, A_2, \ldots A_M$ (with M possibly infinite) be a set of events that satisfy the following conditions:

1. Only one event A_i can occur at a time; that is, its occurrence precludes the occurrence of the other events.
2. Some one of the events A_i must always occur.

If the events satisfy these two conditions, they are said to be correspondingly (1)

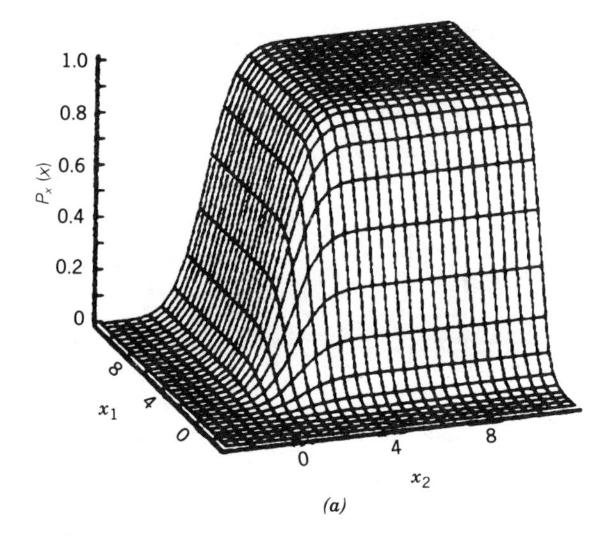

(a)

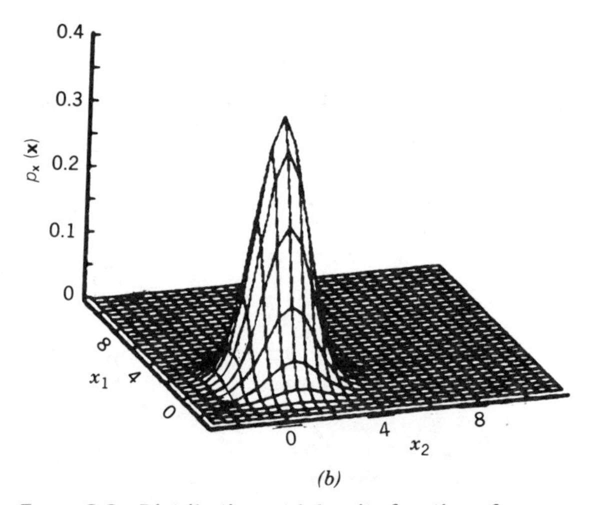

(b)

FIGURE 2.2 Distribution and density functions for a two-dimensional random vector $\mathbf{x}$. (*a*) Distribution function. (*b*) Density function.

mutually exclusive and (2) *collectively exhaustive*. The probabilities of these events then satisfy the relations:

$$\sum_{i=1}^{M} \Pr[A_i] = 1 \tag{2.4a}$$

and

$$\sum_{i=1}^{M} \Pr[A_i \textit{ and } B] = \Pr[B] \tag{2.4b}$$

2.2 DISTRIBUTION AND DENSITY FUNCTIONS

2.2.1 Distribution and Density Functions for a Single Random Vector

Let $\mathbf{x}$ be a *random vector*

$$\mathbf{x} = \begin{bmatrix} x_1 \\ x_2 \\ x_3 \\ \vdots \\ x_n \end{bmatrix} \tag{2.5}$$

where the *components* $x_1, x_2, \ldots, x_n$ of $\mathbf{x}$ are random variables. Let $\hat{\mathbf{x}}$ be a particular instance of $\mathbf{x}$

$$\hat{\mathbf{x}} = \begin{bmatrix} \hat{x}_1 \\ \hat{x}_2 \\ \vdots \\ \hat{x}_n \end{bmatrix} \tag{2.6}$$

In other words, the components $\hat{x}_1, \hat{x}_2, \ldots, \hat{x}_n$ are fixed real numbers. The probability of the event

$$\mathbf{x} \leqslant \hat{\mathbf{x}} : x_1 \leqslant \hat{x}_1, x_2 \leqslant \hat{x}_2, \ldots, x_n \leqslant \hat{x}_n$$

is obviously a function of $\hat{\mathbf{x}}$. This function is called the *distribution function* for the random vector $\mathbf{x}$ and is defined by

$$P_{\mathbf{x}}(\hat{\mathbf{x}}) \equiv P_{x_1 x_2 \ldots x_n}(\hat{x}_1, \hat{x}_2, \ldots, \hat{x}_n) \equiv \Pr[\mathbf{x} \leqslant \hat{\mathbf{x}}] \tag{2.7}$$

Equation 2.7 serves also to define notation. $P_{\mathbf{x}}$ is a *function* and $\hat{\mathbf{x}}$ (in ordinary parentheses) is its argument. The *value* of the *function* is defined by the *probability* of the *event* $\mathbf{x} \leqslant \hat{\mathbf{x}}$.

Figure 2.2(a) shows a typical distribution function for a two-dimensional random vector $\mathbf{x}$. Note that the following relations are a direct consequence of the definition (2.7).

$$P_{\mathbf{x}}(-\infty) = 0 \tag{2.8a}$$

$$P_{\mathbf{x}}(+\infty) = 1 \tag{2.8b}$$

The probability *density function* is defined as the derivative of the distribution function with respect to all of the vector components

$$p_{\mathbf{x}}(\hat{\mathbf{x}}) = \frac{\partial}{\partial x_1} \frac{\partial}{\partial x_2} \cdots \frac{\partial}{\partial x_n} P_{\mathbf{x}}(\mathbf{x}) \big|_{\mathbf{x} = \hat{\mathbf{x}}} \tag{2.9}$$

The distribution and density functions also satisfy the equivalent relation

$$P_{\mathbf{x}}(\hat{\mathbf{x}}) = \int_{-\infty}^{\hat{\mathbf{x}}} p_{\mathbf{x}}(\mathbf{x}) d\mathbf{x} \equiv \int_{-\infty}^{\hat{x}_1} \int_{-\infty}^{\hat{x}_2} \cdots \int_{-\infty}^{\hat{x}_n} p_{\mathbf{x}}(\mathbf{x}) dx_1\, dx_2 \cdots dx_n \tag{2.10}$$

The probability density function corresponding to the distribution function of Fig. 2.2(a) is shown in Fig. 2.2(b). Note from Eqs. 2.8b and 2.10 that

$$\int_{-\infty}^{\infty} p_{\mathbf{x}}(\mathbf{x})\, d\mathbf{x} = 1 \tag{2.11}$$

Note also that for the event

$$\hat{\mathbf{x}} < \mathbf{x} \leqslant \hat{\mathbf{x}} + \Delta\mathbf{x} : \hat{x}_1 < x_1 \leqslant \hat{x}_1 + \Delta x_1, \ldots, \hat{x}_n < x_n \leqslant \hat{x}_n + \Delta x_n \tag{2.12}$$

one has from Eqs. 2.1 and 2.10

$$\Pr[\hat{\mathbf{x}} < \mathbf{x} \leqslant \hat{\mathbf{x}} + \Delta\mathbf{x}\,] = \int_{\hat{\mathbf{x}}}^{\hat{\mathbf{x}}+\Delta\mathbf{x}} p_{\mathbf{x}}(\mathbf{x})\, d\mathbf{x} \approx p_{\mathbf{x}}(\hat{\mathbf{x}})\, \Delta x_1\, \Delta x_2 \cdots \Delta x_n \tag{2.13}$$

This approximation is valid, of course, if the Δx_i are sufficiently small so that $p_{\mathbf{x}}(\hat{\mathbf{x}})$ does not vary appreciably over the region of space represented by Eq. 2.12. In other words, the density function, evaluated at a point $\hat{\mathbf{x}}$, is proportional to the probability that a random vector $\mathbf{x}$ will fall in the small region near $\hat{\mathbf{x}}$ represented by Eq. 2.12. The higher the density, the larger is the probability. However, note this very important distinction. Although the probability that $\mathbf{x}$ is in a small region around $\hat{\mathbf{x}}$ is given by Eq. 2.13, the probability that $\mathbf{x}$ is *equal* to the value $\hat{\mathbf{x}}$ is zero.[2] This is implied by Eq. 2.13 in the limit as the Δx_i approach zero.

2.2.2 Joint Distribution and Density Functions

If $\mathbf{x}$ and $\mathbf{y}$ are both random vectors (perhaps of different dimensionality), then definitions and relations similar to those just defined for single random vectors exist. In fact, in one sense these definitions and relations have already been presented, since the distribution or density function or a random vector is indeed a joint distribution or density function for its components. Thus most of the results follow directly and will be stated without too much discussion.

Let $\mathbf{y}$ be a random vector

$$\mathbf{y} = \begin{bmatrix} y_1 \\ y_2 \\ \vdots \\ y_m \end{bmatrix} \tag{2.14}$$

and let $\hat{\mathbf{y}}$ be a particular instance of $\mathbf{y}$. The joint distribution function for random

[2]If certain types of singularities are allowed to exist in the density function, then the probability of a particular value $\hat{\mathbf{x}}$ may not be zero. However, for continuous densities of the type we shall be considering, the statement holds.

vectors $\mathbf{x}$ and $\mathbf{y}$ is defined by the probability of the joint event "$\mathbf{x} \leq \hat{\mathbf{x}}$ *and* $\mathbf{y} \leq \hat{\mathbf{y}}$, that is,

$$P_{\mathbf{xy}}(\hat{\mathbf{x}}, \hat{\mathbf{y}}) = \Pr[\mathbf{x} \leq \hat{\mathbf{x}} \textit{ and } \mathbf{y} \leq \hat{\mathbf{y}}] \tag{2.15}$$

The joint density for $\mathbf{x}$ and $\mathbf{y}$ is then defined by

$$p_{\mathbf{xy}}(\hat{\mathbf{x}}, \hat{\mathbf{y}}) = \frac{\partial}{\partial x_1}\frac{\partial}{\partial x_2} \cdots \frac{\partial}{\partial x_n}\frac{\partial}{\partial y_1}\frac{\partial}{\partial y_2} \cdots \frac{\partial}{\partial y_m} P_{\mathbf{xy}}(\mathbf{x}, \mathbf{y})\Big|_{\substack{\mathbf{x} = \hat{\mathbf{x}} \\ \mathbf{y} = \hat{\mathbf{y}}}} \tag{2.16}$$

An equivalent relation to (2.16) is

$$P_{\mathbf{xy}}(\hat{\mathbf{x}}, \hat{\mathbf{y}}) = \int_{-\infty}^{\hat{\mathbf{x}}} \int_{-\infty}^{\hat{\mathbf{y}}} p_{\mathbf{xy}}(\mathbf{x}, \mathbf{y})\, d\mathbf{x}\, d\mathbf{y} \tag{2.17}$$

The following relations follow directly from the definition (2.15):

$$P_{\mathbf{xy}}(-\infty, -\infty) = 0 \tag{2.18a}$$

$$P_{\mathbf{xy}}(+\infty, +\infty) = 1 \tag{2.18b}$$

$$P_{\mathbf{xy}}(\mathbf{x}, +\infty) = P_{\mathbf{x}}(\hat{\mathbf{x}}) \tag{2.18c}$$

$$P_{\mathbf{xy}}(+\infty, \hat{\mathbf{y}}) = P_{\mathbf{y}}(\hat{\mathbf{y}}) \tag{2.18d}$$

Equation 2.18b implies that the joint density must integrate to 1, that is,

$$\int_{-\infty}^{+\infty} \int_{-\infty}^{+\infty} p_{\mathbf{xy}}(\mathbf{x}, \mathbf{y})\, d\mathbf{x}\, d\mathbf{y} = 1 \tag{2.19}$$

Equations 2.18c and 2.18d imply that the probability densities of $\mathbf{x}$ and $\mathbf{y}$ can be obtained from the joint density of $\mathbf{x}$ and $\mathbf{y}$ through the relations

$$p_{\mathbf{x}}(\hat{\mathbf{x}}) = \int_{-\infty}^{\infty} p_{\mathbf{xy}}(\hat{\mathbf{x}}, \mathbf{y})\, d\mathbf{y} \tag{2.20a}$$

$$p_{\mathbf{y}}(\hat{\mathbf{y}}) = \int_{-\infty}^{+\infty} p_{\mathbf{xy}}(\mathbf{x}, \hat{\mathbf{y}})\, d\mathbf{x} \tag{2.20b}$$

Equations 2.20 are very important and useful relations. They state that the density for a random vector $\mathbf{x}$ [or $\mathbf{y}$] can be obtained from the joint density of $\mathbf{x}$ and $\mathbf{y}$ by integrating over the other random vector. The resulting densities $p_{\mathbf{x}}(\mathbf{x})$ and $p_{\mathbf{y}}(\hat{\mathbf{y}})$ obtained from Eqs. 2.20a and 2.20b are referred to as the *marginal densities* for $\mathbf{x}$ and $\mathbf{y}$.

One final relation that applies to jointly distributed random vectors is

$$\Pr[\hat{\mathbf{x}} < \mathbf{x} \leq \hat{\mathbf{x}} + \Delta\mathbf{x} \textit{ and } \hat{\mathbf{y}} < \mathbf{y} \leq \hat{\mathbf{y}} + \Delta\mathbf{y}] \simeq p_{\mathbf{xy}}(\hat{\mathbf{x}}, \hat{\mathbf{y}})\, \Delta x_1\, \Delta x_2 \ldots \Delta x_n\, \Delta y_1\, \Delta y_2 \ldots \Delta y_m \tag{2.21}$$

Equation 2.21 states that the probability that $\mathbf{x}$ is in a small rectangular region around $\hat{\mathbf{x}}$ and $\mathbf{y}$ is simultaneously in a small rectangular region around $\hat{\mathbf{y}}$ is given by the density function evaluated at $\hat{\mathbf{x}}$ and $\hat{\mathbf{y}}$ multiplied by all of the increments in $\mathbf{x}$ and all of the increments in $\mathbf{y}$ defining the respective regions. This result is a direct analog of Eq. 2.13 defined for single random vectors.

■ EXAMPLE 2.1

Joint Density

The joint density function for a two-dimensional random vector $\mathbf{x}$ and a one-dimensional random vector $\mathbf{y}$ is

$$p_{\mathbf{xy}}(\hat{\mathbf{x}}, \hat{\mathbf{y}}) = \begin{cases} (\hat{x}_1 + 3\hat{x}_2)\hat{y}_1 & 0 \leq \hat{x}_1, \hat{x}_2, \hat{y}_1 \leq 1 \\ 0 & \text{otherwise} \end{cases}$$

It is desired to determine the probability of the event $\mathbf{y} \leq \mathbf{y}^0$ and the marginal densities $p_{\mathbf{x}}(\hat{\mathbf{x}})$ and $p_{\mathbf{y}}(\hat{\mathbf{y}})$. First observe that (see Eqs. 2.17 and 2.18c)

$$\begin{aligned} \Pr[\mathbf{y} \leq \mathbf{y}^0] = P_{\mathbf{y}}(\mathbf{y}^0) &= \int_{-\infty}^{\infty} \int_{-\infty}^{\mathbf{y}^0} p_{\mathbf{xy}}(\mathbf{x}, \mathbf{y})\, d\mathbf{x}\, d\mathbf{y} \\ &= \int_0^1 \int_0^1 \int_0^{y_1{}^0} (x_1 + 3x_2)y_1\, dx_1\, dx_2\, dy_1 \\ &\qquad \text{(for } 0 \leq y_1^0 \leq 1\text{)} \\ &= \begin{cases} (y_1^0)^2 & 0 \leq y_1^0 \leq 1 \\ 0 & y_1^0 < 0 \\ 1 & y_1^0 > 1 \end{cases} \end{aligned}$$

Note that the limits on $\mathbf{y}^0$ that define the region of validity for the distribution function $P_{\mathbf{y}}(\mathbf{y}^0)$ are very important. Without these limits, one might conclude that $P_{\mathbf{y}}(\pm\,\infty) = \infty$. Note also that the limits in the original joint density function were important for carrying out the integration.

To compute the marginal densities, we merely apply Eq. 2.20.

$$\begin{aligned} p_{\mathbf{x}}(\hat{\mathbf{x}}) &= \int_0^1 (\hat{x}_1 + 3\hat{x}_2)\, y_1\, dy_1 \qquad 0 \leq \hat{x}_1, \hat{x}_2 \leq 1 \\ &= \begin{cases} \frac{1}{2}(\hat{x}_1 + 3\hat{x}_2) & 0 \leq \hat{x}_1, \hat{x}_2 \leq 1 \\ 0 & \text{otherwise} \end{cases} \\ p_{\mathbf{y}}(\hat{\mathbf{y}}) &= \int_0^1 \int_0^1 (x_1 + 3x_2)\hat{y}_1\, dx_1\, dx_2, \qquad 0 \leq \hat{y}_1 \leq 1 \\ &= \begin{cases} 2\hat{y}_1 & 0 \leq \hat{y}_1 \leq 1 \\ 0 & \text{otherwise} \end{cases} \end{aligned}$$

The marginal density function $p_{\mathbf{y}}(\hat{\mathbf{y}})$ can also be obtained by differentiating the distribution function obtained in the first part of this example. ■

2.2.3 Distribution and Density Functions Defined Jointly with Events

One more subject needs to be discussed before we go on to other topics. This subject is the joint distribution and the joint density of a random vector with an event.

The joint distribution of a random vector **x** and an event A is defined by

$$P_{\mathbf{x}A}(\hat{\mathbf{x}}, A) = \Pr[\mathbf{x} \leqslant \hat{\mathbf{x}} \text{ and } A] \tag{2.22}$$

Although the distribution is usually just a function of **x**, the event A is included in parentheses as an argument for symmetry and consistency of notation. The joint density is defined by the relation

$$p_{\mathbf{x}A}(\hat{\mathbf{x}}, A) = \frac{\partial}{\partial x_1}\frac{\partial}{\partial x_2}\cdots\frac{\partial}{\partial x_n} P_{\mathbf{x}A}(\mathbf{x}, A)\big|_{\mathbf{x}=\hat{x}} \tag{2.23}$$

or implicitly by the equivalent relation

$$P_{\mathbf{x}A}(\hat{\mathbf{x}}, A) = \int_{-\infty}^{\hat{\mathbf{x}}} p_{\mathbf{x}A}(\mathbf{x}, A)\, d\mathbf{x} \tag{2.24}$$

The joint probability of the events $\hat{\mathbf{x}} < \mathbf{x} \leqslant \hat{\mathbf{x}} + \Delta\mathbf{x}$ and A is given by

$$\Pr[\hat{\mathbf{x}} < \mathbf{x} \leqslant \hat{\mathbf{x}} + \Delta\mathbf{x} \text{ and } A\,] \simeq p_{\mathbf{x}A}(\hat{\mathbf{x}}, A)\, \Delta x_1 \ldots \Delta x_n. \tag{2.25}$$

If $A_1, A_2, \ldots A_M$ is a set of mutually exclusive and collectively exhaustive events, then the marginal distribution function is given by

$$P_{\mathbf{x}}(\hat{\mathbf{x}}) = \sum_{i=1}^{M} P_{\mathbf{x}A_i}(\hat{\mathbf{x}}, A_i) \tag{2.26}$$

and the marginal density function is given by

$$p_{\mathbf{x}}(\hat{\mathbf{x}}) = \sum_{i=1}^{M} p_{\mathbf{x}A_i}(\hat{\mathbf{x}}, A_i) \tag{2.27}$$

Equation 2.26 follows directly from the definitions of the distribution functions and from Eq. 2.4b for probabilities of events. Equation 2.27 follows directly from the definitions of density functions and Eq. 2.26. Equation 2.27 is analogous to the relations given by Eqs. 2.20 for random vectors.

2.3 CONDITIONAL PROBABILITY AND BAYES'S RULE

2.3.1 Conditional Probability of Events

If A and B are two events, then the probability of event A when it is known that event B has occurred is defined by the relation

$$\Pr[\mathrm{A}|\mathrm{B}] = \frac{\Pr[\mathrm{A}\ \textit{and}\ \mathrm{B}]}{\Pr[\mathrm{B}]} \tag{2.28}$$

The probability Pr[A|B] is called the "probability of A *conditioned on* B," or simply the "probability of A *given* B." In the special situation that the probability Pr[A|B] is the same as the (unconditional) probability Pr[A], the events A and B are said to be *statistically independent* and as a result of Eq. 2.28, the joint probability is given by

$$\Pr[\mathrm{A}\ \textit{and}\ \mathrm{B}] = \Pr[\mathrm{A}] \cdot \Pr[\mathrm{B}] \tag{2.29}$$

for A and B independent.

2.3.2 Conditional Distribution and Density Functions

A few of the many types of conditional distribution and density functions that can be derived from the basic relation, Eq. 2.28, will be described here. Since the results are obtained in a manner similar to the derivation of results for unconditional distribution and density functions, they will once again be presented without much discussion.

Distribution and Density Functions Conditioned on an Event. Let A be the event $\mathbf{x} \leq \hat{\mathbf{x}}$ and let B be any other event. The conditional distribution function $P_{\mathbf{x}|\mathrm{B}}$ is given by

$$P_{\mathbf{x}|\mathrm{B}}(\hat{\mathbf{x}}|\mathrm{B}) \equiv \Pr[\mathbf{x} \leq \hat{\mathbf{x}}|\mathrm{B}] = \frac{\Pr[\mathbf{x} \leq \hat{\mathbf{x}}\ \textit{and}\ \mathrm{B}]}{\Pr[\mathrm{B}]} = \frac{1}{\Pr[\mathrm{B}]} P_{\mathbf{x}\mathrm{B}}(\hat{\mathbf{x}}, \mathrm{B}) \tag{2.30}$$

By differentiating both sides of Eq. 2.30, one can obtain the corresponding relation for the conditional density function.

$$p_{\mathbf{x}|\mathrm{B}}(\hat{\mathbf{x}}|\mathrm{B}) = \frac{1}{\Pr[\mathrm{B}]} p_{\mathbf{x}\mathrm{B}}(\hat{\mathbf{x}}, \mathrm{B}) \tag{2.31}$$

Probability of Event Conditioned on a Random Vector. Let A be any event and let B be the event $\hat{\mathbf{x}} \leq \mathbf{x} \leq \hat{\mathbf{x}} + \Delta\mathbf{x}$. Then the probability of A given that $\mathbf{x}$ is within the small region (2.12) is denoted by $\Pr[\mathrm{A}|\hat{\mathbf{x}}]$ and follows from Eqs. 2.13, 2.25, and 2.28.

$$\Pr[\mathrm{A}|\hat{\mathbf{x}}] = \frac{p_{\mathbf{x}\mathrm{A}}(\hat{\mathbf{x}}, \mathrm{A})\ \Delta x_1\ \Delta x_2 \ldots \Delta x_n}{p_{\mathbf{x}}(\hat{\mathbf{x}})\ \Delta x_1\ \Delta x_2 \ldots \Delta x_n} = \frac{p_{\mathbf{x}\mathrm{A}}(\hat{\mathbf{x}}, \mathrm{A})}{p_{\mathbf{x}}(\hat{\mathbf{x}})} \tag{2.32}$$

The result is analogous but opposite to Eqs. 2.30 and 2.31.

Conditional Density Function for Random Vectors. Let A be the event $\hat{\mathbf{x}} < \mathbf{x} \leq \hat{\mathbf{x}} + \Delta\mathbf{x}$ and B be the event $\hat{\mathbf{y}} < \mathbf{y} \leq \hat{\mathbf{y}} + \Delta\mathbf{y}$. Then from Eqs. 2.13, 2.21, and 2.28, one can obtain

$$\Pr[A|B] = \frac{p_{\mathbf{xy}}(\hat{\mathbf{x}}, \hat{\mathbf{y}})\, \Delta x_1 \ldots \Delta x_n\, \Delta y_1 \ldots \Delta y_m}{p_{\mathbf{y}}(\hat{\mathbf{y}})\, \Delta y_1 \ldots \Delta y_m}$$

$$= \frac{p_{\mathbf{xy}}(\hat{\mathbf{x}}, \hat{\mathbf{y}})}{p_{\mathbf{y}}(\hat{\mathbf{y}})} \Delta x_1\, \Delta x_2 \ldots \Delta x_n \tag{2.33}$$

The conditional density of $\mathbf{x}$ given $\mathbf{y}$ is *defined* as

$$p_{\mathbf{x}|\mathbf{y}}(\hat{\mathbf{x}}|\hat{\mathbf{y}}) \equiv \frac{p_{\mathbf{xy}}(\hat{\mathbf{x}}, \hat{\mathbf{y}})}{p_{\mathbf{y}}(\hat{\mathbf{y}})} \tag{2.34}$$

and it has the interpretation that $p_{x|y}(\hat{\mathbf{x}}|\hat{\mathbf{y}})\, \Delta x_1, \Delta x_2 \ldots \Delta x_n$ is the probability that $\mathbf{x}$ is in the range of $\hat{\mathbf{x}} < \mathbf{x} \leq \hat{\mathbf{x}} + \Delta\mathbf{x}$ given $\mathbf{y}$ is in the range of $\hat{\mathbf{y}} < \mathbf{y} \leq \hat{\mathbf{y}} + \Delta\mathbf{y}$.

Observe that if the events A and B defined above are independent for all values $\hat{\mathbf{x}}$ and $\hat{\mathbf{y}}$, then the conditional density $p_{\mathbf{x}|\mathbf{y}}(\hat{\mathbf{x}}|\hat{\mathbf{y}})$ is identical to the unconditional density $p_{\mathbf{x}}(\hat{\mathbf{x}})$. In this case the random vectors $\mathbf{x}$ and $\mathbf{y}$ are said to be independent and it follows from Eq. 2.34 that

$$p_{\mathbf{xy}}(\hat{\mathbf{x}}, \hat{\mathbf{y}}) = p_{\mathbf{x}}(\hat{\mathbf{x}}) \cdot p_{\mathbf{y}}(\hat{\mathbf{y}})$$

for $\mathbf{x}$ and $\mathbf{y}$ independent.

2.3.3 Bayes's Rule

Since the joint probability of events A and B is the same as the joint probability of events B and A, it follows directly from Eq. 2.28 that

$$\Pr[A|B] = \frac{\Pr[B|A]\Pr[A]}{\Pr[B]} \tag{2.36}$$

Equation 2.36 is called Bayes's rule and is one of the most useful relations in probability and statistical theory. Bayes's rule can be expressed in several special forms by defining events appropriately. In particular, if B is the event $\hat{\mathbf{x}} < \mathbf{x} \leq \hat{\mathbf{x}} + \Delta\mathbf{x}$, Bayes's rule takes the form:

$$\Pr[A|\hat{\mathbf{x}}] = \frac{p_{\mathbf{x}|A}(\hat{\mathbf{x}}|A)\Pr[A]}{p_{\mathbf{x}}(\hat{\mathbf{x}})} \tag{2.37}$$

If A_i is one of a set of mutually exclusive and collectively exhaustive events A_1, $A_2, \ldots, A_M$, then Eq. 2.37 can be rewritten using Eqs. 2.27 and 2.31 as

$$\Pr[A_i|\hat{\mathbf{x}}] = \frac{p_{\mathbf{x}|A_i}(\hat{\mathbf{x}}|A_i)\Pr[A_i]}{\sum_{j=1}^{M} p_{\mathbf{x}|A_j}(\hat{\mathbf{x}}|A_j)\Pr[A_j]} \tag{2.38}$$

If B is the event $\hat{\mathbf{x}} < \mathbf{x} \leq \hat{\mathbf{x}} + \Delta\mathbf{x}$ and A is the event $\hat{\mathbf{y}} < \mathbf{y} \leq \hat{\mathbf{y}} + \Delta\mathbf{y}$, then Bayes's rule becomes

$$p_{\mathbf{y}|\mathbf{x}}(\hat{\mathbf{y}}|\hat{\mathbf{x}}) = \frac{p_{\mathbf{x}|\mathbf{y}}(\hat{\mathbf{x}}|\hat{\mathbf{y}})p_{\mathbf{y}}(\hat{\mathbf{y}})}{p_{\mathbf{x}}(\hat{\mathbf{x}})} \tag{2.39}$$

By applying Eqs. 2.20 and 2.34, one can obtain the equivalent result:

$$p_{\mathbf{y}|\mathbf{x}}(\hat{\mathbf{y}}|\hat{\mathbf{x}}) = \frac{p_{\mathbf{x}|\mathbf{y}}(\hat{\mathbf{x}}|\hat{\mathbf{y}})\, p_{\mathbf{y}}(\hat{\mathbf{y}})}{\int_{-\infty}^{+\infty} p_{\mathbf{x}|\mathbf{y}}(\hat{\mathbf{x}}|\mathbf{y})p_{\mathbf{y}}(\mathbf{y})\, d\mathbf{y}} \tag{2.40}$$

Equations 2.36 through 2.40 are fundamental to much of the work in statistical pattern recognition. For example, Eq. 2.40 is used when one wishes to refine one's estimate of a density function $p_{\mathbf{y}}(\hat{\mathbf{y}})$ by observing the value of another random variable $\mathbf{x}$ related in some way to $\mathbf{y}$. In this application the density function $p_{\mathbf{y}}(\hat{\mathbf{y}})$ is called the *prior* density, and the density function $p_{\mathbf{y}|\mathbf{x}}(\hat{\mathbf{y}}|\hat{\mathbf{x}})$ is called the *posterior* density. Equation 2.38 is used in an analogous application and forms the basis for an optimal rule in pattern classification discussed in Chapter 3. In this case, $\Pr[A_i]$ is called the *prior* probability of the event A_i and $\Pr[A_i|\hat{\mathbf{x}}]$ is called the *posterior* probability of A_i.

■ EXAMPLE 2.2

Calculation of Posterior Density

A two-dimensional random vector $\mathbf{y}$ has the density function

$$p_{\mathbf{y}}(\mathbf{y}) = \begin{cases} \dfrac{1}{a^2} & 0 \leq y_1,\, y_2 \leq a \\ 0 & \text{otherwise} \end{cases}$$

Another two-dimensional random vector $\mathbf{x}$ related to $\mathbf{y}$ has the conditional density function:

$$p_{\mathbf{x}|\mathbf{y}}(\hat{\mathbf{x}}|\hat{\mathbf{y}}) = \frac{1}{2\pi\sigma_1\sigma_2} \exp\left\{ -\left[\frac{(\hat{x}_1 - \hat{y}_1)^2}{2\sigma_1^2} + \frac{(\hat{x}_2 - \hat{y}_2)^2}{2\sigma_2^2} \right] \right\}$$

It is desired to compute the joint density $p_{\mathbf{xy}}(\hat{\mathbf{x}},\hat{\mathbf{y}})$ and use this to compute the *posterior* density $p_{\mathbf{y}|\mathbf{x}}(\hat{\mathbf{y}}|\hat{\mathbf{x}})$. The joint density is

$$p_{\mathbf{xy}}(\hat{\mathbf{x}},\, \hat{\mathbf{y}}) = \begin{cases} \dfrac{1}{2\pi\sigma_1\sigma_2 a^2} \exp\left\{ -\left[\dfrac{(\hat{x}_1 - \hat{y}_1)^2}{2\sigma_1^2} + \dfrac{(\hat{x}_2 - \hat{y}_2)^2}{2\sigma_2^2} \right] \right\} & 0 \leq \hat{y}_1,\, \hat{y}_2 \leq a \\ 0 & \text{otherwise} \end{cases}$$

The *posterior* density of **y** then follows from Eqs. 2.20 and 2.34 or directly from Eq. 2.40.

$$p_{\mathbf{y}|\mathbf{x}}(\hat{\mathbf{y}}|\hat{\mathbf{x}}) = \begin{cases} \dfrac{\exp\left\{ -\left[\dfrac{(\hat{y}_1 - \hat{x}_1)^2}{2\sigma_1^2} + \dfrac{(\hat{y}_2 - \hat{x}_2)^2}{2\sigma_2^2} \right] \right\}}{\displaystyle\int_0^a \int_0^a \exp\left\{ \left[\dfrac{(\hat{x}_1 - y_1)^2}{2\sigma_1^2} + \dfrac{(\hat{x}_2 - y_2)^2}{2\sigma_2^2} \right] \right\} dy_1\, dy_2} & 0 \leqslant \hat{y}_1, \hat{y}_2 \leqslant a \\ 0 & \text{otherwise} \end{cases}$$

Note that as in the earlier example the limits on **y** for which the density is defined are extremely important. Note also that because of these limits, the denominator in the above equation is a function of $\hat{\mathbf{x}}$ that can only be evaluated numerically. Thus the posterior density in this example does not have a simple closed-form expression. If the original (prior) density for **y** had instead been of the form

$$p_{\mathbf{y}}(\hat{\mathbf{y}}) = \frac{1}{2\pi\eta^2} \exp\left[-\frac{(\hat{y}_1^2 + \hat{y}_2^2)}{2\eta^2} \right] \qquad -\infty < \hat{y}_1, \hat{y}_2 < \infty$$

a closed form for the posterior density would be obtainable. The density function resulting is a special form of the multivariate Gaussian density to be introduced in Chapter 4. ■

2.4 EXPECTATION

The *expectation* or mean of a random vector **x** is a constant vector **m** defined by

$$\mathbf{m} = E[\mathbf{x}] = \int_{-\infty}^{\infty} \mathbf{x} p_{\mathbf{x}}(\mathbf{x})\, d\mathbf{x} \tag{2.41}$$

The notation used in Eq. 2.41 means that the ith component of **m**, which is the mean of the ith component of **x**, is given by

$$\begin{aligned} m_i = E[x_i] &= \int_{-\infty}^{\infty} x_i\, p_{\mathbf{x}}(\mathbf{x})\, d\mathbf{x} \\ &= \int_{-\infty}^{\infty} \int_{-\infty}^{\infty} \cdots \int_{-\infty}^{\infty} x_i p_{\mathbf{x}}(\mathbf{x})\, dx_1\, dx_2 \ldots dx_n \end{aligned} \tag{2.42}$$

By carrying out the integration over all vector components x_j, $j \neq i$, one can express this result as

$$m_i = \int_{-\infty}^{\infty} x_i p_{x_i}(x_i)\, dx_i \tag{2.43}$$

where $p_{x_i}(x_i)$ is the marginal density of ith component of **x**.

The expectation of products of terms of the random vector is also important but will be deferred to Chapter 4, where we do a review of ideas in linear algebra. For the components however, as for any set of scalar random variables, we can define the variance as the expectation of the squared difference of the random variable and its mean. That is

$$\mathrm{Var}(x_i) = E[(x_i - m_i)^2] = \int_{-\infty}^{\infty} (x_i - m_i)^2 \, p_{x_i}(x_i) \, dx_i. \tag{2.44}$$

The expectation of a sum of random vectors or random variables is equal to the sum of the expectations. Furthermore, it is easy to show for a set of independent random variables that the variance of their sum is equal to the sum of the variances.

On occasion it will be necessary to consider expectations for random variables that can take on only a discrete set of values. Such discrete random variables do not formally have density functions associated with them unless certain types of singularity functions are allowed. However, the expectation can be defined by summing over the possible values of the discrete random variable. If r is a random variable that can take on values r_i, $i = 0, 1, 2, \ldots M$, with M possibly infinite, then the mean of r is defined by

$$\bar{r} = E[r] = \sum_{i=0}^{M} r_i \Pr[r = r_i] \tag{2.45}$$

and the variance is given by

$$\mathrm{Var}(r) = E[(r - \bar{r})^2] = \sum_{i=0}^{M} (r_i - \bar{r})^2 \Pr[r = r_i]. \tag{2.46}$$

By expanding and summing, one can write Eq. 2.46 in the alternative form

$$\mathrm{Var}(r) = \sum_{i=0}^{M} r_i^2 \Pr[r = r_i] - \bar{r}^2. \tag{2.47}$$

The mean and variance for a random variable are important parameters of the probability distribution, since the mean represents the central point of the distribution or density and the variance represents the spread about that central point. We shall discuss analogous concepts for random vectors, but that discussion will be left for Chapter 4.

2.5 SUMMARY

This chapter reviews some results from probability theory as applied to events and random vectors. Some basic relations from the probability of events are first presented. The concepts of distribution functions and density functions are then defined and several important relations are derived. Both joint and conditional distributions are derived from their counterparts in the probability of events and the concept of statistical independence is defined. Next, Bayes's rule is presented in several forms. This relation follows almost trivially from the definition of conditional probability, but it is one of the most important results in probability and statistics. Finally, the idea of expectation for random vectors and random variables is discussed. The variance of a random variable is also defined, and the mean and variance are related to properties of the density function.

Although the readers should not be expected to memorize all of the formulas and equations in this chapter, they should understand the ideas used to derive them. In particular, they should understand clearly how the various distribution and density functions relate to the probability of events. The readers should, in addition, understand the meaning of joint and conditional probability and the distinction between these two concepts (they are often confused). They should also understand independence of events and random variables and what this concept implies about probabilities, distribution functions, and density functions. Finally, the readers should be thoroughly familiar with Bayes's rule.

REFERENCES

1. E. PARZEN. *Modern Probability Theory and Its Applications*. New York: John Wiley & Sons, Inc., 1960.
2. J. B. THOMAS. *Introduction to Probability*. New York: Springer-Verlag, 1986.

PROBLEMS

2.1 Let x and y be random variables (one-dimensional random vectors) with density functions

$$p_{x|y}(\hat{x}|\hat{y}) = \begin{cases} e^{-(\hat{x}-\hat{y})} & \hat{y} \leqslant \hat{x} < \infty \\ 0 & \hat{x} < \hat{y} \end{cases}$$

and

$$p_y(\hat{y}) = \begin{cases} 1 & 0 \leqslant \hat{y} \leqslant 1 \\ 0 & \text{otherwise} \end{cases}$$

(a) What is $p_{xy}(\hat{x}, \hat{y})$? Specify the region where the joint density is nonzero and sketch this region in the xy plane.

(b) What is $p_x(\hat{x})$? (Don't forget regions of definition.)

2.2 The joint density for two-dimensional random vectors $\mathbf{x}$ and $\mathbf{y}$ is

$$p_{\mathbf{xy}}(\hat{\mathbf{x}}, \hat{\mathbf{y}}) = \begin{cases} \hat{x}_1\hat{x}_2 + 3\hat{y}_1\hat{y}_2 & 0 \leqslant \hat{x}_1,\hat{x}_2, \hat{y}_1,\hat{y}_2 \leqslant 1 \\ 0 & \text{otherwise} \end{cases}$$

Are **x** and **y** statistically independent? (Show why or why not.)

2.3 A probability density function $p_{\mathbf{x}}(\hat{\mathbf{x}}) = p_{x_1x_2}(\hat{x}_1, \hat{x}_2)$ is defined by

$$p_{x_1x_2}(\hat{x}_1, \hat{x}_2) = \begin{cases} A\hat{x}_1^2\,\hat{x}_2 & \text{if } \hat{x}_1, \hat{x}_2 \geqslant 0 \text{ and } \hat{x}_1 + \hat{x}_2 \leqslant 1 \\ 0 & \text{otherwise} \end{cases}$$

(a) What is the marginal density $p_{x_2}(\hat{x}_2)$?

(b) What is the distribution function $P_{\mathbf{x}}(\hat{\mathbf{x}})$?

(c) What is the constant A?

2.4 The components x_1 and x_2 of a random vector **x** are statistically independent and have the following marginal densities:

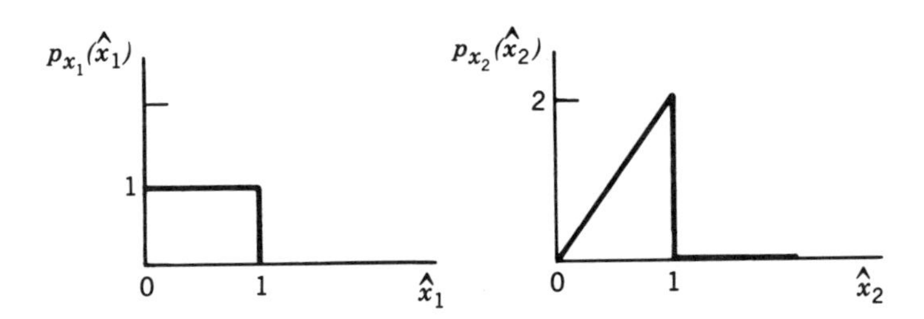

Let A be the event $x_1 \leqslant x_2$. What are the following?

(a) $p_{\mathbf{x}}(\hat{\mathbf{x}})$ (sketch it).

(b) $p_{\mathbf{x}|\mathrm{A}}(\hat{\mathbf{x}}|\mathrm{A})$.

(c) $p_{x_2|\mathrm{A}}(\hat{x}_2|A)$.

2.5 Patterns from a given glass ω_1 are described by a single feature y with the probability density function

$$p_{y|\omega_1}(\hat{y}|\omega_1) = \begin{cases} 1 & 0 \leqslant \hat{y} \leqslant 1 \\ 0 & \text{otherwise} \end{cases}$$

Patterns from a second class ω_2 are described by the same feature y but with the density

$$p_{y|\omega_2}(\hat{y}|\omega_2) = \begin{cases} 1 & 0.8 \leqslant \hat{y} \leqslant 1.8 \\ 0 & \text{otherwise} \end{cases}$$

Let $\hat{y}$ be the value of a feature resulting from some pattern. The following decision rule is used:

$$\begin{array}{ll} \text{if } \hat{y} \leqslant 0.9 & \text{say } \omega_1 \\ \text{if } \hat{y} > 0.9 & \text{say} \omega_2 \end{array}$$

(a) Sketch the two conditional densities on the y-line and indicate the decision regions R_1 and R_2.

(b) What is the probability that a sample from class 2 will be misclassified? (Shade it in on the sketch and evaluate it.)

CHAPTER 3

Simple Statistical Decision Procedures

The field of statistics deals with drawing inferences from data. Consequently, it provides the theory upon which all decision procedures involving random observations are based. The ideas developed in the previous chapter are sufficient to discuss some basic statistical decision procedures. The procedures presented here are fundamental to most of the decision and classification algorithms discussed in later chapters.

3.1 BAYES DECISION THEORY

In Chapter 1, we introduced the concept of a decision rule for the classification of patterns. Recall that the decision rule induced a partitioning of the measurement space into a number of disjoint regions. The rule could thus be stated as "when a measurement vector $\hat{\mathbf{y}}$ falls in region R_i, say that the pattern belongs to class ω_i." This is illustrated in Fig. 3.1.

In this section, we shall discover how the decision regions can be derived from statistical properties of the measurement vectors through procedures known in statistics as hypothesis testing. The hypotheses to be tested in this situation are that a given pattern belongs to one of N_c possible classes. We shall restrict attention in this chapter mostly to the two-class (i.e., $N_c = 2$) case. Decision rules for $N_c > 2$ are discussed briefly in the last section. One measure of the performance of the decision rule is the probability of making an incorrect decision or the *probability of error*. The decision rules described here are optimal in the sense that they minimize either the probability of error or another quantity closely related to it.

Consider first this heuristic approach. One is given a measurement vector $\hat{\mathbf{y}}$ to be classified. In order to classify this vector, one might simply evaluate the posterior probability of each class $\Pr[\omega_i|\hat{\mathbf{y}}]$ and choose the class with the largest posterior

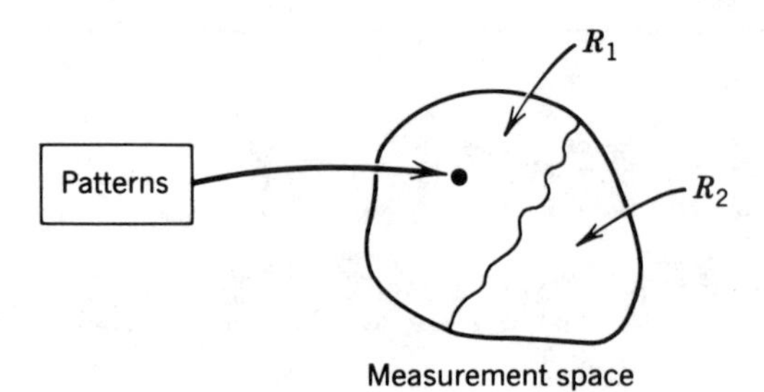

FIGURE 3.1 The partitioning of measurement space induced by a decision rule.

probability.[1] Let us examine the consequences of this decision rule for the two-class case. From Bayes's rule (Eq. 2.37) one can write

$$\text{if } \frac{p_{\mathbf{y}|\omega_1}(\hat{\mathbf{y}}|\omega_1)\Pr[\omega_1]}{p_{\mathbf{y}}(\hat{\mathbf{y}})} > \frac{p_{\mathbf{y}|\omega_2}(\hat{\mathbf{y}}|\omega_2)\Pr[\omega_2]}{p_{\mathbf{y}}(\hat{\mathbf{y}})} \quad \text{choose } \omega_1 \qquad \text{else} \quad \text{choose } \omega_2 \tag{3.1}$$

Thus the decision rule can be stated as

$$\text{if } \ell(\hat{\mathbf{y}}) \triangleq \frac{p_{\mathbf{y}|\omega_1}(\hat{\mathbf{y}}|\omega_1)}{p_{\mathbf{y}|\omega_2}(\hat{\mathbf{y}}|\omega_2)} > \frac{\Pr[\omega_2]}{\Pr[\omega_1]} \quad \text{choose } \omega_1$$
$$< \frac{\Pr[\omega_2]}{\Pr[\omega_1]} \quad \text{choose } \omega_2. \tag{3.2}$$

The quantity $\ell(\hat{\mathbf{y}})$ defined in Eq. 3.2 is called the *likelihood ratio* and the decision rule of Eq. 3.2 is called a *likelihood ratio test*. The likelihood ratio is simply the ratio of the two-*class conditional density functions* $p_{\mathbf{y}|\omega_i}$ evaluated at the point $\hat{\mathbf{y}}$. Therefore, when the class conditional densities are known, the likelihood ratio is a fixed function of $\hat{\mathbf{y}}$.

■ EXAMPLE 3.1

Likelihood Ratio Test for One-Dimensional Gaussian Densities

Assume that a single measurement y has the class conditional densities

$$p_{y|\omega_1}(\hat{y}|\omega_1) = \frac{1}{\sqrt{2\pi}} e^{-1/2(\hat{y}-4)^2}$$

$$p_{y|\omega_2}(\hat{y}|\omega_2) = \frac{1}{\sqrt{2\pi}} e^{-1/2(\hat{y}-10)^2}$$

[1] We use $\Pr[\omega_i|\hat{\mathbf{y}}]$, $\Pr[\omega_i]$, and so on, to represent probabilities of the class ω_i. In terms of the event notations used in the previous chapter, one can think of ω_i as the event that the object belongs to class i.

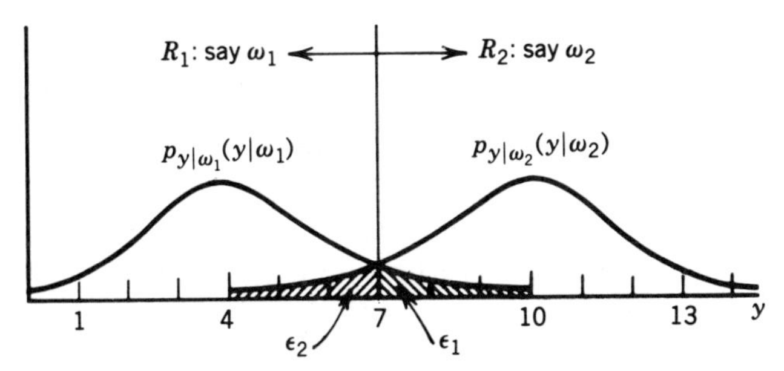

FIGURE 3.2 Class conditional densities and decision regions for Example 3.1.

Figure 3.2 shows the two densities plotted on the y-axis. Suppose that initially the two classes are equally likely so that $\Pr[\omega_1] = \Pr[\omega_2] = \frac{1}{2}$. Then the strategy of choosing the class with the largest a posteriori probability leads to the likelihood ratio test:

$$\ell(\hat{y}) = \frac{e^{-1/2(\hat{y}-4)^2}}{e^{-1/2(\hat{y}-10)^2}} \underset{\omega_2}{\overset{\omega_1}{\gtrless}} 1$$

In this case, the decision rule is considerably simplified if one takes minus twice the log of both sides of the inequality to obtain

$$(\hat{y} - 4)^2 - (y - 10)^2 \underset{\omega_2}{\overset{\omega_1}{\lessgtr}} 0$$

or

$$\hat{y} \underset{\omega_2}{\overset{\omega_1}{\lessgtr}} 7$$

■

Note that the decision rule in this example makes sense from an intuitive point of view, since the class conditional densities are identical in form and symmetric, and differ only in their mean value. Thus one might expect the decision rule to set a threshold for y that is halfway between the means of the two density functions as it does.

Note also that the point $y = 7$ is the point at which the two density functions intersect. This happens whenever the prior probabilities $\Pr[\omega_i]$ are equal. In general, the decision boundaries are the set of points that satisfy

$$p_{\mathbf{y}|\omega_1}(\mathbf{y}|\omega_1)\Pr[\omega_1] = p_{\mathbf{y}|\omega_2}(\mathbf{y}|\omega_2)\Pr[\omega_2]$$

Therefore, if one plots the class conditional density functions weighted by the prior probabilities $\Pr[\omega_i]$, their points (or lines, or planes) of intersection are the decision boundaries. In addition, the region R_i where class ω_i is to be chosen is the region where the corresponding weighted class conditional density is largest. Thus the weighted density forms a discriminant function (see Chapter 1).

It was mentioned earlier that the performance of a decision rule can be measured by its probability of error. A lower value for this probability implies a better decision rule. The probability of error can be expressed in a number of ways using the results of Chapter 2. For example, one can write

$$\Pr[\text{error}] = \int_{-\infty}^{\infty} \Pr[\text{error}|\mathbf{y}]\, p_{\mathbf{y}}(\mathbf{y})\, d\mathbf{y} \tag{3.3}$$

As we shall see, it is relatively straightforward to compute the conditional probability of error $\Pr[\text{error}|\mathbf{y}]$, and the (unconditional) probability of error can be easily computed from Eq. 3.3.

An alternate way to express the probability of error is

$$\Pr[\text{error}] = \Pr[\text{error}|\omega_1]\Pr[\omega_1] + \Pr[\text{error}|\omega_2]\Pr[\omega_2] \tag{3.4}$$

Equation 3.4 is a very useful relation. The terms $\Pr[\text{error}|\omega_i]$ are the probabilities of error for each class and will be denoted by the variables ε_i. These *class error probabilities* are easily computed from the relations

$$\varepsilon_1 = \Pr[\text{error}|\omega_1] = \Pr[\text{choose } \omega_2|\omega_1] = \int_{R_2} p_{\mathbf{y}|\omega_1}(\mathbf{y}|\omega_1)\, d\mathbf{y} \tag{3.5a}$$

$$\varepsilon_2 = \Pr[\text{error}|\omega_2] = \Pr[\text{choose } \omega_1|\omega_2] = \int_{R_1} p_{\mathbf{y}|\omega_2}(\mathbf{y}|\omega_2)\, d\mathbf{y}. \tag{3.5b}$$

Thus ε_i is the integral of the density $p_{\mathbf{y}|\omega_i}$ over the region where we choose ω_j. The class error probabilities for Example 4.1 are shown shaded in Fig. 3.2.

It will now be shown that the decision rule (3.2) minimizes the probability of error $\Pr[\text{error}]$ and thus that Eq. 3.2 is an *optimal* decision rule. This will be shown in two different ways.

Approach No. 1

For any decision rule, let R_i be the region of measurement space, where vectors are classified as ω_i. Then the conditional error probability is given by

$$\Pr[\text{error}|\hat{\mathbf{y}}] = \begin{cases} \Pr[\omega_2|\hat{\mathbf{y}}] & \text{if } \hat{\mathbf{y}} \in R_1 \\ \Pr[\omega_1|\hat{\mathbf{y}}] & \text{if } \hat{\mathbf{y}} \in R_2 \end{cases} \tag{3.6}$$

If one thinks carefully about Eq. 3.6, it becomes clear that a decision rule that chooses the class with the largest *posterior* probability minimizes the conditional error probability for every $\hat{\mathbf{y}}$. For any other decision rule, there would be points $\hat{\mathbf{y}}$ for which the conditional error probability $\Pr[\text{error}|\hat{\mathbf{y}}]$ is not as small as possible. This is illustrated in Fig. 3.3. For the decision rule shown there the point $\hat{\mathbf{y}}$ has a

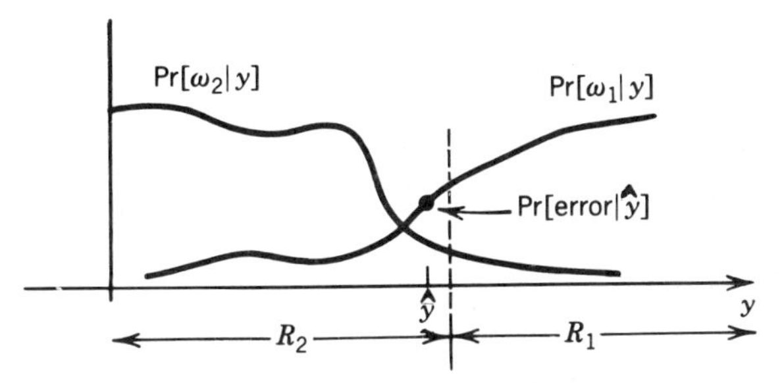

FIGURE 3.3 The error probabilities for a nonoptimal decision rule.

larger conditional error probability (see Eq. 3.6) than it would have if it were placed in R_1. Defining the decision regions according to the class with largest *posterior* probability, however, guarantees that the conditional error probability (3.6) is minimum for every point **y**. Since the decision rule (3.2) minimizes Eq. 3.6 for every point $\hat{\mathbf{y}}$, then by Eq. 3.3, it also minimizes the (unconditional) probability of error. This approach easily extends to decision rules involving more than two classes (see Section 3.4).

Approach No. 2

Let us generalize the previous two-class decision rule by assigning a cost to each of the four possible outcomes of the decision process. In particular, let the cost C take on values

$$C = C_{ij} \tag{3.7a}$$

if we decide on ω_i when $\hat{\mathbf{y}}$ is actually from ω_j and assume that for $i \neq j$

$$C_{ij} > C_{jj} \tag{3.7b}$$

that is, the cost of making an incorrect classification is higher than the cost of making a correct classification. Since the cost depends on the measurement $\hat{\mathbf{y}}$, the cost is a discrete random variable. The *Bayes risk* $\mathcal{R}$ is defined as the expected value of the cost, that is,

$$\begin{aligned}\mathcal{R} = E[C] &= \sum_{i=1}^{2}\sum_{j=1}^{2} C_{ij} \Pr[\text{decide } \omega_i \textit{ and } \mathbf{y} \text{ from } \omega_j] \\ &= \sum_{i=1}^{2}\sum_{j=1}^{2} C_{ij} \Pr[\mathbf{y} \in R_i|\omega_j] \cdot \Pr[\omega_j] \end{aligned} \tag{3.8}$$

Let us determine the decision rule that minimizes the Bayes risk.

Observe first that Eq. 3.8 can be written as

$$\begin{aligned}\mathcal{R} = &\int_{R_1} [C_{11} \Pr[\omega_1]\, p_{\mathbf{y}|\omega_1}(\mathbf{y}|\omega_1) + C_{12} \Pr[\omega_2]\, p_{\mathbf{y}|\omega_2}(\mathbf{y}|\omega_2)]\, d\mathbf{y} \\ + &\int_{R_2} [C_{21} \Pr[\omega_1]\, p_{\mathbf{y}|\omega_1}(\mathbf{y}|\omega_1) + C_{22} \Pr[\omega_2]\, p_{\mathbf{y}|\omega_2}(\mathbf{y}|\omega_2)]\, d\mathbf{y}\end{aligned} \tag{3.9}$$

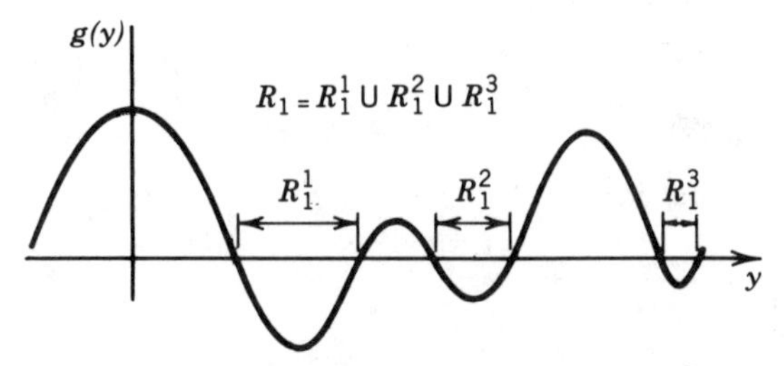

FIGURE 3.4 A selection of regions to minimize the integral for the optimal decision rule.

Then note that for either class conditional density function one can write (see Eq. 2.11)

$$\int_{R_1} p_{\mathbf{y}|\omega_i}(\mathbf{y}|\omega_i)\, d\mathbf{y} + \int_{R_2} p_{\mathbf{y}|\omega_i}(\mathbf{y}|\omega_i)\, d\mathbf{y} = 1 \tag{3.10}$$

Applying Eq. 3.10 to 3.9, one obtains

$$\mathcal{R} = \Pr[\omega_1]\, C_{21} + \Pr[\omega_2]\, C_{22} + \int_{R_1} [-(C_{21} - C_{11}) \Pr[\omega_1]\, p_{\mathbf{y}|\omega_1}(\mathbf{y}|\omega_1) + (C_{12} - C_{22}) \Pr[\omega_2]\, p_{\mathbf{y}|\omega_2}(\mathbf{y}|\omega_2)]\, d\mathbf{y} \tag{3.11}$$

where $\mathcal{R}$ is to be minimized by appropriately choosing the region R_1. Since the first two terms in Eq. 3.11 are not a function of R_1, minimizing $\mathcal{R}$ is equivalent to minimizing the integral

$$\mathcal{I} = \int_{R_1} g(\mathbf{y})d\mathbf{y} \tag{3.12}$$

where

$$g(\mathbf{y}) = -(C_{21} - C_{11}) \Pr[\omega_1]\, p_{\mathbf{y}|\omega_1}(\mathbf{y}|\omega_1) + (C_{12} - C_{22}) \Pr[\omega_2]\, p_{\mathbf{y}|\omega_2}(\mathbf{y}|\omega_2). \tag{3.13}$$

Let us temporarily ignore the form (3.13) of the integrand and show how to minimize the integral (3.12) when $g(\mathbf{y})$ is arbitrary. Figure 3.4 shows an arbitrary function $g(\mathbf{y})$ with both positive and negative values. If one integrates $g(\mathbf{y})$ over regions where the function is positive, the integral increases; if one integrates over regions where $g(\mathbf{y})$ is negative, the integral decreases. Clearly then, to minimize the integral (3.12) one should define the region R_1 to include all of the points and only the points where $g(\mathbf{y})$ is negative. In other words, since R_1 is the region where one chooses ω_1, then one should choose ω_1 whenever $g(\mathbf{y})$ as defined by Eq. 3.13 is negative. Therefore, the decision rule can be expressed as

$$\ell(\hat{\mathbf{y}}) = \frac{p_{\mathbf{y}|\omega_1}(\hat{\mathbf{y}}|\omega_1)}{p_{\mathbf{y}|\omega_2}(\hat{\mathbf{y}}|\omega_2)} \underset{\omega_2}{\overset{\omega_1}{\gtrless}} \lambda_B \tag{3.14a}$$

where

$$\lambda_B = \frac{\Pr[\omega_2](C_{12} - C_{22})}{\Pr[\omega_1](C_{21} - C_{11})} \tag{3.14b}$$

Thus minimization of the Bayes risk also leads to a likelihood ratio test.

The value of the risk can be expressed in terms of the class error probabilities ε_1 and ε_2. If we apply Eq. 3.10 to the first term in the integral of Eq. 3.11 and use the definitions of Eq. 3.5, we have

$$\begin{aligned}\mathcal{R} &= \Pr[\omega_1]\, C_{21} + \Pr[\omega_2]\, C_{22} \\ &\quad - \Pr[\omega_1](C_{21} - C_{11})(1 - \varepsilon_1) + \Pr[\omega_2](C_{12} - C_{22})\varepsilon_2 \\ &= \Pr[\omega_1]C_{11} + \Pr[\omega_2]C_{22} \\ &\quad + \Pr[\omega_1](C_{21} - C_{11})\varepsilon_1 + \Pr[\omega_2]\,(C_{12} - C_{22})\varepsilon_2 \end{aligned} \tag{3.15}$$

Now if one defines the costs to be

$$C_{ij} = \begin{cases} 0 & \text{if } i = j \\ 1 & \text{if } i \neq j \end{cases} \tag{3.16}$$

then the risk becomes

$$\mathcal{R} = \Pr[\omega_1]\varepsilon_1 + \Pr[\omega_2]\varepsilon_2 = \Pr[\text{error}]$$

and Eq. 3.14 becomes identical to Eq. 3.2. Thus the decision rule (3.2) minimizes the probability of error.

3.2 NEYMAN–PEARSON THEORY

In the preceding section it was shown that when one seeks to minimize the probability of error or the more general Bayes risk, one is led to a likelihood ratio test. In this section a third criterion for hypothesis testing—the Neyman–Pearson criterion [1]—will be considered. It will be shown that this criterion also leads to a likelihood ratio test.

The Neyman–Pearson criterion fixes one of the class error probabilities, say ε_2, to satisfy

$$\varepsilon_2 = \int_{R_1} p_{\mathbf{y}|\omega_2}(\mathbf{y}|\omega_2)\,d\mathbf{y} = \alpha \tag{3.17}$$

where α is some predetermined small number and seeks to minimize the other class error probability

$$\varepsilon_1 = \int_{R_2} p_{\mathbf{y}|\omega_1}(\mathbf{y}|\omega_1)d\mathbf{y}. \tag{3.18}$$

In order to minimize Eq. (3.18) subject to the constraint (3.17), one can instead minimize the quantity

$$\mathcal{J} = \varepsilon_1 + \lambda(\varepsilon_2 - \alpha) \tag{3.19}$$

where λ is a Lagrange multiplier. Substituting Eqs. 3.17 and 3.18 into Eq. 3.19 and using Eq. 3.10 to express the result as a single integral over the region R_1, one obtains

$$\begin{aligned} \mathcal{J} &= \int_{R_2} p_{\mathbf{y}|\omega_1}(\mathbf{y}|\omega_1)\, d\mathbf{y} + \lambda \left[\int_{R_1} p_{\mathbf{y}|\omega_2}(\mathbf{y}|\omega_2) d\mathbf{y} - \alpha \right] \\ &= 1 - \lambda\alpha + \int_{R_1} \left[\lambda p_{\mathbf{y}|\omega_2}(\mathbf{y}|\omega_2) - p_{\mathbf{y}|\omega_1}(\mathbf{y}|\omega_1) \right] d\mathbf{y} \end{aligned} \tag{3.20}$$

Since the first two terms in Eq. 3.20 do not depend on R_1, one is once again led to minimize an integral of the form of Eq. 3.12, where $g(\mathbf{y})$ is now given by

$$g(\mathbf{y}) = \lambda p_{\mathbf{y}|\omega_2}(\mathbf{y}|\omega_2) - p_{\mathbf{y}|\omega_1}(\mathbf{y}|\omega_1)$$

Then as before, to minimize the integral, one must define R_1 to be the region where $g(\mathbf{y})$ is negative. Thus one is led to the decision rule

$$\ell(\hat{\mathbf{y}}) = \frac{p_{\mathbf{y}|\omega_1}(\hat{\mathbf{y}}|\omega_1)}{p_{\mathbf{y}|\omega_2}(\hat{\mathbf{y}}|\omega_2)} \underset{\omega_2}{\overset{\omega_1}{\gtrless}} \lambda \tag{3.21}$$

It remains now only to evaluate the Lagrange multiplier λ, which is called the *threshold* of the decision rule (3.21). This can be done (at least implicitly) by noting that since the likelihood ratio is a prescribed function of the random vector $\mathbf{y}$, its value [call it $l = \ell(\mathbf{y})$] is a random variable and can be characterized by some density functions $p_{\ell|\omega_i}(l|\omega_i)$. The decision regions R_1 and R_2 in $\mathbf{y}$ space are mapped, respectively, into the intervals (λ, ∞) and $(-\infty, \lambda)$ in the ℓ space. The condition (3.17) can thus be expressed as

$$\alpha = \int_{\lambda}^{\infty} p_{\ell|\omega_2}(l|\omega_2)\, dl \tag{3.22}$$

and one has an implicit relation that can be solved for λ.

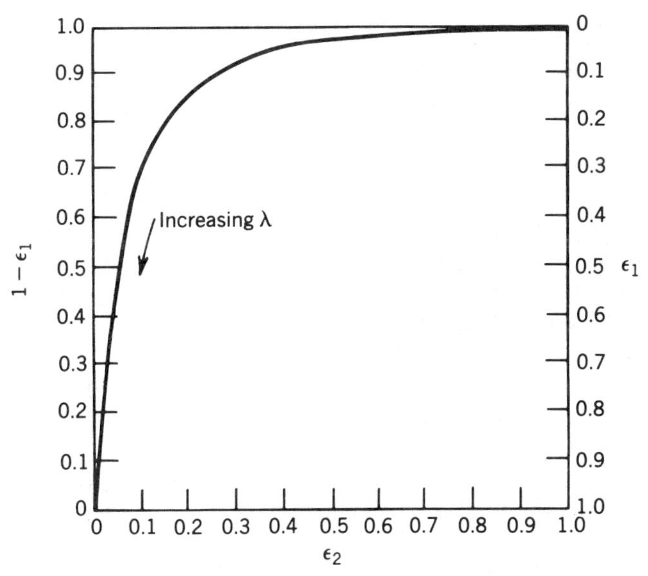

FIGURE 3.5 **The operating characteristic for a two-class decision rule.**

Although Eq. 3.22 may sometimes be difficult to solve in applications, the philosophy of the Neyman–Pearson method is quite sound. One often wishes to formulate the decision rule in terms of the desired class error probabilities rather than in terms of the class prior probabilities, since the latter may be difficult or impossible to estimate. One practical approach to the Neyman–Pearson criterion is derived from noticing that if one varies the threshold λ in Eq. 3.21, a locus of points can be obtained in $\varepsilon_1\varepsilon_2$ space. The resulting curve, an example of which is shown in Fig. 3.5, is known as an *operating characteristic* for the decision rule. Because of its traditional use for signal and radar detection problems, where it is desired to identify one class and reject the other, the operating characteristic generally shows the probability of correctly identifying the first class $(1 - \varepsilon_1)$ on the vertical scale and the probability of misclassifying the second class (ε_2) on the horizontal scale. The quantity $1 - \varepsilon_1$ is called the *power* of the test in statistics. A decision rule that produces low class error probabilities will have an operating characteristics high in the upper left-hand corner of the graph.

An interesting property of the operating characteristic is that the threshold λ used to obtain a point on the curve is equal to the slope of the curve at that point (e.g., Ref. 2). This would be one way to obtain the threshold if the operating characteristic for a given problem were known in a closed form. Usually, the operating characteristic is obtained experimentally by applying the decision rule to a set of test samples and counting the errors. The threshold is then chosen empirically as the value of λ resulting in the desired combination of errors for the test samples.

3.3 SEQUENTIAL DECISION THEORY

In the previous sections, we assumed that the number of measurements was fixed and represented by a vector **y**. The optimal decision procedure then involved a likelihood ratio test and the performance of the test was described by its operating characteristic. Since the number of measurements is fixed, such tests are referred to as *fixed sample-size* tests.

If the number of measurements is allowed to vary, then one can improve the performance of the decision precedure (i.e., reduce the probability of error) by taking more measurements; or equivalently, one may be able to reduce thc number of measurements needed to achieve some specified level of performance. In this section, we discuss a statistical test that employs a variable number of measurements and show how the *number* of measurements can be traded off for lower error probabilities of both classes. A test of this type is known as a *sequential* test [3].

Let $\hat{\mathbf{y}}_m$ represent a vector of m measurements $\hat{y}_1, \hat{y}_2, \ldots, \hat{y}_m$ on an object to be classified. Then we attempt to classify $\hat{\mathbf{y}}_m$ according to

$$\ell_m(\hat{\mathbf{y}}_m) = \frac{p_{\mathbf{y}_m|\omega_1}(\hat{\mathbf{y}}_m|\omega_1)}{p_{\mathbf{y}_m|\omega_2}(\hat{\mathbf{y}}_m|\omega_2)} \quad \begin{matrix} > & A \text{ choose } \omega_1 \\ < & B \text{ choose } \omega_2 \end{matrix} \tag{3.23}$$

where A and B are thresholds with $A > B$. If the value of the likelihood ratio falls between A and B, we take another measurement and repeat the test for $m + 1$.

Equation 3.23 is known as a *Sequential Probability Ratio Test* (SPRT). The SPRT is optimal in the sense that it minimizes the number of observations necessary to achieve specified error probabilities ε_1 and ε_2 for the two classes. In what follows, we shall examine the performance of this test and relate the thresholds A and B to the error probabilities ε_1 and ε_2.

Observe that since the SPRT involves evaluation of a likelihood ratio of increasing order, its advantages are considerably mitigated if the likelihood ratio cannot be computed recursively. Thus, although the theory does not require the individual measurements y_k to be independent, the test has its greatest utility if they are. In this case, we have

$$\ell_m(\hat{\mathbf{y}}_m) = \prod_{k=1}^{m} \frac{p_{y_k|\omega_1}(\hat{y}_k|\omega_1)}{p_{y_k|\omega_2}(\hat{y}_k|\omega_2)} \tag{3.24}$$

and the computation of ℓ_m is clearly recursive. One notable exception occurs. If the original measurements are jointly Gaussian but not independent, they can be converted to a set of independent measurements $\hat{y}'_k$ by a linear transformation of the type discussed in Section 4.7.2. Since, for this type of transformation, y'_k depends on y_j only for $j \leq k$, the advantages of the sequential test are not destroyed. The entire procedure will be described in detail in Chapter 10, where we discuss classification of random signals.

Now consider the SPRT where the measurements are independent. Applying Eq. 3.24 to Eq. 3.23 and taking logarithms leads to the equivalent test:

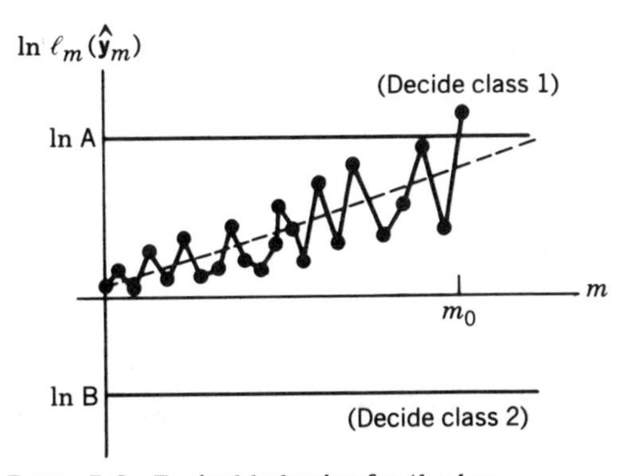

FIGURE 3.6 Typical behavior for the log likelihood ratio assuming class 1 measurements.

$$\ln \ell_m(\hat{\mathbf{y}}_m) = \sum_{k=1}^{m} \ln \frac{p_{y_k|\omega_1}(\hat{y}_k|\omega_1)}{p_{y_k|\omega_2}(\hat{y}_k|\omega_2)} \begin{array}{lll} > & \ln A & \text{choose } \omega_1 \\ < & \ln B & \text{choose } \omega_2 \end{array} \tag{3.25}$$

The quantity on the left-hand side of Eq. 3.25 is referred to as the *log likelihood ratio*. Suppose now that the observed measurements are from class i. Each term in the sum is a random variable with mean and variance that we shall denote by $\delta_k^{(i)}$ and $\eta_k^{(i)}$. Since the terms are statistically independent,

$$E[\ln \ell_m(\mathbf{y}_m)|\omega_i] = \sum_{k=1}^{m} \delta_k^{(i)} \tag{3.26a}$$

and

$$\text{Var}\,(\ln \ell_m(\mathbf{y}_m)|\omega_i) = \sum_{k=1}^{m} \eta_k^{(i)}. \tag{3.26b}$$

Since for $i = 1$ the terms $\delta_k^{(i)}$ are never negative (see Problem 3.5), the mean and variance of the log likelihood ratio for class 1 measurements are monotonically increasing functions of m. Typical behavior for the log likelihood ratio for class 1 measurements is shown in Fig. 3.6. Corresponding behavior is exhibited for samples from class 2. In this case, the expected value of the log likelihood is monotonically decreasing.

Let us now relate the thresholds A and B to the class error probabilities ε_1 and ε_2. Suppose that at some stage m_o of the decision process we find that

$$\ell_{m_o}(\hat{\mathbf{y}}_{m_o}) \gtrsim A \tag{3.27}$$

(The notation $\gtrsim$ means "greater than but approximately equal to.") As discussed earlier in this chapter, the condition $\ell_{m_o}(\mathbf{y}_{m_o}) \geq A$ defines a region R_1 in the m_o-

dimensional measurement space, where vectors are classified as belonging to class 1. If $p_{\mathbf{y}_{m_o}|\omega_1}$ is integrated over this region and Eqs. 3.23 and 3.27 are applied, we have

$$\int_{R_1} p_{\mathbf{y}_{m_o}|\omega_1}(\mathbf{y}_{m_o}|\omega_1)d\mathbf{y}_{m_o} \gtrsim A \int_{R_1} p_{\mathbf{y}_{m_o}|\omega_2}(\mathbf{y}_{m_o}|\omega_2)\, d\mathbf{y}_{m_o} \tag{3.28}$$

Observe that the integral on the left-hand side of this equation is simply the probability of correctly classifying class 1 vectors $(1 - \varepsilon_1)$ while the integral on the right-hand side is the error in classifying class 2 vectors (ε_2). Thus Eq. 3.28 can be written as

$$(1 - \varepsilon_1) \gtrsim A\, \varepsilon_2 \tag{3.29}$$

or

$$A \lesssim \frac{1 - \varepsilon_1}{\varepsilon_2} \tag{3.30a}$$

From similar considerations, it is found that

$$B \gtrsim \frac{\varepsilon_1}{1 - \varepsilon_2} \tag{3.30b}$$

Equations 3.30a and 3.30b provide a direct method of choosing the threshold to achieve any desired class 1 and class 2 error probabilities. Observe that unlike the Neyman–Pearson test (see Eq. 3.22), the relations between the thresholds and the error probabilities are algebraic and simple to evaluate.

Performance of the SPRT is most conveniently described by the expected value of m_o, the number of measurements needed for classification. If the individual measurements are identically distributed, then we can obtain an expression for the expected value of m_o as follows. The expected value of the log likelihood ratio for any fixed value of m is given by Eq. 3.26a. If the measurements are identically distributed, then for each k, $\delta_k^{(i)}$ is equal to the same constant. Denoting this constant as $\delta^{(1)}$ for class 1 and $\delta^{(2)}$ for class 2, we have

$$E\,[\ln \ell_m(\mathbf{y}_m)|\omega_i]|_{m \text{ fixed}} = m\delta^{(i)} \qquad i = 1, 2 \tag{3.31}$$

Now let m_o be the value at which the log likelihood exceeds one of the thresholds. Clearly, m_o is a random variable and from Eq. 3.31, we have

$$E[\ln \ell_{m_o}(\mathbf{y}_{m_o})|\omega_i] = E[m_o|\omega_i]\delta^{(i)} \tag{3.32}$$

Next observe that at m_o the log likelihood ratio has a (approximate) value of either $\ln A$ or $\ln B$. If the measurements are from class 1, we have

$$\Pr[\ln \ell_{m_o}(\mathbf{y}_{m_o}) = \ln A] = \Pr[\text{correct decision}] = 1 - \varepsilon_1 \tag{3.33a}$$

and

$$\Pr[\ln \ell_{m_o}(\mathbf{y}_{m_o}) = \ln B] = \Pr[\text{incorrect decision}] = \varepsilon_1 \tag{3.33b}$$

If the measurements are from class 2, we have

$$\Pr[\ln \ell_{m_o}(\mathbf{y}_{m_o}) = \ln A] = \Pr[\text{incorrect decision}] = \varepsilon_2 \tag{3.34a}$$

$$\Pr[\ln \ell_{m_o}(\mathbf{y}_{m_o}) = \ln B] = \Pr[\text{correct decision}] = 1 - \varepsilon_2 \tag{3.34b}$$

Thus the expected value of the log likelihood ratio for each class is given by

$$E[\ln \ell_{m_o}(\mathbf{y}_{m_o})|\omega_1] = (1 - \varepsilon_1)\ln A + \varepsilon_1 \ln B \tag{3.35a}$$

$$E[\ln \ell_{m_o}(\mathbf{y}_{m_o})|\omega_2] = \varepsilon_2 \ln A + (1 - \varepsilon_2)\ln B \tag{3.35b}$$

Combining Eq. 3.35 with Eq. 3.32, we have the results

$$E[m_o|\omega_1] = \frac{(1 - \varepsilon_1)\ln A + \varepsilon_1 \ln B}{\delta^{(1)}} \tag{3.36a}$$

$$E[m_o|\omega_2] = \frac{\varepsilon_2 \ln A + (1 - \varepsilon_2)\ln B}{\delta^{(2)}} \tag{3.36b}$$

These equations give quantitative measures of performance of the test. Clearly, as $\delta^{(1)}$ or $\delta^{(2)}$ gets larger, the expected number of measurements is smaller. This corresponds to our intuition and to our description of the test as depicted in Fig. 3.6. For the case when the measurements are not identically distributed, such simple relations do not exist. However, the average number of measurements can be computed in any empirical evaluation of the test and serves with the error probabilities as an important measure of performance.

3.4 DECISION AMONG MULTIPLE HYPOTHESES

The decision procedures discussed so far in this chapter dealt only with the case of two hypotheses. Most of the procedures described here can be extended to the case of multiple hypotheses. We shall discuss the extension briefly here, since it relates to classification involving multiple classes that is considered in later chapters.

When the goal is to minimize probability of error, the procedure developed in Section 3.1 (Approach No. 1) extends easily. In the general N_c-class case, the conditional error probability is given by

$$\begin{aligned} \Pr[\text{error}|\hat{\mathbf{y}}] &= \sum_{\substack{j=1 \\ j \neq i}}^{N_c} \Pr[\omega_j|\hat{\mathbf{y}}] \\ &= 1 - \Pr[\omega_i|\hat{\mathbf{y}}] \quad \text{if } \hat{\mathbf{y}} \in R_i \qquad i = 1, 2, \ldots, N_c \end{aligned} \tag{3.37}$$

From Eq. 3.37, it is clear that if $\Pr[\text{error}|\hat{\mathbf{y}}]$ is to be minimized, then R_i should be defined to be the region of measurement space where $\Pr[\omega_i|\hat{\mathbf{y}}]$ is largest. Thus the decision rule that minimizes the probability of error is

$$\text{choose } \omega_i \text{ where } \Pr[\omega_i|\hat{\mathbf{y}}] = \max_j \Pr[\omega_j|\hat{\mathbf{y}}]. \tag{3.38}$$

The implications of this multiclass decision rule will be discussed at greater length in Chapter 6.

The more general Bayes decision procedure (Section 3.1, Approach No. 2) also extends to multiple hypotheses in a more-or-less straightforward way. The general procedure will not be discussed here; however, a good treatment of Bayes decision theory for multiple hypotheses can be found in Ref. 4.

Sequential decision theory has also been extended to multiple hypotheses in the form of a Generalized Sequential Probability Ratio Test (GSPRT) [5]. The GSPRT involves comparing a set of "generalized likelihood ratios" to a set of thresholds, and results in a successive elimination or rejection of hypotheses. Although the test is neatly formulated and consistent with the two-hypothesis case, there has unfortunately been no proof of its optimality.

The reader interested in the details of any of these procedures is encouraged to consult the references.

3.5 SUMMARY

This chapter describes some simple statistical decision procedures for two-class decision problems. Procedures to minimize the probability of error, the Bayes risk, and the Neyman–Pearson criterion are discussed. It is shown that each of these procedures leads to a likelihood ratio test with a suitably defined threshold. The concept of an operating characteristic is introduced, and we describe how that can be used to set the threshold for the Neyman–Pearson type of decision rule. Following that, it is shown that if a variable number of measurements can be used, then the probability of error can be traded off for the *number* of measurements by employing a sequential hypothesis test. The threshold values of the test are related to the desired error probabilities through simple algebraic expressions. Expressions for the expected number of measurements for decision are derived in the case of identically distributed measurements. The generalization of all of these procedures to multiple-class problems is discussed briefly.

REFERENCES

1. J. NEYMAN, and E. S. PEARSON. "On the Problem of the Most Efficient Tests of Statistical Hypotheses." *Phil. Trans. Roy. Soc. London,* Vol. 231, pp. 289–337 (1933).
2. J. D. GIBSON, and J. L. MELSA. *Introduction of Nonparametric Detection with Applications*. New York: Academic Press, 1975.
3. A. WALD. *Sequential Analysis*. New York: John Wiley & Sons, Inc., 1947.
4. H. L. VANTREES. *Decision, Estimation, and Modulation Theory,* Part I, New York: John Wiley & Sons, Inc. 1968, Chapter 2.
5. F. C. REED. "A Sequential Multidecision Procedure." Proc. Symp. on Decision Theory

and Electronic Equipment Development, Rome Air Development Center, Griffiss AFB, New York, DDC AD-236338, April 1960.

PROBLEMS

3.1 The conditional density for patterns of class 1 in a one-dimensional measurement space is Gaussian with mean 0 and variance 3; the conditional density of patterns of class 2 is Gaussian with mean 2 and variance 1. That is,

$$p_{y|\omega_1}(\hat{y}|\omega_1) = \frac{1}{\sqrt{3}\sqrt{2\pi}} e^{\left[\frac{-1}{2}\left(\frac{\hat{y}^2}{3}\right)\right]}$$

$$p_{y|\omega_2}(\hat{y}|\omega_2) = \frac{1}{\sqrt{2\pi}} e^{\left[\frac{-1}{2}(\hat{y}-2)^2\right]}$$

(a) Sketch the two densities on the same line (the y line).

(b) What is the likelihood ratio?

(c) Assume that $\Pr[\omega_1] = \Pr[\omega_2] = 0.5$, $C_{11} = C_{22} = 0$, $C_{12} = 1$, and $C_{21} = \sqrt{3}$. Write an expression (in integral form) for the probability of error with a Bayes decision rule.

3.2 The class conditional densities for two classes of patterns described by a one-dimensional feature are

$$p_{y|\omega_1}(\hat{y}|\omega_1) = \frac{1}{\sigma\sqrt{2\pi}} e^{-\left[\frac{(\hat{y}-m_1)^2}{2\sigma^2}\right]}$$

$$p_{y|\omega_2}(\hat{y}|\omega_2) = \frac{1}{\sigma\sqrt{2\pi}} e^{-\left[\frac{(\hat{y}-m_2)^2}{2\sigma^2}\right]}$$

Show that if λ is the threshold in a likelihood ratio test of either the Neyman–Pearson type or the Bayes type, then the decision rule reduces to

$$\text{choose } \omega_1 \quad \text{if } \hat{y} > c$$

$$\text{choose } \omega_2 \quad \text{if } \hat{y} \le c$$

where c is a constant. Express c in terms of the parameters of this problem.

3.3 The probability densities for a feature y representing two classes of patterns are

$$p_{y|\omega_1}(\hat{y}|\omega_1) = \begin{cases} e^{\hat{y}-2} & \hat{y} \le 2 \\ 0 & \text{otherwise} \end{cases}$$

$$p_{y|\omega_2}(\hat{y}|\omega_2) = \begin{cases} e^{-(\hat{y}-b)} & \hat{y} \le b \\ 0 & \text{otherwise} \end{cases}$$

The prior probabilities are $\Pr[\omega_1] = \Pr[\omega_2] = \frac{1}{2}$

(a) Sketch the two densities on the same line for $b < 2$. Show the regions corresponding to the decision rule that minimizes the probability of error.

(b) What is Pr[error|ω_1] in terms of b? (Consider all values of b from $-\infty$ to $+\infty$.)

(c) What is the value of b that maximizes Pr[error|ω_1]? Does this value also maximize the unconditional probability of error?

3.4 The individual measurements y_k in a sequential test are independent and identically distributed with probability density functions

$$p_{y|\omega_1}(\hat{y}|\omega_1) = \frac{1}{\sqrt{2\pi}\,\sigma} e^{\left[-\frac{(\hat{y}-\alpha)^2}{2\sigma^2}\right]}$$

$$p_{y|\omega_2}(\hat{y}|\omega_2) = \frac{1}{\sqrt{2\pi}\,\sigma} e^{\left[-\frac{(\hat{y}-\beta)^2}{2\sigma^2}\right]}$$

(a) Write the SPRT in the simplest form possible and give a geometric interpretation of the result.

(b) Derive an expression for the variables $\delta^{(1)}$ and $\delta^{(2)}$ appearing in Eq. 3.31 and 3.36 and show that these variables are positive and negative, respectively.

3.5 Show that if the measurements are from class 1, the variables $\delta_k^{(1)}$ appearing in Eq. 3.26a can never be negative. Likewise show that if the measurements are from class 2, $\delta_k^{(2)}$ can never be positive. *Hint:* Start with

$$\delta_k^{(1)} = E\left[\ln \frac{p_{y_k|\omega_1}(y_k|\omega_1)}{p_{y_k|\omega_2}(y_k|\omega_2)}\middle|\,\omega_1\right] = \int_{-\infty}^{\infty} \ln \frac{p_{y_k|\omega_1}(y_k|\omega_1)}{p_{y_k|\omega_2}(y_k|\omega_2)}\, p_{y_k|\omega_1}(y_k|\omega_1)\, dy_k$$

and by using the bound $\ln x \leq x - 1$ for any $x \geq 0$, show that $\delta_k^{(1)} \geq 0$.

CHAPTER 4

Operations upon Random Vectors

The applications of pattern recognition involve not only probabilistic and statistical methods, but also ideas from linear algebra. This chapter presents and reviews concepts related to vectors, vector spaces, and their transformations as these concepts apply to random vectors.

4.1 INNER PRODUCTS, VECTOR SPACES AND BASES

Let $\mathbf{x}$ and $\mathbf{y}$ be vectors with real-valued components x_i and y_i, $i = 1, 2, \ldots, n$. The *inner product* (sometimes called the scalar product or dot product in physics) of $\mathbf{x}$ and $\mathbf{y}$ is defined by

$$\langle \mathbf{x}, \mathbf{y} \rangle = \mathbf{x}^T\mathbf{y} = \mathbf{y}^T\mathbf{x} = \sum_{i=1}^{n} x_i y_i \tag{4.1}$$[1]

If $\mathbf{x}^T\mathbf{y} = 0$, then $\mathbf{x}$ and $\mathbf{y}$ are said to be *orthogonal*. The *magnitude* of a vector is defined by

$$|\mathbf{x}| = \sqrt{\mathbf{x}^T\mathbf{x}} = \left[\sum_{i=1}^{n} x_i^2 \right]^{1/2} \tag{4.2}$$

If a vector $\mathbf{u} = \mathbf{x}/|\mathbf{x}|$ is defined, this vector has unit magnitude and direction the same as $\mathbf{x}$. The inner product (4.1) can be written as

$$\langle \mathbf{x}, \mathbf{y} \rangle = (\mathbf{y}^T\mathbf{u}) \cdot |\mathbf{x}| \tag{4.3}$$

and represents the orthogonal *projection* of $\mathbf{y}$ on $\mathbf{u}$ multiplied by the magnitude of $\mathbf{x}$ (see Fig. 4.1).

[1]Note that a vector is represented by a column matrix (see Eq. 2.5) so that the vector transpose is represented by a row of matrix $\mathbf{x}^T = [x_1 x_2 \ldots x_n]$.

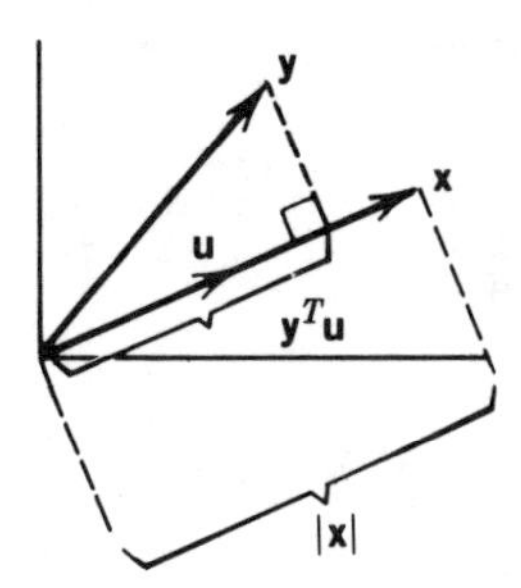

FIGURE 4.1 The inner product of vectors.

The n-dimensional space in which the vectors **x** reside will be called the vector space and denoted by X.[2] If there exists a set of vectors $\mathbf{u}_1, \mathbf{u}_2, \ldots, \mathbf{u}_n$ in X such that an arbitrary vector **x** can be represented by a linear combination

$$\mathbf{x} = a_1\mathbf{u}_1 + a_2\mathbf{u}_2 + \ldots + a_n\mathbf{u}_n \tag{4.4}$$

where the a_i are real numbers, and *any* vector **x** in X has such a representation, then the $\{\mathbf{u}_i\}$ are said to form a *basis* for X. The $\{a_i\}$ are called the *components* of **x** with respect to the basis $\{\mathbf{u}_i\}$.

To form a basis, it is necessary and sufficient that the $\{\mathbf{u}_i\}$ be *linearly independent*; that is, no member of the set can be written as a linear combination of the other vectors. Furthermore, if the $\{\mathbf{u}_i\}$ satisfy

$$\mathbf{u}_i^T\mathbf{u}_j = \begin{cases} 1 & i = j \\ 0 & i \neq j \end{cases} \tag{4.5}$$

then the basis vectors are said to be *orthonormal* and can be interpreted as defining the axes of a Cartesian coordinate system. This is illustrated in Fig. 4.2. If the basis is orthonormal, then by premultiplying both sides of Eq. 4.4 by $\mathbf{u}_i^T$ and applying Eq. 4.5 one obtains the relation

$$\mathbf{u}_i^T\,\mathbf{x} = a_i \qquad i = 1, 2, \ldots, n \tag{4.6}$$

which provides a direct approach to determining the vector components $\{a_i\}$ with respect to the basis $\{\mathbf{u}_i\}$.

4.2 DISTANCE FUNCTIONS

It is frequently useful to define the "distance" between two points in a vector space. The usual way to define distance is as the magnitude of the vector difference between the points. That is, if **x** and **y** are vectors representing points in the same

[2]Formal definitions for a vector space exist (e.g., Ref. 1) However, since these do not add to the understanding of the ideas presented here, we forego the formal definitions.

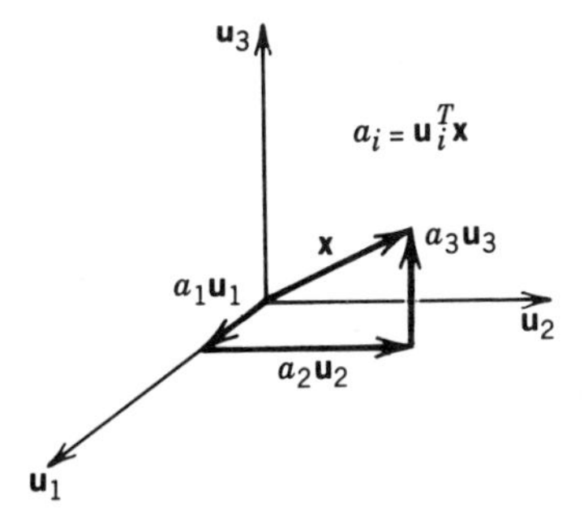

FIGURE 4.2 A set of basis vectors.

n-dimensional vector space, we define the distance $d_E(\mathbf{x}, \mathbf{y})$ between the two points as

$$d_E(\mathbf{x}, \mathbf{y}) = |\mathbf{x} - \mathbf{y}| = \left[\sum_{i=1}^{n} (x_i - y_i)^2 \right]^{1/2} \tag{4.7}$$

This is called the *Euclidean distance*.

More generally, a distance function $d(\mathbf{x}, \mathbf{y})$ is any scalar-valued function that satisfies the following conditions

$$d(\mathbf{x}, \mathbf{y}) \begin{cases} > 0 & \mathbf{x} \neq \mathbf{y} \\ = 0 & \mathbf{x} = \mathbf{y} \end{cases} \tag{4.8a}$$

$$d(\mathbf{x}, \mathbf{y}) = d(\mathbf{y}, \mathbf{x}) \tag{4.8b}$$

$$d(\mathbf{x}, \mathbf{y}) + d(\mathbf{y}, \mathbf{z}) \geqslant d(\mathbf{x}, \mathbf{z}) \tag{4.8c}$$

The last condition is known as the triangular inequality and is a particularly strong constraint. Functions meeting only the first two conditions can be useful in many analyses, although they are not true distance functions.

Two other commonly used distance functions are the maximum value distance

$$d_M(\mathbf{x}, \mathbf{y}) = \max_i |x_i - y_i| \tag{4.9}$$

and the absolute value or "city block" distance

$$d_A(\mathbf{x}, \mathbf{y}) = \sum_{i=1}^{n} |x_i - y_i| \tag{4.10}$$

Both of these are computationally simpler than the Euclidean distance.

Figure 4.3 shows the locus of points $\mathbf{x}$ such that $d(\mathbf{x}, \mathbf{y}) \leqslant a$ for each of the three distance functions in a two-dimensional space ($\mathbf{y}$ is held fixed). The locus for the city block distance is smaller than that for the Euclidean distance, which in turn is smaller than that for the maximum value distance.

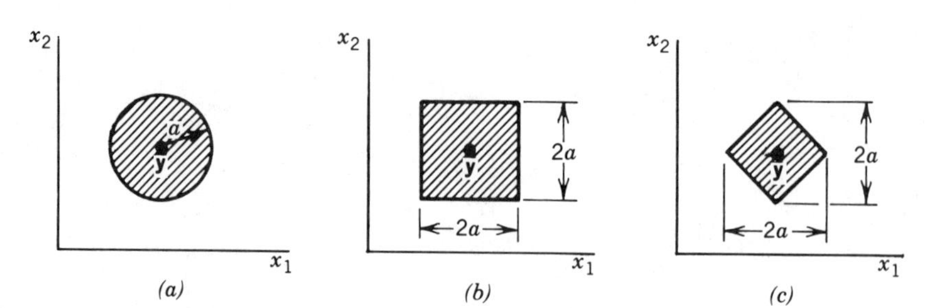

FIGURE 4.3 The locus of points $\mathbf{x} : d(\mathbf{x},\mathbf{y}) \leq a$.
(a) $d_E(\mathbf{x},\mathbf{y}) \leq a$.
(b) $d_M(\mathbf{x},\mathbf{y}) \leq a$.
(c) $d_A(\mathbf{x},\mathbf{y}) \leq a$.

4.3 LINEAR TRANSFORMATIONS

4.3.1 General Linear Transformations

A linear transformation is a mapping from a vector space X to another vector space Y and is represented by a matrix. If $\mathbf{x}$ is a vector in X and $\mathbf{y}$ is the corresponding (mapped) vector in Y, then one can write

$$\mathbf{y} = \mathbf{A}\mathbf{x} \tag{4.11}$$

where $\mathbf{A}$ is the matrix that defines the linear transformation. The transformation is said to be *one-to-one* if given vector $\mathbf{y}$ in Y can be derived from one and only one vector $\mathbf{x}$ in X [see Fig. 4.4(a)]. The transformation is said to be *onto* if every vector

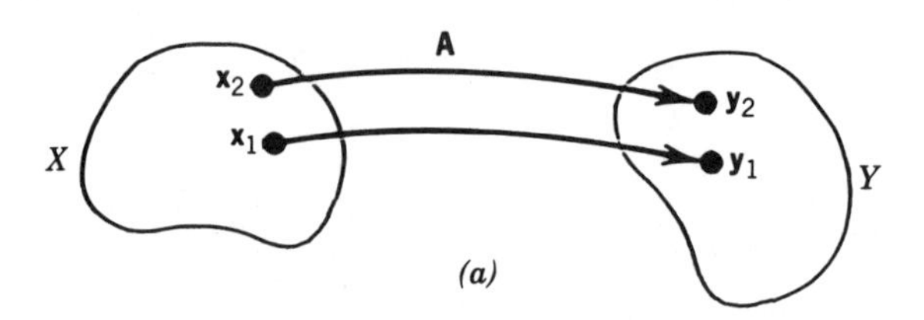

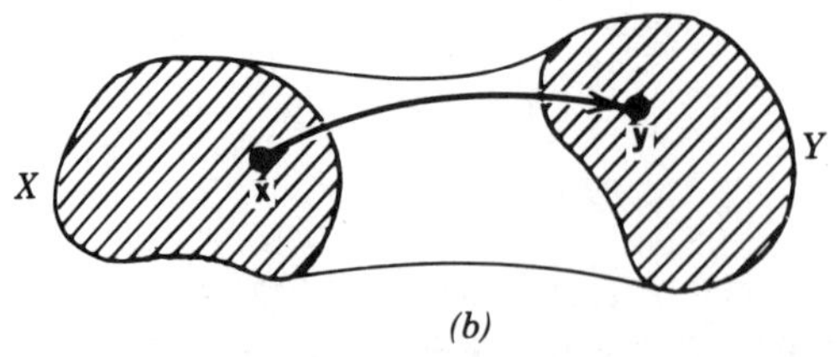

(b)

FIGURE 4.4 Definitions of one-to-one and onto. (*a*) *One-to-one*—different points in *X* always map to different points in *Y*. (*b*) Onto—some subset (or all) of *X* when mapped to *Y* includes every point in *Y*.

$\mathbf{y}$ in Y can be derived by applying the transformation to some vector $\mathbf{x}$ in X. In other words, the set of all transformed vectors from the X space is the entire Y space [see Fig. 4.4(b)]. If the linear transformation is both one-to-one and onto, then an inverse transformation $\mathbf{A}^{-1}$ exists and one can write

$$\mathbf{x} = \mathbf{A}^{-1}\mathbf{y}. \tag{4.12}$$

Note that if $\mathbf{A}$ is to be invertible, it is necessary (but *not* sufficient) that the dimension of $\mathbf{y}$ is the same as the dimension of $\mathbf{x}$, that is, $\mathbf{A}$ is a square matrix. If this were not the case, the linear transformation would not be one-to-one.

Let us review a few important definitions and relations for matrices. For the following development, the elements of a matrix $\mathbf{A}$ will be denoted by a_{ij}.

The *transpose* of a matrix $\mathbf{A}$ is denoted by $\mathbf{A}^T$ and represents the matrix with its rows and columns interchanged. In other words, if a_{ij}^T are the elements of the transposed matrix, then $a_{ij}^T = a_{ji}$ for all values of the indices i and j. A square matrix is *symmetric* if

$$\mathbf{A}^T = \mathbf{A} \tag{4.13}$$

A square matrix $\mathbf{A}$ whose inverse $\mathbf{A}^{-1}$ exists satisfies the relation

$$\mathbf{A}\mathbf{A}^{-1} = \mathbf{A}^{-1}\mathbf{A} = \mathbf{I} \tag{4.14}$$

where $\mathbf{I}$ is the identity matrix. The *trace* is defined for a square matrix by

$$\operatorname{tr} \mathbf{A} = \sum_{i=1}^{n} a_{ii} \tag{4.15}$$

where a_{ii} are the diagonal elements of $\mathbf{A}$. The *determinant* of a square matrix is denoted by det $\mathbf{A}$ or $|\mathbf{A}|$ and is defined as the *sum* of all signed permutations of products of terms where one term is selected from each row or column. The sign is positive for an even and negative for an odd permutation [2]. A necessary and sufficient condition for the inverse of a square matrix to exist is that the determinant of the matrix be nonzero.

A common way to evaluate the determinant of an $n \times n$ matrix is expansion by cofactors. The minor $|\mathbf{A}_{ij}|$ is the determinant of the $(n - 1) \times (n - 1)$ matrix formed by removing the ith row and the jth column. The *cofactor* A_{ij} is $(-1)^{i+j}$ times the minor. One method of evaluating the determinant is to take the sum of all elements in the first row and their cofactors, that is,

$$|\mathbf{A}| = \sum_{j=1}^{n} a_{1j}A_{1j} = \sum_{j=1}^{n} (-1)^{1+j} a_{1j}|A_{1j}| \tag{4.16}$$

Note that we begin with a plus sign and alternate signs in the sums. A similar expression exists for expansion by cofactors of the elements in any row or column.

The cofactor is also used in computing the inverse of a matrix. If a_{ij}^{-1} is any element of the inverse matrix $\mathbf{A}^{-1}$, then

$$a_{ij}^{-1} = \frac{A_{ji}}{|\mathbf{A}|} = (-1)^{j+i} \frac{|A_{ji}|}{|\mathbf{A}|} \tag{4.17}$$

■ EXAMPLE 4.1

Determinant and Inverse of a 3 × 3 Matrix

To compute the determinant of the matrix

$$\mathbf{A} = \begin{bmatrix} 3 & 2 & 1 \\ 2 & 3 & 2 \\ 1 & 2 & 3 \end{bmatrix}$$

expand by cofactors of the first row.

$$\begin{aligned} |\mathbf{A}| &= +(3)\begin{vmatrix} 3 & 2 \\ 2 & 3 \end{vmatrix} - (2)\begin{vmatrix} 2 & 2 \\ 1 & 3 \end{vmatrix} + (1)\begin{vmatrix} 2 & 3 \\ 1 & 2 \end{vmatrix} \\ &= 3(5) - 2(4) + (1)(1) = 8 \end{aligned}$$

The inverse matrix is computed term by term as

$$a_{11}^{-1} = \frac{+\begin{vmatrix} 3 & 2 \\ 2 & 3 \end{vmatrix}}{|\mathbf{A}|} = \frac{5}{8} = 0.625$$

$$a_{12}^{-1} = \frac{-\begin{vmatrix} 2 & 1 \\ 2 & 3 \end{vmatrix}}{|\mathbf{A}|} = -\frac{4}{8} = -0.5$$

$$a_{13}^{-1} = \frac{+\begin{vmatrix} 2 & 1 \\ 3 & 2 \end{vmatrix}}{|\mathbf{A}|} = \frac{1}{8} = 0.125$$

and so on. (The other terms are $a_{21}^{-1} = a_{23}^{-1} = a_{32}^{-1} = -0.5$, $a_{22}^{-1} = 1.0$, $a_{31}^{-1} = 0.125$, and $a_{33}^{-1} = 0.625$.) ■

If $\mathbf{A}$ and $\mathbf{B}$ are any two matrices such that the number of columns in $\mathbf{A}$ is equal to the number of rows in $\mathbf{B}$, then $\mathbf{A}$ is said to be *conformable* with $\mathbf{B}$. In this case the matrix product $\mathbf{AB}$ is another matrix $\mathbf{C}$ whose elements c_{ij} are defined by

$$c_{ij} = \sum_{k=1}^{m} a_{ik} b_{kj} \tag{4.18}$$

where m is the number of columns in **A** (rows in **B**). If **A** and **B** are two conformable matrices, then one has

$$(\mathbf{AB})^T = \mathbf{B}^T\mathbf{A}^T \tag{4.19}$$

Furthermore, if **B** is conformable with **A**, then

$$\mathrm{tr}(\mathbf{AB}) = \mathrm{tr}(\mathbf{BA}) \tag{4.20}$$

(This is easy to prove from definitions.) If **A** and **B** are square matrices, then one has the additional relation

$$|\mathbf{AB}| = |\mathbf{A}| \cdot |\mathbf{B}| \tag{4.21}$$

Finally, if **A** and **B** both possess inverses, then one has the relation

$$(\mathbf{AB})^{-1} = \mathbf{B}^{-1}\mathbf{A}^{-1} \tag{4.22}$$

A very important concept for square matrices is that of positive definiteness. A matrix **A** is said to be *positive definite* if the *quadratic product*, $\mathbf{x}^T\mathbf{A}\mathbf{x}$ (which is a scalar quantity) is strictly greater than zero for all vectors $\mathbf{x}$ in X not equal to the all zero vector $\mathbf{0}$. The matrix is said to be *positive semidefinite* if the quadratic product is greater than or equal to zero for all vectors $\mathbf{x}$ not equal to $\mathbf{0}$. The quadratic product can be expressed in terms of the elements a_{ij} of **A** and the components x_i of $\mathbf{x}$ as

$$\mathbf{x}^T\mathbf{A}\mathbf{x} = \sum_{i=1}^{n}\sum_{j=1}^{n} a_{ij}\, x_i x_j \tag{4.23}$$

A matrix cannot be positive definite if its determinant is equal to zero.

■ EXAMPLE 4.2

Positive Definite Matrix

To determine if the matrix

$$\mathbf{A} = \begin{bmatrix} 1 & -1 \\ -1 & 2 \end{bmatrix}$$

is positive definite, form the quadratic product $\mathbf{x}^T\mathbf{A}\mathbf{x}$ (see Eq. 4.23)

$$x_1^2 - 2x_1x_2 + 2x_2^2 = (x_1 - x_2)^2 + x_2^2$$

Since this expression is greater than zero for all values of x_1 and x_2 except $x_1 = x_2 = 0$, the matrix is positive definite. ■

■ **EXAMPLE 4.3**

Non-Positive Definite Matrix

To determine if the matrix

$$\mathbf{B} = \begin{bmatrix} 2 & 1 & 1 \\ 1 & 2 & -1 \\ 3 & 3 & 0 \end{bmatrix}$$

is positive definite, form the quadratic product $\mathbf{x}^T\mathbf{B}\mathbf{x}$

$$2x_1^2 + 2x_2^2 + 2x_1x_2 + 4x_1x_3 + 2x_2x_3$$

Note that if $x_1 = 0$, the quadratic form is

$$2x_2^2 + 2x_2x_3 = 2x_2(x_2 + x_3)$$

Thus one can choose, for example, $x_2 = 1, x_3 = -2$ to make the quadratic product negative. Therefore, the matrix $\mathbf{B}$ is not positive definite (or even positive semidefinite). ■

4.3.2 Orthonormal Transformations

If $\mathbf{S}$ is a square matrix that satisfies the relation

$$\mathbf{S}\mathbf{S}^T = \mathbf{S}^T\mathbf{S} = \mathbf{I} \tag{4.24}$$

then $\mathbf{S}$ is said to be an *orthonormal transformation*. It is clear from a comparison of Eqs. 4.24 and 4.14 that for an orthonormal transformation $\mathbf{S}^{-1} = \mathbf{S}^T$.

An orthonormal transformation preserves the magnitude of vectors because if $\mathbf{y}$ is given by

$$\mathbf{y} = \mathbf{S}\mathbf{x} \tag{4.25}$$

then

$$|\mathbf{y}| = \sqrt{\mathbf{y}^T\mathbf{y}} = \sqrt{\mathbf{x}^T\mathbf{S}^T\mathbf{S}\mathbf{x}} = \sqrt{\mathbf{x}^T\mathbf{x}} = |\mathbf{x}| \tag{4.26}$$

One can also say that the magnitude of the vector is *invariant* under an orthonormal transformation.

It will now be shown that an orthonormal transformation can be thought of as a rotation of the basis or the coordinate frame in which the vector is represented. In other words, if $\mathbf{x}$ is a column matrix of the vector components with respect to the original coordinate frame, then $\mathbf{y}$ is a column matrix of the vector components with respect to the rotated coordinate frame (see Fig. 4.5).

Let $\mathbf{r}_i^T$ represent the ith row of $\mathbf{S}$. Thus $\mathbf{y}$ can be represented as

$$\mathbf{y} = \begin{bmatrix} \leftarrow \mathbf{r}_1^T \rightarrow \\ \leftarrow \mathbf{r}_2^T \rightarrow \\ \vdots \\ \leftarrow \mathbf{r}_n^T \rightarrow \end{bmatrix} \mathbf{x} \tag{4.27}$$

so that

$$y_i = \mathbf{r}_i^T\mathbf{x} \tag{4.28}$$

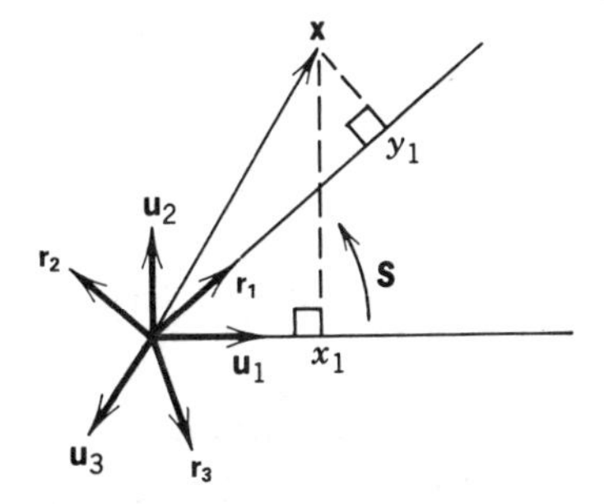

FIGURE 4.5 The interpretation of an orthonormal transformation as a rotation of the coordinate frame.

In addition, since $\mathbf{S}^T = \mathbf{S}^{-1}$, one can write

$$\mathbf{x} = \begin{bmatrix} \uparrow & \uparrow & & \uparrow \\ \mathbf{r}_1 & \mathbf{r}_2 & \ldots & \mathbf{r}_n \\ \downarrow & \downarrow & & \downarrow \end{bmatrix} \mathbf{y} \tag{4.29}$$

or

$$\mathbf{x} = \sum_{i=1}^{n} y_i \mathbf{r}_i \tag{4.30}$$

By comparing Eqs. 4.30 with 4.4 and 4.28 with 4.6, one can observe that the $\{\mathbf{r}_i\}$ form a set of orthonormal basis vectors and that $\{y_i\}$ are the components of $\mathbf{x}$ with respect to that basis.

4.4 DIFFERENTIATION WITH RESPECT TO VECTORS

If s is a scalar function of an N-dimensional vector quantity $\mathbf{a}$, then the derivative of s with respect to $\mathbf{a}$ is defined as the vector

$$\frac{ds}{d\mathbf{a}} = \left[\frac{\partial s}{\partial a_1}, \frac{\partial s}{\partial a_2}, \ldots, \frac{\partial s}{\partial a_N}\right]^T \tag{4.31}$$

This vector is sometimes called the *gradient*. If $\mathbf{s}$ is an M-dimensional vector, all of whose components depend on $\mathbf{a}$, the foregoing definition can be extended. The derivative of $\mathbf{s}^T$ with respect to $\mathbf{a}$ is a matrix

$$\frac{d\mathbf{s}^T}{d\mathbf{a}} = \begin{bmatrix} \dfrac{\partial s_1}{\partial a_1} & \dfrac{\partial s_2}{\partial a_1} & \ldots & \dfrac{\partial s_M}{\partial a_1} \\ \vdots & \vdots & & \vdots \\ \dfrac{\partial s_1}{\partial a_N} & \dfrac{\partial s_2}{\partial a_N} & \ldots & \dfrac{\partial s_M}{\partial a_N} \end{bmatrix} \tag{4.32}$$

Some important relations arise when transformations of the vectors are involved. If $\mathbf{r}$ is a linear function of $\mathbf{s}$, that is, $\mathbf{r} = \mathbf{B}\mathbf{s}$, then

$$\frac{d\mathbf{r}^T}{d\mathbf{a}} = \frac{d\mathbf{s}^T}{d\mathbf{a}} \mathbf{B}^T \tag{4.33}$$

If $\mathbf{r}$ is a general nonlinear differentiable function of $\mathbf{s}$, then a chain rule of the form

$$\frac{d\mathbf{r}^T}{d\mathbf{a}} = \left[\frac{d\mathbf{s}^T}{d\mathbf{a}}\right]\left[\frac{d\mathbf{r}^T}{d\mathbf{s}}\right] \tag{4.34}$$

applies where each of the terms is a matrix. These results can be shown from the definition (4.32) and the ordinary chain rule for scalar variables.

Finally, it is useful to be able to take derivatives of a quadratic product. If we have the quadratic product $\mathbf{a}^T\mathbf{B}\mathbf{a}$, then by writing out terms and using the definition (4.31), one can show that

$$\frac{d}{d\mathbf{a}} (\mathbf{a}^T\mathbf{B}\mathbf{a}) = (\mathbf{B} + \mathbf{B}^T)\mathbf{a}. \tag{4.35}$$

For a symmetric matrix $\mathbf{B}$, this simplifies to

$$\frac{d}{d\mathbf{a}} (\mathbf{a}^T\mathbf{B}\mathbf{a}) = 2\mathbf{B}\mathbf{a} \qquad \text{if } \mathbf{B} = \mathbf{B}^T \tag{4.36}$$

4.5 EXPECTATION OF RANDOM VECTORS

4.5.1 The Expectation Operator

The expectation or mean of a random vector was defined in Section 2.4. This section treats expectation more generally.

Let $\mathbf{x}$ be a random vector and let $\psi(\mathbf{x})$ represent any quantity derived from $\mathbf{x}$ [$\psi(\mathbf{x})$ may be a scalar, vector, matrix, and so on]. The expectation of ψ is denoted by $E[\psi(\mathbf{x})]$ and defined by the operation

$$E[\psi(\mathbf{x})] = \int_{-\infty}^{\infty} \psi(\mathbf{x})p_{\mathbf{x}}(\mathbf{x})\, d\mathbf{x} \tag{4.37}$$

If ψ is a vector or matrix, Eq. 4.37 is interpreted as an application of the expectation operation to every component of the vector or element of the matrix. Thus the result of taking the expectation of a vector or matrix is another vector or matrix of the same size.

In order to be more explicit, one could attach a subscript $\mathbf{x}$ to the expectation operator to indicate that the density function $p_{\mathbf{x}}(\mathbf{x})$ should be used to carry out the expectation. However, this is usually clear from the form of the operand. For example, if $\mathbf{y}$ is defined by a vector-valued function of $\mathbf{x}$, that is,

$$\mathbf{y} = \mathbf{f}(\mathbf{x}) \tag{4.38}$$

then it can be shown that

$$\int_{-\infty}^{\infty} \mathbf{y}\, p_{\mathbf{y}}(\mathbf{y})\, d\mathbf{y} = \int_{-\infty}^{\infty} \mathbf{f}(\mathbf{x})\, p_{\mathbf{x}}(\mathbf{x})\, d\mathbf{x} \tag{4.39}$$

Thus the notation $E[\mathbf{y}]$ represents the same quantity as the notation $E[\mathbf{f}(\mathbf{x})]$, although the former implies that the expectation is carried out using the density of $\mathbf{y}$ while the latter implies that the integration is to be carried out using the density of $\mathbf{x}$.

4.5.2 Moments of a Distribution

The expectation of various powers of the components of a random vector $\mathbf{x}$ are referred to as *moments* of the distribution of $\mathbf{x}$ (because of the analogy of the equations to those used for determining the moments of a rigid body in mechanics). The first moment is the mean of the random vector defined by Eq. 2.41. The second moments are described by matrices.

The *correlation matrix* is defined by[3]

$$\mathbf{R} = E[\mathbf{x}\mathbf{x}^T] \tag{4.40}$$

The elements r_{ij} of $\mathbf{R}$ are the second moments of the vector components and are given by

$$r_{ij} = E[x_i x_j] \tag{4.41}$$

The *covariance matrix* is defined by

$$\mathbf{K} = E[(\mathbf{x} - \mathbf{m})(\mathbf{x} - \mathbf{m})^T] \tag{4.42}$$

The elements k_{ij} of this matrix are the second central moments of the vector components and are given by

$$k_{ij} = E[(x_i - m_i)(x_j - m_j)] \tag{4.43}$$

The diagonal elements $E[(x_i - m_i)^2]$ are the variances of the vector components (see Eq. 2.44) and are sometimes denoted by

$$k_{ii} = \sigma_i^2 = \mathrm{Var}(x_i) \tag{4.44}$$

Note from Eqs. 4.40 and 4.42 or from Eqs. 4.41 and 4.43 that both the correlation and the covariance matrices are symmetric matrices. Both matrices are also positive semidefinite (see Problem 4.4). In addition, the correlation matrix and the covariance matrix can be related by noting that since E is a linear operator and $\mathbf{m}$ is a constant vector, one has

$$\begin{aligned} E[(\mathbf{x} - \mathbf{m})(\mathbf{x} - \mathbf{m})^T] &= \mathbf{E}[\mathbf{x}\mathbf{x}^T - \mathbf{x}\mathbf{m}^T - \mathbf{m}\mathbf{x}^T + \mathbf{m}\mathbf{m}^T] \\ &= E[\mathbf{x}\mathbf{x}^T] - E[\mathbf{x}]\mathbf{m}^T - \mathbf{m}E[\mathbf{x}^T] + \mathbf{m}\mathbf{m}^T \\ &= E[\mathbf{x}\mathbf{x}^T] - \mathbf{m}\mathbf{m}^T \end{aligned} \tag{4.45}$$

Thus it is seen from Eqs. 4.40, 4.42, and 4.45 that the correlation and covariance matrices are related by

$$\mathbf{R} = \mathbf{K} + \mathbf{m}\mathbf{m}^T \tag{4.46}$$

[3]Note. The quantity $\mathbf{x}\mathbf{x}^T$ represents a matrix, not the scalar product. The scalar product of $\mathbf{x}$ with itself is given by $\mathbf{x}^T\mathbf{x}$.

Consider now a random vector $\mathbf{y}$ defined by Eq. 4.11, where $\mathbf{A}$ represents any linear transformation. Let $\mathbf{m}_x$ be the mean vector of $\mathbf{x}$ and $\mathbf{m}_y$ be the mean vector of $\mathbf{y}$. Then since E is a linear operator, we have the relation

$$\mathbf{m_y} = E[\mathbf{Ax}] = \mathbf{A}E[\mathbf{x}] = \mathbf{Am_x} \tag{4.47}$$

The correlation matrix $\mathbf{R_y}$ of $\mathbf{y}$ can be derived from the correlation matrix $\mathbf{R_x}$ of $\mathbf{x}$ by noting that

$$\mathbf{R_y} = E[(\mathbf{Ax})(\mathbf{Ax})^T] = \mathbf{A}E[\mathbf{xx}^T]\mathbf{A}^T = \mathbf{AR_xA}^T \tag{4.48}$$

A similar relation can be derived for the covariance matrix, that is

$$\mathbf{K_y} = \mathbf{AK_xA}^T \tag{4.49}$$

If $\mathbf{A}$ is an orthonormal transformation, then it can be shown that the following relations are valid:

$$|\mathbf{R_y}| = |\mathbf{R_x}| \tag{4.50a}$$

$$\text{tr } \mathbf{R_y} = \text{tr } \mathbf{R_x} \tag{4.50b}$$

$$|\mathbf{K_y}| = |\mathbf{K_x}| \tag{4.50c}$$

$$\text{tr } \mathbf{K_y} = \text{tr } \mathbf{K_x} \tag{4.50d}$$

The proof of these results will be left as an exercise (see Problem 4.8).

4.5.3 Uncorrelated Random Vectors

If $\mathbf{x}$ and $\mathbf{y}$ are two random vectors, then the expectation of their outer product $\mathbf{xy}^T$ is the matrix defined by

$$E[\mathbf{xy}^T] = \int_{-\infty}^{\infty}\int_{-\infty}^{\infty} (\mathbf{xy}^T)p_{\mathbf{xy}}(\mathbf{x}, \mathbf{y})\, d\mathbf{x}\, d\mathbf{y} \tag{4.51}$$

The random vectors $\mathbf{x}$ and $\mathbf{y}$ are said to be *uncorrelated* if

$$E[\mathbf{xy}^T] = E[\mathbf{x}]\, E[\mathbf{y}^T] = \mathbf{m_x}\, \mathbf{m_y}^T \tag{4.52}$$

or equivalently if

$$E[(\mathbf{x} - \mathbf{m_x})(\mathbf{y} - \mathbf{m_y})^T] = [\mathbf{0}] \tag{4.53}$$

It is almost trivial to show from Eq. 4.51 that if $\mathbf{x}$ *and* $\mathbf{y}$ are independent random vectors, then $\mathbf{x}$ and $\mathbf{y}$ are uncorrelated. *The converse of this statement is generally not true.*

The concept of uncorrelated can be defined in an analogous way for the components x_i of a vector $\mathbf{x}$. In fact, given any random vector $\mathbf{x}$ with any distribution, a basis of coordinate frame can be found where the vector components are uncorrelated. We shall address this concept in Section 4.7 and show how this basis can be derived.

4.5.4 Approximating the Expectation

The expectation of any quantity $\psi(\mathbf{x})$ derived from $\mathbf{x}$ can always be computed from Eq. 4.37 if one knows the density $p_\mathbf{x}(\mathbf{x})$. However, one can also obtain a good

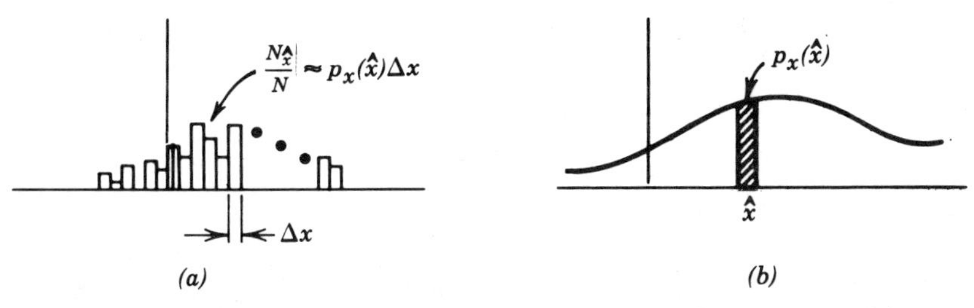

FIGURE 4.6 The comparison of a normalized histogram of a random variable to the probability density function. (a) Histogram. (b) Corresponding density.

approximation to the expectation if one does not know the density but instead has a number of samples $\mathbf{x}^{(1)}, \mathbf{x}^{(2)}, \ldots, \mathbf{x}^{(N)}$ of the random vector $\mathbf{x}$. To illustrate how this would be done, consider a simple case in one dimension.

Figure 4.6(a) shows a histogram constructed from the samples with intervals Δx wide and Fig. 4.6(b) shows the actual (unknown) probability density $p_x(x)$. Let $N_{\hat{x}}$ be the number of samples in the interval $\hat{x} < x \leqslant \hat{x} + \Delta x$. If the total number of samples N is sufficiently large and the interval size Δx is sufficiently small, then both $N_{\hat{x}}/N$ and $p_x(\hat{x})\Delta x$ are good estimates of the probability that x is in the given interval. Thus one has

$$p_x(\hat{x})\ \Delta x = \frac{N_{\hat{x}}}{N} \tag{4.54}$$

If both $p_x(\hat{x})$ and $\psi(x)$ do not vary much over each interval, then Eq. 4.37 can be approximated by

$$E[\psi(x)] \simeq \sum_{\text{all } \hat{x}} \psi(\hat{x})p_x(\hat{x})\ \Delta x \simeq \frac{1}{N} \sum_{\text{all } \hat{x}} \psi(\hat{x})\ N_{\hat{x}} \tag{4.55}$$

Now note that the last summation in Eq. 4.55 has a contribution equal to $N_{\hat{x}}\psi(\hat{x})$ corresponding to the $N_{\hat{x}}$ samples in the interval $\hat{x} < x \leqslant \hat{x} + \Delta x$. This contribution can be replaced by summing just $\psi(x^{(i)})$ over all samples in the same interval (assuming that for these samples $\psi\ (x^{(i)}) \simeq \psi(\hat{x})$). If this procedure is followed for all such intervals, then Eq. 4.55 can be written as

$$E[\psi(\mathbf{x})] \simeq \frac{1}{N} \sum_{i=1}^{N} \psi(\mathbf{x}^{(i)}) \tag{4.56}$$

which has now been written in vector form, since the derivation for vectors follows directly from similar arguments.

Equation 4.56 shows how expectations can be computed from samples of the random vector; this is generally the way in which mean vectors, correlation, and covariance matrices are computed in practice. When this procedure is applied to compute some parameter (such as the mean or covariance), the result of the computation is called an *estimate* of the parameter. If the samples $\mathbf{x}^{(i)}$ are considered to be random vectors, the estimate itself is also a random variable. Estimation theory deals with the statistical properties of estimates and establishes some guides for measuring how "good" a particular estimate is. This topic will be discussed further in Chapter 7.

■ EXAMPLE 4.4

Computation of Sample Mean

Given four sample vectors

$$\mathbf{x}^{(1)} = \begin{bmatrix} 2 \\ 1 \end{bmatrix}, \quad \mathbf{x}^{(2)} = \begin{bmatrix} 1 \\ 2 \end{bmatrix}, \quad \mathbf{x}^{(3)} = \begin{bmatrix} 3 \\ 0 \end{bmatrix}, \quad \mathbf{x}^{(4)} = \begin{bmatrix} 2 \\ 5 \end{bmatrix}$$

an estimate of the mean vector can be computed using Eq. 4.56

$$\mathbf{m} = \frac{1}{4}\left\{\begin{bmatrix} 2 \\ 1 \end{bmatrix} + \begin{bmatrix} 1 \\ 2 \end{bmatrix} + \begin{bmatrix} 3 \\ 0 \end{bmatrix} + \begin{bmatrix} 2 \\ 5 \end{bmatrix}\right\} = \begin{bmatrix} 2 \\ 2 \end{bmatrix}$$

The mean vector computed in this way is sometimes called the "sample mean." ■

4.6 GAUSSIAN RANDOM VECTORS

4.6.1 The Gaussian Density Function

A Gaussian random vector is one characterized by a multivariate Normal or Gaussian distribution. The probability density function for an n-dimensional Gaussian random vector $\mathbf{x}$ is defined by

$$p_{\mathbf{x}}(\hat{\mathbf{x}}) = \frac{1}{(2\pi)^{n/2}|\mathbf{K}_x|^{1/2}} e^{[-\frac{1}{2}(\hat{\mathbf{x}} - \mathbf{m}_\mathbf{x})^T \mathbf{K}_\mathbf{x}^{-1}(\hat{\mathbf{x}} - \mathbf{m}_\mathbf{x})]} \tag{4.57}$$

Note that this density is characterized by only two parameters, the mean vector $\mathbf{m}_\mathbf{x}$ and the covariance matrix $\mathbf{K}_\mathbf{x}$. Equation 4.57 is the multidimensional form of the one-dimensional Normal density given by

$$p_x(\hat{x}) = \frac{1}{\sqrt{2\pi\sigma^2}} e^{-\frac{(\hat{x}-m)^2}{2\sigma^2}} \tag{4.58}$$

If a random vector $\mathbf{x}$ is known (or suspected) to be Gaussian, then estimates of the mean and covariance can be derived from samples of the vector using the procedure of Section 4.5.4 and the resulting parameter estimates can be used in Eq. 4.57 to obtain an estimate of the density function.

If one forms any vector $\mathbf{x}'$ consisting of some number of the components of $\mathbf{x}$, then that vector will also be a Gaussian random vector. Also, the conditional density of $\mathbf{x}'$ given the remaining components of $\mathbf{x}$ is Gaussian. These facts will prove useful in later chapters.

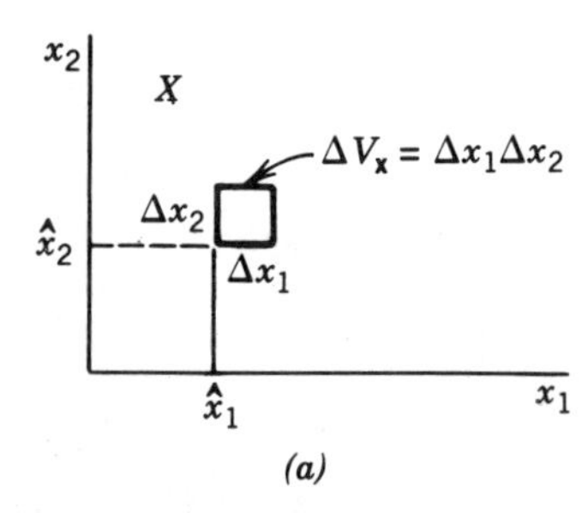

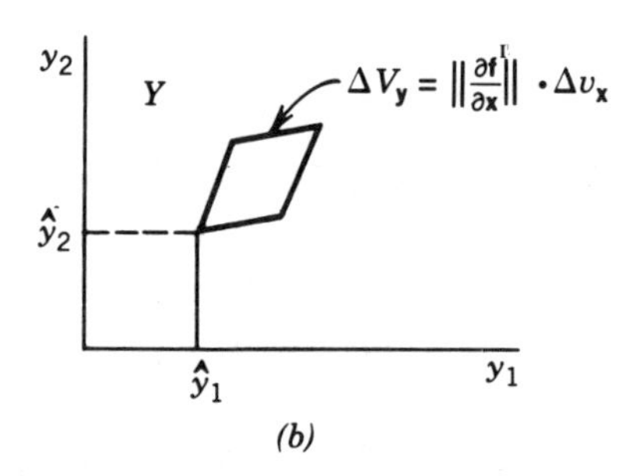

FIGURE 4.7 **Mapping of a small region of *X* space to *Y* space. (*a*) Small region of *X* space. (*b*) Corresponding image in *Y* space.**

4.6.2 Linear Transformations of Gaussian Random Vectors

One of the most basic facts about Gaussian random vectors is that any vector derived as a linear transformation of a Gaussian random vector is also Gaussian. That is, let $\mathbf{x}$ be a Gaussian random vector and let $\mathbf{y}$ be given by Eq. 4.11. Then $\mathbf{y}$ is also a Gaussian random vector.

We can assume without loss of generality that $\mathbf{y}$ is of the same dimension as $\mathbf{x}$, that is, $\mathbf{A}$ is a square matrix. If $\mathbf{y}$ were smaller than $\mathbf{x}$, one could always form a vector $\mathbf{z}$ by appending some rows to the matrix $\mathbf{A}$ and show that the vector $\mathbf{z}$ is a Gaussian random vector. Then, since $\mathbf{y}$ consists of selected components of $\mathbf{z}$, it too would be a Gaussian random vector. If $\mathbf{y}$ were larger than $\mathbf{x}$, one could form the vector

$$\mathbf{x}_{\mathrm{II}} = \begin{bmatrix} \mathbf{x} \\ \mathbf{x} \end{bmatrix} \tag{4.59}$$

which is also a Gaussian random vector and proceed as just described. We also assume that $\mathbf{A}$ is a nonsingular matrix. If this were not the case, the distribution of $\mathbf{y}$ would not be defined except in a subspace of the Y space.

To show the claimed result, let us begin with the more general transformation (Eq. 4.38). For the moment, no assumptions are made on the form of the function or on the distribution of the random vector $\mathbf{x}$. It will be assumed, however, that $\mathbf{f}$ is one-to-one and onto so that the inverse relation

$$\mathbf{x} = \mathbf{f}^{-1}(\mathbf{y}) \tag{4.60}$$

exists. Assume now that $\mathbf{x}$ is in a small rectangular region shown in Fig. 4.7(a) (for $n = 2$) with volume

$$\Delta V_x = \Delta x_1 \, \Delta x_2 \, . \, . \, . \, \Delta x_n \tag{4.61}$$

The rectangular region in X maps into a generally nonrectangular region in Y whose volume is given by

$$\Delta V_y = J(\mathbf{y}, \mathbf{x}) \, \Delta V_x \tag{4.62}$$

where the Jacobian $J(\mathbf{y}, \mathbf{x})$ is defined by

$$J(\mathbf{y}, \mathbf{x}) = \left|\det \frac{\partial \mathbf{f}^T}{\partial \mathbf{x}}\right| \tag{4.63}$$

(For a proof and discussion of this result, see Ref. 3.) Since the event that $\mathbf{x}$ is in the small region of X is the same as the event that $\mathbf{y}$ is in the corresponding small region of Y, one can equate the two probabilities to obtain

$$p_{\mathbf{x}}(\hat{\mathbf{x}})\,\Delta V_{\mathbf{x}} = p_{\mathbf{y}}(\hat{\mathbf{y}})\,\Delta V_y = p_{\mathbf{y}}(\hat{\mathbf{y}})\,J(\mathbf{y}, \mathbf{x})\,\Delta V_{\mathbf{x}} \tag{4.64}$$

Since the region with volume $\Delta V_{\mathbf{x}}$ is small but arbitrary, Eq. 4.64 must be independent of $\Delta V_{\mathbf{x}}$ and one therefore has the result

$$p_{\mathbf{y}}(\hat{\mathbf{y}}) = \frac{1}{J(\mathbf{y}, \mathbf{x})}\,p_{\mathbf{x}}(\mathbf{f}^{-1}(\hat{\mathbf{y}})) \tag{4.65}$$

Equation 4.65 is a useful result that holds for any invertible (nonlinear) transformation $\mathbf{f}$ and any probability density $p_{\mathbf{x}}$. If $\mathbf{f}$ is the linear transformation defined by Eq. 4.11 and $p_{\mathbf{x}}$ is the Gaussian density (4.57), then the Jacobian $J(\mathbf{y}, \mathbf{x})$ is simply the absolute value of the determinant of $\mathbf{A}$ and one obtains the result

$$\begin{aligned} p_{\mathbf{y}}(\hat{\mathbf{y}}) &= \frac{1}{|\det \mathbf{A}|} \cdot \frac{1}{(2\pi)^{n/2}|\mathbf{K}_{\mathbf{x}}|^{1/2}} \exp\left[-\frac{1}{2}(\mathbf{A}^{-1}\hat{\mathbf{y}} - \mathbf{m}_x)^T\mathbf{K}_{\mathbf{x}}^{-1}(\mathbf{A}^{-1}\hat{\mathbf{y}} - \mathbf{m}_x)\right] \\ &= \frac{1}{(2\pi)^{n/2}|\mathbf{K}_{\mathbf{y}}|^{1/2}} \exp\left[-\frac{1}{2}(\hat{\mathbf{y}} - \mathbf{m}_y)^T\,\mathbf{K}_{\mathbf{y}}^{-1}(\hat{\mathbf{y}} - \mathbf{m}_y)\right] \end{aligned} \tag{4.66}$$

where $\mathbf{m}_y$ and $\mathbf{K}_{\mathbf{y}}$ are defined by Eqs. 4.47 and 4.49, respectively. Thus it has been shown that when $\mathbf{x}$ is a Gaussian random vector, $\mathbf{y}$ is also a Gaussian random vector.

Before concluding this section, we shall just remark that if $\mathbf{y}$ is defined by the relation

$$\mathbf{y} = \mathbf{A}\mathbf{x} + \mathbf{b} \tag{4.67}$$

where $\mathbf{A}$ is a linear transformation and $\mathbf{b}$ is a constant vector, then $\mathbf{y}$ is a Gaussian random vector whose density is given by Eq. 4.66, where $\mathbf{K}_{\mathbf{y}}$ is defined by Eq. 4.49 and $\mathbf{m}_{\mathbf{y}}$ is defined by

$$\mathbf{m}_{\mathbf{y}} = \mathbf{A}\mathbf{m}_{\mathbf{x}} + \mathbf{b} \tag{4.68}$$

The proof of this fact follows directly again from Eq. 4.65.

4.7 DIAGONALIZATION OF THE COVARIANCE MATRIX

4.7.1 Diagonalization by Orthonormal Transformation

Sometimes it is desirable to find a basis for which the components of a random vector $\mathbf{x}$ are uncorrelated. That is, if x'_i $i = 1, 2, \ldots, n$, are the components with respect to the basis, then

$$E[x'_i x'_j] = m'_i m'_j \qquad i \neq j \tag{4.69}$$

or

$$E[(x'_i - m'_i)(x'_j - m'_j)] = 0 \qquad i \neq j \tag{4.70}$$

It will be shown that the *eigenvectors* of the covariance matrix for $\mathbf{x}$ form such a basis.

If $\mathbf{K}$ is the covariance matrix, an eigenvector $\mathbf{e}$ and an *eigenvalue* λ satisfy the relation

$$\mathbf{Ke} = \lambda\mathbf{e} \tag{4.71}$$

That is, $\mathbf{K}$, when regarded as a linear transformation, maps the eigenvector $\mathbf{e}$ into a scaled version of itself. It is a fact that if the matrix $\mathbf{K}$ is positive semidefinite (as all covariance matrices are), then there exist n linearly independent eigenvectors (usually corresponding to different eigenvalues). Thus these eigenvectors form a basis for X. One can further show that it is always possible to find a set of eigenvectors $\mathbf{e}_1, \mathbf{e}_2, \ldots, \mathbf{e}_n$ that are orthonormal. Hence one can show that

$$\mathbf{e}_i^T\mathbf{K}\mathbf{e}_j = \mathbf{e}_i^T(\lambda_j\mathbf{e}_j) = \lambda_j\,\mathbf{e}_i^T\mathbf{e}_j = \begin{cases} \lambda_i & \text{if } i = j \\ 0 & \text{if } i \neq j \end{cases} \tag{4.72}$$

and therefore one has the relation

$$\mathbf{E}^T\mathbf{K}\mathbf{E} = \begin{bmatrix} \leftarrow \mathbf{e}_1^T \rightarrow \\ \leftarrow \mathbf{e}_2^T \rightarrow \\ \vdots \\ \leftarrow \mathbf{e}_n^T \rightarrow \end{bmatrix} \mathbf{K} \begin{bmatrix} \uparrow & \uparrow & & \uparrow \\ \mathbf{e}_1 & \mathbf{e}_2 & \cdots & \mathbf{e}_n \\ \downarrow & \downarrow & & \downarrow \end{bmatrix} = \begin{bmatrix} \lambda_1 & & & 0 \\ & \lambda_2 & & \\ & & \ddots & \\ 0 & & & \lambda_n \end{bmatrix} = \mathbf{\Lambda} \tag{4.73}$$

($\mathbf{E}$ is the matrix whose columns are the eigenvectors.) Now observe from Eqs. 4.11 and 4.49 that $\mathbf{\Lambda}$ is the covariance matrix for the transformed variable $\mathbf{x}'$ defined by

$$\mathbf{x}' = \mathbf{E}^T\mathbf{x} \tag{4.74}$$

and thus that the components x'_i must satisfy Eq. 4.70. Thus $\mathbf{E}^T$ is the desired transformation and, since it is orthonormal (see Section 4.3.2), its application amounts to a rotation of the coordinate system to one defined by the eigenvectors of $\mathbf{K}$. The eigenvalues λ_i are the variances $\sigma_i'^2$ of the vector components in the new coordinate system.

Before proceeding, let us just note a few additional facts about the eigenvector transformation (4.74). First, by using Eq. 4.24 in Eq. 4.73, one can express the covariance matrix as

$$\mathbf{K} = \mathbf{E}\mathbf{\Lambda}\mathbf{E}^T \tag{4.75}$$

Then, since $\mathbf{E}^{-1} = \mathbf{E}^T$, one can immediately obtain the relation

$$\mathbf{K}^{-1} = \mathbf{E}\boldsymbol{\Lambda}^{-1}\mathbf{E}^T \tag{4.76}$$

which is useful for inverting the covariance matrix, since $\boldsymbol{\Lambda}^{-1}$ is simply a diagonal matrix with diagonal elements $1/\lambda_j$. In addition, it can be shown that since $\mathbf{E}$ is an orthonormal transformation, the determinant and trace of $\mathbf{K}$ are the same as the determinant and trace of $\boldsymbol{\Lambda}$ (see Eqs. 4.50c and 4.50d). Thus one has the relations

$$|\mathbf{K}| = |\boldsymbol{\Lambda}| = \prod_{j=1}^{n} \lambda_j \tag{4.77a}$$

$$\text{tr}\,\mathbf{K} = \text{tr}\,\boldsymbol{\Lambda} = \sum_{j=1}^{n} \lambda_j \tag{4.77b}$$

In order to find the eigenvectors of a matrix, notice that Eq. 4.71 can be written in the equivalent form

$$(\mathbf{K} - \lambda\mathbf{I})\mathbf{e} = \mathbf{0} \tag{4.78}$$

In order for nontrivial solutions of Eq. 4.78 to exist, it is required that

$$\det(\mathbf{K} - \lambda\mathbf{I}) = 0 \tag{4.79}$$

Equation 4.79 is the *characteristic equation* corresponding to Eq. 4.71 and its roots (values of λ that satisfy it) are the eigenvalues of $\mathbf{K}$. (This result is known as the Cayley–Hamilton theorem.) Once these eigenvalues are found, one can use each one in Eq. 4.78 to determine its corresponding eigenvector.[5]

■ EXAMPLE 4.5

Calculation of Eigenvalues and Eigenvectors

Consider the 2×2 covariance matrix

$$\mathbf{K} = \begin{bmatrix} 21 & -8 \\ -8 & 9 \end{bmatrix}$$

The characteristic equation for the eigenvalues is

$$\begin{vmatrix} 21 - \lambda & -8 \\ -8 & 9 - \lambda \end{vmatrix} = \lambda^2 - 30\lambda + 125 = 0$$

which has the two roots[6]

[5] In practice, numerically more efficient methods exist for finding the eigenvectors. See, for example, Ref. 4.

[6] It is conventional to number the eigenvalues from largest to smallest.

$$\lambda_1 = 25$$

$$\lambda_2 = 5$$

To find the first eigenvector, one can substitute $\lambda_1 = 25$ in Eq. 4.78 and solve

$$\begin{bmatrix} -4 & -8 \\ -8 & -16 \end{bmatrix} \mathbf{e}_1 = \mathbf{0}$$

which yields (noting that $\mathbf{e}_1^T \mathbf{e}_1 = 1$) the result

$$\mathbf{e}_1 = \begin{bmatrix} \dfrac{2}{\sqrt{5}} \\ \\ \dfrac{-1}{\sqrt{5}} \end{bmatrix}$$

The second eigenvector can be found in a similar manner by substituting $\lambda_2 = 5$ in Eq. 4.78 and solving

$$\begin{bmatrix} 16 & -8 \\ -8 & 4 \end{bmatrix} \mathbf{e}_2 = \mathbf{0}$$

which yields

$$\mathbf{e}_2 = \begin{bmatrix} \dfrac{1}{\sqrt{5}} \\ \\ \dfrac{2}{\sqrt{5}} \end{bmatrix}$$

To check the result, note that

$$\begin{bmatrix} \dfrac{2}{\sqrt{5}} & \dfrac{-1}{\sqrt{5}} \\ \\ \dfrac{1}{\sqrt{5}} & \dfrac{2}{\sqrt{5}} \end{bmatrix} \begin{bmatrix} 21 & -8 \\ \\ -8 & 9 \end{bmatrix} \begin{bmatrix} \dfrac{2}{\sqrt{5}} & \dfrac{1}{\sqrt{5}} \\ \\ \dfrac{-1}{\sqrt{5}} & \dfrac{2}{\sqrt{5}} \end{bmatrix} = \begin{bmatrix} 25 & 0 \\ \\ 0 & 5 \end{bmatrix}$$

so Eq. 4.73 is satisfied. ■

The procedure described here leads to vectors with uncorrelated vector components regardless of the form of the density characterizing the random vectors in the original coordinate frame. However, for Gaussian random vectors, it is easy to show that the density of the transformed vector takes the form of a product of one-dimensional Gaussian density functions

$$p_{\mathbf{x}'}(\mathbf{x}') = \prod_{i=1}^{n} \frac{1}{\sqrt{2\pi \lambda_i}} \exp -\frac{(x_i' - m_i')^2}{2\lambda_i} \tag{4.80}$$

and therefore the components of $\mathbf{x}'$ are statistically independent.

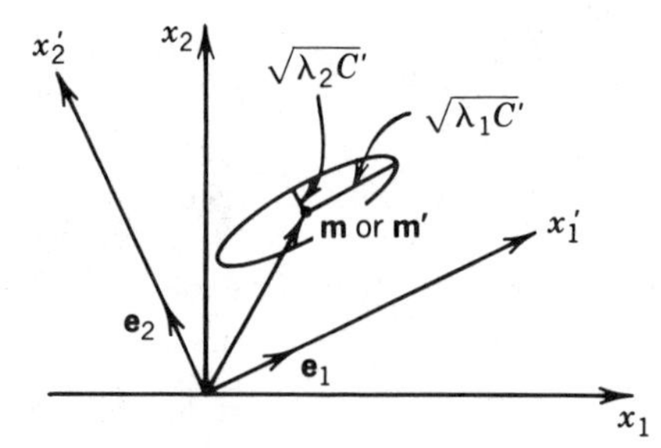

FIGURE 4.8 Contours of a Gaussian density.

The results of this section can also be used to plot the contours of the Gaussian density function. That is, suppose that it is desired to plot the curves defined by the relation

$$p_{\mathbf{x}}(\mathbf{x}) = \frac{1}{(2\pi)^{n/2}\,|\mathbf{K}|^{1/2}} \cdot e^{\,[-\frac{1}{2}(\mathbf{x}-\mathbf{m})^T\mathbf{K}^{-1}(\mathbf{x}-\mathbf{m}]} = C \tag{4.81}$$

where C is a constant. Equation 4.81 reduces to

$$(\mathbf{x}-\mathbf{m})^T\mathbf{K}^{-1}(\mathbf{x}-\mathbf{m}) = C' \tag{4.82}$$

where C' is another constant related to C in an obvious way. The quantity on the left-hand side of Eq. 4.82 has all the properties of a distance function between the random vector $\mathbf{x}$ and the mean $\mathbf{m}$ and is called the *Mahalanobis distance* [5]. Thus Eq. 4.82 is the locus of all points at a given Mahalanobis distance from the mean. We shall see that this locus is an elipse in n dimensions.

Note now that if the transformation of Eq. 4.74 is applied to Eq. 4.82, one can write the latter equation as

$$(\mathbf{x}'-\mathbf{m}')^T\mathbf{\Lambda}^{-1}(\mathbf{x}'-\mathbf{m}') = C' \tag{4.83}$$

Equation 4.83 can be written in expanded form as

$$\frac{(x_1'-m_1')^2}{\lambda_1} + \frac{(x_2'-m_2')^2}{\lambda_2} + \ldots + \frac{(x_n'-m_n')^2}{\lambda_n} = C' \tag{4.84}$$

This is the equation of a hyperellipse with center at $\mathbf{m}'$ (or $\mathbf{m}$ with respect to the original coordinate system; see Fig. 4.8). The principal axes of the ellipse are aligned with the eigenvectors, and their sizes are given by $2\sqrt{\lambda_j C'}$ $j = 1, 2, \ldots, n$. Diagonalization of the covariance matrix and plotting of the distribution contours can also be applied to densities that are not Gaussian, but well described by their first and second moments. This is an important method for gaining insight about the statistical character of a random vector.

4.7.2 Diagonalization by LU Decomposition

The eigenvector transformation is not the only way to diagonalize a covariance matrix. Another useful way to perform the diagonalization is by LU (triangular) decomposition [6].

Let **A** be a nonsingular square matrix such that all of the submatrices formed by taking only the first k rows and columns of **A** are also nonsingular. Then **A** can be expressed as a product

$$\mathbf{A} = \mathbf{L}\mathbf{U} \tag{4.85}$$

where **L** is *lower triangular* (i.e., all elements above the main diagonal are zero) and **U** is *upper triangular* (all elements below the diagonal are zero). If we require that the diagonal elements of **L** are all ones, that is, that **L** is *unit lower triangular*, then this factoring is unique and can be effected by Gaussian elimination of the elements in the lower triangular portion of **A**.

We can further note that if **D** is a diagonal matrix consisting of the diagonal elements of **U** then Eq. 4.85 can be written as

$$\mathbf{A} = \mathbf{L}\mathbf{D}\mathbf{U}' \tag{4.86}$$

where $\mathbf{U}'$ is *unit upper triangular* (ones on the diagonal). If the matrix **A** is symmetric, then clearly $\mathbf{U}' = \mathbf{L}^T$.

The foregoing considerations suggest another way to diagonalize the covariance matrix. Since the covariance matrix **K** is positive definite, the conditions stated above for the **LU** decomposition are satisfied. Furthermore, since the covariance matrix is symmetric, we can write

$$\mathbf{K} = \mathbf{L}\mathbf{D}\mathbf{L}^T \tag{4.87}$$

and thus

$$\mathbf{L}^{-1}\mathbf{K}(\mathbf{L}^T)^{-1} = \mathbf{L}^{-1}\mathbf{K}(\mathbf{L}^{-1})^T = \mathbf{D} \tag{4.88}$$

From our earlier considerations, it can be seen that **D** is the covariance matrix for a random vector $\mathbf{x}''$ defined by

$$\mathbf{x}'' = \mathbf{L}^{-1}\mathbf{x} \tag{4.89}$$

and thus the components of $\mathbf{x}''$ are uncorrelated. The diagonal elements of **D** represent the variances of the transformed variables. Unlike the eigenvector transformation, Eq. 4.89 cannot be interpreted as a simple rotation of the coordinate axes. However, we can observe that since **L** is unit lower triangular, $\mathbf{L}^{-1}$ will have the same property. One way to see this is by induction. Suppose that the property holds for inverse matrices of dimension $n - 1$. Then for a unit lower triangular matrix of dimension n, we can write

$$\underbrace{\left[\begin{array}{c|c} \mathbf{L}_{n-1}^{-1} & \begin{matrix} 0 \\ \beta \end{matrix} \\ \hline \gamma & \alpha \end{array}\right]}_{\mathbf{L}^{-1}} \underbrace{\left[\begin{array}{c|c} \mathbf{L}_{n-1} & \begin{matrix} 0 \\ 0 \\ \vdots \\ 0 \end{matrix} \\ \hline \mathbf{l}_n & 1 \end{array}\right]}_{\mathbf{L}} = \underbrace{\begin{bmatrix} 1 & & & & \\ & 1 & & & \\ & & 1 & & \\ \times & \times & \times & \times\times\times\times & \\ & & 0 & \ddots & \\ & & & & 1 \end{bmatrix}}_{\mathbf{I}} \tag{4.90}$$

(Row j → indicated at the row containing β.)

Clearly, in order for the product to be the identity matrix, the element α must be one. Also, if any element in the last column of $\mathbf{L}^{-1}$ such as β is nonzero, then the elements in the corresponding row of the product (denoted by the symbols x) will be nonzero. Thus the inverse cannot have nonzero elements (except α) in the last column, and $\mathbf{L}^{-1}$ must be lower triangular. Since the unit lower triangular property is trivially true for $n = 1$, it is therefore true for all n.

Because $\mathbf{L}^{-1}$ is lower triangular, we observe from Eq. 4.89 that an element x''_k of the new random vector $\mathbf{x}''$ is a function of only the variables x_j for $j \leq k$. The importance of this form of covariance diagonalization is that if the original random variables represent measurements observed in the sequence $x_1, x_2, x_3 \ldots$, then the transformed variables depend only on those measurements already observed. If the variables x_j represent a discrete-time signal or time series, then $\mathbf{L}^{-1}$ represents a *causal* transformation of the signal. Such a transformation is important for real-time applications and for the sequential classification procedures discussed in Chapter 10.

Before we close this section, observe that since $\mathbf{L}$ is unit lower triangular, its determinant is equal to one. Thus, from Eq. 4.87, one can write

$$|\mathbf{K}| = |\mathbf{L}|\,|\mathbf{D}|\,|\mathbf{L}^T| = |\mathbf{D}| = \prod_{k=1}^{n} d_k \tag{4.91}$$

where d_k are the diagonal elements of D. Since the d_k represent the variances of the transformed variables x''_k, we see that as in the case of diagonalization by the eigenvector transformation, the determinant of the covariance matrix can be expressed as a product of the variances of the transformed variables.

4.8 SUMMARY

This chapter reviews important concepts related to random vectors and operations upon them. The concepts of vector space, inner product, and bases are discussed together with the notions of general and orthonormal linear transformations. The ideas of singularity and positive definiteness of a linear transformation are also defined. The expectation of a quantity derived from a random vector is discussed, and the correlation and covariance matrices for random vectors are defined. The notion of uncorrelated random vectors is discussed briefly, and the procedure of computing expectations from samples of a random vector is described. Following that, the Gaussian density function is introduced and some properties of Gaussian random vectors are explored. The eigenvectors and eigenvalues of the covariance matrix are then studied in the context of a transformation leading to a set of uncorrelated random variables. These concepts are used to plot contours of the Gaussian density function. Finally, LU matrix decomposition is described as leading to an alternative transformation for producing a set of uncorrelated random variables. It is pointed out that the resulting transformation is ideally suited to situations where the components of the random vector are measurements observed sequentially and the transformed variables must depend only on measurements previously observed.

REFERENCES

1. G. Birkhoff, and S. MacLane. *A Survey of Modern Algebra*, 4th ed. New York: Macmillan Publishing Company, 1977.
2. G. B. Thomas. *Calculus and Analytic Geometry*, 5th ed. Reading, MA: Addison Wesley Publishing Company, 1979.
3. A. E. Taylor. *Advanced Calculus*, 3rd ed. New York: John Wiley & Sons, Inc., 1983.
4. Y. N. Faddeeva. *Computational Methods of Linear Algebra*. New York: Dover Publications, 1959.
5. P. C. Mahalanobis. "On the Generalized Distance in Statistics." *Proc. Nat. Inst. Sci. Calcutta*, Vol. 12, pp. 49–55 (1936).
6. D. M. Young, and R. T. Gregory. *A Survey of Numerical Mathematics*. Reading, MA: Addison-Wesley Publishing Company, 1973.

PROBLEMS

4.1 Are the vectors

$$\mathbf{u}_1 = \begin{bmatrix} \frac{2}{\sqrt{5}} \\ \\ \frac{-1}{\sqrt{5}} \end{bmatrix} \qquad \mathbf{u}_2 = \begin{bmatrix} \frac{2}{\sqrt{13}} \\ \\ \frac{3}{\sqrt{13}} \end{bmatrix}$$

linearly independent? Are they orthonormal?

4.2 **(a)** Find the determinant and trace of the matrix

$$\begin{bmatrix} \frac{1}{\sqrt{2}} & \frac{1}{\sqrt{2}} \\ \frac{-1}{\sqrt{2}} & \frac{1}{\sqrt{2}} \end{bmatrix}$$

Is the matrix positive definite? Can the matrix represent an orthonormal transformation?

(b) Repeat part (a) for the matrix

$$\begin{bmatrix} -2 & 1 \\ 1 & 3 \end{bmatrix}$$

4.3 Show that if $\mathbf{F}$ is any matrix with real elements, the matrix $\mathbf{F}\mathbf{F}^T$ is symmetric and positive semidefinite.

4.4 By starting with the definitions, show that the correlation matrix $\mathbf{R}$ and the covariance matrix $\mathbf{K}$ are always positive semidefinite matrices.

4.5 Calculate the expected vector, covariance matrix, and correlation matrix of the data given by

$$\mathbf{x}^{(1)} = \begin{bmatrix} 1 \\ 1 \end{bmatrix} \quad \mathbf{x}^{(2)} = \begin{bmatrix} 1 \\ 2 \end{bmatrix} \quad \mathbf{x}^{(3)} = \begin{bmatrix} 2 \\ 0 \end{bmatrix} \quad \mathbf{x}^{(4)} = \begin{bmatrix} 0 \\ 1 \end{bmatrix}$$

If the data are known to be Gaussian, what is the density function?

4.6 A random variable x has the probability density

$$p_x(x) = \frac{1}{\sigma\sqrt{2\pi}} \exp\left[-\frac{(x-\mu)^2}{2\sigma^2}\right]$$

(a) What is the density of y in the following equation?

$$y = ax + b$$

(b) What is the density of z in the following equation?

$$z = x^3$$

4.7 A covariance matrix is

$$\mathbf{K} = E[(\mathbf{x} - \mathbf{m})(\mathbf{x} - \mathbf{m})^T] = \begin{bmatrix} 1 & 0.5 \\ 0.5 & 1 \end{bmatrix} \text{ with } \mathbf{m} = \begin{bmatrix} 1 \\ 0 \end{bmatrix}$$

(a) What are its eigenvalues and eigenvectors?

(b) Sketch the ellipse representing this covariance in the $\mathbf{x}$ plane.

4.8 **(a)** Show that if $\mathbf{A}$ represents an orthonormal transformation, then $|\mathbf{A}| = \pm 1$. Use this to prove Eqs. 4.50a and 4.50c.

(b) Show that if $\mathbf{A}$ and $\mathbf{B}$ are any two conformable matrices, $\text{tr}(\mathbf{AB}) = \text{tr}(\mathbf{BA})$. Use this result to prove Eqs. 4.50b and 4.50d when $\mathbf{A}$ is an orthonormal transformation.

4.9 **(a)** What can be said about the eigenvalues of a matrix if the matrix is not singular? What can be said about the eigenvalues of a matrix if it is positive definite?

(b) Show that the determinant of a matrix must be positive if the matrix is to be positive definite. Use this fact to show that the matrix of Problem 4.2(b) cannot be positive definite.

4.10 By multiplying rows by a constant and subtracting them from higher numbered rows, show that the matrix

$$\mathbf{A} = \begin{bmatrix} 3 & 2 & 1 \\ 2 & 3 & 2 \\ 1 & 2 & 3 \end{bmatrix}$$

can be expressed as

$$\mathbf{A} = \begin{bmatrix} 1 & 0 & 0 \\ \frac{2}{3} & 1 & 0 \\ \frac{1}{3} & \frac{4}{5} & 1 \end{bmatrix} \begin{bmatrix} 3 & 2 & 1 \\ 0 & \frac{5}{3} & \frac{4}{3} \\ 0 & 0 & \frac{8}{5} \end{bmatrix}$$

$$= \begin{bmatrix} 1 & 0 & 0 \\ \frac{2}{3} & 1 & 0 \\ \frac{1}{3} & \frac{4}{5} & 1 \end{bmatrix} \begin{bmatrix} 3 & 0 & 0 \\ 0 & \frac{5}{3} & 0 \\ 0 & 0 & \frac{8}{5} \end{bmatrix} \begin{bmatrix} 1 & \frac{2}{3} & \frac{1}{3} \\ 0 & 1 & \frac{4}{5} \\ 0 & 0 & 1 \end{bmatrix}$$

and thus is of the form $\mathbf{LDL}^T$.

Show also that the matrix $\mathbf{L}^{-1}$ has the following lower triangular form

$$\mathbf{L}^{-1} = \begin{bmatrix} 1 & 0 & 0 \\ -\frac{2}{3} & 1 & 0 \\ \frac{1}{5} & -\frac{4}{5} & 1 \end{bmatrix}$$

and that it can be obtained by performing the same multiplication and subtraction operations that are used to reduce $\mathbf{A}$ on rows of the identity matrix.

4.11 The means and covariances for two classes of *Gaussian* observation vectors are

$$\mathbf{m}_1 = \begin{bmatrix} 1 \\ 0 \end{bmatrix}, \quad \mathbf{m}_2 = \begin{bmatrix} 0 \\ 1 \end{bmatrix}, \quad \mathbf{K}_1 = \mathbf{K}_2 = \begin{bmatrix} 2 & -1 \\ -1 & 2 \end{bmatrix}$$

The prior probabilities of the classes are

$$\Pr[\omega_1] = \frac{2}{3}, \quad \Pr[\omega_2] = \frac{1}{3}$$

(a) What is the decision rule that minimizes the probability of error? (Write it in the simplest form possible.)

(b) Let h be the random variable that represents the value of minus twice the log of the likelihood ratio. Determine the density $p_{h|\omega_1}(\hat{h}|\omega_1)$ and express the error $e_1 = \Pr[\text{error}|\omega_1]$ as an integral of the density $p_{h|\omega_1}(\hat{h}|\omega_1)$.

CHAPTER 5

Feature Extraction and Nonlinear Mapping

In Chapter 1, we saw that observations made on patterns were usually transformed into a set of features before classification. Although these features are often suggested by the nature of the problem (this was the case for the examples of Chapter 1), it is sometimes useful to have formal automatic methods for finding features. These methods, which are generally applicable to any problem, are the topic of the present chapter.

Nonlinear mapping is a related topic. Although its main purpose is to explore the structure of data by mapping it into a lower dimensional space, the mappings if explicit, can be used as feature transformations. Some basic forms of nonlinear mapping are also discussed here.

5.1 GENERAL APPROACHES TO FEATURE EXTRACTION

The goal of feature extraction is to find a transformation from an n-dimensional observation space X to a smaller m-dimensional feature space Y that retains most of the information needed for pattern classification. The coordinate axes that define the feature space Y are called *features*. There are two main reasons for performing feature extraction. First, the computational complexity for pattern classification is reduced by dealing with the data in a lower dimensional space. Secondly, for a given number of training samples, one can generally obtain more accurate estimates of the class-conditional density functions and thus formulate a more reliable decision rule. Whether or not this decision rule actually performs better than one applied in the observation space depends on how much information was lost in the feature transformation. In some cases, it is possible to derive features that sacrifice *none* of the information needed for classification. We will refer to these as "optimal" features (see the next section).

In many cases features are simply postulated (as in Chapter 1) on the basis of characteristics peculiar to the problem at hand or on the basis of intuition. These features may then be ranked according to their level of performance and the best m features can be selected for use thereafter. However, the m features that produce the best classification results when used jointly may not be the same as the m highest-ranking individual features. In fact, selecting these jointly optimal features is a rather tedious combinatorial problem.[1] Often this problem is simply ignored and the m highest ranking features are chosen with the rationale that unless these features are linearly dependent, or nearly so, then each new feature will contribute some new information to the problem and this amalgamation will perform very nearly as well as the best set of m features. This approach to deriving features will be called *feature selection* and is valid for many practical problems in spite of its lack of mathematical elegance.

In order to rank features, it is not always necessary to design and test individual classifiers based on each combination of features. More often, one would use various analytical expressions that bound the probability of error or otherwise relate to class separability (see Chapter 9) to evaluate the features. There is a danger in this procedure, however. The error bounds or measures of separability usually depend upon the probability density function, which may not be known. It is tempting, therefore, to use formulas that make specific assumptions about the form of the density (e.g., that it is Gaussian). *This can give misleading results*. Hence feature selection and ranking, although not generally considered an analytical process, should be approached with care and thoughtfulness.

The approaches described in this chapter are true feature extraction techniques in that they involve mathematical procedures to derive or construct features from the statistical characteristics of the data. Although the features can usually be related to characteristics peculiar to the problem from which the data was derived, no special consideration is given to these characteristics in deriving the features.

The procedures optimize various criteria. The most desirable procedures optimize a measure of class separability, but others merely optimize a criterion related to *representation* of the data. Examples of both types of feature extraction procedures are described in the following sections.

5.2 "OPTIMAL" FEATURES

An *optimal* set of features will be defined as a set of features that results in no increase in the minimum probability of error. That is, the probability of error is the same when a Bayes decision rule is applied in both the observation and the feature spaces. Loosely speaking, one finds that an optimal set of features contains all the information present in the observation vector that is relevant to the classification of the patterns.

[1]See Devijver and Kittler [1] for a comprehensive discussion of search methods for feature selection.

Optimal features are also known as *sufficient statistics*. A sufficient statistic $\mathbf{y}$ is defined as one for which

$$p_{\mathbf{x}|\mathbf{y},\omega_i}(\mathbf{x}|\mathbf{y},\omega_i) = p_{\mathbf{x}|\mathbf{y},\omega_j}(\mathbf{x}|\mathbf{y},\omega_j) \qquad \text{all } i, j \tag{5.1}$$

That is, the density for $\mathbf{x}$ conditioned on $\mathbf{y}$ is *independent of the class* ω. Since the decision rule that minimizes the probability of error in the observation space chooses the class with the largest posterior probability $\Pr[\omega_i|\hat{\mathbf{x}}]$, it can be shown that if $\mathbf{y}$ is a sufficient statistic, then the optimal decision rule can be made independent of $\mathbf{x}$. In particular, since $\mathbf{y}$ is derived from $\mathbf{x}$, one has

$$\begin{aligned} \Pr[\omega_i|\hat{\mathbf{x}}] &= \Pr[\omega_i|\hat{\mathbf{y}}, \hat{\mathbf{x}}] \\ &= p_{\mathbf{y}|\omega_i}(\hat{\mathbf{y}}|\omega_i)\Pr[\omega_i] \cdot \left(\frac{p_{\mathbf{x}|\mathbf{y}\omega_i}(\hat{\mathbf{x}}|\hat{\mathbf{y}},\omega_i)}{p_{\mathbf{xy}}(\hat{\mathbf{x}},\hat{\mathbf{y}})}\right) \end{aligned} \tag{5.2}$$

Since $\mathbf{y}$ is a sufficient statistic, the term in parentheses does not depend on ω_i and thus does not influence the decision rule. The first two terms in Eq. 5.2 (which depend only on $\mathbf{y}$) therefore constitute a discriminant function in the feature space that achieves the minimum probability of error. The converse of this result is also true. If the optimal decision rule in the observation space depends only on a quantity $\mathbf{y}$, then $\mathbf{y}$ is a sufficient statistic. This follows because if the optimal decision rule depends only on $\mathbf{y}$, then the term in parentheses in Eq. 5.2 must not enter into the decision rule. Thus $p_{\mathbf{x}|\mathbf{y},\omega_i}$ must satisfy Eq. 5.1 and so $\mathbf{y}$ is a sufficient statistic.

■ EXAMPLE 5.1

Zero-Mean Gaussian Random Vectors

Consider two classes of zero-mean Gaussian observation vectors with covariance matrices $\mathbf{K}_1 = \sigma_1^2\mathbf{I}$ and $\mathbf{K}_2 = \sigma_2^2\mathbf{I}$.

It is easy to show (see Problem 5.1) that the optimal decision rule in the observation space can be expressed as

$$\left(\frac{1}{\sigma_1^2} - \frac{1}{\sigma_2^2}\right)\sum_{i=1}^{n} x_i^2 + n\ln\frac{\sigma_1^2}{\sigma_2^2} \underset{\omega_2}{\overset{\omega_1}{\lessgtr}} T$$

where $T = 2\ln(\Pr[\omega_1]/\Pr[\omega_2])$. The decision rule thus depends only on the single feature

$$y = \sum_{i=1}^{n} x_i^2 = |\mathbf{x}|^2$$

which is the sufficient statistic. ■

5.3 FEATURE EXTRACTION BASED ON EIGENVECTOR ANALYSIS

A large number of feature extraction techniques involving linear transformations are based in one way or another on the eigenvectors of the correlation or covariance matrices. Some of the more general results will be derived here. The techniques to be described are very closely related to the topic in statistics known as principle component analysis and to the Karhunen–Loève expansion in stochastic process theory. In fact, because of the latter relations, these feature extraction techniques are often (somewhat inappropriately) called Karhunen–Loève methods.

5.3.1 Choosing Features for Optimal Representation

Suppose that it is desired to approximate a random vector $\mathbf{x}$ of dimension n by a linear combination of $m < n$ vectors from some orthonormal basis $\{\mathbf{u}_j, j = 1, 2, \ldots, n\}$. The approximation is

$$\tilde{\mathbf{x}} = y_1\mathbf{u}_1 + y_2\mathbf{u}_2 + \cdots + y_m\mathbf{u}_m \tag{5.3}$$

where

$$y_j = \mathbf{u}_j^T\mathbf{x} \tag{5.4}$$

Equations 5.3 and 5.4 can be written more concisely as

$$\tilde{\mathbf{x}} = \mathbf{U}_m\mathbf{y} \tag{5.5}$$

and

$$\mathbf{y} = \mathbf{U}_m^T\mathbf{x} \tag{5.6}$$

where $\mathbf{y}$ is the m-dimensional vector whose components are y_j and $\mathbf{U}_m$ is the matrix of basis vectors

$$\mathbf{U}_m = \begin{bmatrix} \uparrow & \uparrow & & \uparrow \\ \mathbf{u}_1 & \mathbf{u}_2 & \cdots & \mathbf{u}_m \\ \downarrow & \downarrow & & \downarrow \end{bmatrix} \tag{5.7}$$

Since $\{\mathbf{u}_j, j = 1, 2, \ldots, n\}$ is an orthonormal basis, the residual error in representing $\mathbf{x}$ by $\tilde{\mathbf{x}}$ is given by

$$\boldsymbol{\varepsilon} = \mathbf{x} - \tilde{\mathbf{x}} = \sum_{j=m+1}^{n} y_j\mathbf{u}_j \tag{5.8}$$

where the y_j for $j > m$ are still defined according to Eq. 5.4. The problem now is to choose the basis $\{\mathbf{u}_j\}$ such that the *mean-square error*

$$\mathscr{E} = E[|\boldsymbol{\varepsilon}|^2] = E[|\mathbf{x} - \tilde{\mathbf{x}}|^2] \tag{5.9}$$

is as small as possible. The y_j can then be regarded as features derived from the random vector $\mathbf{x}$ and Eq. 5.6 represents the feature transformation.

It follows from Eqs. 5.8 and 5.9 and the condition that the basis is orthonormal that

$$\mathscr{E} = E[\boldsymbol{\varepsilon}^T\boldsymbol{\varepsilon}] = E\left[\left(\sum_{i=m+1}^{n} y_i\mathbf{u}_i^T\right)\left(\sum_{j=m+1}^{n} y_j\mathbf{u}_j\right)\right] = \sum_{j=m+1}^{n} E[y_j^2] \tag{5.10}$$

If one writes

$$y_j^2 = (y_j)(y_j) = (\mathbf{u}_j^T\mathbf{x})(\mathbf{x}^T\mathbf{u}_j) \tag{5.11}$$

it then follows that

$$E[y_j^2] = \mathbf{u}_j^T\, E[\mathbf{x}\mathbf{x}^T]\, \mathbf{u}_j = \mathbf{u}_j^T\, \mathbf{R}\, \mathbf{u}_j \tag{5.12}$$

where $\mathbf{R}$ is the correlation matrix for $\mathbf{x}$. By substituting Eq. 5.12 into Eq. 5.10, one finds that the quantity to be minimized is

$$\mathscr{E} = \sum_{j=m+1}^{n} \mathbf{u}_j^T\, \mathbf{R}\mathbf{u}_j \tag{5.13}$$

subject, of course, to the constraint

$$\mathbf{u}_j^T\, \mathbf{u}_j = 1 \qquad j = m + 1, \ldots, n \tag{5.14}$$

The constraints of Eq. 5.14 can be incorporated directly into the minimization problem by using a set of Lagrange multipliers λ_j and seeking to minimize the quantity

$$\mathscr{E}' = \sum_{j=m+1}^{n} \mathbf{u}_j^T\, \mathbf{R}\mathbf{u}_j + \sum_{j=m+1}^{n} \lambda_j(1 - \mathbf{u}_j^T\mathbf{u}_j) \tag{5.15}$$

A *necessary* condition for the minimum is that

$$\frac{\partial \mathscr{E}'}{\partial \mathbf{u}_j} = 2(\mathbf{R}\mathbf{u}_j - \lambda_i\mathbf{u}_j) = \mathbf{0}, \qquad j = m + 1, \ldots, n \tag{5.16}$$

Equation 5.16 states that the $\mathbf{u}_j$ must be *eigenvectors* of $\mathbf{R}$. Under the condition that the $\mathbf{u}_j$ are eigenvectors, Eq. 5.13 can be expressed (see Eq. 4.72) as

$$\mathscr{E} = \sum_{j=m+1}^{n} \lambda_j \tag{5.17}$$

and the solution to the minimization problem is now obvious. To minimize E, the eigenvectors $\mathbf{u}_{m+1}, \ldots, \mathbf{u}_n$ must be those corresponding to the smallest eigenvalues. Thus the vectors used for Eq. 5.3 should be the eigenvectors of $\mathbf{R}$ corresponding to the m largest eigenvalues.

The features just derived can be shown to have another optimal property that will be stated only briefly here. The *entropy* or *information* for a distribution is defined by

$$H = -E[\ln p_{\mathbf{y}}(\mathbf{y})] \tag{5.18}$$

and, loosely speaking, is largest for distributions where the probability is evenly spread out over a wide range of values for the random vector. If the random vector $\mathbf{x}$ is characterized by a zero-mean Gaussian distribution, then the features selected can be shown to be those with maximum entropy. In other words, since the directions of the original space chosen to represent the vectors are the directions for which the variances (eigenvalues of R) are largest, these are also the directions for which the vector is "most random" or has maximum entropy. Since these directions are the directions of greatest uncertainty about the random vector, these directions should be retained as features. That is, any new information or measurements made on the vector are best made along these directions.

Another entropy function [2] is sometimes referred to in discussions of the Karhunen–Loève expansion. If the diagonal elements of the correlation matrix $r_{jj} = E[x_i^2]$ are normalized so that they sum to one, then these variables resemble discrete probabilities. The function

$$H_R = -\sum_{j=1}^{N} r_{jj} \log r_{jj}$$

then resembles a discrete form of the entropy function and is *minimized* when the Karhunen–Loève coordinate system is used. The quantity, which is sometimes referred to as *representation entropy,* serves only to measure the distribution of the second moments in the chosen coordinate system and does not represent a true measure of information in the information-theoretic sense.

■ EXAMPLE 5.2

Features for a Three-Dimensional Observation Vector

Consider a three-dimensional observation vector with correlation matrix

$$\mathbf{R} = \begin{bmatrix} 3 & -1 & 0 \\ -1 & 3 & 0 \\ 0 & 0 & 3 \end{bmatrix}$$

The eigenvalues and eigenvectors are

$$\lambda_1 = 4, \lambda_2 = 3, \lambda_3 = 2$$

$$\mathbf{e}_1 = \begin{bmatrix} \frac{1}{\sqrt{2}} \\ \frac{-1}{\sqrt{2}} \\ 0 \end{bmatrix}, \mathbf{e}_2 = \begin{bmatrix} 0 \\ 0 \\ 1 \end{bmatrix}, \mathbf{e}_3 = \begin{bmatrix} \frac{1}{\sqrt{2}} \\ \frac{1}{\sqrt{2}} \\ 0 \end{bmatrix}$$

To select one feature, one would choose the $\mathbf{e}_1$ direction. The corresponding mean-square error in representation would be $\lambda_2 + \lambda_3 = 5$. To select two features, one

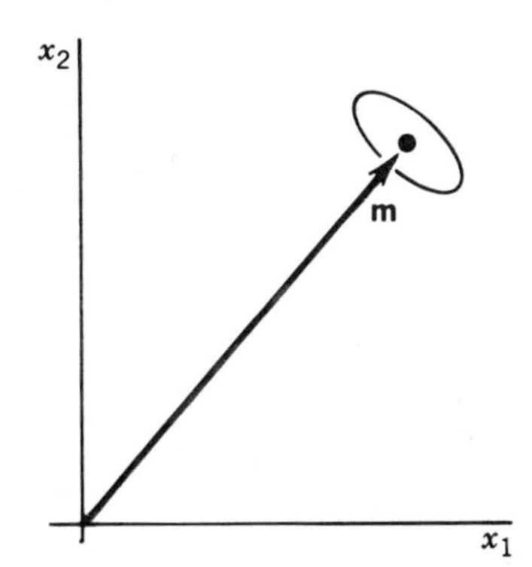

FIGURE 5.1 A distribution with a large mean vector.

would choose the $\mathbf{e}_1$ and $\mathbf{e}_2$ directions. The corresponding mean-square error would then be $\lambda_3 = 2$. ■

5.3.2 Representation Versus Classification

The method for choosing features just described is clearly sensitive to the mean vector for the data. If the mean vector is large compared to the variances of the distribution (see Fig. 5.1), then the features chosen *should* be in the general direction of the mean vector to optimally represent the data. Since, in this case, the correlation matrix is strongly influenced by the mean (see Eq. 4.46) the features chosen via the Karhunen–Loève expansion *will* tend to be in the direction of the mean. If we are using the features to classify two sets of data with different means, then these features are desirable. However, if the mean vectors for both distributions are similar, the chosen features may not be good for classification.

It is also possible to seek an optimal representation of the data about the mean. In this case, the analysis of Section 5.3.1 leads to features that correspond to eigenvectors of the *covariance* matrix. Thus the feature values represent projections on coordinate axes that are parallel to the principle axes of the density function. This is quite satisfying in one sense, since the features with largest eigenvalues represent the directions of greatest uncertainty; therefore, measurements along these directions should be retained. However, the choice of representation directions based on the covariance matrix may also be poor for *classification* of data from two distributions. A simple example is shown in Fig. 5.2. The direction $\mathbf{e}_1$ is best, for representing both classes. Yet the densities projected along this direction overlap and are almost completely inseparable. If, instead, the direction $\mathbf{e}_2$ is chosen as a feature, the classes can be easily separated. In this example there is also a problem if the correlation matrix is used, since both classes have similar mean vectors and the mean is not in the direction of greatest separability. The problem is alleviated, however, if the center of the coordinate system is chosen close to the mean of one of the distributions. In this case, eigenvectors of the correlation matrix corresponding to the largest eigenvalues will tend to align with the direction between the two means.

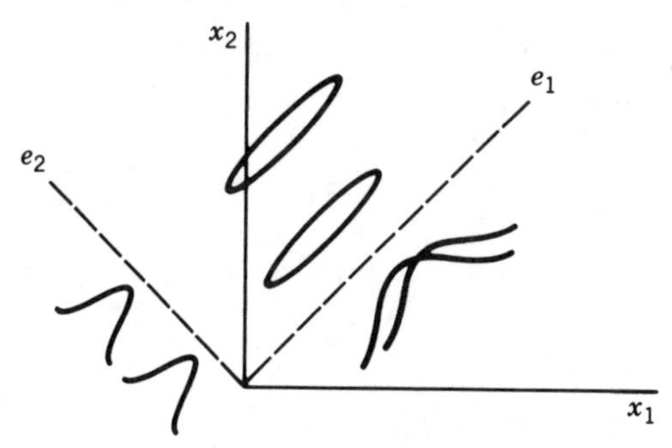

FIGURE 5.2 An illustration showing that directions for representation are not always best for classification.

5.4 A FEATURE EXTRACTION METHOD FOR MULTIPLE CLASSES

The method described here derives features by simultaneous consideration of all classes of interest. The method was first described for two-class problems by Fukunaga and Koontz [3].

5.4.1 The Two-Class Case

Let $\mathbf{R}_1$ and $\mathbf{R}_2$ represent the correlation matrices for two classes of observation vectors. That is,

$$\mathbf{R}_i = E_i[\mathbf{x}\mathbf{x}^T] \tag{5.19}$$

where E_i denotes expectation using the density of class ω_i. Let $\mathbf{Q}$ be defined as

$$\mathbf{Q} = \mathbf{R}_1 + \mathbf{R}_2 \tag{5.20}$$

and let $\mathbf{S}$ be a linear transformation such that

$$\mathbf{S}^T\mathbf{Q}\mathbf{S} = \mathbf{S}^T\mathbf{R}_1\mathbf{S} + \mathbf{S}^T\mathbf{R}_2\mathbf{S} = \mathbf{I} \tag{5.21}$$

From the considerations of Section 4.5.3, such a transformation can be expressed as

$$\mathbf{S} = \begin{bmatrix} \uparrow & \uparrow & & \uparrow \\ \mathbf{v}_1 & \mathbf{v}_2 & \cdots & \mathbf{v}_n \\ \downarrow & \downarrow & & \downarrow \end{bmatrix} \begin{bmatrix} \frac{1}{\sqrt{\mu_1}} & & & 0 \\ & \frac{1}{\sqrt{\mu_2}} & & \\ & & \ddots & \\ 0 & & & \frac{1}{\sqrt{\mu_n}} \end{bmatrix} \tag{5.22}$$

where $\mathbf{v}_i$ are the eigenvectors and μ_i are the eigenvalues of $\mathbf{Q}$. The transformation

R_1'	λ_1	$\mathbf{e}_1$	$1 - \lambda_1$	
↓	λ_2	$\mathbf{e}_2$	$1 - \lambda_2$	
Decreasing importance	λ_3	$\mathbf{e}_3$	$1 - \lambda_3$	Decreasing importance
	.	.		
	.	.		↑
	.	.		
	λ_{n-1}	$\mathbf{e}_{n-1}$	$1 - \lambda_{n-1}$	R_2'
	λ_n	$\mathbf{e}_n$	$1 - \lambda_n$	

FIGURE 5.3 Ordering of eigenvalues for two-class feature extraction.

$\mathbf{S}$ does not in general diagonalize either $\mathbf{R}_1$ or $\mathbf{R}_2$. It does, however, transform the observation vector to

$$\mathbf{x}' = \mathbf{S}^T\mathbf{x} \tag{5.23}$$

where the correlation matrices are given by

$$\mathbf{R}_i' = \mathbf{S}^T\mathbf{R}_i\mathbf{S} \tag{5.24}$$

which, by virtue of Eq. 5.21 satisfies

$$\mathbf{R}_1' + \mathbf{R}_2' = \mathbf{I} \tag{5.25}$$

Consider now the features to be defined in this new coordinate system. First note that the eigenvectors of $\mathbf{R}_1'$ and $\mathbf{R}_2'$ are identical, because if $\mathbf{e}$ is an eigenvector of $\mathbf{R}_1'$ corresponding to an eigenvalue λ, then from Eq. 5.25

$$\mathbf{R}_2'\mathbf{e} = (\mathbf{I} - \mathbf{R}_1')\,\mathbf{e} = \mathbf{e} - \lambda\mathbf{e} = (1 - \lambda)\mathbf{e} \tag{5.26}$$

Thus $\mathbf{e}$ is also an eigenvector of $\mathbf{R}_2'$ corresponding to eigenvalue $1 - \lambda$. Since the correlation matrices $\mathbf{R}_1'$ and $\mathbf{R}'_2$ must both be positive semidefinite, the eigenvalues of both must be nonnegative (see Problem 4.9) and so λ must lie in the interval

$$0 \leqslant \lambda \leqslant 1 \tag{5.27}$$

As a result, the eigenvectors that are best for the representation of class 1 are worst for the representation of class 2, and vice versa. This relationship is illustrated in Fig. 5.3.

There remains the question of how to choose the features. Two possible approaches are as follows:

1. Select $m/2$ eigenvectors corresponding to the $m/2$ largest eigenvalues of each class. If m is odd, select for the remaining feature the eigenvector corresponding to the largest remaining eigenvalue regardless of class.
2. Select the eigenvectors corresponding to the m largest eigenvalues regardless of class.

Neither of these schemes can be proven to be superior; in general, the scheme yielding the best results will depend on the problem at hand. Once the eigenvectors have been chosen, then the feature transformation can be expressed as

$$\mathbf{y} = \mathbf{T}\mathbf{x} = \begin{bmatrix} \longleftarrow & \mathbf{e}_{j_1}^T & \longrightarrow \\ \longleftarrow & \mathbf{e}_{j_2}^T & \longrightarrow \\ & \vdots & \\ \longleftarrow & \mathbf{e}_{j_m}^T & \longrightarrow \end{bmatrix} \mathbf{S}^T\mathbf{x} \tag{5.28}$$

where $\mathbf{S}$ is the linear transformation that satisfies Eq. 5.21.

5.4.2 The N_c-Class Case

Consider now the problem of generating features to classify patterns into one of N_c distinct classes. The patterns are originally represented by vectors $\mathbf{x}$ in an n-dimensional linear vector space (the observation space). The correlation matrix for each class is defined in Eq. 5.19.

Let it be assumed that the largest eigenvalue $\lambda_{\max}$ of the correlation matrices satisfies the condition

$$\lambda_{\max} \leqslant 1 \tag{5.29}$$

(This results in no loss of generality, since Eq. 5.29 can always be achieved by a linear scaling of the observation space.) Thus, since each correlation matrix is positive definite, all of the eigenvalues of $\mathbf{R}_i$ lie between 0 and 1.

As in Section 5.3.1, let $\{\mathbf{u}_j, j = 1, 2, \ldots, n\}$ be an orthonormal basis for the observation space. Furthermore, let $\mathbf{x}$ be any observation vector and let $\tilde{\mathbf{x}}$ be the truncated expansion of $\mathbf{x}$ defined by Eq. 5.3. A suitable set of features for the ith class would result if one could choose the $\mathbf{u}_j$ such that the mean-square error with respect to class i

$$\mathscr{E}_i = E_i[|\mathbf{x} - \tilde{\mathbf{x}}|^2] = \int_{-\infty}^{\infty} |\mathbf{x} - \tilde{\mathbf{x}}|^2\, p_{\mathbf{x}|\omega_i}(\mathbf{x}|\omega_i)\, d\mathbf{x} \tag{5.30}$$

were minimum and simultaneously the mean-square error with respect to class k

$$\mathscr{E}_k = E_k\,[|\mathbf{x} - \tilde{\mathbf{x}}|^2] = \int_{-\infty}^{\infty} |\mathbf{x} - \tilde{\mathbf{x}}|^2\, p_{\mathbf{x}|\omega_k}(\mathbf{x}|\omega_k)\, d\mathbf{x} \qquad \begin{matrix} k = 1, 2, \ldots, N_c \\ k \neq i \end{matrix} \tag{5.31}$$

were maximum. Minimizing Eq. 5.30 without conditions (5.31) leads to the features derived in Section 5.3. The additional conditions (5.31), however, if satisfied, would insure that the basis chosen to optimally represent a vector as a member of a class i would simultaneously be nonoptimal for representing it as a member of the other classes.

Since it is usually not possible to minimize Eq. 5.30 and maximize Eq. 5.31

simultaneously, a related criterion will be derived. Proceeding along the same lines that were followed to derive Eq. 5.13, one can write

$$\mathscr{E}_k = \sum_{j=m+1}^{n} \mathbf{u}_j^T \mathbf{R}_k \mathbf{u}_j \qquad k = 1, 2, \ldots, N_c \tag{5.32}$$

Then by virtue of Eq. 5.29 and the positive definite property of $\mathbf{R}_k$, $\mathscr{E}_k$ is bounded by

$$n - m \geqslant \mathscr{E}_k \geqslant 0; \qquad k = 1, 2, \ldots, N_c \tag{5.33}$$

As a result, maximizing Eq. 5.31 for $k \neq i$ is equivalent to minimizing

$$(n - m) - \mathscr{E}_k = \sum_{j=m+1}^{n} \left(\mathbf{u}_j^T \mathbf{u}_j - \mathbf{u}_j^T \mathbf{R}_k \mathbf{u}_j \right) = \sum_{j=m+1}^{n} \mathbf{u}_j^T (\mathbf{I} - \mathbf{R}_k) \mathbf{u}_j \tag{5.34}$$

A single combined criterion is taken, therefore, as the sum of Eq. 5.30 and 5.34 normalized by the number of classes, that is,

$$C_i = \frac{1}{N_c} \left\{ \mathscr{E}_i + \sum_{\substack{k=1 \\ k \neq i}}^{N_c} (n - m - \mathscr{E}_k) \right\} \tag{5.35}$$

where C_i is to be minimized. If Eqs. 5.32 and 5.34 are substituted into Eq. 5.35, then C_i can be expressed as

$$C_i = \sum_{j=m+1}^{n} \mathbf{u}_j^T \mathbf{G}_i \mathbf{u}_j \tag{5.36}$$

where

$$\mathbf{G}_i = \frac{1}{N_c} \left[\mathbf{R}_i + \sum_{\substack{k=1 \\ k \neq i}}^{N_c} (\mathbf{I} - \mathbf{R}_k) \right] \tag{5.37}$$

This is identical in form to the problem considered in Section 5.3 and thus the m vectors $\mathbf{u}_i$ chosen to represent $\tilde{\mathbf{x}}$ in order to minimize C_i should be the eigenvectors of $\mathbf{G}_i$ corresponding to its m largest eigenvalues. Indeed, note that if $\mathbf{e}$ is a normalized eigenvector of $\mathbf{G}_i$, then the corresponding eigenvalue λ can be expressed as

$$\lambda = \mathbf{e}^T \mathbf{G}_i \mathbf{e} = \frac{1}{N_c} \left[\mathbf{e}^T \mathbf{R}_i \mathbf{e} + \sum_{\substack{k=1 \\ k \neq i}}^{N_c} (1 - \mathbf{e}^T \mathbf{R}_k \mathbf{e}) \right] \tag{5.38}$$

Equation 5.29 and the positive definite property imply that each of the quadratic products in Eq. 5.38 has a value between 0 and 1. Thus λ lies between 0 and 1 and is close to 1 only if $\mathbf{e}^T \mathbf{R}_i \mathbf{e}$ is close to 1 and all of the $\mathbf{e}^T \mathbf{R}_k \mathbf{e}$ $(k \neq i)$ are simultaneously close to 0. Thus the eigenvectors of $\mathbf{G}_i$ corresponding to eigenvalues near 1 relate to important distinguishing features of class i.

Note that for the special case of $N_c = 2$, Eq. 5.37 implies that

$$\mathbf{G}_1 + \mathbf{G}_2 = \mathbf{I}$$

Thus the eigenvectors of $\mathbf{G}_1$ are identical to those of $\mathbf{G}_2$ and the eigenvalues are related in the same manner as those of the transformed correlation matrices $\mathbf{R}_1'$ and $\mathbf{R}_2'$ employed in Section 5.4.1. For $N_c > 2$, however, the eigenvectors and eigenvalues of the $\mathbf{G}_i$ matrices are not related in any simple way.

A further simplification of this method can result if the correlation matrices are transformed to satisfy the condition

$$\sum_{k=1}^{N_c} \mathbf{S}^T\mathbf{R}_k\mathbf{S} = \sum_{k=1}^{N_c} \mathbf{R}_k' = \mathbf{I} \tag{5.39}$$

The required linear transformation $\mathbf{S}$ is derived as discussed in Section 5.4.1. When the transformed correlation matrices are used, the matrices $\mathbf{G}_i$ simplify to

$$\mathbf{G}_i' = \frac{1}{N_c}\left[2\,\mathbf{R}_i' + (N_c - 2)\mathbf{I}\right] \tag{5.40}$$

which reduces to $\mathbf{G}_i' = \mathbf{R}_i'$ for $N_c = 2$.

5.5 A FEATURE EXTRACTION METHOD FOR IMAGES

Digital pictures or images are represented by an array of cells known as pixels (picture elements). If this array of pixels has N rows and N columns, then the observation vector would consist of the N^2 brightness values of the pixels arranged in some prescribed order. Since the observation vector can be very large, it is worthwhile to consider the representation of images in terms of features.

There are many ways to derive features for images. Typical features may be derived from the two-dimensional frequency spectrum or may be measures of the spread of an estimated joint density function for pixels separated by a fixed vector distance within the image. Another approach involves representation of the image as a weighted sum of other images that form a basis for the expansion. Since this method closely resembles the eigenvalue feature extraction methods that were discussed earlier, we develop the method here.

Assume that a given image is represented by an $N \times N$ matrix $\mathbf{B}$, where the elements of $\mathbf{B}$ represent brightness values of the pixels. Consider two $N \times N$ orthonormal matrices $\mathbf{U}$ and $\mathbf{V}$. The matrix $\mathbf{B}$ can be transformed to another matrix $\mathbf{A}$ by the operation

$$\mathbf{A} = \mathbf{U}^T\mathbf{B}\mathbf{V} \tag{5.41}$$

Since $\mathbf{U}$ and $\mathbf{V}$ are orthonormal, no information is lost and $\mathbf{B}$ can be recovered by the inverse transformation

$$\mathbf{B} = \mathbf{U}\mathbf{A}\mathbf{V}^T \tag{5.42}$$

Equation 5.42 can further be written as

$$\mathbf{B} = \sum_{i=1}^{N} \sum_{j=1}^{N} a_{ij} \mathbf{u}_i \mathbf{v}_j^T \tag{5.43}$$

where a_{ij} are the elements of $\mathbf{A}$ and $\mathbf{u}_i$ and $\mathbf{v}_j$ are the columns of $\mathbf{U}$ and $\mathbf{V}$, respectively. Since each of the products $\mathbf{u}_i \mathbf{v}_j^T$ is itself an $N \times N$ matrix, one can think of Eq. 5.43 as an expansion of the image in a basis set of images, where the a_{ij} are the coefficients.

The idea of feature extraction is to find a basis where only a few of the a_{ij} are necessary to represent the image. The image $\mathbf{B}$ then can be represented by an appropriately truncated form of Eq. 5.43 and the a_{ij} become the features. Several specific transformations (e.g., Hadamard, Harr, Fourier [4]) are useful for this purpose. However, one such transformation leads to a representation where only the diagonal terms a_{ii} of the matrix $\mathbf{A}$ are nonzero. In this basis the image can be represented with only N (or fewer) coefficients. This representation is known as *singular-value decomposition.*

To see how singular-value decomposition works, consider the matrix product

$$\mathbf{B}\mathbf{B}^T = \mathbf{U}\mathbf{A}\mathbf{V}^T\mathbf{V}\mathbf{A}^T\mathbf{U}^T = \mathbf{U}\mathbf{A}\mathbf{A}^T\mathbf{U}^T \tag{5.44}$$

It is easy to show (see Problem 4.3) that the matrix $\mathbf{B}\mathbf{B}^T$ is symmetric and positive semidefinite. Thus it has N nonnegative real eigenvalues and N linearly independent eigenvectors (recall the discussion in Section 4.7.1). Now compare Eq. 5.44 to Eq. 4.75 of Chapter 4. If $\mathbf{U}$ is taken to be the matrix whose columns are the eigenvectors of $\mathbf{B}\mathbf{B}^T$, then $\mathbf{A}\mathbf{A}^T$ must be the diagonal matrix of eigenvalues of $\mathbf{B}\mathbf{B}^T$. For later convenience we write $\mathbf{A}\mathbf{A}^T$ in the form

$$\mathbf{A}\mathbf{A}^T = \begin{bmatrix} \lambda_1^2 & & & & 0 \\ & \lambda_2^2 & & & \\ & & \cdot & & \\ & & & \cdot & \\ & & & & \cdot \\ 0 & & & & \lambda_N^2 \end{bmatrix} \tag{5.45}$$

In a similar manner, one can form the matrix $\mathbf{B}^T\mathbf{B}$ and write

$$\mathbf{B}^T\mathbf{B} = \mathbf{V}\mathbf{A}^T\mathbf{U}^T\mathbf{U}\mathbf{A}\mathbf{V}^T = \mathbf{V}\mathbf{A}^T\mathbf{A}\mathbf{V}^T \tag{5.46}$$

Now if $\mathbf{V}$ is the matrix whose columns are the eigenvectors of $\mathbf{B}^T\mathbf{B}$, then $\mathbf{A}^T\mathbf{A}$ must also have the diagonal form

$$\mathbf{A}^T\mathbf{A} = \begin{bmatrix} \lambda_1'^2 & & & & 0 \\ & \lambda_2'^2 & & & \\ & & \cdot & & \\ & & & \cdot & \\ & & & & \cdot \\ 0 & & & & \lambda_N'^2 \end{bmatrix} \tag{5.47}$$

The only way that Eqs. 5.45 and 5.47 can both be satisfied is if $\lambda_i = \lambda_i'$ and $\mathbf{A}$ is a diagonal matrix with diagonal elements $\lambda_1, \lambda_2, \ldots, \lambda_N$. In this case Eq. 5.43 reduces to

$$\mathbf{B} = \sum_{i=1}^{N} \lambda_i \mathbf{u}_i \mathbf{v}_i^T \tag{5.48}$$

where $\mathbf{u}_i$ and $\mathbf{v}_i$ are eigenvectors of $\mathbf{BB}^T$ and $\mathbf{B}^T\mathbf{B}$, respectively, and the $\{\lambda_i\}$ are given by

$$\lambda_i = \mathbf{u}_i^T \mathbf{B} \mathbf{v}_i \qquad i = 1, 2, \ldots, N \tag{5.49}$$

The $\{\lambda_i\}$ are called the *singular values* of **B**.

The transformation of Eq. 5.49 can be used to compute a set of N features to represent an image **B** or any similar array of data. Alternatively, one can select the features corresponding to the m ($<N$) largest singular values and discard the others. In the case where **B** is not a square matrix, the singular-value decomposition can still be performed, but the largest number of singular values that can exist is equal to the smaller dimension of **B**.

5.6 OTHER LINEAR METHODS OF FEATURE EXTRACTION

It is possible to derive features based on a number of different criteria. Often linear transformations can be found that produce features that are optimal with respect to these criteria. For example, one can seek to find a linear transformation that minimizes the quantity

$$\operatorname{tr}(\boldsymbol{\Sigma}_1 + \boldsymbol{\Sigma}_2)^{-1} [(\boldsymbol{\mu}_1 - \boldsymbol{\mu}_2)(\boldsymbol{\mu}_1 - \boldsymbol{\mu}_2)^T] \tag{5.50}$$

where $\boldsymbol{\Sigma}_1$, $\boldsymbol{\Sigma}_2$, $\boldsymbol{\mu}_1$, and $\boldsymbol{\mu}_2$ are the class covariance matrices and means for the *features*. This quantity is a form of the Fisher criterion (discussed further in Chapter 6). The term $\boldsymbol{\Sigma}_1 + \boldsymbol{\Sigma}_2$ is a measure of the spread of the data around the mean of each class, and is generically referred to as a *within-class* scatter matrix. The second term $(\boldsymbol{\mu}_1 - \boldsymbol{\mu}_2)(\boldsymbol{\mu}_1 - \boldsymbol{\mu}_2)^T$ is a measure of the spread between classes and is generically referred to as a *between-class* scatter matrix. Intuitively, minimizing the Fisher criterion results in choosing directions in the observation space such that the spread of the data around each mean vector is small relative to the spread between the two classes. It can be shown [5] by analyses similar to those in the preceding sections that the features chosen should correspond to eigenvectors of the matrix

$$\mathbf{F} = (\mathbf{K}_1 + \mathbf{K}_2)^{-1} (\mathbf{m}_1 - \mathbf{m}_2)(\mathbf{m}_1 - \mathbf{m}_2)^T \tag{5.51}$$

where $\mathbf{K}_1$, $\mathbf{K}_2$, $\mathbf{m}_1$, and $\mathbf{m}_2$ are the class covariance matrices and mean vectors in the *observation space*. Other possible criteria are obtained by taking the determinant of the matrix in Eq. 5.50 instead of the trace, or by taking the ratio of the determinants or traces of the two scatter matrices. All of these problems have (at least approximate) solutions involving eigenvectors of the matrix **F**.

The *entropy,* Eq. 5.18, has also been used as a criterion for feature extraction. For Gaussian distributions, it can be shown (see Problem 5.6) that for any class:

$$H = \frac{1}{2} \ln |\mathbf{K}_i| + \frac{n}{2}(1 + \ln 2\pi) \tag{5.52}$$

However, since this expression depends only on the covariance matrix and not the mean, using the entropy for feature extraction can be ambiguous. If the mean vectors of the classes are all zero, then one may want to select features that *maximize* the entropy. As we mentioned earlier, this is the same as choosing features to optimally represent the data in the Karhunen–Loève sense. Or on the other hand, when there is a difference in the mean vectors but equal covariances, some authors have suggested choosing features to *minimize* the entropy. This amounts to choosing directions with the smallest variance and may result in less overlap in the distributions. Although this would appear to work well for the example of Fig. 5.2, it is easy to construct counterexamples where the directions of *largest* entropy are preferred because of a larger mean separation.

A better procedure is to use the relative information

$$H(i, j) = E\left[\ln \frac{p_{\mathbf{x}|\omega_i}}{p_{\mathbf{x}|\omega_j}} \;\middle|\; \omega_i \right] \tag{5.53}$$

which is the mean of the log likelihood ratio when class ω_i is present. The quantity $H(1, 2) + H(2, 1)$ is known as the *divergence* and represents the difference in the expected values of the log likelihood ratio for each of the two classes. Quantities such as the divergence and the Bhattacharyya distance, both discussed in Chapter 9, can serve as suitable criteria for feature extraction, and several authors have studied linear and nonlinear methods based on these criteria.

5.7 NONLINEAR MAPPING

Linear feature transformations are easy to apply and relatively easy to derive. However, the most desirable features are seldom linear transformations of the observation data. Nonlinear mapping deals with attempting to discover the inherent structure of the data in the (high-dimensional) observation space and to find a nonlinear transformation to a lower-dimensional space that more-or-less preserves that structure. The transformations are not always useful for feature extraction. In some cases, the transformations are iteratively generated or otherwise nonexplicit so that they can only be used to better understand the structure of the data. In these cases, the transformed data is usually displayed as a scatter plot in a two- or three-dimensional subspace.

The fundamental ideas involved in nonlinear mapping are discussed briefly in the next subsection. Following that, a noniterative transformation is described that can be used to explicitly generate features.

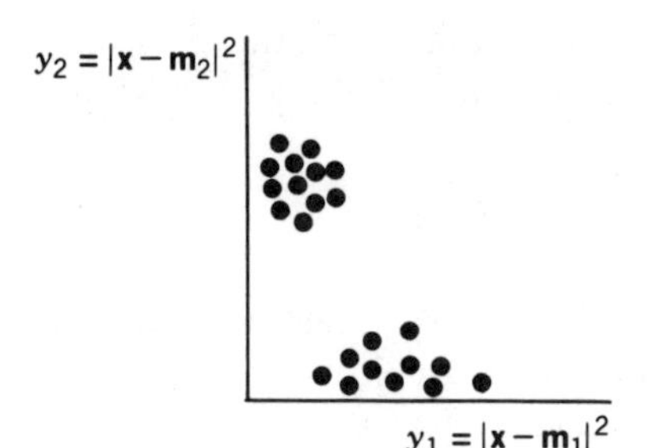

FIGURE 5.4 A scatter plot for distance features.

5.7.1 Principles of Nonlinear Mapping

The simplest form of nonlinear mapping involves measuring distances of the data from fixed points in the observation space. For example, if there are two classes of data, one could choose the features

$$y_1 = |\mathbf{x} - \mathbf{m}_1|^2 = d_E(\mathbf{x}, \mathbf{m}_1) \tag{5.54a}$$

$$y_2 = |\mathbf{x} - \mathbf{m}_2|^2 = d_E(\mathbf{x}, \mathbf{m}_2) \tag{5.54b}$$

where $\mathbf{m}_1$ and $\mathbf{m}_2$ are the means of the two classes. Distances other than the Euclidean distance can also be used, and suitable normalization of the coordinate system or use of the Mahalanobis distance may be helpful. If the data in the observation space are well separated in mean, then these features result in a scatter plot similar to that of Fig. 5.4. This method of nonlinear mapping is easy to apply and generates explicit features but, in general, may have little else in its favor. The distance features give relatively little information about the true structure of the data in the observation space.

A method that better displays the structure is based on preserving the intersample distances. This method was developed by J. W. Sammon [6] and is called the Sammon mapping. For convenience of notation, let $d_x(i, j)$ denote the distance $d(\mathbf{x}^i, \mathbf{x}^j)$ between samples $\mathbf{x}^i$ and $\mathbf{x}^j$ in the observation space where $d(\cdot, \cdot)$ is any appropriate distance function. Also, let $d_y(i, j)$ denote the distance $d(\mathbf{y}^i, \mathbf{y}^j)$ between the corresponding samples in a postulated two- or three-dimensional feature space. The Sammon mapping attempts to place the samples in the feature space so as to best match the distances $d_x(i, j)$ to $d_y(i, j)$ for all of the samples. This implicitly determines a nonlinear mapping of the data.

If one defines a normalized error for the distances as

$$\mathscr{E} = \frac{\sum_{i<j} (d_x(i, j) - d_y(i, j))^2 \Big/ d_x(i, j)}{\sum_{i<j} d_x(i, j)} \tag{5.55}$$

the distances $d_y(i, j)$ can be regarded as variables and $\mathscr{E}$ can be minimized by steepest descent or gradient techniques.

The Sammon mapping pays no particular attention to the classes of the samples but merely seeks to represent the structure in a global sense. This is appropriate, since the mapping is not intended to be used as a feature transformation. Nonlinear mapping applied for purposes of feature extraction, however, should acknowledge class representation of the training samples. This allows the mapping to emphasize separability instead of overall data representation. The method to be described next subscribes to this theory.

5.7.2 A Nonlinear Feature Extraction Method

A nonlinear method for feature extraction was proposed by Koontz and Fukunaga [7]. This procedure generates a mapping that attempts to preserve class separability while reducing dimensionality. Since the mapping is explicit, it can be used as a feature transformation. We give a brief summary of the method here. More details can be found in the original paper [7] and in the book by Fukunaga [5].

Let the classes of samples $\mathbf{x}^i$ and $\mathbf{x}^j$ be ω_{k_i} and ω_{k_j} and let $d_x(i, j)$ and $d_y(i, j)$ represent distances between samples in the observation and feature spaces. A criterion C_1 is first chosen which when minimized will tend to keep the distances between each class in the feature space as small as possible. The criterion selected has the form

$$C_1 = \sum_{i,j} \frac{d_y^2(i, j)}{d_x^2(i, j)} \delta(\omega_{k_i}, \omega_{k_j}) \tag{5.56}$$

where $\delta(\omega_{k_i}, \omega_{k_j})$ is one when ω_{k_i} is equal to ω_{k_j} and is zero otherwise. A second criterion C_2 is then chosen that seeks to preserve the overall structure of the data (both within classes and between classes). This second criterion has the form

$$C_2 = \sum_{i,j} \frac{(d_y(i, j) - d_x(i, j))^2}{d_x^2(i, j)} \tag{5.57}$$

and is similar to Eq. 5.55. If one now takes a combined criterion of the form

$$C = C_1 + \mu C_2 \tag{5.58}$$

where μ is a constant of proportionality, one can manipulate the last three equations into the form

$$C = \sum_{i,j} k_{ij} \, (d_y(i, j) - q_{ij})^2 + \text{const} \tag{5.59}$$

where

$$k_{ij} = \frac{1}{d_x^2(i, j)} [\delta(\omega_{k_i}, \omega_{k_j}) + \mu] \tag{5.60}$$

$$q_{ij} = \frac{\mu}{\delta(\omega_{k_i}, \omega_{k_j}) + \mu} \cdot d_x(i, j) \tag{5.61}$$

The goal is now to find a mapping that minimizes Eq. 5.59. Koontz and Fukunaga approached this by finding a mapping of the distances $d_y(i, j) = f(d_x(i, j))$.

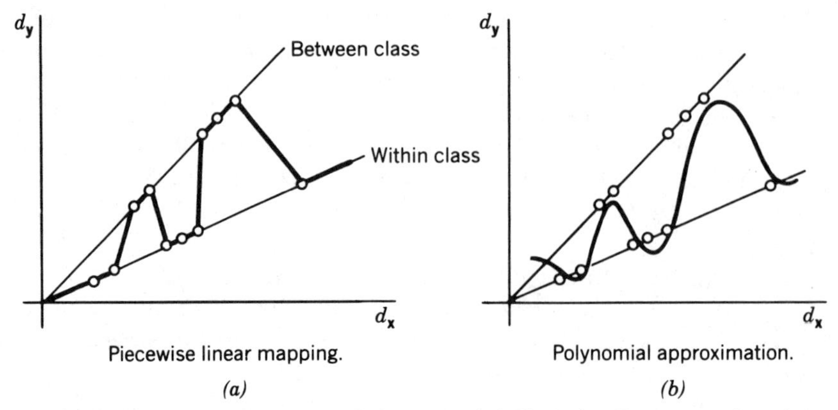

FIGURE 5.5 Functional mapping of distances. (*a*) Piecewise linear mapping. (*b*) Polynomial approximation.

First observe that if the mapping is to be used as a feature extraction method and the given samples are regarded as training data with known classes, then finding the desired mapping is very simple. One minimizes Eq. 5.59 by choosing $d_y(i, j) = q_{ij}$ for all i and j. This implies the two relations

$$d_y(i, j) = d_x(i, j) \qquad \omega_{k_i} \neq \omega_{k_j} \tag{5.62a}$$

$$d_y(i, j) = \frac{1}{1 + \mu} d_x(i, j) \qquad \omega_{k_i} = \omega_{k_j} \tag{5.62b}$$

which represent two linear mappings of the distances as shown in Fig. 5.5(*a*). A piecewise linear function that implements this mapping for the training data is also shown in Fig. 5.5(*a*). Any new data points can now have their intersample distances mapped through this function.

For reasons of efficiency, the authors chose not to use the piecewise linear function but instead elected to approximate it by a low-order polynomial. Thus the function f that maps the distances d_x to d_y is taken to be of the form

$$f(d) = a_0 + a_1 d + \cdots + a_p d^p \tag{5.63}$$

and the coefficients a_i needed to minimize Eq. 5.59 can be found by a standard least-squares method (see Problem 5.7). Such a least-squares polynomial function is shown in Fig. 5.5(*b*).

Observe now that although the intersample distances in the observation space can be mapped to intersample distances in the feature space through the function f, it will generally *not* be possible to find a set of *samples* in the feature space that are actually located at the desired distances from one another. Since the distance requirement cannot be met, a smaller set of representative points called "pivot points" are chosen in the observation space and mapped into the feature space via the distance transformation. Specifically, if the feature space has m dimensions, it is always possible to locate $m + 1$ or fewer pivot points in the feature space to

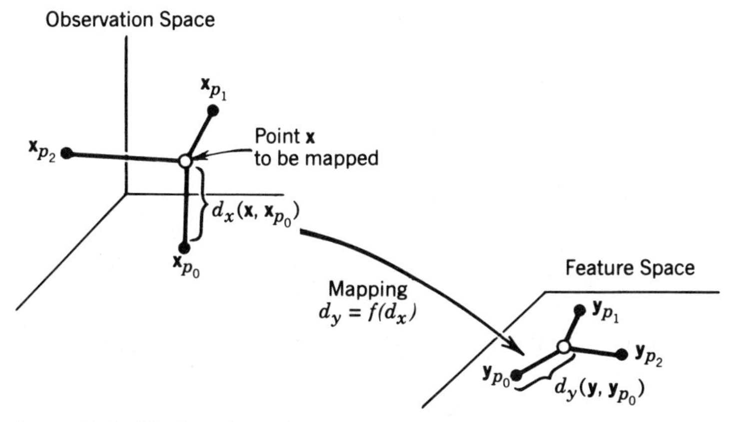

FIGURE 5.6 The location of a point in the feature space through mapping of distances.

have the required interpoint distances. These points are typically chosen at locations in the observation space where the data has high concentration. The intersample distances of the pivot points are mapped through Eq. 5.63, and the corresponding pivot points are located in the feature space.

Once the pivot points are set up, the mapping of a new point into the feature space proceeds as follows:

1. Find the distances between the given point and each of the pivot points in the observation space.
2. Map the distances according to Eq. 5.63.
3. Locate the data in the feature space according to distances from the pivot points.

This procedure is illustrated in Fig. 5.6. Note that if the number of pivot points is less than or equal to the number of dimensions m, then step 3 is always possible. Koontz and Fukunaga, however, suggested choosing $m + 1$ pivot points and locating the samples according to the conditions

$$d_y^2(\mathbf{y}, \mathbf{y}_{P_i}) - d_y^2(\mathbf{y}, \mathbf{y}_{P0}) = D_{\mathbf{y}}^2(i) - D_{\mathbf{y}}^2(0), \quad i = 1,2, \ldots m \tag{5.64}$$

where $D_y(i)$ is the distance to the pivot point $\mathbf{y}_{P_i}$ as determined by the mapping. Although these equations do not guarantee that the points $\mathbf{y}$ will be located at all of the prescribed distances, analytic geometrical arguments [7, 5] can be generated to show that the solution to Eq. 5.64 does indeed represent a reasonable compromise.

If d_y is taken to be the Euclidean distance function, then one can obtain from Eq. 5.64 the equivalent set of linear equations

$$2(\mathbf{y}_{P0} - \mathbf{y}_{P_i})^T\mathbf{y} = |\mathbf{y}_{P0}|^2 - |\mathbf{y}_{P_i}|^2 + D_{\mathbf{y}}^2(i) - D_{\mathbf{y}}^2(0) \tag{5.65}$$

$$i = 1, 2, \ldots, m$$

which can be easily solved for $\mathbf{y}$.

5.8 SUMMARY

This chapter describes some methods of feature extraction. So-called "optimal" features or sufficient statistics are described to give impetus to the development of (other) feature extraction methods. Certain optimal properties of the eigenvectors of the correlation matrix are discussed and a method to choose features to represent a given class of patterns is considered. A general method for extracting features for multiple-class problems is then described. Each of the features chosen by this method are designed to be best representative of one class and also least representative of the other classes. The chapter goes on to describe the singular-value decomposition as a method of deriving features for images (or other arrays of data). The features so derived are based on considerations of representation that are similar in many ways to those involved in the linear feature transformations for general data described earlier. Further general feature extraction methods designed to optimize various other criteria are discussed. Finally, the chapter describes some methods for nonlinear mapping that can be used to study the structure of data, and a method of nonlinear mapping that results in an explicit (noniterative) transformation of the data that can be used for feature extraction.

REFERENCES

1. P. A. DEVIJVER, and J. KITTLER. *Pattern Recognition: A Statistical Approach.* Englewood Cliffs, NJ: Prentice-Hall, Inc., 1982.
2. S. WATANABE. *Pattern Recognition: Human and Mechanical.* New York: John Wiley & Sons, 1985.
3. K. FUKUNAGA, and W. L. G. KOONTZ. "Applications of the Karhunen–Loève Expansion to Feature Selection and Ordering." *IEEE Trans. Computers,* Vol. C-19, pp. 917–923 (1970).
4. W. K. PRATT. *Digital Image Processing.* New York: John Wiley & Sons, Inc., 1978.
5. K. FUKUNAGA. *Introduction to Statistical Pattern Recognition.* New York: Academic Press, 1972.
6. J. W. SAMMON. "A Nonlinear Mapping Algorithm for Data Structure Analysis." *IEEE Trans. Computers,* Vol. C-18, No. 5, pp. 401–409 (May 1969).
7. W. L. G. KOONTZ, and K. FUKUNAGA. "A Nonlinear Feature Extraction Algorithm Using Distance Transformation." *IEEE Trans. Computers,* Vol. C-21, No. 1, pp. 56–63 (1972).

PROBLEMS

5.1 The covariance matrices for two classes of zero-mean n-dimensional Gaussian random vectors are $\mathbf{K}_1 = \sigma_1^2\mathbf{I}$ and $\mathbf{K}_2 = \sigma_2^2\mathbf{I}$. Show that the likelihood ratio test to minimize the probability of error

$$\frac{p_{\mathbf{x}|\omega_1}(\mathbf{x}|\omega_1)}{p_{\mathbf{x}|\omega_2}(\mathbf{x}|\omega_2)} \underset{\omega_2}{\overset{\omega_1}{\gtrless}} \frac{\Pr[\omega_2]}{\Pr[\omega_1]}$$

reduces to the form

$$\left(\frac{1}{\sigma_1^2} - \frac{1}{\sigma_2^2}\right)\sum_{i=1}^{n} x_i^2 + n \ln \frac{\sigma_1^2}{\sigma_2^2} \underset{\omega_2}{\overset{\omega_1}{\lessgtr}} T$$

where

$$T = 2 \ln \frac{\Pr[\omega_2]}{\Pr[\omega_1]}$$

5.2 Find the eigenvalues and eigenvectors of the matrix

$$\mathbf{R}_i = \begin{bmatrix} 1 & 0.5 & 0 \\ 0.5 & 1 & 0 \\ 0 & 0 & 2 \end{bmatrix}$$

(a) What is the mean-square error in representing a vector $\mathbf{x}$ by

$$\tilde{\mathbf{x}} = c_1\mathbf{e}_1$$

where $\mathbf{e}_1$ is the eigenvector corresponding to the largest eigenvalue?

(b) What is the mean-square error in representing a vector by

$$\tilde{\mathbf{x}} = c_1\mathbf{e}_1 + c_2\mathbf{e}_2$$

where $\mathbf{e}_1$ and $\mathbf{e}_2$ are the eigenvectors corresponding to the two largest eigenvalues?

5.3 The correlation matrix $\mathbf{R}$ for observation vectors from a class ω is

$$\mathbf{R} = \begin{bmatrix} 2 & 1 & 0 \\ 1 & 2 & 0 \\ 0 & 0 & 7 \end{bmatrix}$$

What is the mean-square error in representing a vector $\mathbf{x}$ from the class by

$$\tilde{\mathbf{x}} = c_1\mathbf{e}_1$$

where $\mathbf{e}_1$ is the eigenvector of $\mathbf{R}$ corresponding to the *largest* eigenvalue and $c_1 = \mathbf{x}^T\mathbf{e}_1$? Is this a larger or smaller error than would be encountered in representing $\mathbf{x}$ by

$$\tilde{\mathbf{x}} = c_2\mathbf{e}_2 + c_3\mathbf{e}_3$$

where $\mathbf{e}_i$ are the remaining two eigenvectors and $c_i = \mathbf{x}^T\mathbf{e}_i$?

5.4 Let $\mathbf{R}_1$ be the correlation matrix of Problem 5.2, let $\mathbf{R}_2$ be

$$\mathbf{R}_2 = \begin{bmatrix} 1 & -0.5 & 0 \\ -0.5 & 1 & 0 \\ 0 & 0 & 2 \end{bmatrix}$$

(a) What is the transformation $\mathbf{S}$ in the feature extraction method of Section 5.4.1?

(b) Given that we wish to pick one eigenvector from each class to represent the features, what is the feature transformation? Write it as

$$\mathbf{y} = \mathbf{T}\mathbf{x} = \begin{bmatrix} \longleftarrow & \mathbf{e}_i^T & \longrightarrow \\ \longleftarrow & \mathbf{e}_j^T & \longrightarrow \end{bmatrix} \mathbf{S}^T\mathbf{x}$$

where $\mathbf{e}_i$ and $\mathbf{e}_j$ are selected eigenvectors.

5.5 Suppose that a feature vector for the method of Section 5.4.2 is chosen as

$$\mathbf{y} = \begin{bmatrix} y_1 \\ \cdot \\ \cdot \\ \cdot \\ y_k \end{bmatrix} = \begin{bmatrix} \longleftarrow & \mathbf{e}_1^{(1)T} & \longrightarrow \\ & \cdot & \\ & \cdot & \\ & \cdot & \\ \longleftarrow & \mathbf{e}_j^{(N_c)T} & \longrightarrow \end{bmatrix} \mathbf{x} = \mathbf{T}\mathbf{x}$$

where $\mathbf{e}_1^{(1)}$ through $\mathbf{e}_1^{(N_c)}$ are the first eigenvectors of the matrices $\mathbf{G}_1$ through $\mathbf{G}_{N_c}$. Show that if the correlation matrices are transformed to satisfy Eq. 5.39 before performing the feature extraction, then the resulting feature vector $\mathbf{y}$ is independent of the original coordinate system used to represent the data. That is, if a different coordinate system is chosen for the observation space

$$\mathbf{z} = \mathbf{A}\mathbf{x}$$

where $\mathbf{z}$ is the data in the new coordinate system and $\mathbf{A}$ is the coordinate transformation matrix (whose inverse $\mathbf{A}^{-1}$ exists), then the feature extraction procedure leads to the same feature vector $\mathbf{y}$.

5.6 Beginning with Eqs. 5.18 and 4.57, show that the entropy for a Gaussian random vector is given by Eq. 5.52. *Hint:* Take note of Eq. 4.20 and observe that

$$E[(\mathbf{x} - \mathbf{m})^T\mathbf{K}^{-1}(\mathbf{x} - \mathbf{m})] = E[\mathrm{tr}\,\mathbf{K}^{-1}(\mathbf{x} - \mathbf{m})(\mathbf{x} - \mathbf{m})^T] = \mathrm{tr}\mathbf{K}^{-1}\mathbf{K} = n$$

5.7 Define the following vectors and matrices:

$$\mathbf{a} = \begin{bmatrix} a_0 \\ a_1 \\ \cdot \\ \cdot \\ \cdot \\ a_{p-1} \end{bmatrix}, \quad \mathbf{D} = \begin{bmatrix} 1 & d_{21} & \cdots & d_{21}^p \\ 1 & d_{31} & \cdots & d_{31}^p \\ & \cdot & & \cdot \\ & \cdot & & \cdot \\ & \cdot & & \cdot \\ 1 & d_{N,N-1} & \cdots & d_{N,N-1}^p \end{bmatrix}$$

$$\mathbf{q} = \begin{bmatrix} q_{21} \\ q_{31} \\ \cdot \\ \cdot \\ \cdot \\ q_{N,N-1} \end{bmatrix}, \quad \mathbf{H} = \begin{bmatrix} k_{21} & & & & 0 \\ & k_{31} & & & \\ & & \cdot & & \\ & & & \cdot & \\ & & & & \cdot \\ 0 & & & & k_{N,N-1} \end{bmatrix}$$

Then the feature extraction criterion Eq. (5.59) can be written as

$$C = (\mathbf{Da} - \mathbf{q})^T \mathbf{H}(\mathbf{Da} - \mathbf{q}) + \text{const}$$

By taking derivatives with respect to the vector **a** and setting the result equal to zero, show that the optimum choice for **a** is given by

$$\mathbf{a} = (\mathbf{D}^T\mathbf{HD})^{-1} \mathbf{D}^T \mathbf{Hq}$$

CHAPTER 6

Quadratic and Linear Classifiers

The theory presented in the earlier chapters (2 through 4) provides the basis for developing specific forms of classifiers. Quadratic and linear classifiers are so named because of the mathematical form of their decision boundaries. These classifiers are parametric, in that they are specified in terms of parameters (mean and covariance) of the class distributions. Nonparametric classifiers, whose form does not depend on estimating particular parameters, are discussed in Chapter 8.

6.1 QUADRATIC AND LINEAR CLASSIFIERS FOR TWO-CLASS PROBLEMS

It was shown in Chapter 3 that various decision criteria led to a likelihood ratio test, that is, a decision rule of the form

$$\ell(\hat{\mathbf{y}}) = \frac{p_{\mathbf{y}|\omega_1}(\hat{\mathbf{y}}|\omega_1)}{p_{\mathbf{y}|\omega_2}(\hat{\mathbf{y}}|\omega_2)} \underset{\omega_2}{\overset{\omega_1}{\gtrless}} \lambda \tag{6.1}$$

The threshold λ is defined explicitly in terms of the prior probabilities and the Bayes costs for criteria that minimize the probability of error or the Bayes risk (see Eqs. 3.2 and 3.14), and defined implicitly by Eq. 3.22 for the Neyman–Pearson criterion. If the measurement vectors $\mathbf{y}$ from the ith class are characterized by a Gaussian density (Eq. 4.57) with mean $\mathbf{m}_i$ and covariance $\mathbf{K}_i$, then Eq. 6.1 becomes

$$\ell(\hat{\mathbf{y}}) = \sqrt{\frac{|\mathbf{K}_2|}{|\mathbf{K}_1|}} \exp\left[-\frac{1}{2}(\hat{\mathbf{y}} - \mathbf{m}_1)^T\mathbf{K}_1^{-1}(\hat{\mathbf{y}} - \mathbf{m}_1) + \frac{1}{2}(\hat{\mathbf{y}} - \mathbf{m}_2)^T\mathbf{K}_2^{-1}(\hat{\mathbf{y}} - \mathbf{m}_2)\right] \underset{\omega_2}{\overset{\omega_1}{\gtrless}} \lambda \tag{6.2}$$

If the quantity $h(\hat{\mathbf{y}})$ is defined as

$$h(\hat{\mathbf{y}}) = -2 \ln \ell(\hat{\mathbf{y}}) \tag{6.3}$$

then the quantity rule (6.2) can be expressed as

$$h(\hat{\mathbf{y}}) = (\hat{\mathbf{y}} - \mathbf{m}_1)^T\mathbf{K}_1^{-1}(\hat{\mathbf{y}} - \mathbf{m}_1) - (\hat{\mathbf{y}} - \mathbf{m}_2)^T\mathbf{K}_2^{-1}(\hat{\mathbf{y}} - \mathbf{m}_2) + \ln\frac{|\mathbf{K}_1|}{|\mathbf{K}_2|} \underset{\omega_2}{\overset{\omega_1}{\lessgtr}} T \tag{6.4}$$

where

$$T = -2 \ln \lambda \tag{6.5}$$

The decision rule (6.4) is called a Gaussian classifier or a *quadratic classifier* and T is called the threshold of the classifier. Observe that the quadratic classifier essentially computes the Mahalanobis distances to the mean of each class using the class covariance matrix and compares the difference in those distances to a threshold $(T - \ln|\mathbf{K}_1|/\mathbf{K}_2|)$. For the case of a one-dimensional measurement y, the Mahalanobis distance becomes equal to $(y - m_i)^2/\sigma_i^2$ and the classifier simply compares the ordinary distance to the mean of each class in standard deviation units.

By expanding Eq. 6.4, one can express the quadratic classifier in the form

$$h(\hat{\mathbf{y}}) = \hat{\mathbf{y}}^T\mathbf{A}\hat{\mathbf{y}} + \mathbf{b}^T\mathbf{y} + c \quad \underset{\omega_2}{\overset{\omega_1}{\lessgtr}} \quad T \tag{6.6}$$

where

$$\mathbf{A} = \mathbf{K}_1^{-1} - \mathbf{K}_2^{-1} \tag{6.7a}$$

$$\mathbf{b} = 2(\mathbf{K}_2^{-1}\mathbf{m}_2 - \mathbf{K}_1^{-1}\mathbf{m}_1) \tag{6.7b}$$

$$c = (\mathbf{m}_1^T\mathbf{K}_1^{-1}\mathbf{m}_1 - \mathbf{m}_2^T\mathbf{K}_2^{-1}\mathbf{m}_2 + \ln\frac{|\mathbf{K}_1|}{|\mathbf{K}_2|} \tag{6.7c}$$

Thus, the decision boundary $h(\hat{\mathbf{y}}) = T$ defined by the quadratic classifier is a general second order or quadratic surface; it may be an ellipsoid, hyperboloid, paraboloid, or some combination of these.[1] Vectors $\hat{\mathbf{y}}$ falling on one side of the decision boundary are classified as ω_1 and vectors falling on the other side are classified as ω_2.

The quadratic classifier can also be applied to vectors that are not characterized by Gaussian density functions. In this case, the probability of error is not necessarily minimized, but one can interpret the classifier as defining a decision boundary that

[1]To determine the form of the surface and plot it in the general case, one must first eliminate all cross-product terms of the components of $\hat{\mathbf{y}}$. This can be done by rotating the coordinate system to one represented by the eigenvectors of $\mathbf{A}$. The geometric form of the decision surface is determined by the eigenvalues of $\mathbf{A}$. If all eigenvalues are positive, the surface will be an ellipsoid; if some are positive and some are negative, the surface will be a hyperboloid; if some of the eigenvectors are zero, the surface will exhibit parabolic behavior in planes containing the corresponding eigenvectors.

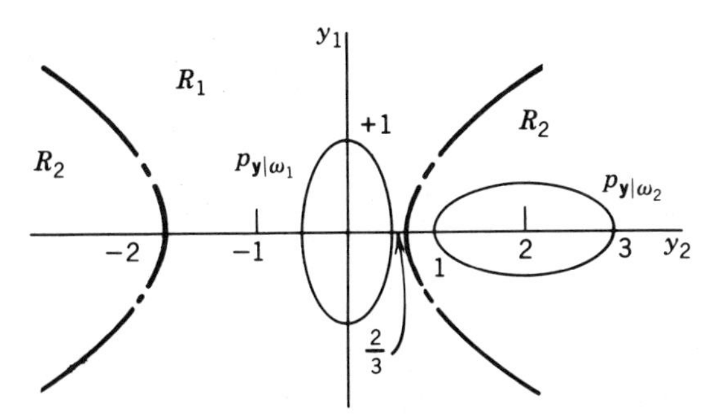

FIGURE 6.1 The decision boundary for Example 6.1.

is best matched to the second moment statistics (i.e., the mean and covariance) of the random vectors.

In general, any decision rule of the form of Eq. 6.6 can be called a quadratic classifier regardless of how the parameters $\mathbf{A}$, $\mathbf{b}$, and c are defined. The classifier is called a Gaussian classifier only when the parameters are defined by Eq. 6.7. Unless otherwise specified, we shall use the term *quadratic classifier* to mean a classifier of the specific form of Eq. 6.4 that is, a quadratic classifier whose parameters are defined by Eq. 6.7.

■ EXAMPLE 6.1

Decision Boundary for a Two-Dimensional Quadratic Classifier

Suppose that the measurement vectors for each class are Gaussian and characterized by parameters

$$\mathbf{K}_1 = \begin{bmatrix} 1 & 0 \\ 0 & \frac{1}{4} \end{bmatrix}, \qquad \mathbf{m}_1 = \begin{bmatrix} 0 \\ 0 \end{bmatrix}$$

$$\mathbf{K}_2 = \begin{bmatrix} \frac{1}{4} & 0 \\ 0 & 1 \end{bmatrix}, \qquad \mathbf{m}_2 = \begin{bmatrix} 0 \\ 2 \end{bmatrix}$$

then, from Eq. 6.4 $h(\hat{\mathbf{y}})$ is given by

$$\begin{aligned} h(\hat{\mathbf{y}}) &= (\hat{y}_1^2 + 4\hat{y}_2^2) - (4\hat{y}_1^2 + (\hat{y}_2 - 2)^2) + \ln \frac{\frac{1}{4}}{\frac{1}{4}} \\ &= -3\hat{y}_1^2 + 3\hat{y}_2^2 + 4\hat{y}_2 - 4 \end{aligned}$$

The decision boundary $h(\hat{\mathbf{y}}) = T$ is a hyperbola that is plotted in Fig. 6.1 for $T = 0$. Typical contours of the Gaussian class densities are also shown. ■

One may at first be surprised to see that the region labeled R_2 in the left half plane of Fig. 6.1 exists. Recall that when the prior probabilities are equal, the decision rule that minimizes the probability of error chooses the class whose density is largest. Since the variance in the y_2 direction is larger for class 2 than for class 1, the density $p_{\mathbf{y}|\omega_2}$ will actually be larger than $p_{\mathbf{y}|\omega_1}$ at the left half plane points in the R_2 region, although these points are closer to the mean of class 1.

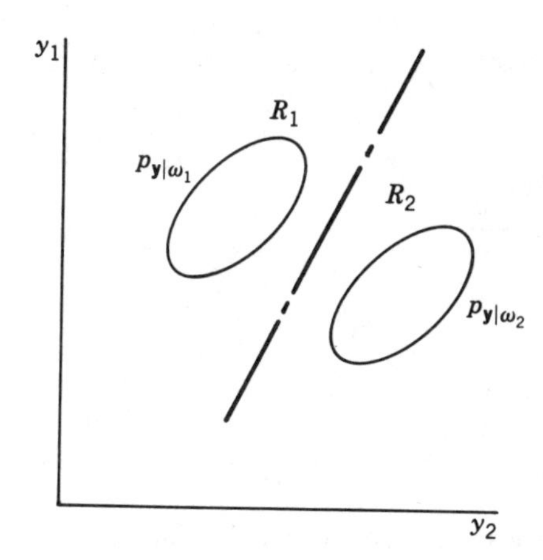

FIGURE 6.2 The decision boundary for equal covariances.

Note that if the two covariance matrices are equal, that is, $\mathbf{K}_1 = \mathbf{K}_2 = \mathbf{K}$, then the matrix $\mathbf{A}$ of Eq. 6.6 is identically zero and the decision rule becomes

$$h(\hat{\mathbf{y}}) = \mathbf{b}^T\hat{\mathbf{y}} + c \quad \underset{\omega_2}{\overset{\omega_1}{\lesseqgtr}} \quad T \tag{6.8}$$

where

$$\mathbf{b} = 2\mathbf{K}^{-1}(\mathbf{m}_2 - \mathbf{m}_1) \tag{6.9a}$$

$$c = \mathbf{m}_1^T\mathbf{K}^{-1}\mathbf{m}_1 - \mathbf{m}_2^T\mathbf{K}^{-1}\mathbf{m}_2. \tag{6.9b}$$

The decision boundary thus reduces to a linear boundary (hyperplane) and the classifier is correspondingly called a *linear classifier*. A typical case is illustrated in Fig. 6.2. The decision boundary is orthogonal to the vector $\mathbf{b}$ and moves parallel to itself as the threshold is varied.

6.2 DISCRIMINANT FUNCTIONS AND MULTICLASS CLASSIFIERS

6.2.1 Discriminant Functions

It was shown in Chapter 3 that when patterns are derived from one of N_c classes where $N_c \geqslant 2$, then the decision rule that minimizes the probability of error was given by Eq. 3.38, which can be expressed as

$$\text{choose } \omega_i \text{ when } g_i(\hat{\mathbf{y}}) = \max_k g_k(\hat{\mathbf{y}}) \tag{6.10}$$

where

$$g_k(\hat{\mathbf{y}}) = \Pr[\omega_k|\hat{\mathbf{y}}], \qquad k = 1, 2, \ldots, N_c \tag{6.11}$$

Recall from Chapter 1 that when a decision rule is expressed in this form, the functions g_k are called *discriminant functions*.

It is clear from Bayes's rule that the functions

$$g'_k(\hat{\mathbf{y}}) = p_{\mathbf{y}|\omega_k}(\hat{\mathbf{y}}|\omega_k) \Pr[\omega_k], \qquad k = 1, 2, \ldots, N_c \tag{6.12}$$

are *equivalent* to those of (6.11) in that when they are used in Eq. 6.10, they result in the same decision rule. In addition, when the prior probabilities $\Pr[\omega_k]$ of all of the classes are equal, then the class conditional densities $p_{\mathbf{y}|\omega_k}$ form a set of discriminant functions equivalent to those in Eqs. 6.11 or 6.12. In general, if $\{g_k\}$ is any set of discriminant functions, then the functions defined by

$$g'_k(\mathbf{y}) = a g_k(\mathbf{y}) + b, \qquad k = 1, 2, \ldots, N_c \tag{6.13}$$

where a is any positive constant and b is any positive or negative constant,[2] and also the functions defined by

$$g''_k(\mathbf{y}) = f(g_k(\mathbf{y})), \qquad k = 1, 2, \ldots, N_c \tag{6.14}$$

where f is any strictly monotonically increasing function, are equivalent to the $\{g_k\}$. These results are useful for deriving from one set of discriminant functions another set that may be computationally more convenient and/or provide more insight into the decision process. The principles expressed by Eqs. 6.13 and 6.14 will be used to manipulate discriminant functions in the next section although we may not always refer to Eqs. 6.13 and 6.14 explicitly.

6.2.2 Multiclass Quadratic and Linear Classifiers

When the feature vectors of the kth class are characterized by a Gaussian density function (Eq. 4.57) with mean $\mathbf{m}_k$ and covariance $\mathbf{K}_k$, a set of discriminant functions that minimizes the probability of error is, from Eq. 6.12,

$$g'_k(\hat{\mathbf{y}}) = \frac{\Pr[\omega_k]}{(2\pi)^{m/2}|\mathbf{K}_k|^{1/2}} \exp\left[-\frac{1}{2}(\hat{\mathbf{y}} - \mathbf{m}_k)^T\mathbf{K}_k^{-1}(\hat{\mathbf{y}} - \mathbf{m}_k)\right] \qquad k = 1, 2, \ldots, N_c \tag{6.15}$$

Since the natural logarithm is a strictly monotonically increasing function, one can define a set of equivalent discriminant functions as

$$\begin{aligned} g_k(\hat{\mathbf{y}}) &= 2 \ln g'_k(\hat{\mathbf{y}}) + m \ln 2\pi \\ &= -(\hat{\mathbf{y}} - \mathbf{m}_k)^T\mathbf{K}_k^{-1}(\hat{\mathbf{y}} - \mathbf{m}_k) - \ln|\mathbf{K}_k| + 2 \ln \Pr[\omega_k] \end{aligned} \tag{6.16}$$

The g_k of Eq. 6.16 are called *quadratic discriminant functions*. When used with Eq. 6.10, they implement the multiclass form of the quadratic classifier and minimize the probability of error for Gaussian feature vectors. Of course, when the

[2]The parameters a and b in Eq. 6.13 may be a function of $\mathbf{y}$, but must not be a function of the class index k.

prior probabilities of all of the classes are equal, the last term in Eq. 6.16 can be dropped without any loss of optimality.

It was shown in the two-class case that when the covariance matrices of both classes are identical, the quadratic classifier reduces to a linear classifier. The result also holds true in the multiclass case. The quadratic discriminant functions, and thus the decision boundary between any two classes (see Eq. 1.5) is a linear one. When $\mathbf{K}_1 = \mathbf{K}_2 = \cdots = \mathbf{K}_{N_c} = \mathbf{K}$, Eq. 6.16 can be written as

$$g_k(\hat{\mathbf{y}}) = -\hat{\mathbf{y}}^T\mathbf{K}^{-1}\hat{\mathbf{y}} + 2\mathbf{m}_k^T\mathbf{K}^{-1}\hat{\mathbf{y}} - \mathbf{m}_k^T\mathbf{K}^{-1}\mathbf{m}_k - \ln|\mathbf{K}| + 2\ln \Pr[\omega_k] \qquad k = 1, 2, \ldots, N_c \tag{6.17}$$

Since the first and fourth terms are common to all of the g_k, an equivalent set of discriminant functions is

$$g_k(\hat{\mathbf{y}}) = 2\mathbf{m}_k^T\mathbf{K}^{-1}\hat{\mathbf{y}} - \mathbf{m}_k^T\mathbf{K}^{-1}\mathbf{m}_k + 2\ln \Pr[\omega_k] \qquad k = 1, 2, \ldots, N_c \tag{6.18}$$

which are *linear* functions of $\hat{\mathbf{y}}$.

Let us consider some special cases to provide some interpretation of decision procedures involving quadratic and linear classifiers. Assume that in the following two examples all of the prior probabilities are equal.

■ EXAMPLE 5.2

Nearest Mean Classifier

Assume that the components of **y** for each class are uncorrelated and have a common variance σ^2. Then $\mathbf{K}_k = \sigma^2\mathbf{I}$ for $k = 1, 2, \ldots, N_c$ and the discriminant functions (6.16) reduce to

$$g_k(\hat{\mathbf{y}}) = -\frac{|\hat{\mathbf{y}} - \mathbf{m}_k|^2}{\sigma^2} - 2m \ln \sigma + 2 \ln \Pr[\omega_k]$$

Since the prior probabilities are all equal, one can drop the last two terms and scale the result by σ^2 to obtain the equivalent discriminant functions

$$g_k(\hat{\mathbf{y}}) = -|\hat{\mathbf{y}} - \mathbf{m}_k|^2$$

Thus the decision rule (6.10) results in assigning $\hat{\mathbf{y}}$ to the class to whose mean it is closest. ■

We have observed earlier that the decision boundary between any two classes is orthogonal to the vector **b** in Eq. 6.9a. For this example, **b** is proportional to the difference in the means, and so the decision boundary is orthogonal to a vector between the means of the two classes.

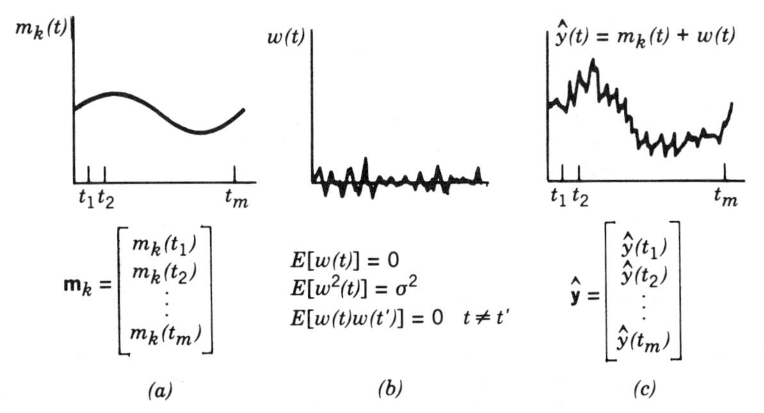

FIGURE 6.3 Signals in white noise. (a) Signal. (b) Noise. (c) Signal plus noise.

■ EXAMPLE 5.3

Inner Product Classifier

Assume that $\mathbf{K}_k = \sigma^2\mathbf{I}$, $k = 1, 2, \ldots, N_c$ as in the previous example and use the linear discriminant functions (6.18). One has

$$g_k(\hat{\mathbf{y}}) = \frac{2\mathbf{m}_k^T\hat{\mathbf{y}}}{\sigma^2} - \frac{|\mathbf{m}_k|^2}{\sigma^2} + 2\ \ln \Pr[\omega_k]$$

Assume further that the magnitude of each mean vector $|\mathbf{m}_k|$ is the same, that is, the means are distributed on a hypersphere with radius $|\mathbf{m}_k|$. Since the prior probabilities are equal, an equivalent set of discriminant functions is defined by

$$g_k(\hat{\mathbf{y}}) = \mathbf{m}_k^T\hat{\mathbf{y}} = \sum_{j=1}^{n} m_{k_j}\hat{y}_j$$

Thus the classifier can be considered as performing an inner product or a *correlation* between the mean vector of each class and the measurement vector and choosing the class with the highest value. ■

The last example serves as a model for a classical communications problem involving the detection of one of N_c known signals in additive white Gaussian noise. Let $y(t)$ represent a received waveform and $m_k(t)$ a known signal (see Fig. 6.3). When $m_k(t)$ is transmitted, the received waveform is given by

$$y(t) = m_k(t) + w(t)$$

where $w(t)$ is a zero-mean uncorrelated Gaussian noise process. That is, for any value of t, say t_i, the sample $w(t_i)$ is a Gaussian random variable with mean zero and variance σ^2 and for any $t_j \neq t_i$ the correlation $E[w(t_i)w(t_j)]$ is zero. If random vectors $\mathbf{y}$ and $\mathbf{m}_i$ are formed from m samples of the corresponding time functions,

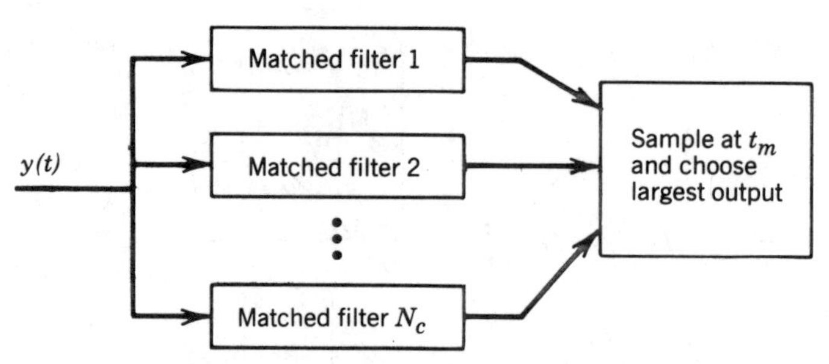

FIGURE 6.4 Matched filter detector structure.

then one has the pattern recognition problem described in this example. The assumption that the terms $|m_i|^2$ are all equal corresponds to the assumption that all signals have equal energy. A well-known result in communication theory is that the optimal detector involves a correlation of the received waveform with the known signals. This is often implemented as a "matched filter." The filter's impulse response[3] is the signal reversed in time, so its output at the end of the observation interval is the inner product $\mathbf{m}_k^T\hat{\mathbf{y}}$. The optimal detector selects the signal corresponding to the filter whose output is largest (see Fig. 6.4).

These examples provide interpretations that can be carried over to the general forms of the linear and quadratic classifiers. The linear classifier involves a comparison of terms of the form $\mathbf{m}_k^T\mathbf{K}^{-1}\hat{\mathbf{y}}$ (see Eq. 6.18 or Eqs. 6.8 and 6.9). If all vectors are represented in a coordinate system corresponding to the eigenvectors of the covariance matrix and scaled so that all components of the transformed vectors have unit variance, then the linear classifier can be shown to compare correlation between the measurement vector and each mean vector in this transformed coordinate system. In terms of the communication problem, one has signals in a more general type of noise whose time samples are correlated and whose variance may change from sample to sample. The optimal detector can be shown to be a filter that makes the noise sample uncorrelated (corresponding to the coordinate transformation) followed by a correlation or matched filter detector [e.g., Ref. 1].

The "nearest-mean" decision rule interpretation can also be applied to the general multiclass quadratic classifier. It was already pointed out that the two-class quadratic classifier compares the Mahalanobis distances between the vectors to be classified and both means. The Mahalanobis distance

$$d_{\mathbf{K}_i}(\hat{\mathbf{y}}, \mathbf{m}_i) = [(\hat{\mathbf{y}} - \mathbf{m}_i)^T\mathbf{K}_i^{-1}(\hat{\mathbf{y}} - \mathbf{m}_i)]^{1/2} \tag{6.19}$$

is also seen to be the essential ingredient of the discriminant functions for the multiclass quadratic classifier (see Eq. 6.16). Thus the multiclass quadratic classifier can be interpreted as comparing the squared Mahalanobis distance of the vector to the mean of each class. If the vectors are represented in the coordinate system

[3]Linear filters are further discussed in Chapter 10. (See Section 10.6.1)

corresponding to the eigenvectors of the covariance matrix $\mathbf{K}_i$, then by a procedure identical to the one leading to Eq. 4.84, the squared Mahalanobis distance can be expressed as

$$d^2_{\mathbf{K}_i}(\hat{\mathbf{y}}, \mathbf{m}_i) = \sum_{j=1}^{m} \frac{(\hat{y}'_j - m'_{ij})^2}{(\sigma^i_j)^2} \tag{6.20}$$

where $(\sigma^i_j)^2 = \lambda^i_j$ are the eigenvalues of $\mathbf{K}_i$ and $\hat{y}'_j$ and m'_{ij} are the components of $\hat{\mathbf{y}}$ and $\mathbf{m}_i$ with respect to the eigenvector coordinate system. The squared Mahalanobis distance thus measures the squared distance of each vector component from the corresponding mean component in standard deviation units and the quadratic classifier selects the class whose mean is, in this sense, closest.

6.3 OTHER DECISION CRITERIA—THE FISHER LINEAR CLASSIFIER

In the preceding sections two forms of classifiers were derived and interpreted as decision boundaries in an m-dimensional measurement space. The parameters in these classifiers (e.g., $\mathbf{A}$, $\mathbf{b}$, c, and T in Eq. 6.6) were determined such that if the measurement vectors were Gaussian, the classifiers would minimize the probability of error, the Bayes risk, or the Neyman–Pearson criterion. In some cases, one may not know the class conditional probability densities for the vectors and thus one cannot derive a classifier that optimizes these criteria. In other cases, one may be able to estimate the class conditional densities, but one may not want to tolerate the complexity of the optimal classifier. In such cases it may be more desirable to postulate a particular form of the classifier, such as a linear or quadratic form, and find the parameters of that form that optimize a suitable criterion of separability. Usually, the criterion is not the probability of error but one that is somewhat simpler and more tractable analytically. A considerable amount of attention has been given to linear *classifiers* in this regard [2–5]. The concentration on linear classifiers is not only because of the simplicity of analysis, but also because combinations of linear classifiers can realize very complex decision boundaries [5]. Linear classifiers were central to an early form of neural network called the Perceptron [6].

An example of this linear classifier designed to optimize a simple criterion can be found in the Fisher linear classifier for two-class problems. One assumes a linear structure for the classifier in the form of Eq. 6.8 and seeks to determine the classifier parameters to maximize the Fisher criterion [7]

$$F = \frac{(\mu_1 - \mu_2)^2}{\sigma_1^2 + \sigma_2^2} \tag{6.21}$$

where

$$\mu_i = E[h(\mathbf{y})|\omega_i] \tag{6.22a}$$

$$\sigma_i^2 = E[(h(\mathbf{y}) - \mu_i)^2|\omega_i] \qquad i = 1, 2 \tag{6.22b}$$

That is, the mean classifier outputs for the two classes should be as well separated as possible and the variances of those outputs should be as small as possible.

From Eqs. 4.47 and 4.49, the means and variances of the classifier outputs can be expressed as

$$\mu_i = \mathbf{b}^T\mathbf{m}_i + c \tag{6.23a}$$

$$\sigma_i^2 = \mathbf{b}^T\mathbf{K}_i\mathbf{b} \qquad i = 1, 2 \tag{6.23b}$$

It is clear, therefore, from Eq. 6.23 that Eq. 6.21 does not depend on the parameter c. As a result, this parameter can be included with the threshold T, and one needs only to determine the vector parameter **b** to maximize Eq. 6.21. The threshold can be determined to minimize the probability of error once **b** is chosen (e.g., Ref. 3, Section 4.2) or determined experimentally from the classifier operating characteristic to achieve the desired class error probabilities (see Section 3.2).

A necessary condition for the maximum is that the gradient $\partial F/\partial \mathbf{b}$ vanish. Applying this condition to Eq. 6.21 and employing Eq. 6.23, we have

$$\begin{aligned}\frac{\partial F}{\partial \mathbf{b}} &= \frac{\partial \mu_1}{\partial \mathbf{b}}\frac{\partial F}{\partial \mu_1} + \frac{\partial \mu_2}{\partial \mathbf{b}}\frac{\partial F}{\partial \mu_2} + \frac{\partial \sigma_1^2}{\partial \mathbf{b}}\frac{\partial F}{\partial \sigma_1^2} + \frac{\partial \sigma_2^2}{\partial \mathbf{b}}\frac{\partial F}{\partial \sigma_2^2} \\ &= \frac{2(\mu_1 - \mu_2)}{\sigma_1^2 + \sigma_2^2}(\mathbf{m}_1 - \mathbf{m}_2) - \frac{2(\mu_1 - \mu_2)^2}{(\sigma_1^2 + \sigma_2^2)^2}(\mathbf{K}_1\mathbf{b} + \mathbf{K}_2\mathbf{b}) = \mathbf{0}\end{aligned} \tag{6.24}$$

Thus **b** is given by

$$\mathbf{b} = \left[\frac{\sigma_1^2 + \sigma_2^2}{\mu_1 - \mu_2}\right][\mathbf{K}_1 + \mathbf{K}_2]^{-1}(\mathbf{m}_1 - \mathbf{m}_2) \tag{6.25}$$

Although the quantities μ_1, μ_2, σ_1^2, and σ_2^2 can be explicitly evaluated from Eqs. 6.23, it is generally more convenient to define **b** as simply

$$\mathbf{b} = \left[\tfrac{1}{2}(\mathbf{K}_1 + \mathbf{K}_2)\right]^{-1}(\mathbf{m}_1 - \mathbf{m}_2) \tag{6.26}$$

where the first term on the right of Eq. 6.26 is an average of the two covariance matrices, and redefine the threshold T to include the term $(\sigma_1^2 + \sigma_2^2)/(\mu_1 - \mu_2)$. The classifier thus has the form

$$(\mathbf{m}_1 - \mathbf{m}_2)^T\left[\tfrac{1}{2}(\mathbf{K}_1 + \mathbf{K}_2)\right]^{-1}\hat{\mathbf{y}} \underset{\omega_2}{\overset{\omega_1}{\gtrless}} T \tag{6.27}$$

Note that when $\mathbf{K}_1 = \mathbf{K}_2 = \mathbf{K}$ the value of **b** determined by Eq. 6.26 is proportional to that determined by Eq. 6.9a. Thus when the features are characterized by Gaussian probability densities with equal covariances, the decision rule that optimizes the Fisher criterion also minimizes the probability of error.

6.4 SUMMARY

This chapter describes some approaches to pattern classification based on the mean and covariance of the measurement vectors. Quadratic and linear forms of classifiers for two-class problems are derived from the likelihood ratio for Gaussian random vectors. Discriminant functions are discussed for multiclass pattern recognition problems, and quadratic and linear discriminant functions are described in detail. Quadratic and linear classifiers are interpreted as implementing a "nearest-mean" and "correlation" type of decision rule. Finally, a linear form of classifier for two-class problems based on the Fisher criterion is derived. The Fisher classifier is shown to reduce to the linear classifier that minimizes the probability of error for random vectors characterized by Gaussian probability densities with equal covariance matrices.

REFERENCES

1. H. L. Van Trees. *Detection, Estimation, and Modulation Theory*, Part I. New York: John Wiley & Sons, Inc., 1968, Chapter 4.
2. D. W. Peterson, and R. L. Mattson. "A Method of Finding Linear Discriminant Functions for a Class of Performance Criteria." *IEEE Transactions on Information Theory*, Vol. IT-12, pp. 380–387 (1966).
3. K. Fukunaga. *Introduction to Statistical Pattern Recognition*. New York: Academic Press, 1972, Chapters 4 and 7.
4. R. O. Duda, and P. E. Hart. *Pattern Classification and Scene Analysis*. New York: John Wiley & Sons, Inc., 1973, Chapter 5.
5. K. Fukunaga, and D. R. Olsen. "Piecewise Linear Discriminant Functions and Classification Errors for Multiclass Problems." *IEEE Transactions on Information Theory*, Vol. IT-16, pp. 99–100 (1970).
6. N. J. Nilsson. *Learning Machines*. New York: McGraw Hill Book Company, 1965.
7. R. A. Fisher. "The Use of Multiple Measurements in Taxonomic Problems." *Ann. Eugenics*, Vol. 7, Part II, pp. 179–188 (1936). Also in *Contributions to Mathematical Statistics*, New York: John Wiley & Sons, Inc., 1950.

PROBLEMS

6.1 Two classes of feature vectors are characterized by

$$\mathbf{K}_1 = \mathbf{K}_2 = \begin{bmatrix} 1 & 0 \\ 0 & \frac{1}{4} \end{bmatrix}; \quad \mathbf{m}_1 = \begin{bmatrix} 0 \\ 0 \end{bmatrix}; \quad \mathbf{m}_2 = \begin{bmatrix} 0 \\ 2 \end{bmatrix}$$

Determine and plot the equation for the decision boundary induced by a quadratic classifier with threshold

(a) $T = 0$.

(b) $T = -2$.

Label the decision regions R_1 and R_2.

6.2 Repeat Problem 6.1 for

$$\mathbf{K}_1 = \mathbf{K}_2 = \begin{bmatrix} 2 & 1 \\ 1 & 2 \end{bmatrix}; \quad \mathbf{m}_1 = \begin{bmatrix} 0 \\ 0 \end{bmatrix}; \quad \mathbf{m}_2 = \begin{bmatrix} 0 \\ 2 \end{bmatrix}$$

6.3 Repeat Problem 6.1 for

$$\mathbf{K}_1 = \begin{bmatrix} 2 & 1 \\ 1 & 2 \end{bmatrix}; \quad \mathbf{m}_1 = \begin{bmatrix} 0 \\ 0 \end{bmatrix}$$

$$\mathbf{K}_2 = \begin{bmatrix} 2 & -1 \\ -1 & 2 \end{bmatrix}; \quad \mathbf{m}_2 = \begin{bmatrix} 0 \\ 2 \end{bmatrix}$$

6.4 Three classes of patterns are characterized by a single feature y. The class conditional densities are

$$p_{y|\omega_1}(\hat{y}|\omega_1) = \frac{1}{\sqrt{2\pi}} \exp\left[\frac{-(\hat{y}+2)^2}{2}\right]$$

$$p_{y|\omega_2}(\hat{y}|\omega_2) = \frac{1}{\sqrt{2\pi}} \exp\left(\frac{-\hat{y}^2}{2}\right)$$

$$p_{y|\omega_3}(\hat{y}|\omega_3) = \frac{1}{\sqrt{2\pi}} \exp\left[\frac{-(\hat{y}-2)^2}{2}\right]$$

Assume that $\Pr[\omega_k] = \frac{1}{3}$, $k = 1, 2, 3$, and take the discriminant functions to be

$$g_k(y) = p_{y|\omega_k}(y|\omega_k)\Pr[\omega_k] \qquad k = 1, 2, 3$$

(a) Plot the discriminant functions on the y-axis and identify the regions R_i where the corresponding classes ω_i will be chosen.

(b) Discuss what happens if $\Pr[\omega_2]$ is increased while $\Pr[\omega_1]$ is held equal to $\Pr[\omega_3]$.

(c) How do the decision regions change if $p_{y|\omega_2}$ is changed to

$$p_{y|\omega_2}(\hat{y}|\omega_2) = \frac{1}{\sqrt{4\pi}} e^{-\hat{y}^2/4}$$

that is, the variance increases from 1 to $\sqrt{2}$?

6.5 Repeat Problem 6.4 for discriminant functions defined by

$$g_k(y) = 2 \ln\left[p_{y|\omega_k}(y|\omega_k)\Pr[\omega_k]\right] + \tfrac{1}{2} \ln 2\pi$$

6.6 Three classes of feature vectors are characterized by

$$\mathbf{K}_1 = \mathbf{K}_2 = \begin{bmatrix} 1 & 0 \\ 0 & \frac{1}{4} \end{bmatrix}; \quad \mathbf{m}_1 = \begin{bmatrix} 0 \\ 2 \end{bmatrix}; \quad \mathbf{m}_2 = \begin{bmatrix} 0 \\ 0 \end{bmatrix}$$

$$\mathbf{K}_3 = \begin{bmatrix} 4 & 0 \\ 0 & 2 \end{bmatrix}; \quad \mathbf{m}_3 = \begin{bmatrix} 0 \\ 2 \end{bmatrix}$$

Assume that $\Pr[\omega_1] = \Pr[\omega_2] = \Pr[\omega_3] = \frac{1}{3}$ and determine the quadratic discriminant functions $g_1(\mathbf{y})$, $g_2(\mathbf{y})$, and $g_3(\mathbf{y})$. Plot the covariance ellipses in the $y_1\,y_2$ plane and determine and plot the interclass boundaries

$$g_1(\mathbf{y}) = g_2(\mathbf{y})$$

$$g_1(y) = g_3(\mathbf{y})$$

$$g_2(\mathbf{y}) = g_3(\mathbf{y})$$

Identify the regions R_1, R_2, and R_3 in your sketch where the corresponding classes are chosen.

6.7 For the data of Problem 6.3, determine the parameter

$$\mathbf{b} = \left[\tfrac{1}{2}(\mathbf{K}_1 + \mathbf{K})_2\right]^{-1}(\mathbf{m}_1 - \mathbf{m}_2)$$

in the Fisher classifier. Plot the decision boundary induced by the classifier when $T = 1$.

6.8 The nonlinear feature extraction method described in Section 5.7.2 resulted in a linear transformation of the distances $D_{\mathbf{y}}^2(i) - D_{\mathbf{y}}^2(0)$ (see Eq. 5.65). To put the equations in matrix form, define a matrix $\mathbf{P}$ whose ith row is equal to $2(\mathbf{y}_{P0} - \mathbf{y}_{P_i})$, a vector $\mathbf{q}$ whose ith element is equal to $|\mathbf{y}_{P0}|^2 - |\mathbf{y}_{P_i}|^2$, and a new feature $\mathbf{z}$ whose ith element is equal to $D_{\mathbf{y}}^2(i) - D_{\mathbf{y}}^2(0)$. Then Eq 5.65 can be written as

$$\mathbf{P}\mathbf{y} = \mathbf{q} + \mathbf{z}$$

Show that if a linear classifier is used, then the classifier designed in the Z feature space is equivalent to one designed in the Y feature space. Thus the features $\mathbf{z}$ are just as useful for classification as the features $\mathbf{y}$.

CHAPTER 7

Parameter Estimation

It was seen in Chapter 3 that decision rules can be designed to minimize the probability of error, the Bayes risk, or the Neyman–Pearson criterion whenever the class conditional density functions for the features are known. Density functions sufficiently common to have been described by mathematical formulas always involve a set of parameters whose values determine the size and shape of the density. (For the Gaussian density, the parameters are the mean vector and the covariance matrix.) This chapter deals with estimation of those parameters from data.

7.1 ESTIMATION OF CONSTANT PARAMETERS

In many problems in pattern recognition, the form of the densities may be known (or assumed), but the values of the associated parameters are usually not known. The process of determining the values of the parameters from samples of the random vectors is known as *parameter estimation* and the value of the parameter that results is called an *estimate*. In general, the parameters to be estimated may be scalars, vectors, or matrices. However, for purposes of the present discussion, it will be assumed that the set of parameters is represented by a single vector parameter $\boldsymbol{\rho}$ of appropriate dimension. This represents no loss of generality but provides a convenient way to describe and discuss properties of estimates. In the present section, it will be assumed that the parameters are constants which are simply unknown. In Section 7.2, we shall revise that assumption by considering the parameters to be random variables for which a prior density function is given.

7.1.1 Maximum Likelihood Estimation

Let $\boldsymbol{\rho}$ represent the vector whose components $\rho_1, \rho_2, \ldots, \rho_L$ are the scalar parameters of a density function $p_{\mathbf{y};\boldsymbol{\rho}}(\mathbf{y};\boldsymbol{\rho})$ for a random vector $\mathbf{y}$. Let $\mathbf{y}^{(1)}, \mathbf{y}^{(2)}, \ldots, \mathbf{y}^{(N)}$ represent a set of N observed samples of the random vector $\mathbf{y}$. In the context of an estimation problem, these outcomes are themselves viewed as random variables, which are characterized by the joint density $p_{\mathbf{y}^{(1)}\mathbf{y}^{(2)}\ldots\mathbf{y}^{(N)};\boldsymbol{\rho}}(\mathbf{y}^{(1)}, \mathbf{y}^{(2)}, \ldots, \mathbf{y}^{(N)}; \boldsymbol{\rho})$.[1] When viewed as a function of $\boldsymbol{\rho}$, that is, for fixed values of the samples $\hat{\mathbf{y}}^{(1)}, \hat{\mathbf{y}}^{(2)}, \ldots, \hat{\mathbf{y}}^{(N)}$, $p_{\mathbf{y}^{(1)}\mathbf{y}^{(2)},\ldots,\mathbf{y}^{(N)};\boldsymbol{\rho}}$ is called a *likelihood function*. (It is thus clear why Eq. 3.2 is called a likelihood ratio test.) If we denote an estimate based on N samples as $\tilde{\boldsymbol{\rho}}_N$ then the *maximum likelihood* estimation procedure chooses, as its estimate, that value of the parameter that maximizes the likelihood function. In other words, $\tilde{\boldsymbol{\rho}}_N$ is chosen such that the event that the samples $\mathbf{y}^{(i)}$ fall in small regions about their observed values $\hat{\mathbf{y}}^{(i)}$ is the most likely event. It will be seen in Section 7.2 that this procedure is equivalent to estimating the value of $\boldsymbol{\rho}$ that has the highest probability of occurrence when the parameter is considered to be a random vector with a uniform density (all values of $\boldsymbol{\rho}$ are equally likely).

As long as the necessary derivatives exist, one can obtain the maximum of the likelihood function by setting

$$\frac{\partial p_{\mathbf{y}^{(1)}\mathbf{y}^{(2)}\ldots\mathbf{y}^{(N)};\boldsymbol{\rho}}}{\partial \boldsymbol{\rho}} = \mathbf{0} \tag{7.1}$$

or since the logarithm is a strictly monotonically increasing function, by setting

$$\frac{\partial \ln p_{\mathbf{y}^{(1)}\mathbf{y}^{(2)}\ldots\mathbf{y}^{(N)};\boldsymbol{\rho}}}{\partial \boldsymbol{\rho}} = \mathbf{0} \tag{7.2}$$

Equations 7.1 and 7.2 are sometimes called the *likelihood equation* and the *log likelihood equation,* respectively. They are entirely equivalent conditions and one will usually be more convenient than the other for a given estimation problem.

■ EXAMPLE 7.1

Arrival Time for Output Requests on a Computer

The time T between requests for output on a particular channel of a computer is described by the exponential density function

$$p_T(\hat{T}) = \begin{cases} \alpha e^{-\alpha \hat{T}} & \hat{T} > 0 \\ 0 & \text{otherwise} \end{cases}$$

The times between $N + 1$ requests on this channel are measured and found to be $\hat{T}^{(1)}, \hat{T}^{(2)}, \ldots, \hat{T}^{(N)}$. It is desired to estimate the parameter α (the "arrival rate")

[1]Unless otherwise noted, the samples $\mathbf{y}^{(i)}$ will be assumed to be independent. Thus the joint density can be expressed as the product of the density functions $p_{\mathbf{y}^{(i)};\boldsymbol{\rho}}$ $i = 1, 2, \ldots, N$.

of the distribution. Since the times between requests can be assumed to be independent, the likelihood function is

$$p_{T^{(1)}\,T^{(2)}\,\ldots\,T^{(N)};\,\alpha}(\hat{T}^{(1)}, \hat{T}^{(2)}, \ldots, \hat{T}^{(N)}; \alpha) = \prod_{i=1}^{N} \alpha\, e^{-\alpha \hat{T}^{(i)}} = \alpha^N e^{-\alpha \sum_{i=1}^{N} \hat{T}^{(i)}}$$

To find the value of α that maximizes this, one can use Eq. 7.2:

$$\frac{\partial}{\partial \alpha}\left[N \ln \alpha - \alpha \sum_{i=1}^{N} \hat{T}^{(i)}\right] = 0$$

or

$$\tilde{\alpha}_N = \frac{1}{\frac{1}{N}\sum_{i=1}^{N} \hat{T}^{(i)}}$$

Thus the maximum likelihood estimate for the arrival rate is simply the reciprocal of the average time between requests. ■

The previous example involved estimating a scalar parameter, but it illustrated the general procedure. For a case involving a vector parameter consider the following example.

■ EXAMPLE 7.2

Mean of a Multivariate Gaussian Density Function

A random vector $\mathbf{y}$ is described by a Gaussian density with known covariance $\mathbf{K}$ and unknown mean $\mathbf{m}$. The N samples $\mathbf{y}^{(1)}, \mathbf{y}^{(2)}, \ldots, \mathbf{y}^{(N)}$ are given and it is desired to estimate the mean.

The likelihood function is obtained from the joint density of the samples

$$p_{\mathbf{y}^{(1)}\,\mathbf{y}^{(2)}\,\ldots\,\mathbf{y}^{(N)};\,\mathbf{m}}(\hat{\mathbf{y}}^{(1)}, \hat{\mathbf{y}}^{(2)}, \ldots, \hat{\mathbf{y}}^{(N)}; \mathbf{m})$$
$$= \prod_{i=1}^{N} \frac{1}{(2\pi)^{\frac{m}{2}} |\mathbf{K}|^{\frac{1}{2}}} \exp\left[-\frac{1}{2}(\hat{\mathbf{y}}^{(i)} - \mathbf{m})^T \mathbf{K}^{-1} (\hat{\mathbf{y}}^{(i)} - \mathbf{m})\right]$$

The log likelihood function is thus

$$\ln p_{\mathbf{y}^{(1)}\,\mathbf{y}^{(2)}\,\ldots\,\mathbf{y}^{(N)};\mathbf{m}}(\hat{\mathbf{y}}^{(1)}, \hat{\mathbf{y}}^{(2)}, \cdots, \hat{\mathbf{y}}^{(N)}; \mathbf{m})$$
$$= \sum_{i=1}^{N} -\frac{m}{2}\ln 2\pi - \frac{1}{2}\ln |\mathbf{K}| - \frac{1}{2}(\hat{\mathbf{y}}^{(i)} - \mathbf{m})^T \mathbf{K}^{-1} (\hat{\mathbf{y}}^{(i)} - \mathbf{m})$$

Taking the derivative with respect to $\mathbf{m}$ and setting it equal to zero, we find

$$\frac{\partial \ln p_{\mathbf{y}^{(1)}\mathbf{y}^{(2)} \cdots \mathbf{y}^{(N)};\, \mathbf{m}}}{\partial \mathbf{m}} = \sum_{i=1}^{N} \mathbf{K}^{-1} (\hat{\mathbf{y}}^{(i)} - \mathbf{m}) = \mathbf{0}$$

or since $\mathbf{K}^{-1}$ is a constant matrix

$$\tilde{\mathbf{m}}_N = \frac{1}{N} \sum_{i=1}^{N} \hat{\mathbf{y}}^{(i)}$$

Thus the maximum likelihood estimate of $\mathbf{m}$ is the sample mean (see Example 4.4 in Section 4.5.4). ■

7.1.2 Properties of Estimates

An estimate of a parameter $\boldsymbol{\rho}$ can be considered as being a vector-valued function of the samples, that is,

$$\tilde{\boldsymbol{\rho}}_N = \tilde{\boldsymbol{\rho}}_N (\mathbf{y}^{(1)}, \mathbf{y}^{(2)}, \ldots, \mathbf{y}^{(N)}) \tag{7.3}$$

Since the estimate is a function of the samples, it is itself a random vector and one can describe its properties in a statistical sense. The following properties are useful in characterizing estimates.

1. An estimate $\tilde{\boldsymbol{\rho}}_N$ is said to be *unbiased* if

$$E[\tilde{\boldsymbol{\rho}}_N] = \boldsymbol{\rho} \tag{7.4}$$

Otherwise, it is said to be *biased*. An estimate is said to be *asymptotically unbiased* if

$$\lim_{N\to\infty} E[\tilde{\boldsymbol{\rho}}_N] = \boldsymbol{\rho} \tag{7.5}$$

2. An estimate $\tilde{\boldsymbol{\rho}}_N$ is said to be *consistent* if

$$\lim_{N\to\infty} \Pr[|\tilde{\boldsymbol{\rho}}_N - \boldsymbol{\rho}| < \varepsilon] = 1 \tag{7.6}$$

for any arbitrarily small number ε. The sequence of estimates $\{\tilde{\boldsymbol{\rho}}_N\}$ is said to *converge in probability* to the parameter $\boldsymbol{\rho}$. Some authors have also defined an estimate to be consistent if

$$\lim_{N\to\infty} E[|\tilde{\boldsymbol{\rho}}_N - \boldsymbol{\rho}|^2] = 0 \tag{7.7}$$

This is called convergence in *mean square*. For most purposes, we can consider the two definitions to be equivalent, although Eq. 7.6 is actually a stronger condition than Eq. 7.7.

3. An estimate is said to be *efficient* with respect to another estimate if it has a lower variance. Thus, if $\tilde{\boldsymbol{\rho}}_N$ is unbiased and efficient with respect to $\tilde{\boldsymbol{\rho}}_{N-1}$ for all N, then $\tilde{\boldsymbol{\rho}}_N$ is a consistent estimate.

It can be shown [1] that the maximum likelihood estimate is consistent and asymptotically the most efficient. Further, if $\tilde{\boldsymbol{\rho}}_N$ is any unbiased estimate, then the variance of any component $\tilde{\rho}_i$ of the estimate is bounded by

$$E[(\tilde{\rho}_i - \rho_i)^2] \geq j_{ii}^{-1} \qquad i = 1, 2, \ldots, L \tag{7.8}$$

where j_{ii}^{-1} is the ith diagonal element of the inverse of the matrix $\mathbf{J}$, where $\mathbf{J}$ is defined by

$$\mathbf{J} = E[\mathbf{a}\mathbf{a}^T] \tag{7.9}$$

and where

$$\mathbf{a} = \frac{\partial \ln p_{\mathbf{y}^{(1)}\mathbf{y}^{(2)} \ldots \mathbf{y}^{(N)};\, \boldsymbol{\rho}}}{\partial \boldsymbol{\rho}} \tag{7.10}$$

The matrix $\mathbf{J}$ is known as the Fisher information matrix [2].

For the case of a scalar parameter ρ, Eq. 7.8 reduces to

$$E[(\tilde{\rho}_N - \rho)^2] \geq \frac{1}{E[[\partial \ln p_{\mathbf{y}^{(1)}\,\mathbf{y}^{(2)} \ldots \mathbf{y}^{(N)};\,\rho}/\partial\rho]^2]} \tag{7.11}$$

which is called the Cramer–Rao inequality [3, 4]. An estimate that satisfies Eq. 7.8 or Eq. 7.11 with equality is the most efficient of all estimates and is called a *minimum variance estimate*. A minimum variance estimate, when it exists, is the maximum likelihood estimate [3].

A necessary and sufficient condition for $\tilde{\boldsymbol{\rho}}_N$ to be a minimum variance estimate is that

$$\mathbf{a} = \mathbf{B}(\boldsymbol{\rho})(\tilde{\boldsymbol{\rho}}_N - \boldsymbol{\rho}) \tag{7.12}$$

where $\mathbf{B}(\boldsymbol{\rho})$ is a matrix whose elements can be a function of $\boldsymbol{\rho}$ (but not of $\tilde{\boldsymbol{\rho}}_N$). The proof of these results is as follows.

Since $\tilde{\boldsymbol{\rho}}_N$ is unbiased, one has[2]

$$E[(\tilde{\boldsymbol{\rho}}_N - \boldsymbol{\rho})^T]$$
$$= \int_{-\infty}^{\infty}\int_{-\infty}^{\infty} \cdots \int_{-\infty}^{\infty} (\tilde{\boldsymbol{\rho}}_N - \boldsymbol{\rho})^T p_{\mathbf{y}^{(1)}\mathbf{y}^{(2)} \ldots \mathbf{y}^{(N)};\,\boldsymbol{\rho}}\, d\mathbf{y}^{(1)}\, d\mathbf{y}^{(2)} \ldots d\mathbf{y}^{(N)} = \mathbf{0}$$

and thus

[2]The arguments of the functions are deliberately left out to simplify the notation.

$$\frac{\partial E(\tilde{\boldsymbol{\rho}}_N - \boldsymbol{\rho})^T}{\partial \boldsymbol{\rho}}$$

$$= \int_{-\infty}^{\infty}\int_{-\infty}^{\infty}\cdots\int_{-\infty}^{\infty} \frac{\partial p_{\mathbf{y}^{(1)}\mathbf{y}^{(2)}\cdots\mathbf{y}^{(N)};\boldsymbol{\rho}}}{\partial \boldsymbol{\rho}} (\tilde{\boldsymbol{\rho}}_N - \boldsymbol{\rho})^T\, d\mathbf{y}^{(1)}\, d\mathbf{y}^{(2)} \cdots d\mathbf{y}^{(N)}$$

$$- \mathbf{I}\int_{-\infty}^{\infty}\int_{-\infty}^{\infty}\cdots\int_{-\infty}^{\infty} p_{\mathbf{y}^{(1)}\mathbf{y}^{(2)}\cdots\mathbf{y}^{(N)}}\, d\mathbf{y}^{(1)}\, d\mathbf{y}^{(2)} \cdots d\mathbf{y}^{(N)}$$

$$= \int_{-\infty}^{\infty}\int_{-\infty}^{\infty}\cdots\int_{-\infty}^{\infty} \frac{\partial \ln p_{\mathbf{y}^{(1)}\mathbf{y}^{(2)}\cdots\mathbf{y}^{(N)};\boldsymbol{\rho}}}{\partial \boldsymbol{\rho}} (\tilde{\boldsymbol{\rho}} - \boldsymbol{\rho})^T \cdot$$

$$p_{\mathbf{y}^{(1)}\mathbf{y}^{(2)}\cdots\mathbf{y}^{(N)};\boldsymbol{\rho}}\, d\mathbf{y}^{(1)}\, d\mathbf{y}^{(2)} \cdots d\mathbf{y}^{(N)} \qquad (7.14)$$

$$-\mathbf{I} = [\mathbf{0}]$$

It follows, therefore, using the definition of Eq. 7.10 that

$$E[\mathbf{a}(\tilde{\boldsymbol{\rho}}_N - \boldsymbol{\rho})^T] = \mathbf{I} \qquad (7.15)$$

Consider now the random vector defined by

$$\mathbf{z}_i = \begin{bmatrix} \tilde{\rho}_i - \rho_i \\ \hline \mathbf{a} \end{bmatrix} \qquad (7.16)$$

It follows from Eqs. 7.9 and 7.15 that the correlation matrix for $\mathbf{z}_i$ is given by

$$E[\mathbf{z}_i\, \mathbf{z}_i^T] = \left[\begin{array}{c|c} E[(\tilde{\rho}_i - \rho_i)^2] & 0, 0, \cdots 1 \cdots 0 \\ \hline 0 & \\ 0 & \\ \vdots & \\ 1 & \mathbf{J} \\ \vdots & \\ 0 & \end{array}\right] \qquad (7.17)$$

where the 1s appear in the $i+1^{\text{th}}$ position in the first row and column and 0s appear elsewhere. Since the correlation matrix is a positive semidefinite matrix, the determinant of Eq. 7.17 must be nonnegative. Thus

$$|E[\mathbf{z}_i\, \mathbf{z}_i^T]| = E[(\tilde{\rho}_i - \rho_i)^2] \cdot |\mathbf{J}| - J_{ii} \geq 0 \qquad (7.18)$$

where J_{ii} is the iith cofactor of $\mathbf{J}$. Thus we have (see Eq. 4.17)

$$E[\tilde{\rho}_i - \rho_i)^2] \geq \frac{J_{ii}}{|\mathbf{J}|} = j_{ii}^{-1} \qquad (7.19)$$

which is the desired result. To prove Eq. 7.12, one only need note that when the determinant of the covariance is zero, the components of $\mathbf{z}_i$ are linearly dependent and thus Eq. 7.12 applies.

■ EXAMPLE 7.3

Sample Mean

The sample mean of Example 7.2 is unbiased because

$$E[\tilde{\mathbf{m}}_N] = \frac{1}{N} \sum_{i=1}^{N} E[\mathbf{y}^{(i)}] = \frac{1}{N}(N\mathbf{m}) = \mathbf{m}$$

If the samples $\mathbf{y}^{(i)}$ are independent, they are also uncorrelated and so the covariance matrix for the estimate $\tilde{\mathbf{m}}_N$ is given by

$$E[(\tilde{\mathbf{m}}_N - \mathbf{m})(\tilde{\mathbf{m}}_N - \mathbf{m})^T] = \frac{1}{N^2} E\left[\left(\sum_{i=1}^{N} (\mathbf{y}^{(i)} - \mathbf{m})\right)\left(\sum_{j=1}^{N} (\mathbf{y}^{(j)} - \mathbf{m})^T\right)\right]$$

$$= \frac{1}{N^2} \sum_{i=1}^{N} E\left[(\mathbf{y}^{(i)} - \mathbf{m})(\mathbf{y}^{(i)} - \mathbf{m})^T\right]$$

$$= \frac{1}{N}\mathbf{K}$$

Since the covariance of $\tilde{\mathbf{m}}_N$ decreases as $1/N$, the estimate $\tilde{\mathbf{m}}_N$ is efficient relative to $\tilde{\mathbf{m}}_{N-1}$ and thus (since the estimate is also unbiased) $\tilde{\mathbf{m}}_N$ is a consistent estimate of $\mathbf{m}$. Note also that since the samples are independent, we have as in Example 7.2,

$$\mathbf{a} = \frac{\partial \ln p_{\mathbf{y}^{(1)}\,\mathbf{y}^{(2)}\,\ldots\,\mathbf{y}^{(N)};\,\mathbf{m}}}{\partial \mathbf{m}}$$

$$= \mathbf{K}^{-1} \sum_{i=1}^{N} (\mathbf{y}^{(i)} - \mathbf{m}) = N\,\mathbf{K}^{-1}(\tilde{\mathbf{m}}_N - \mathbf{m})$$

which is in the form of Eq. 7.12. Thus $\tilde{\mathbf{m}}_N$ is a minimum-variance estimate. ■

7.2 BAYES ESTIMATION

Maximum likelihood estimation can be thought of as a procedure to be used when one has no prior knowledge (or is willing to assume none) about the probability of various values of the parameter. If one *does* have some prior knowledge concerning the parameter $\boldsymbol{\rho}$, then one can treat the parameter as a random vector characterized by a density function $p_{\boldsymbol{\rho}}(\boldsymbol{\rho})$ and apply a procedure known as *Bayes estimation*. A continuous function $C(\tilde{\boldsymbol{\rho}}, \boldsymbol{\rho})$ is defined that assigns a "cost" to every pair of variables $\tilde{\boldsymbol{\rho}}$ and $\boldsymbol{\rho}$, and the Bayes *risk* $\mathcal{R}$ is defined as the expected value of the cost function.[3] An estimate $\tilde{\boldsymbol{\rho}}$ is then chosen to minimize the risk. (This procedure is entirely analogous to the Bayes hypothesis testing procedure discussed in Chapter 3.)

The Bayes risk can be expressed as[4]

$$
\begin{aligned}
\mathcal{R} &= E[C(\tilde{\boldsymbol{\rho}} - \boldsymbol{\rho})] \\
&= \int_{-\infty}^{\infty}\int_{-\infty}^{\infty} \cdots \int_{-\infty}^{\infty}\int_{-\infty}^{\infty} C(\tilde{\boldsymbol{\rho}}, \boldsymbol{\rho}) p_{\mathbf{y}^{(1)}\,\mathbf{y}^{(2)}\,\cdots\,\mathbf{y}^{(N)}\boldsymbol{\rho}}\, d\mathbf{y}^{(1)}\, d\mathbf{y}^{(2)} \cdots d\mathbf{y}^{(N)}\, d\boldsymbol{\rho} \\
&= \int_{-\infty}^{\infty}\int_{-\infty}^{\infty} \cdots \int_{-\infty}^{\infty} I(\tilde{\boldsymbol{\rho}}) p_{\mathbf{y}^{(1)}\mathbf{y}^{(2)}\cdots\mathbf{y}^{(N)}}\, d\mathbf{y}^{(1)}\, d\mathbf{y}^{(2)} \cdots d\mathbf{y}^{(N)}
\end{aligned}
\tag{7.20}
$$

where

$$
I(\tilde{\boldsymbol{\rho}}) = \int_{-\infty}^{\infty} C(\tilde{\boldsymbol{\rho}}, \boldsymbol{\rho}) p_{\boldsymbol{\rho}|\mathbf{y}^{(1)}\mathbf{y}^{(2)}\cdots\mathbf{y}^{(N)}}(\boldsymbol{\rho}|\mathbf{y}^{(1)}\,\mathbf{y}^{(2)} \cdots \mathbf{y}^{(N)})\, d\boldsymbol{\rho} \tag{7.21}
$$

If $C(\tilde{\boldsymbol{\rho}}, \boldsymbol{\rho})$ is assumed to be nonnegative, then $I(\tilde{\boldsymbol{\rho}})$ is also nonnegative, and minimizing $I(\tilde{\boldsymbol{\rho}})$ is equivalent to minimizing the risk.

7.2.1 Mean-Square and Maximum a Posteriori Estimates

As a specific case of Bayes estimation consider the quadratic cost function shown in Fig. 7.1. This function depends only on the distance $|\tilde{\boldsymbol{\rho}} - \boldsymbol{\rho}|$ of the estimated parameter from the true parameter and assigns costs that increase with the square of the distance. For the quadratic cost function Eq. 7.21 becomes

$$
I(\tilde{\boldsymbol{\rho}}) = \int_{-\infty}^{\infty} |\tilde{\boldsymbol{\rho}} - \boldsymbol{\rho}|^2\, p_{\boldsymbol{\rho}|\mathbf{y}^{(1)}\mathbf{y}^{(2)}\cdots\mathbf{y}^{(N)}}(\boldsymbol{\rho}|\mathbf{y}^{(1)}\mathbf{y}^{(2)} \cdots \mathbf{y}^{(N)})\,d\boldsymbol{\rho} \tag{7.22}
$$

[3]To make the notation less cumbersome in the following discussion we drop the subscript N on the estimate.

[4]Again the arguments of the density function are left out for simplicity. Note that $p_{\mathbf{y}^{(1)}\,\mathbf{y}^{(2)}\,\cdots\,\mathbf{y}^{(N)}\boldsymbol{\rho}}$ used in Eq. 7.20 is a joint density between the samples $\mathbf{y}^{(1)}\,\mathbf{y}^{(2)} \cdots \mathbf{y}^{(N)}$ *and* the random parameter $\boldsymbol{\rho}$. This is very different from the parameterized density function $p_{\mathbf{y}^{(1)}\,\mathbf{y}^{(2)}\,\cdots\,\mathbf{y}^{(N)};\,\boldsymbol{\rho}}$ used in Section 7.1. The joint density can be expressed as

$$
p_{\mathbf{y}^{(1)}\mathbf{y}^{(2)}\cdots\mathbf{y}^{(N)},\,\boldsymbol{\rho}} = p_{\mathbf{y}^{(1)}\mathbf{y}^{(2)}\cdots\mathbf{y}^{(N)}|\boldsymbol{\rho}}\, p_{\boldsymbol{\rho}}(\boldsymbol{\rho})
$$

where the conditional density function $p_{\mathbf{y}^{(1)}\mathbf{y}^{(2)}\cdots\mathbf{y}^{(N)}|\boldsymbol{\rho}}$ is for all practical purposes the same as the parameterized density function $p_{\mathbf{y}^{(1)}\mathbf{y}^{(2)}\cdots\mathbf{y}^{(N)};\,\boldsymbol{\rho}}$, but the vertical bar is used instead of the semicolon to indicate that $\boldsymbol{\rho}$ is a random vector.

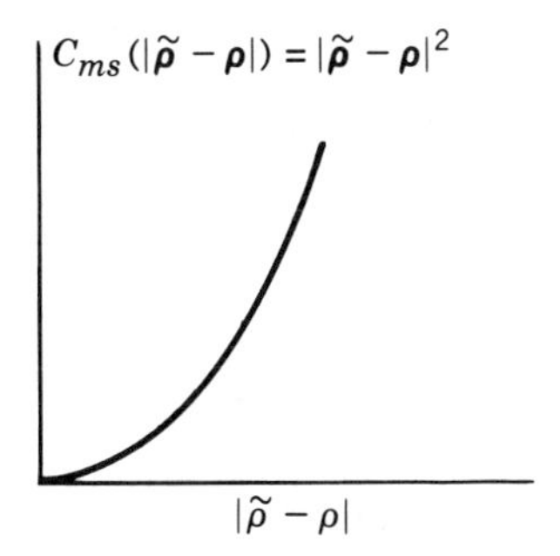

FIGURE 7.1 A quadratic cost function.

To obtain the estimate that minimizes the risk, it is sufficient to find the value of $\tilde{\boldsymbol{\rho}}$ that satisfies

$$\frac{\partial I(\tilde{\boldsymbol{\rho}})}{\partial \tilde{\boldsymbol{\rho}}} = 2 \int_{-\infty}^{\infty} (\tilde{\boldsymbol{\rho}} - \boldsymbol{\rho})\, p_{\boldsymbol{\rho}|\mathbf{y}^{(1)}\mathbf{y}^{(2)} \ldots \mathbf{y}^{(N)}} (\boldsymbol{\rho}|\mathbf{y}^{(1)}\, \mathbf{y}^{(2)} \ldots \mathbf{y}^{(N)})\, d\boldsymbol{\rho} = \mathbf{0} \tag{7.23}$$

The desired estimate is thus given by

$$\tilde{\boldsymbol{\rho}} = \int_{-\infty}^{\infty} \boldsymbol{\rho}\, p_{\boldsymbol{\rho}|\mathbf{y}^{(1)}\mathbf{y}^{(2)} \ldots \mathbf{y}^{(N)}} (\boldsymbol{\rho}|\mathbf{y}^{(1)}\, \mathbf{y}^{(2)} \ldots \mathbf{y}^{(N)})\, d\boldsymbol{\rho} \tag{7.24}$$

In other words, the estimate $\tilde{\boldsymbol{\rho}}$ is the *mean of the posterior density* $p_{\boldsymbol{\rho}|\mathbf{y}^{(1)}\mathbf{y}^{(2)} \ldots \mathbf{y}^{(N)}}$. This estimate is called the *mean-square* estimate because it minimizes the mean-square error, $\mathcal{R} = E[|\tilde{\boldsymbol{\rho}} - \boldsymbol{\rho}|^2]$. It can be shown [5] that if the posterior density is symmetric about its mean, then the mean-square estimate is the best estimate not only for the quadratic cost function, but also for any cost function that is a convex function[5] of the distance $|\tilde{\boldsymbol{\rho}} - \boldsymbol{\rho}|$.

Another form of cost function commonly employed is the uniform cost function shown in Fig. 7.2. This cost function also depends only on the distance $|\tilde{\boldsymbol{\rho}} - \boldsymbol{\rho}|$

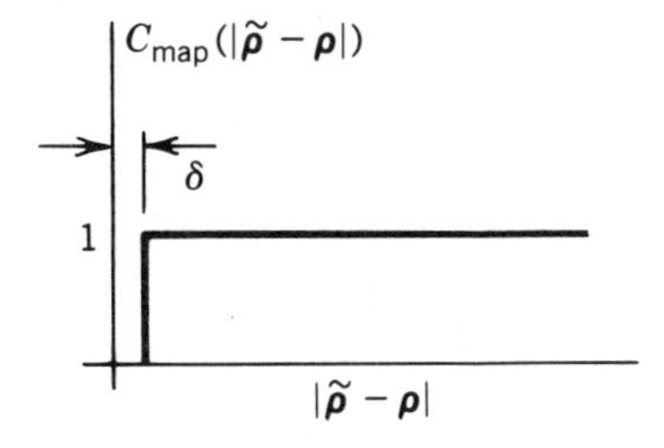

FIGURE 7.2 A uniform cost function.

[5]A convex function is a function that when plotted will always lie below a straight line that connects any two points on the curve.

and assigns zero cost to all estimates that are within an arbitrarily small distance δ from the true value of the parameter and assigns unit cost to all other estimates. For the uniform cost function, Eq. 7.21 becomes

$$I(\tilde{\boldsymbol{\rho}}) = 1 - \int_{R_\delta} p_{\boldsymbol{\rho}|\mathbf{y}^{(1)}\mathbf{y}^{(2)} \ldots \mathbf{y}^{(N)}} (\boldsymbol{\rho}|\mathbf{y}^{(1)}\,\mathbf{y}^{(2)} \ldots \mathbf{y}^{(N)})\, d\boldsymbol{\rho} \qquad (7.25)$$

where R_δ is a region of parameter space where $|\tilde{\boldsymbol{\rho}} - \boldsymbol{\rho}| \leq \delta$. Since δ can be made very small, a good approximation to the integral is the integrand evaluated at $\tilde{\boldsymbol{\rho}}$ multiplied by the volume of R_δ. Thus to minimize $I(\tilde{\boldsymbol{\rho}})$, one should choose the value $\tilde{\boldsymbol{\rho}}$ that *maximizes* the posterior density $p_{\boldsymbol{\rho}|\mathbf{y}^{(1)}\mathbf{y}^{(2)} \ldots \mathbf{y}^{(N)}}$. This estimate is correspondingly called the *maximum a posteriori* (or MAP) estimate.

From Bayes's rule the posterior density can be expressed as

$$p_{\boldsymbol{\rho}|\mathbf{y}^{(1)}\,\mathbf{y}^{(2)} \ldots \mathbf{y}^{(N)}}(\boldsymbol{\rho}|\mathbf{y}^{(1)}\,\mathbf{y}^{(2)} \ldots \mathbf{y}^{(N)}) = \frac{p_{\mathbf{y}^{(1)}\,\mathbf{y}^{(2)} \ldots \mathbf{y}^{(N)}|\boldsymbol{\rho}}(\mathbf{y}^{(1)}, \mathbf{y}^{(2)} \ldots \mathbf{y}^{(N)}|\boldsymbol{\rho})p_{\boldsymbol{\rho}}(\boldsymbol{\rho})}{p_{\mathbf{y}^{(1)}\,\mathbf{y}^{(2)} \ldots \mathbf{y}^{(N)}}(\mathbf{y}^{(1)}, \mathbf{y}^{(2)}, \ldots \mathbf{y}^{(N)})}$$

If the prior density $p_{\boldsymbol{\rho}}(\boldsymbol{\rho})$ is uniform (constant) such that all values of $\boldsymbol{\rho}$ in the region of interest are equally likely, then maximizing $p_{\boldsymbol{\rho}|\mathbf{y}^{(1)}\mathbf{y}^{(2)} \ldots \mathbf{y}^{(N)}}$ is equivalent to maximizing $p_{\mathbf{y}^{(1)}\mathbf{y}^{(2)} \ldots \mathbf{y}^{(N)}|\boldsymbol{\rho}}$. In this situation, the MAP estimate is the same as the maximum likelihood estimate for $\boldsymbol{\rho}$.

■ EXAMPLE 7.4

Mean of a Gaussian Density

Let $\mathbf{y}^{(1)}, \mathbf{y}^{(2)}, \ldots, \mathbf{y}^{(N)}$ be samples from a Gaussian density function with known covariance $\mathbf{K_y}$ and unknown mean $\mathbf{m}$.

$$p_{\mathbf{y}|\mathbf{m}}(\mathbf{y}^{(i)}\,|\mathbf{m}) = \frac{1}{(2\pi)^{m/2}\,|\mathbf{K_y}|^{1/2}} \exp\left[-\frac{1}{2}(\mathbf{y}^{(i)} - \mathbf{m})^T\mathbf{K_y}^{-1}(\mathbf{y}^{(i)} - \mathbf{m})\right]$$

Furthermore, assume that the mean itself has a prior density that is Gaussian with covariance $\mathbf{K_m}$ and mean $\mathbf{m}_0$.

$$p_{\mathbf{m}}(\mathbf{m}) = \frac{1}{(2\pi)^{m/2}\,|\mathbf{K_m}|^{1/2}} \exp\left[-\frac{1}{2}(\mathbf{m} - \mathbf{m}_0)^T\mathbf{K_m}^{-1}(\mathbf{m} - \mathbf{m}_0)\right]$$

By applying Eq. 7.26 (one needs to integrate the numerator over $\boldsymbol{\rho}$ to obtain the denominator; see Eqs. 2.39 and 2.40) one can find after much matrix algebra that the posterior density $p_{\mathbf{m}|\mathbf{y}^{(1)}\,\mathbf{y}^{(2)} \ldots \mathbf{y}^{(N)}}$ is Gaussian with mean vector

$$\tilde{\mathbf{m}} = (\mathbf{K_y}^{-1} + \frac{1}{N}\mathbf{K_m}^{-1})^{-1}(\mathbf{K_y}^{-1}\frac{1}{N}\sum_{i=1}^{N}\mathbf{y}^{(i)} + \frac{1}{N}\mathbf{K_m}^{-1}\,\mathbf{m}_0)$$

Since this is both the mean and the maximum point of the posterior density, $\tilde{\mathbf{m}}$ is both the mean-square estimate and the MAP estimate. Problems 7.4 and 7.5 show a much easier to way to obtain this result. ■

So far we have considered only estimation of *parameters*. Since Bayes estimation deals with estimation of random vectors, it can be used in applications where we need to estimate something other than a parameter of a density. The following example illustrates this.

■ EXAMPLE 7.5

Sample Prediction

Let $y^{(1)}, y^{(2)}, \ldots, y^{(N)}$ be a set of nonindependent (scalar) samples from a random phenomena. It is desired to predict $y^{(N+1)}$, the next sample of the random phenomena. It is known that the samples have zero mean and that any k consecutive samples are Gaussian with covariance matrix $\mathbf{K}_k$.

Although, in this example one is not estimating the parameter of a density function, the principles are identical. First, construct the posterior density function for $y^{(N+1)}$. Let $\mathbf{y}_k$ represent the vector

$$\mathbf{y}_k = \begin{bmatrix} y^{(1)} \\ y^{(2)} \\ \vdots \\ y^{(k)} \end{bmatrix}$$

then

$$p_{y^{(N+1)}|\mathbf{y}_N}(y^{(N+1)}|\mathbf{y}_N)$$

$$= \frac{1/((2\pi)^{(N+1/2)}\,|\mathbf{K}_{N+1}|^{1/2})\exp\left(-\frac{1}{2}\mathbf{y}_{N+1}^T\,\mathbf{K}_{N+1}^{-1}\,\mathbf{y}_{N+1}\right)}{1/((2\pi)^{N}|\mathbf{K}_N|^{1/2})\exp\left(-\frac{1}{2}\mathbf{y}_N^T\,\mathbf{K}_N^{-1}\,\mathbf{y}_N\right)}$$

It is not too difficult to show that this density reduces to the form

$$p_{y^{(N+1)}|\mathbf{y}_N}(y^{(N+1)}|\mathbf{y}_N) = \frac{1}{\sqrt{2\pi}\,\sigma}\exp\left[\frac{-(y^{(N+1)} - \mathbf{g}^T\mathbf{y}_N)^2}{2\sigma^2}\right]$$

where $\sigma = \sqrt{|\mathbf{K}_{N+1}|/|\mathbf{K}_N|}$, $\mathbf{g} = \mathbf{K}_N^{-1}\,\boldsymbol{\phi}$ and $\boldsymbol{\phi} = E[y^{(N+1)}\,\mathbf{y}_N]$

Since this posterior density is Gaussian, both the mean and the maximum occur at the same point. Therefore, both the mean-square estimate and the MAP estimate are the same and are given by

$$\hat{y}^{(N+1)} = \mathbf{g}^T\mathbf{y}_N$$

This shows that when the samples are jointly Gaussian, the best estimate of $y^{(N+1)}$ is a *linear* function of the previous samples. ■

7.2.2 Bounds on the Mean-Square Error

Although it will not be proven here, Eq. 7.8 holds true when the parameter $\boldsymbol{\rho}$ is considered to be a random vector if the matrix $\mathbf{J}$ is defined by

$$\mathbf{J} = E\left[\mathbf{a}\mathbf{a}^T + \mathbf{b}\mathbf{b}^T\right] \tag{7.27}$$

where

$$\mathbf{a} = \frac{\partial \ln p_{\mathbf{y}^{(1)}\mathbf{y}^{(2)} \cdots \mathbf{y}^{N}|\boldsymbol{\rho}}}{\partial \boldsymbol{\rho}} \tag{7.28}$$

and

$$\mathbf{b} = \frac{\partial \ln p_{\boldsymbol{\rho}}}{\partial \boldsymbol{\rho}} \tag{7.29}$$

The bound is satisfied with equality if and only if the estimate satisfies

$$\mathbf{a} + \mathbf{b} = \mathbf{B} \cdot (\tilde{\boldsymbol{\rho}} - \boldsymbol{\rho}) \tag{7.30}$$

where $\mathbf{B}$ is a constant matrix. The quantity on the left-hand side of Eq. 7.8 is now interpreted as the mean-square error instead of the variance of the estimate. The proof of these results is analogous to the proof given for nonrandom parameters.

7.3 SUMMARY

This chapter deals with estimation of the parameters of a density function. Maximum likelihood estimation is described as an approach that requires no prior knowledge of the probability of various values of the parameter. Several properties of estimates are discussed and bounds on the variance of an estimate are derived. Bayes estimation is then described as an approach to be used when prior knowledge about the parameter values is available, and thus the parameter can be treated as a random vector with an associated probability density function. Bounds on the mean square error for estimation of parameters are cited.

REFERENCES

1. S. S. Wilks. *Mathematical Statistics*. New York: John Wiley & Sons, Inc., 1962.
2. R. A. Fisher. *Statistical Methods and Scientific Inference*. London: Oliver & Boyd, 1956.
3. H. Cramer. *Mathematical Methods of Statistics*. Princeton, NJ: Princeton University Press, 1946, Chapter 32.

4. C. R. RAO. "Information and Accuracy Attainable in the Estimation of Statistical Parameters." *Bull. Calcutta Math. Soc.*, Vol. 37, pp 81–91 (1945).
5. H. L. VAN TREES. *Detection, Estimation, and Modulation Theory*. Part I. New York: John Wiley & Sons, Inc., 1968.

PROBLEMS

7.1 **(a)** What is the maximum likelihood estimate for the mean of the exponential distribution of Example 7.1?
(b) Is this estimate unbiased?
(c) Is it consistent?
(d) Is it a minimum-variance estimate?

7.2 A random variable y has the uniform distribution

$$p_y(\hat{y}) = \begin{cases} \dfrac{1}{a} & 0 \leq \hat{y} \leq a \\ 0 & \text{otherwise} \end{cases}$$

(a) Determine the likelihood function $p_{y^{(1)}y^{(2)} \cdots y^{(N)};a}$ for $N = 1$ and $N = 2$ and sketch it.
(b) Determine the maximum likelihood estimate of the parameter a for arbitrary N.

7.3 Assume that the parameter α in the exponential density of Example 7.1 is a random parameter with prior density function

$$p_\alpha(\alpha) = \begin{cases} \alpha\beta^2 e^{-\alpha\beta} & \alpha \geq 0 \\ 0 & \text{otherwise} \end{cases}$$

(a) What is the posterior density function $p_{\alpha|T^{(1)}T^{(2)} \cdots T^{(N)}}$?
(b) What is the mean square estimate of α?
(c) What is the MAP estimate of α?

$$\textit{Note:} \int_0^\infty y^k e^{-y} \, dy = k! \qquad \text{for any integer } k.$$

7.4 Show that a necessary condition for $\tilde{\boldsymbol{\rho}}$ to be the MAP estimate is that

$$\mathbf{a} + \mathbf{b} \,|_{\tilde{\boldsymbol{\rho}}} = \mathbf{0}$$

where **a** and **b** are defined by Eqs. 7.28 and 7.29, respectively.

7.5 Assume that samples $\mathbf{y}^{(i)}$ of a Gaussian random phenomenon are independently distributed with known covariance $\mathbf{K_y}$ and random mean $\mathbf{m}$. Assume that $\mathbf{m}$ is characterized by a Gaussian density with mean $\mathbf{m}_0$ and covariance $\mathbf{K_m}$.

(a) What is the MAP estimate for $\mathbf{m}$? *Hint:* Use the results of Problem 7.4.

(b) What is the expected value (the bias) of the estimate?

CHAPTER 8

Nonparametric Estimation and Classification

Methods were developed in the preceding chapter for estimating the parameters of a density whose generic form is known (or assumed). In this chapter two related methods are discussed for estimating the density function when its generic form is not known. These procedures are called nonparametric estimation procedures. The first nonparametric procedure to be discussed, so-called Parzen estimation (after E. Parzen [1]), provides an estimate of the class conditional densities that can be subsequently used for a likelihood ratio test. The second procedure, the nearest neighbor algorithm [2, 3], leads directly to an approximation of the likelihood ratio test that minimizes the probability of error. In addition, this chapter gives a brief introduction to the area of nonparametric classification, where one does not try to explicitly estimate the density or its parameters but instead develops classification methods that will be optimal in some sense over a broad class of densities. These lead to relatively simple tests involving only the magnitudes or the ordering of the magnitudes of the observations.

8.1 PARZEN ESTIMATION

The Parzen estimation procedure will first be developed for densities of random variables (one-dimensional random vectors). The results will then be generalized to the estimation of the densities of (multidimensional) random vectors.

8.1.1 Estimation of the Density of a Random Variable

To motivate the Parzen estimation procedure, assume that one has N independent samples $y^{(1)}, y^{(2)}, \ldots, y^{(N)}$ of a random variable y, and consider approximating the density p_y by a histogram formed from the samples with bins that are $\Delta y = 2h$

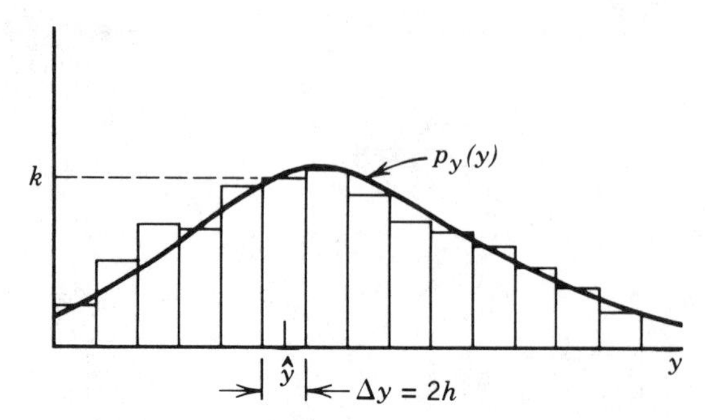

FIGURE 8.1 The approximation of density function by histogram.

wide as shown in Fig. 8.1. Let k be the number of samples in a bin whose midpoint is at $\hat{y}$ and let the probability that a sample is in that bin be approximated by

$$\Pr[|\hat{y} - y| \leq h] = p_y(\hat{y})\, 2h \tag{8.1}$$

If one has a sufficiently large number of samples, then the probability of this event can also be approximated by the relative frequency k/N and thus the density can be approximated at $\hat{y}$ by

$$\tilde{p}_y(\hat{y}) = \frac{k}{2hN} \tag{8.2}$$

Now consider the function

$$\gamma(z) = \begin{cases} \dfrac{1}{2h} & |z| \leq h \\ 0 & \text{otherwise} \end{cases} \tag{8.3}$$

The function $\gamma(\hat{y} - y)$ is plotted as a function of y for a fixed value of $\hat{y}$ in Fig. 8.2. Since the function is equal to $1/2h$ for all samples $y^{(i)}$ in the interval

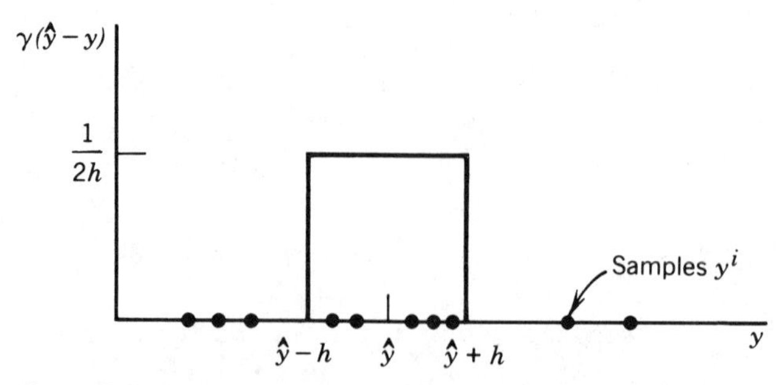

FIGURE 8.2 A rectangular kernal in one dimension.

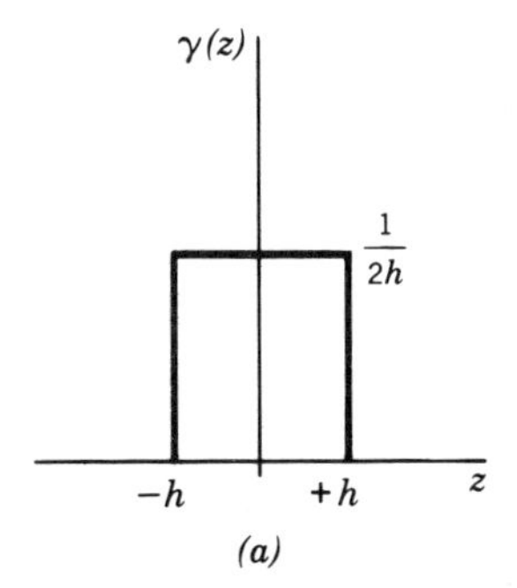

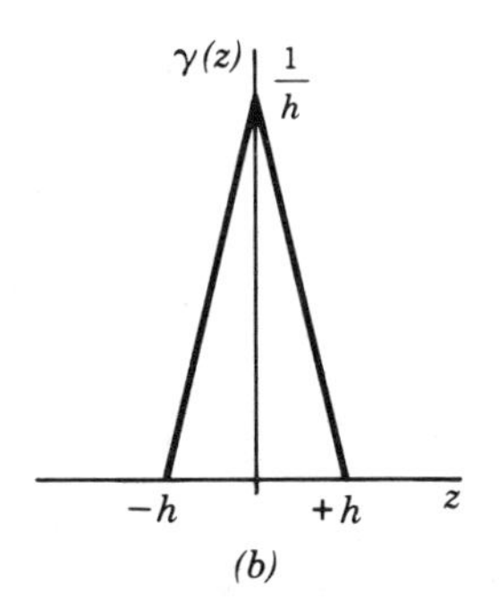

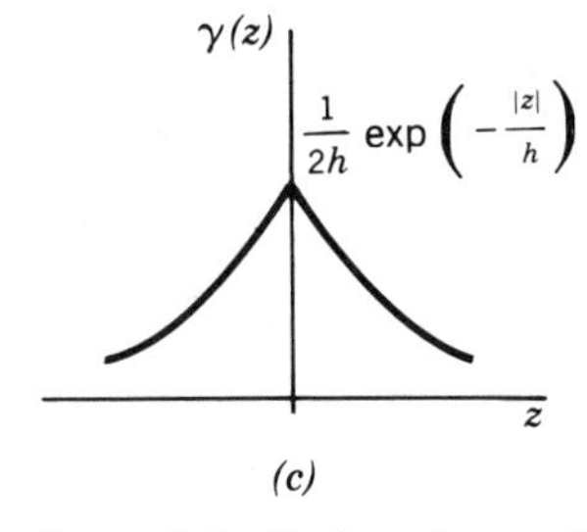

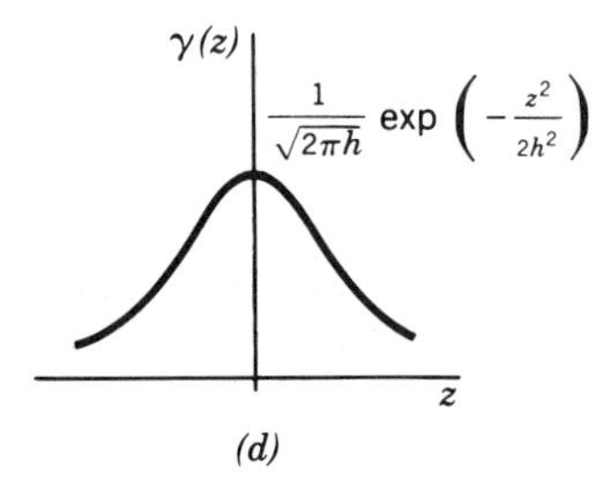

FIGURE 8.3 Various types of kernels in one dimension. (*a*) Rectangular. (*b*) Triangular. (*c*) Expenential. (*d*) Gaussian.

$\hat{y} - h < y^{(i)} \leq \hat{y} + h$ and zero for all samples outside of this interval, one can write Eq. 8.2 as

$$\tilde{p}_y(\hat{y}) = \frac{1}{N} \cdot \frac{k}{2h} = \frac{1}{N} \sum_{i=1}^{N} \gamma(\hat{y} - y^{(i)}) \tag{8.4}$$

The function of γ is called a *kernel, potential function,* or *Parzen window,* and kernels other than the rectangular function of Eq. 8.3 can be chosen. The rectangular kernel produces a density estimate that is highly discontinuous. Other, continuous kernels produce a continuous density estimate. In order to insure that the density estimate $\tilde{p}_y$ is positive and integrates to one, the kernel must satisfy the same conditions. Furthermore, it can be shown [4, 5] that if $\gamma(z)$ is bounded, decreases to zero faster than $1/z$, and satisfies some mild conditions regarding its integrability, then

$$\lim_{N \to \infty} E[\tilde{p}_y(\hat{y})] = p_y(\hat{y}) \tag{8.5}$$

where convergence is defined in the sense of Eqs. 7.6 or 7.7. Some typical kernels are shown in Fig. 8.3.

8.1.2 Estimation of the Density of a Random Vector

Now consider the estimation of a density function for a multidimensional random vector $\mathbf{y}$. The basic approach taken in the foregoing section will be followed, but the results will be derived in a slightly different manner.

Consider a small region R about the point $\hat{\mathbf{y}}$ at which the density is to be estimated. By the mean-value theorem of calculus one can write the probability P that $\mathbf{y}$ is in the region R as

$$P = \int_R p_{\mathbf{y}}(\mathbf{y})\, d\mathbf{y} = p_{\mathbf{y}}(\mathbf{y}')V \tag{8.6}$$

where $V = \int_R d\mathbf{y}$ is the volume of R and $\mathbf{y}'$ is a suitable point within R. Then if $p_{\mathbf{y}}$ is continuous and if R is taken to be sufficiently small, one has, to any desired degree of approximation, $p_{\mathbf{y}}(y') \approx p_{\mathbf{y}}(\hat{y})$ and thus from Eq. 8.6

$$p_{\mathbf{y}}(\hat{\mathbf{y}}) = \frac{P}{V} \tag{8.7}$$

To estimate P from the set of samples $\mathbf{y}^{(1)}, \mathbf{y}^{(2)}, \ldots, \mathbf{y}^{(N)}$, note that since the samples are independent, the probability of finding any k of these samples in R is given by

$$\Pr[k \text{ in } R] = \frac{N!}{k!(N-k)!} P^k(1-P)^{N-k} = \binom{N}{k} P^k(1-P)^{N-k} \tag{8.8}$$

which is the binomial distribution. The mean and variance of this distribution are given by

$$E[k] = \sum_{k=1}^{N} k\binom{N}{k}P^k(1-P)^{N-k} = NP \tag{8.9}$$

and

$$\begin{aligned} \operatorname{Var}(k) &= E[k^2] - (E[k])^2 \\ &= \sum_{k=1}^{N} k^2\binom{N}{k}P^k(1-P)^{N-k} - (NP)^2 \\ &= NP(1-P) \end{aligned} \tag{8.10}$$

The maximum likelihood estimate for P is obtained by finding the value $\hat{P}$ that maximizes Eq. 8.8. Thus differentiating Eq. 8.8 with respect to P and setting the result equal to zero, one obtains

$$\begin{aligned} \frac{d\Pr[k \text{ in } R]}{dk} &= \binom{N}{k}\left[kP^{k-1}(1-P)^{N-k} - P^k(N-k)(1-P)^{N-k-1}\right] \\ &= \binom{N}{k}P^{k-1}(1-P)^{N-k-1}[k(1-P) - P(N-k)] \\ &= 0 \end{aligned} \tag{8.11}$$

Solving for P, one finds

$$\hat{P} = \frac{k}{N} \tag{8.12}$$

The estimate is unbiased because from Eq. 8.9 one has

$$E[\hat{P}] = \frac{E[k]}{N} = P \tag{8.13}$$

The estimate is also consistent, since the variance (using Eqs. 8.9 and 8.10) is

$$E[\hat{P}^2] - (E[\hat{P}])^2 = \frac{E[\hat{k}^2] - (E[\hat{k}])^2}{N^2} = \frac{P(1 - P)}{N} \tag{8.14}$$

which becomes arbitrarily small as N gets large. These considerations more rigorously justify the approximation of the probability P by the relative frequency k/N, which was more loosely asserted in Section 8.1.1. By using $\hat{P}$ from Eq. 8.12 in Eq. 8.7, one arrives at the density estimate

$$\tilde{p}_{\mathbf{y}}(\hat{\mathbf{y}}) = \frac{k}{NV} \tag{8.15}$$

A density estimate of the Parzen form can be obtained by defining the region R to be the hypercube $\{|\hat{y}_j - y_j| \leq h; j = 1, 2, \ldots, m\}$ and defining a kernel as

$$\gamma(\mathbf{z}) = \begin{cases} \frac{1}{V} & |z_j| \leq h; \mathrm{j} = 1,2, \ldots \mathrm{m} \\ 0 & \text{otherwise} \end{cases} \tag{8.16}$$

where $V = (2h)^m$. Equation 8.15 can then be expressed as

$$\tilde{p}_{\mathbf{y}}(\hat{\mathbf{y}}) = \frac{1}{N} \sum_{i=1}^{N} \gamma(\hat{\mathbf{y}} - \mathbf{y}^{(i)}) \tag{8.17}$$

As in the case of density estimation for a single random variable, a continuous estimate can be obtained by choosing a continuous type of kernel. One very popular choice for the kernel is the Gaussian form

$$\gamma(\mathbf{z}) = \frac{1}{(2\pi)^{m/2}\,\sigma^m} \exp\left(-\frac{|\mathbf{z}|^2}{2\sigma^{2m}}\right) \tag{8.18}$$

Some care must be exercised in choosing the kernel (or the parameters of a kernel). If the kernel is chosen to be too narrow, the density estimate will be very discontinuous and "spiked." If the kernel is too broad, the estimate will be overly smooth and will not show enough detail in the density. An example of density estimates using a Gaussian kernel with three different values of σ is shown in Fig. 8.4. In general, the best kernel to estimate a density function depends on the density function

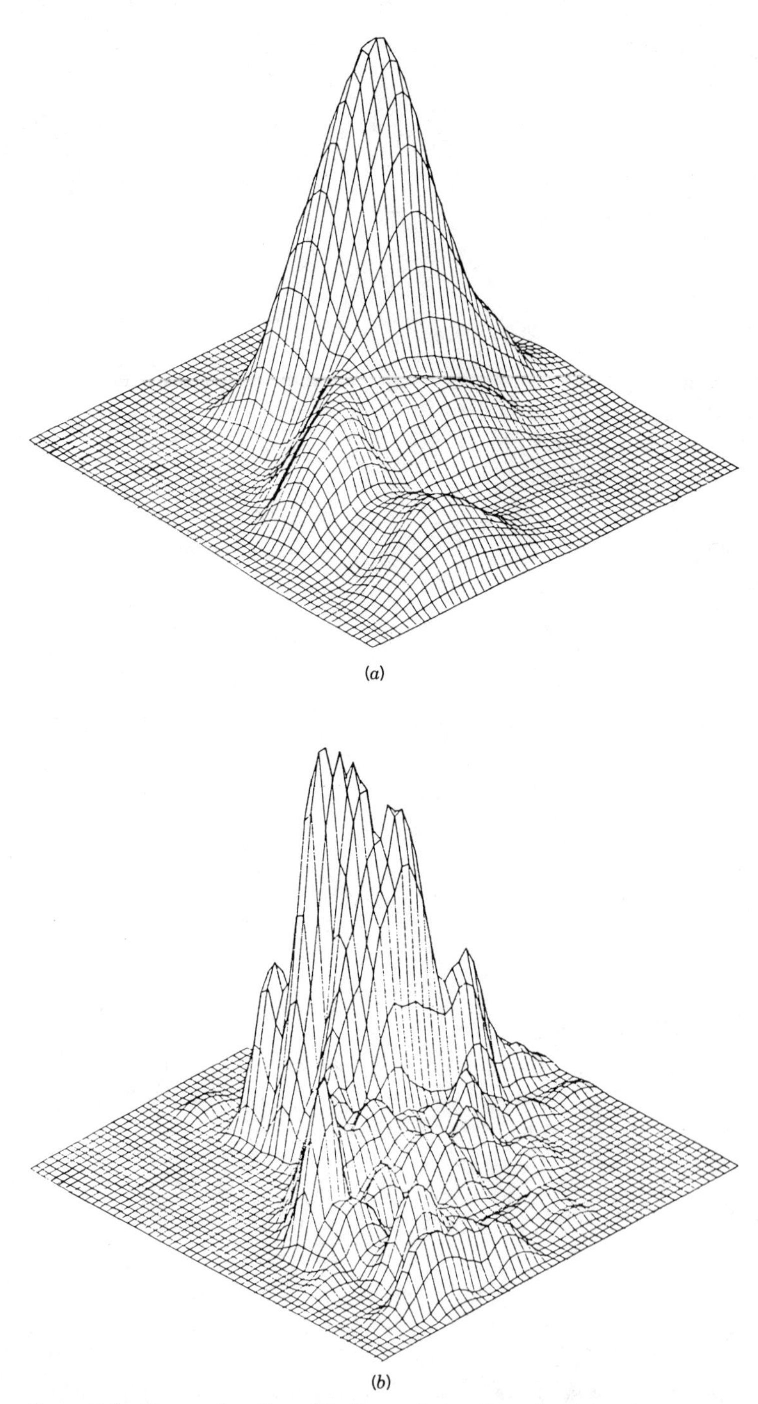

FIGURE 8.4 Parzen density estimates using a Gaussian kernel. (a) A well-chosen kernel. (b) A kernel that is too narrow. (c) A kernel that is too broad.

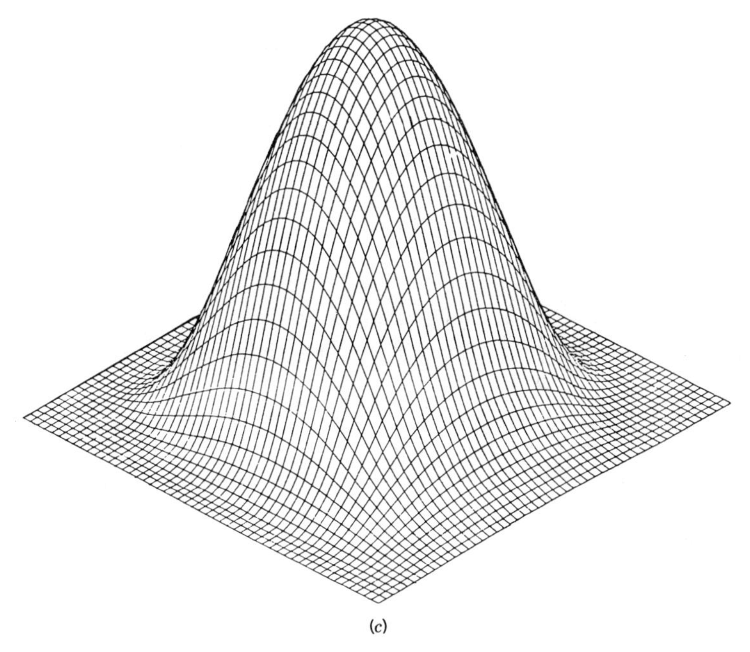

(c)

FIGURE 8.4 Continued

to be estimated and the number of samples available. Thus some judgment is necessary when applying these estimation procedures.

8.2 THE NEAREST NEIGHBOR ALGORITHM

Since the kernel in the Parzen density estimate and thus the effective volume in Eq. 8.15 is a fixed size, it may be difficult to obtain a satisfactory estimate of the density everywhere when the samples are not evenly distributed. One way to overcome this difficulty is to fix the number k of samples in Eq. 8.15 and let the volume V be determined so that the region around $\hat{\mathbf{y}}$ contains just k samples. If this approach is used to estimate densities of two classes of samples ω_1 and ω_2, it leads to a simple and elegant decision rule.

Define the volume V as that of an m-dimensional "hypersphere" centered around $\hat{\mathbf{y}}$. That is, V is the volume of a region of the space defined by

$$d(\hat{\mathbf{y}}, \mathbf{y}) \leq r \tag{8.19}$$

where the distance function d can be any of those defined in Chapter 4, Section 4.2, and r is the radius of the hypersphere. Now let the radius of the hypersphere for each class be determined so that the hypersphere encloses just k samples of the class, that is, let r be the distance to the kth *nearest neighbor* of $\hat{\mathbf{y}}$. Let N_i be the total number of samples of class i and represent the density function by Eq. 8.15. Furthermore, estimate the prior probability $\Pr[\omega_i]$ by $N_i/(N_1 + N_2)$. The decision rule for minimum probability of error (Eq. 3.2)) then becomes

$$\frac{k/N_1V_1}{k/N_2V_2} \mathop{\gtrless}_{\omega_2}^{\omega_1} \frac{N_2/(N_1 + N_2)}{N_1/(N_1 + N_2)}$$

or

$$\frac{V_2}{V_1} \mathop{\gtrless}_{\omega_2}^{\omega_1} 1 \tag{8.20}$$

This decision rule, which fixes the number of samples of each class and compares the volumes of the two hyperspheres, is the *grouped* form of the k-nearest neighbor decision rule. If V_1 is smaller than V_2, this implies that there are more samples of ω_1 in the vicinity of $\hat{\mathbf{y}}$ than there are samples of ω_2. The point $\hat{\mathbf{y}}$ is therefore assigned to ω_1.

The more usual form of the k-nearest neighbor rule is the *pooled* form. The hypersphere around $\hat{\mathbf{y}}$ is determined to include k total samples *regardless* of class. This procedure results in equal volumes for the two classes and a different number of samples k_i for each class. For this case the decision rule of Eq. 3.2 reduces to

$$\frac{k_1}{k_2} \mathop{\gtrless}_{\omega_2}^{\omega_1} 1 \tag{8.21}$$

In other words, $\hat{\mathbf{y}}$ is assigned to the class that has the largest number of samples in the hypersphere (k should be taken to be an odd number to avoid ties). The pooled form of the nearest neighbor rule is surprisingly simple. No volumes have to be computed; one needs only to count the number of points in the hypersphere. It can also be shown (see Chapter 9) that as the number of samples gets large, the probability of error for the pooled nearest neighbor rule with $k = 1$ is less than twice the (Bayes) minimum probability of error as obtained by Eq. 3.2. The upper bound is further reduced for larger values of k.

The main disadvantage of the k-nearest neighbor decision rule is the computation of the distances from the vector $\hat{\mathbf{y}}$ to the samples $\mathbf{y}^{(i)}$. When the number of dimensions is large and the number of vectors to be classified is large, the computation required for classification can be enormous. One way to alleviate this problem is to note that the k-nearest neighbor decision rule, like all other decision rules, induces a decision boundary between the samples. Samples far from the boundary do not affect this boundary; thus distances to these samples do not need to be computed (see Problem 8.4). When such samples are eliminated, one has a so-called condensed or edited form of the nearest neighbor rule. Alternatively, a partial ordering (tree) of the intersample distances can be constructed, and efficient searching such as the branch and bound technique can be used to eliminate many of the distance computations.

The k-nearest neighbor rule generalizes directly to the multiclass case. By taking

$\Pr[\omega_i] = N_i/N$, where N is the total number of samples of all classes, and employing Eq. 8.15, the multiclass discriminant functions of Eq. 6.12 reduce to

$$g_i'(\mathbf{y}) = \frac{k_i}{V_i N} \qquad i = 1, 2, \ldots, N_c \tag{8.22}$$

For the pooled nearest neighbor algorithm a common volume is computed by choosing the hypersphere to include just k samples from among all the classes (i.e., $k_1 + k_2 + \ldots + k_{N_c} = k$). Thus an equivalent discriminant function for the ith class is just the number of samples k_i in the hypersphere and the decision rule of Eq. 6.10 reduces to choosing the class with the largest number of samples.

8.3 NONPARAMETRIC CLASSIFICATION

Nonparametric classification refers to a set of procedures for decision making that can be used when there is only partial information about the class conditional density functions. For example, one may know that a certain parameter of the density such as the mean or variance lies only within a *range* of possible values. Alternatively, one may know nothing about the density function except that it has a positive mean and is symmetric. The approach taken here foregoes any attempts to estimate the unknown properties of the density from training data. Instead it seeks to develop tests that do not depend on the unknown information. Such tests will, of course, not match the performance of a Bayes and Neyman–Pearson test when the densities are completely specified. However, the tests may perform better over a class of densities than likelihood ratio tests designed for one particular type. One can say that the nonparametric tests are more *robust*.

8.3.1 Classification with Unknown Parameters

We begin by considering a problem where the probability density function for each class i has an unknown vector parameter $\boldsymbol{\rho}_i$. As in Chapter 7, the vector parameter $\boldsymbol{\rho}_i$ may actually represent a set of scalar, vector, or matrix parameters for the density. Problems of this type are known in the statistical literature as *composite hypothesis testing problems*.

If the parameter $\boldsymbol{\rho}_i$ is a random variable and its density is known, then the problem has an easy solution. One simply forms the class conditional density needed for the likelihood ratio test by integrating over the unknown parameter. That is,

$$p_{\mathbf{y}|\omega_i}(\mathbf{y}|\omega_i) = \int_{-\infty}^{\infty} p_{\mathbf{y}|\boldsymbol{\rho}_i\omega_i}(\mathbf{y}|\boldsymbol{\rho}_i, \omega_i) p_{\boldsymbol{\rho}_i|\omega_i}(\boldsymbol{\rho}_i|\omega_i)\, d\boldsymbol{\rho}_i \tag{8.23}$$

Although the integration may be difficult, in principle there is no problem.

If applying Eq. 8.23 is not practical or if the density function for the parameter is not known, then one possible approach is to use the following generalized ratio test:

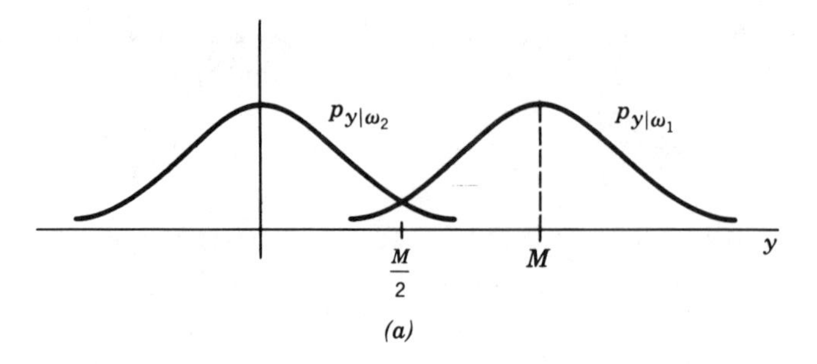

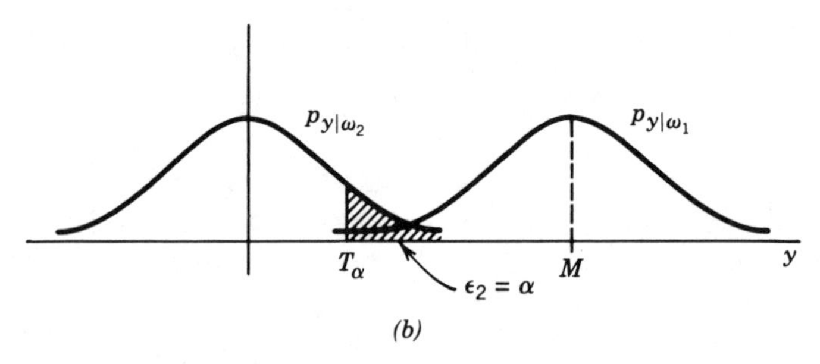

FIGURE 8.5 Tests involving an unknown parameter. (a) A minimum probability of error test, σ^2 unknown. (b) Neyman-Pearson test, M unknown.

$$\frac{p_{\mathbf{y}|\boldsymbol{\rho}_1\omega_1}(\mathbf{y}|\tilde{\boldsymbol{\rho}}_1, \omega_1)}{p_{\mathbf{y}|\boldsymbol{\rho}_2\omega_2}(\mathbf{y}|\tilde{\boldsymbol{\rho}}_2, \omega_2)} \underset{\omega_2}{\overset{\omega_1}{\gtrless}} \lambda \tag{8.24}$$

where $\tilde{\boldsymbol{\rho}}_1$ and $\tilde{\boldsymbol{\rho}}_2$ are MAP or maximum likelihood estimates for the parameters under the assumption that the observed data is from class 1 or class 2. Note that this is quite different from training the classifier. *At the time of classification*, the data to be classified is first used to generate estimates for the parameters $\boldsymbol{\rho}_i$. If maximum likelihood estimation is used, $\tilde{\boldsymbol{\rho}}_i$ will be chosen to maximize $p_{\mathbf{y}|\boldsymbol{\rho}_i\omega_i}$ for the given observations $\mathbf{y}$. These estimates are used together with the data to evaluate Eq. 8.24 and make a class decision. Although this procedure has no theoretical justification, it is intuitively reasonable.

The foregoing procedures attempt to deal with the unknown parameter by averaging over it or estimating it. The best situation that can exist is when the optimal decision procedure simply *does not depend* on the unknown parameter. In this case one can construct a test that is optimal for any value of the parameter (usually within some range) without knowing the actual value of the parameter. For example, consider the case of a single feature with a Gaussian distribution shown in Fig. 8.5(a). The class 1 data has mean M and unknown variance σ^2. The class 2 data has mean zero and the same unknown variance σ^2. If the prior probabilities are equal, then the decision rule that minimizes the probability of error can be expressed simply as

$$y \underset{\omega_2}{\overset{\omega_1}{\gtrless}} \frac{M}{2} \quad \text{if } M > 0 \tag{8.25a}$$

and

$$y \underset{\omega_2}{\overset{\omega_1}{\lessgtr}} \frac{M}{2} \quad \text{if } M < 0 \tag{8.25b}$$

This procedure optimizes the decision at a single point on the operating characteristic (corresponding to a threshold value of 1) and does not depend on the unknown parameter σ^2.

A more general situation arises in terms of the Neyman–Pearson criterion. This is depicted in Fig. 8.5(b). In this example, the two densities have a known equal variance σ^2. The class 1 data have an unknown mean M, which however *is known to be positive* while the class 2 data have a zero mean. A Neyman–Pearson test fixes the class 2 error probability at some fixed level α and maximizes the probability of a correct decision for class 1. Note that as long as M is positive, the Neyman–Pearson test will set a threshold T_α on the positive side of the class 2 density function as shown, such that the integral of the shaded region is equal to α. Thus the optimal test is always of the form

$$y \underset{\omega_2}{\overset{\omega_1}{\gtrless}} T_\alpha \tag{8.26}$$

and does not depend on the unknown parameter M. Since this is true for any chosen value α and any corresponding threshold T_α, the test is optimal at any point on the operating characteristic.

In statistics, the fixed class 2 error probability α is called the *significance* of the test and the probability of correctly choosing class 1 is called the *power* of the test. A test such as the one just described has maximum power for any parameter value in the given range and is called a *uniformly most powerful* (UMP) test.

An UMP test may not always exist and its existence may depend on the range of values allowed for the parameter. It should be clear from the example that if M were known to take on only negative values, a similar but distinct UMP test would exist while if M could take on any positive or negative values a UMP would not exist.

8.3.2 Sign Test

Some common forms of nonparametric tests are able to deal with cases when much less is known about the class conditional densities than in the foregoing examples. One of the simplest nonparametric tests is a sign test. Here the measurement vector

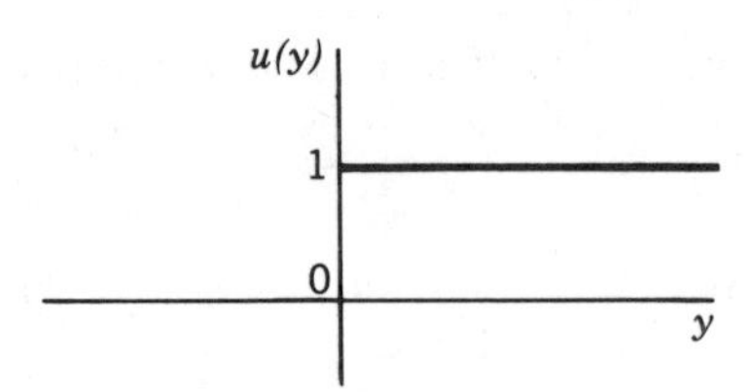

FIGURE 8.6 Unit step function.

is assumed to have independent components $y_1, y_2, \ldots, y_m$. Nothing is known about the class conditional densities of the y_i except that for class 1

$$\Pr[y_i > 0 \mid \omega_1] = P > \frac{1}{2} \tag{8.27a}$$

while for class 2

$$\Pr[y_i > 0 \mid \omega_2] = \frac{1}{2} \tag{8.27b}$$

This problem would occur, for example, if one were observing a signal in noise. If the noise were distributed such that positive and negative values were equally likely and the signal, while unknown in detail, contributed only positive values to the observations, then Eq. 8.27 would hold. Class 1 observations would be the signal plus noise while class 2 would be the noise alone.

Let $u(y)$ represent the unit step function shown in Fig. 8.6. The quantity $u(y_i)$ is equal to 1 when y_i is positive and 0 otherwise. Then the test

$$S(\mathbf{y}) = \sum_{i=1}^{m} u(y_i) \underset{\omega_2}{\overset{\omega_1}{\gtrless}} T \tag{8.28}$$

can be shown to be UMP for the class of distributions satisfying Eqs. (8.27) [6].

The performance of the test can be deduced from the following. If the observations are from class 1 (signal present), then each term in the sum takes a value of $+1$ with probability P and 0 with probability $1 - P$. The probability that the sum $S(\mathbf{y})$ takes on some value k is therefore given by the binomial distribution

$$\Pr[S(\mathbf{y}) = k \mid \omega_1] = \binom{m}{k} P^k (1 - P)^{m-k} \tag{8.29}$$

Similarly, if the observations are from class 2 (noise only), the probability of any value k is

$$\Pr[S(\mathbf{y}) = k \mid \omega_2] = \binom{m}{k} \left(\tfrac{1}{2}\right)^k \left(\tfrac{1}{2}\right)^{m-k} = \binom{m}{k} \left(\tfrac{1}{2}\right)^m \tag{8.30}$$

To fix the class 2 error at some value less than or equal to α, one would pick T such that

$$\Pr[\text{error} \mid \omega_2] = \sum_{k=T}^{m} \binom{m}{k} \left(\tfrac{1}{2}\right)^m \leq \alpha \tag{8.31}$$

The probability of a correct choice for class 1 that is maximized by this test would then be given by

$$\Pr[\text{correct}|\omega_1] = \sum_{k=T}^{m} \binom{m}{k} P^k(1 - P)^{m-k} \tag{8.32}$$

These probabilities are constant for all densities satisfying Eq. 8.27.

8.3.3 Order Statistics

A final type of nonparametric test that will be considered involves the use of *rank* or *order statistics*. Consider the problem posed in Section 8.3.2 but with the additional assumption that each class conditional density function is symmetric about the mean. Then an optimal nonparametric classifier is based on the Wilcoxon test [7]. The features, assumed to be independent, are ordered according to absolute value as

$$|y_{i_1}| < |y_{i_2}| < \ldots < |y_{i_m}| \tag{8.33}$$

The *rank* r_i of feature y_i is defined as the feature's position in this sequence. The Wilcoxon test then can be written as

$$\sum_{i=1}^{m} r_i u(y_i) \quad \underset{\omega_2}{\overset{\omega_1}{\gtrless}} \quad T \tag{8.34}$$

Thus the Wilcoxon test statistic is the sum of the ranks for all of the positive valued features.

The Wilcoxon classifier maintains a constant level of performance for all densities having the postulated symmetry and is rather remarkable in that the features need not be identically distributed. Nonlinear transformations applied to the features do not disturb the performance as long as the symmetry of the density functions is maintained.

When this procedure is applied to the problem of detection of a signal in Gaussian noise, its performance compares very favorably with that of the optimal Gaussian classifier. Moreover, the Wilcoxon classifier maintains its level of performance over a wide range of distributions [8].

8.4 SUMMARY

This chapter deals with procedures that can be applied when the probability density function is in some sense unknown. It begins with two approaches to nonparametric density estimation. The first approach, Parzen estimation, employs a fixed size kernel or window function that is applied to each sample and summed to produce the estimate. The density estimates for two or more classes of data can then be used to derive a decision rule. The second approach, the *k*-nearest neighbor algorithm, computes the density estimate in a region of the space whose volume depends on the local concentration of the samples. When applied to two or more classes of data, the k-nearest neighbor density estimate leads to a simple decision rule that comes very close to minimizing the probability of error. Both techniques are important for classifying patterns when there is no a priori knowledge about the forms of the class conditional density functions. A third procedure is discussed that foregoes any attempts to estimate the density function from training data. This procedure in fact acknowledges that the exact form of the density function is unknown and instead attempts to find decision rules that perform well for a large class of densities. The idea of a uniformly most powerful test is developed, and two examples of nonparametric classification procedures are described.

REFERENCES

1. E. Parzen. "On Estimation of a Probability Density Function and Mode." *Ann. Math. Statistics,* Vol. 33, pp. 1065–1076 (September 1962).
2. D. O. Loftsgaarden, and C. P. Quesenberry. "A Nonparametric Density Function." *Ann. Math. Statistics,* Vol. 36, pp. 1049–1051 (June 1965).
3. T. M. Cover, and P. E. Hart. "Nearest Neighbor Pattern Classification." *IEEE Trans. Information Theory,* Vol. IT-13, pp. 21–27 (January 1967).
4. K. Fukunaga. *Introduction to Statistical Pattern Recognition*. New York: Academic Press, 1972.
5. R. O. Duda, and P. E. Hart. *Pattern Classification and Scene Analysis*. New York: John Wiley & Sons, Inc. (1973).
6. D. A. S. Fraser. *Nonparametric Methods in Statistics*. New York: John Wiley & Sons, Inc. (1957).
7. F. Wilcoxon. "Individual Comparisons by Ranking Methods," *Biometrics,* Vol. 1, pp. 80–83 (1945).
8. J. D. Gibson, and J. L. Melsa. *Introduction to Nonparametric Detection with Applications*. New York: Academic Press, 1975.

PROBLEMS

8.1 Construct the one-dimensional Parzen estimate for a density p_y, given samples

$$y^{(i)}\text{: } 2.5,\ 2.8,\ 3.4,\ 4.2,\ 4.5,\ 4.7,\ 5.2,\ 5.6,\ 7.5$$

8.2 Let $\tilde{p}_{\mathbf{y}}$ be the Parzen estimate for a density function $p_{\mathbf{y}}$ and let the kernel γ satisfy

$$\int_{-\infty}^{\infty} \gamma(\mathbf{z})\, d\mathbf{z} = 1$$

$$\int_{-\infty}^{\infty} \mathbf{z}\, \gamma(\mathbf{z})\, d\mathbf{z} = \mathbf{0}$$

Derive the simplest possible expression for the estimated mean vector

$$\tilde{\mathbf{m}} = \int_{-\infty}^{\infty} \mathbf{y}\tilde{p}_{\mathbf{y}}(\mathbf{y})\, d\mathbf{y}$$

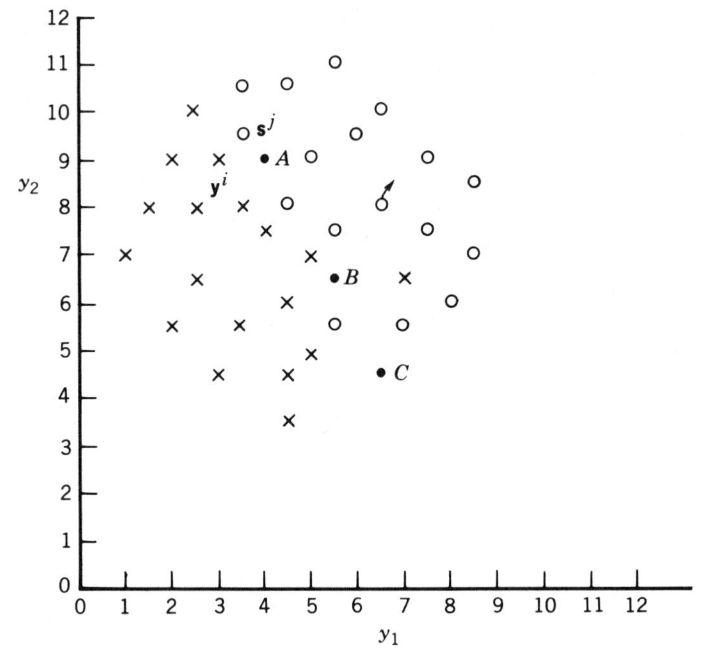

Samples for Problems 8.3 and 8.4.

8.3 Classify the points A, B, and C in the accompanying figure using a pooled 5-nearest neighbor decision rule and a Euclidean distance function. Repeat using the maximum-value distance function (see Eq. 4.9).

8.4 The pooled nearest neighbor classification rule for $k = 1$, applied to the two classes of data, generates decision regions and a decision boundary between these regions. If $\mathbf{y}^{(i)}$ are the samples of class 1 and $\mathbf{s}^{(i)}$ are the samples of class 2, then any point $\hat{\mathbf{y}}$ on the boundary (by definition) satisfies

$$\min_i d(\hat{\mathbf{y}}, \mathbf{y}^{(i)}) = \min_i d(\hat{\mathbf{y}}, \mathbf{s}^{(i)})$$

Assume that the distance function is the Euclidean distance function.

(a) What is the equation of the boundary in a small region of points on the boundary for which a particular sample $\mathbf{y}^{(i)}$ is the nearest sample of class 1, and a particular sample $\mathbf{s}^{(j)}$ is the nearest sample of class 2? What can you infer about the form of the boundary?

(b) Beginning in the region of the labeled points $\mathbf{y}^{(i)}$ and $\mathbf{s}^{(j)}$ in the figure in Problem 8.3, draw the complete decision boundary.

(c) Circle the samples of both classes whose deletion would *not* change the decision boundary. Note that removal of these samples can result in a very substantial savings of both storage and computation time in the practical application of the nearest neighbor classification rule.

8.5 Refer to the example in Section 8.3.1

(a) If the density functions for the two classes were not Gaussian, but the densities were known to be symmetric about their mean and the class 1 density was known to have a positive mean, would an UMP test exist?

(b) If the class 1 density were a two-dimensional Gaussian with mean $\mathbf{m}$ and covariance $\mathbf{K}$, and the class 2 density had zero mean and covariance $\mathbf{K}$, under what conditions would an UMP test exist?

CHAPTER 9

Estimating and Bounding the Probability of Error

The previous chapters have dealt mainly with the *design* of classifiers. This chapter deals with the *performance* of classifiers by developing bounds on the probability of error that can easily be evaluated, and by outlining organized methods for testing the classifier with data in order to estimate the probability of error.

9.1 MEASURES OF SEPARABILITY

This section introduces two important measures of separability, namely the divergence and the Bhattacharyya distance [1, 2]. These quantities are first defined for general density functions in terms of certain integrals. The results are then specialized to the multivariate Gaussian case, where explicit algebraic formulas are derived.

9.1.1 The Divergence and Bhattacharyya Distance

Recall from the discussion in Chapter 3 that the likelihood ratio can be considered as a *statistic,* that is, a function of the observation data that has some density function for class 1 and some other density function for class 2. The log likelihood ratio

$$\Lambda(\mathbf{y}) = \ln \frac{p_1(\mathbf{y})}{p_2(\mathbf{y})} \tag{9.1}$$

is also such a statistic and can be described by a pair of density functions such as those shown in Fig. 9.1. Since a decision using the log likelihood ratio is always made by comparing it to a single threshold τ, the error probability will be low when the density functions are widely separated and high otherwise. One measure of

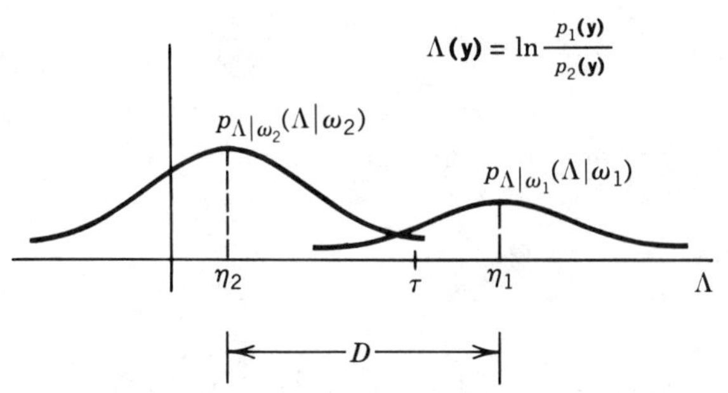

FIGURE 9.1 Typical density functions for the log likelihood ratio.

separability is the difference in the means $\eta_1 - \eta_2$ (see Fig. 9.1). This quantity is called the *divergence*. The divergence is formally defined as

$$\begin{aligned} D &= E[\Lambda(\mathbf{y})|\omega_1] - E[\Lambda(\mathbf{y})|\omega_2] \\ &= \int_{-\infty}^{\infty} \left(\ln \frac{p_1(\mathbf{y})}{p_2(\mathbf{y})}\right) p_1(\mathbf{y})\, d\mathbf{y} - \int_{-\infty}^{\infty} \left(\ln \frac{p_1(\mathbf{y})}{p_2(\mathbf{y})}\right) p_2(\mathbf{y})\, d\mathbf{y} \end{aligned} \tag{9.2}$$

The quantity

$$\begin{aligned} H(i, j) &= \int_{-\infty}^{\infty} \left(\ln \frac{p_i(\mathbf{y})}{p_j(\mathbf{y})}\right) p_i(\mathbf{y})\, d\mathbf{y} \\ &= E\left[\ln \frac{p_i(\mathbf{y})}{p_j(\mathbf{y})} \middle| \omega_i\right] \end{aligned} \tag{9.3}$$

which was mentioned briefly in Chapter 5, is called the directed divergence, or the *relative information* of class i with respect to class j. (Some authors also refer to this quantity as the Kullback–Liebler number [3].) From Eqs. 9.2 and 9.3 it can be seen that

$$D = H(1, 2) + H(2, 1) \tag{9.4}$$

Thus when the relative information is high, the divergence and the separation of the classes are also high.

Another measure of separability is the *Bhattacharyya distance* [4] defined as

$$B = -\ln\left[\int_{-\infty}^{\infty} \sqrt{p_1(\mathbf{y})p_2(\mathbf{y})}\, d\mathbf{y}\right] \tag{9.5}$$

The quantity

$$\rho_B = e^{-B} = \int_{-\infty}^{\infty} \sqrt{p_1(\mathbf{y})p_2(\mathbf{y})}\, d\mathbf{y} \tag{9.6}$$

is sometimes refered to as the *Bhattacharyya coefficient*. These quantities are more difficult to interpret than the divergence. However, if we write Eq. 9.6 as

$$\rho_B = \int_{-\infty}^{\infty} \sqrt{p_1(\mathbf{y})/p_2(\mathbf{y})}\; p_2(\mathbf{y})\, d\mathbf{y} = E\left[\sqrt{p_1(\mathbf{y})/p_2(\mathbf{y})}\middle|\omega_2\right] \tag{9.7}$$

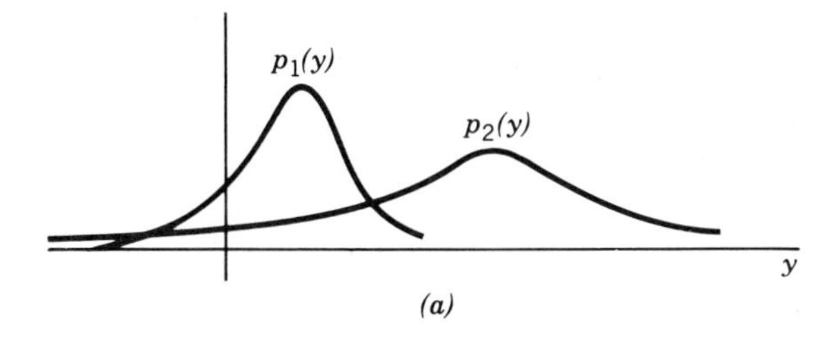

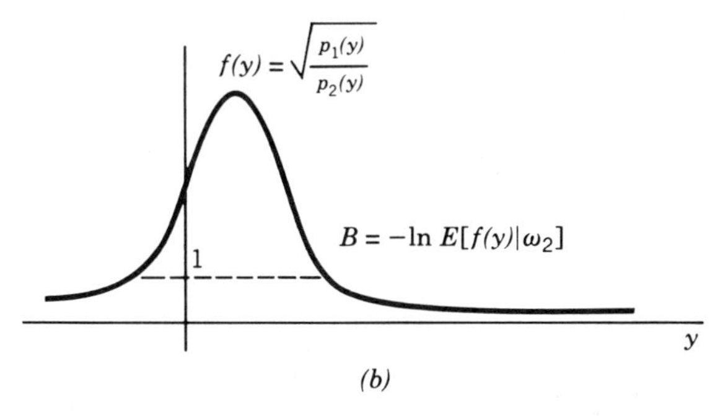

FIGURE 9.2 The interpretation of the Bhattacharyya distance.

then we can begin to give the Bhattacharyya distance an interpretation. Figure 9.2 shows a typical pair of density functions $p_1(y)$ and $p_2(y)$ and a single random variable y and a corresponding plot of the function $f(y) = \sqrt{p_1(y)/p_2(y)}$. Note that if the original density functions are well separated, then the expectation of the function f with respect to ω_2 will give a value that is low ($\ll 1$). Thus the Bhattacharyya distance, which is the negative logarithm of this quantity, will be high. On the other hand, if the densities overlap, then the expectation will tend to give a value that is high (> 1) and the Bhattacharyya distance will correspondingly be low.

Although the divergence seems to have the intuitive qualities of a distance measure, the use of the word "distance" in connection with the Bhattacharyya seems more difficult to accept. However, both the divergence and the Bhattacharyya distance are invariant under a one-to-one transformation of the vector $\mathbf{y}$ (see Problem 9.1), and both are additive when the components of $\mathbf{y}$ are independent (i.e., they can be expressed as a sum of similar terms with each term involving only one of the components of $\mathbf{y}$.) In addition, if $J_m(\omega_1, \omega_2)$ represents either the divergence or the Bhattacharyya distance for classes ω_1 and ω_2 based on a feature vector $\mathbf{y}$ with m components, then both have the following metric properties appropriate to a distance function (see Section 4.2):

$$\left.\begin{array}{ll} J_m(\omega_1, \omega_2) > 0 & \omega_1 \neq \omega_2 \\ J_m(\omega_1\ \omega_1) = J_m(\omega_2, \omega_2) = 0 & \end{array}\right\} \tag{9.8a}$$

$$J_m(\omega_1, \omega_2) = J_m(\omega_2, \omega_1) \tag{9.8b}$$

Neither satisfies the triangular inequality, and so neither can be classified as a true distance function. However, both satisfy the additional property

$$J_m(\omega_1, \omega_2) \leq J_{m+1}(\omega_1, \omega_2) \tag{9.8c}$$

Proof of these properties is left to the reader (see Problem 9.2).

9.1.2 The Divergence and Bhattacharyya Distance for Gaussian Data

A closed-form expression for the divergence for Gaussian data is rather easily derived. The log likelihood ratio can be expressed using Eq. 4.57 as

$$\ln \frac{p_1(\mathbf{y})}{p_2(\mathbf{y})} = \frac{1}{2}(\mathbf{y} - \mathbf{m}_2)^T\mathbf{K}_2^{-1}(\mathbf{y} - \mathbf{m}_2) - \frac{1}{2}(\mathbf{y} - \mathbf{m}_1)^T\mathbf{K}_1^{-1}(\mathbf{y} - \mathbf{m}_1) + \frac{1}{2}\ln\frac{|\mathbf{K}_2|}{|\mathbf{K}_1|} \tag{9.9}$$

and thus it follows from Eqs. 9.3 and 9.9 that

$$\begin{aligned} H(1, 2) = {} & \frac{1}{2}E[(\mathbf{y} - \mathbf{m}_2)^T\mathbf{K}_2^{-1}(\mathbf{y} - \mathbf{m}_2)|\omega_1] \\ & - \frac{1}{2}E[(\mathbf{y} - \mathbf{m}_1)^T\mathbf{K}_1^{-1}(\mathbf{y} - \mathbf{m}_1)|\omega_1] + \frac{1}{2}\ln\frac{|\mathbf{K}_2|}{|\mathbf{K}_1|} \end{aligned} \tag{9.10}$$

Now observe that since $(\mathbf{y} - \mathbf{m}_i)^T\mathbf{K}_i^{-1}(\mathbf{y} - \mathbf{m}_i) = tr\,(\mathbf{y} - \mathbf{m}_i)^T\mathbf{K}_i^{-1}(\mathbf{y} - \mathbf{m}_i)$, Eq. 4.20 can be applied to the terms in Eq. 9.10 to show that

$$\begin{aligned} E[(\mathbf{y} - \mathbf{m}_1)^T\mathbf{K}_1^{-1}(\mathbf{y} - \mathbf{m}_1)|\omega_1] &= E\{tr\,\mathbf{K}_1^{-1}(\mathbf{y} - \mathbf{m}_1)(\mathbf{y} - \mathbf{m}_1^T)|\omega_1] \\ &= tr\,\mathbf{K}_1^{-1}\mathbf{K}_1 = tr\,\mathbf{I} \end{aligned} \tag{9.11}$$

and

$$\begin{aligned} E\,[(\mathbf{y} - \mathbf{m}_2)^T\mathbf{K}_2^{-1}(\mathbf{y} - \mathbf{m}_2)|\omega_1] &= E[tr\,\mathbf{K}_2^{-1}(\mathbf{y} - \mathbf{m}_2)(\mathbf{y} - \mathbf{m}_2)^T|\omega_1] \\ &= tr\,\mathbf{K}_2^{-1}(\mathbf{K}_1 + (\mathbf{m}_1 - \mathbf{m}_2)(\mathbf{m}_1 - \mathbf{m}_2)^T) \\ &= tr\,\mathbf{K}_2^{-1}\mathbf{K}_1 + (\mathbf{m}_1 - \mathbf{m}_2)^T\mathbf{K}_2^{-1}(\mathbf{m}_1 - \mathbf{m}_2) \end{aligned} \tag{9.12}$$

It then follows from Eqs. 9.10 to 9.12 that

$$H(1, 2) = \frac{1}{2}\,tr(\mathbf{K}_2^{-1}\mathbf{K}_1 - \mathbf{I}) + \frac{1}{2}(\mathbf{m}_1 - \mathbf{m}_2)^T\mathbf{K}_2^{-1}(\mathbf{m}_1 - \mathbf{m}_2) + \frac{1}{2}\ln\frac{|\mathbf{K}_2|}{|\mathbf{K}_1|} \tag{9.13}$$

and similarly,

$$H(2, 1) = \frac{1}{2} tr(\mathbf{K}_1^{-1} \mathbf{K}_2 - \mathbf{I}) + \frac{1}{2}(\mathbf{m}_2 - \mathbf{m}_1)^T \mathbf{K}_1^{-1} (\mathbf{m}_2 - \mathbf{m}_1) + \frac{1}{2} \ln \frac{|\mathbf{K}_1|}{|\mathbf{K}_2|} \tag{9.14}$$

Thus it follows from Eqs. 9.13, 9.14, and 9.4 that

$$D = \tfrac{1}{2} tr(\mathbf{K}_1^{-1} \mathbf{K}_2 + \mathbf{K}_2^{-1} \mathbf{K}_1 - 2\mathbf{I}) + \tfrac{1}{2}(\mathbf{m}_1 - \mathbf{m}_2)^T (\mathbf{K}_1^{-1} + \mathbf{K}_2^{-1})(\mathbf{m}_1 - \mathbf{m}_2) \tag{9.15}$$

This is the closed-form expression for the divergence for Gaussian data.

The closed form expression for the Bhattacharyya distance is somewhat more difficult to derive. However, the sequence of steps is straightforward and can be outlined as follows. By a direct substitution of Eq. 4.57 in Eq. 9.5, one can obtain

$$\begin{aligned} B &= -\ln \int_{-\infty}^{\infty} p_1^{1/2}(\mathbf{y}) p_2^{1/2}(\mathbf{y})\, d\mathbf{y} \\ &= -\ln \int_{-\infty}^{\infty} \frac{1}{(2\pi)^{m/2} |\mathbf{K}_1|^{1/4} |\mathbf{K}_2|^{1/4}} \exp\left\{ -\frac{1}{4}\left[(\mathbf{y} - \mathbf{m}_1)^T \mathbf{K}_1^{-1} (\mathbf{y} - \mathbf{m}_1) \right.\right. \\ &\qquad \left.\left. + (\mathbf{y} - \mathbf{m}_2)^T \mathbf{K}_2^{-1} (\mathbf{y} - \mathbf{m}_2) \right] \right\} d\mathbf{y} \end{aligned} \tag{9.16}$$

The term in the exponent can then be expanded and rewritten as

$$\begin{aligned} &\frac{1}{4}\left[(\mathbf{y} - \mathbf{m}_1)^T \mathbf{K}_1^{-1} (\mathbf{y} - \mathbf{m}_1) + (\mathbf{y} - \mathbf{m}_2)^T \mathbf{K}_2^{-1} (\mathbf{y} - \mathbf{m}_2) \right] \\ &= \frac{1}{4}\left[\mathbf{y}^T \mathbf{K}_1^{-1} \mathbf{y} - 2\mathbf{m}_1^T \mathbf{K}_1^{-1} \mathbf{y} + \mathbf{m}_1^T \mathbf{K}_1^{-1} \mathbf{m}_1 \right. \\ &\qquad \left. + \mathbf{y}^T \mathbf{K}_2^{-1} \mathbf{y} - 2\mathbf{m}_2^T \mathbf{K}_2^{-1} \mathbf{y} + \mathbf{m}_2^T \mathbf{K}_2^{-1} \mathbf{m}_2 \right] \\ &= \frac{1}{2}\left[\mathbf{y}^T \mathbf{K}_p^{-1} \mathbf{y} - 2\mathbf{m}_p^T \mathbf{K}_p^{-1} \mathbf{y} + \mathbf{m}_p^T \mathbf{K}_p^{-1} \mathbf{m}_p \right] + C \end{aligned} \tag{9.17}$$

where

$$\mathbf{K}_p^{-1} = \frac{1}{2}(\mathbf{K}_1^{-1} + \mathbf{K}_2^{-1}) \tag{9.18a}$$

$$\mathbf{m}_p = \frac{1}{2}\mathbf{K}_p\left(\mathbf{K}_1^{-1} \mathbf{m}_1 + \mathbf{K}_2^{-1} \mathbf{m}_2 \right) \tag{9.18b}$$

$$C = \frac{1}{4}\left(\mathbf{m}_1^T \mathbf{K}_1^{-1} \mathbf{m}_1 + \mathbf{m}_2^T \mathbf{K}_2^{-1} \mathbf{m}_2 - 2\mathbf{m}_p^T K_p^{-1} m_p \right) \tag{9.18c}$$

Then, by virtue of Eq. 9.17, Eq. 9.16 can be written as

$$B = -\ln\left\{\frac{|\mathbf{K}_p|^{1/2}}{|\mathbf{K}_1|^{1/4}|\mathbf{K}_2|^{1/4}} e^{-C}\right.$$

$$\left.\int_{-\infty}^{\infty} \frac{1}{(2\pi)^{m/2}|\mathbf{K}_p|^{1/2}} \exp\left[-\frac{1}{2}(\mathbf{y} - \mathbf{m}_p)^T\mathbf{K}_p^{-1}(\mathbf{y} - \mathbf{m}_p)\right] d\mathbf{y}\right\}$$

$$= C + \tfrac{1}{2}\ln\frac{|\mathbf{K}_1|^{1/2}|\mathbf{K}_2|^{1/2}}{|\mathbf{K}_p|} \tag{9.19}$$

which follows, since the integral is equal to one. It can then be shown with some algebraic manipulation that C as defined by Eq. 9.18c reduces to

$$C = \frac{1}{8}(\mathbf{m}_1 - \mathbf{m}_2)^T\left(\frac{\mathbf{K}_1 + \mathbf{K}_2}{2}\right)^{-1}(\mathbf{m}_1 - \mathbf{m}_2) \tag{9.20}$$

and that

$$\frac{|\mathbf{K}_1|^{1/2}\,|\mathbf{K}_2|^{1/2}}{|\mathbf{K}_p|} = \frac{|\frac{1}{2}(\mathbf{K}_1 + \mathbf{K}_2)|}{|\mathbf{K}_1|^{1/2}|\mathbf{K}_2|^{1/2}} \tag{9.21}$$

[These steps are left as a problem for the reader (Problem 9.3).] Therefore, it follows from Eqs. 9.19 through 9.21 that

$$B = \frac{1}{8}(\mathbf{m}_1 - \mathbf{m}_2)^T\left(\frac{\mathbf{K}_1 + \mathbf{K}_2}{2}\right)^{-1}(\mathbf{m}_1 - \mathbf{m}_2) + \frac{1}{2}\ln\frac{|(\mathbf{K}_1 + \mathbf{K}_2)/2|}{|\mathbf{K}_1|^{1/2}|\mathbf{K}_2|^{1/2}} \tag{9.22}$$

This is the closed-form expression for the Bhattacharyya distance for Gaussian data.

Note from Eqs. 9.15 and 9.22 that when the two class covariance matrices are equal ($\mathbf{K}_1 = \mathbf{K}_2 = \mathbf{K}$), the divergence and the Bhattacharyya distance are equivalent measures of separability in that

$$D = 8B = (\mathbf{m}_1 - \mathbf{m}_2)^T\mathbf{K}^{-1}(\mathbf{m}_1 - \mathbf{m}_2) \tag{9.23}$$

This quantity is also recognized as the Mahalanobis distance between the two means.

9.2 THE BHATTACHARYYA AND CHERNOFF BOUNDS

This section develops bounds on the probability of error for various likelihood ratio tests. These bounds are based on the Bhattacharyya distance and a certain generalization of this distance. Bounds based on the generalization are known as Chernoff bounds [5].

9.2.1. Bounds on the Minimum Probability of Error

A simple way to derive a bound on the minimum probability of error is to begin with the likelihood ratio test (Eq. 3.2) that achieves this minimum. In this chapter we shall refer to this minimum probability of error as the *Bayes error* probability ε_B. Then the Bayes error, as given by Eqs. 3.4 and 3.5, can be expressed as

$$\begin{aligned}\varepsilon_B &= \int_{R_2} \Pr[\omega_1]p_1(\mathbf{y})\,d\mathbf{y} + \int_{R_1} \Pr[\omega_2]p_2(\mathbf{y})\,d\mathbf{y} \\ &= \int_{-\infty}^{\infty} \min\{\Pr[\omega_1]p_1(\mathbf{y}), \Pr[\omega_2]p_2(\mathbf{y})\}\,d\mathbf{y}\end{aligned} \tag{9.24}$$

If one now applies the identity

$$\min\{a, b\} \leq \sqrt{ab} \tag{9.25}$$

which is true for any positive values of a and b, to Eq. 9.24, one obtains

$$\varepsilon_B \leq \Pr[\omega_1]^{1/2}\Pr[\omega_2]^{1/2} \int_{-\infty}^{\infty} \sqrt{p_1(\mathbf{y})p_2(\mathbf{y})}\,d\mathbf{y} \tag{9.26}$$

or from Eq. 9.6,

$$\varepsilon_B \leq \Pr[\omega_1]^{1/2}\Pr[\omega_2]^{1/2}\, e^{-B} \leq \tfrac{1}{2}e^{-B} \tag{9.27}$$

This result is known as the *Bhattacharyya bound.*

A somewhat more general result can be obtained by using the identity

$$\min\{a, b\} \leq a^s b^{1-s} \tag{9.28}$$

which is true for $0 \leq a, b, s \leq 1$. Following through the steps leading to Eq. 9.27, one obtains the more general result known as a *Chernoff bound*:

$$\varepsilon_B \leq \Pr[\omega_1]^s \Pr[\omega_2]^{1-s}\, e^{\mu(s)} \qquad 0 \leq s \leq 1 \tag{9.29}$$

where

$$\mu(s) = \ln \int_{-\infty}^{\infty} p_1^s(\mathbf{y})p_2^{1-s}(\mathbf{y})\,d\mathbf{y}; \qquad 0 \leq s \leq 1 \tag{9.30}$$

For Gaussian density functions, it is possible to evaluate the integral explicitly (see Problem 9.5). The result is that for Gaussian density functions $\mu(s)$ is given by

$$\begin{aligned}\mu(s) = -\frac{1}{2}s(1-s)(\mathbf{m}_1 - \mathbf{m}_2)^T[(1-s)\mathbf{K}_1 + s\mathbf{K}_2]^{-1}(\mathbf{m}_1 - \mathbf{m}_2) \\ -\frac{1}{2}\ln\frac{|(1-s)\mathbf{K}_1 + s\mathbf{K}_2|}{|\mathbf{K}_1|^{1-s}|\mathbf{K}_2|^s}\end{aligned} \tag{9.31}$$

This gives an explicit, more general bound on the probability of error.

Observe from Eqs. 9.5 and 9.30 that the Bhattacharyya distance is given by

$$B = -\mu(\tfrac{1}{2}) \tag{9.32}$$

and that for $s = \frac{1}{2}$ the Chernoff bound reduces to the Bhattacharyya bound. The advantage of the Chernoff bound is that there are generally values of $s \neq \frac{1}{2}$ that give tighter bounds on the probability of error. In addition, the quantity $\mu(s)$ can

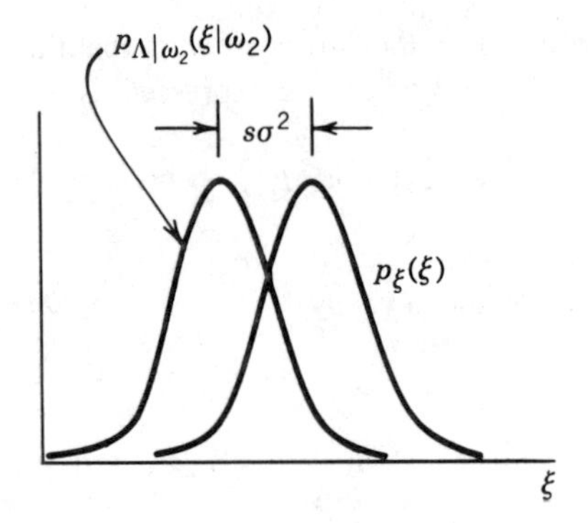

FIGURE 9.3 Density functions used in deriving Chernoff bound. ($p_{\Lambda|\omega_2}$ shown Gaussian with variance σ^2).

be used to bound the individual class error probabilities ε_1 and ε_2 and the total error for a Neyman–Pearson test or any likelihood ratio involving an arbitrary threshold τ. This leads us to consider an alternative derivation of the Chernoff bounds in the following subsection.

9.2.2 Chernoff Bounds for General Likelihood Ratio Tests

Consider now the general log likelihood ratio test

$$\Lambda(\mathbf{y}) = \ln \frac{p_1(\mathbf{y})}{p_2(\mathbf{y})} \underset{\omega_2}{\overset{\omega_1}{\gtrless}} \tau \tag{9.33}$$

which defines the statistic $\Lambda(\mathbf{y})$. It follows from Eqs. 9.30 and 9.33 and properties of the expectation that

$$\begin{aligned}\mu(s) &= \ln \int_{-\infty}^{\infty} \left(\frac{p_1(\mathbf{y})}{p_2(\mathbf{y})}\right)^s p_2(\mathbf{y})\, d\mathbf{y} = \ln \int_{-\infty}^{\infty} e^{s\Lambda(\mathbf{y})} p_2(\mathbf{y})\, d\mathbf{y} \\ &= \ln \int_{-\infty}^{\infty} e^{s\Lambda} p_{\Lambda|\omega_2}(\Lambda|\omega_2)\, d\Lambda \end{aligned} \tag{9.34}$$

or

$$\int_{-\infty}^{\infty} e^{s\Lambda}\, p_{\Lambda|\omega_2}(\Lambda|\omega_2)\, d\Lambda = e^{\mu(s)} \tag{9.35}$$

where $p_{\Lambda|\omega_2}$ is the class conditional density function of the log likelihood ratio.

Now consider a new family of density functions defined by

$$p_\xi(\xi) = e^{s\xi - \mu(s)}\, p_{\Lambda|\omega_2}(\xi|\omega_2) \tag{9.36}$$

Since from Eq. 9.35 the integral of $e^{s\xi} p_{\Lambda|\omega_2}(\xi|\omega_2)$ is equal to $e^{\mu(s)}$, the density functions defined by Eq. 9.36 clearly integrate to one. Figure 9.3 shows a typical density function for Λ and one of these "skewed" density functions derived from it.

Now consider the class error probability ε_2. Recall that this quantity is given by

$$\varepsilon_2 = \int_{\tau}^{\infty} p_{\Lambda|\omega_2}(\xi|\omega_2)\, d\xi = \int_{\tau}^{\infty} e^{-s\xi+\mu(s)} p_{\xi}(\xi)\, d\xi \tag{9.37}$$

(the second expression follows from Eq. 9.36). Observe that if s is a real number between 0 and 1, then the function $e^{-s\xi}$ is a monotonically decreasing function of ξ. Therefore, for values of ξ in the region of integration we have

$$e^{-s\xi} < e^{-s\tau} \tag{9.38}$$

Then from Eqs. 9.37 and 9.38

$$\varepsilon_2 \leq e^{-s\tau+\mu(s)} \int_{\tau}^{\infty} p_{\xi}(\xi)\, d\xi \tag{9.39}$$

Since the integral is always less than one, Eq. 9.39 gives the bound

$$\varepsilon_2 < e^{\mu(s)-s\tau} \tag{9.40}$$

A similar bound can be established for ε_1. This is probably most easily done from symmetry arguments. [An alternate method is given in Problem 9.6(a).] Consider the equivalent test to Eq. 9.33,

$$\ln \frac{p_2(\mathbf{y})}{p_1(\mathbf{y})} \underset{\omega_1}{\overset{\omega_2}{\gtrless}} -\tau \tag{9.41}$$

and the quantity

$$\mu'(s') = \ln \int_{-\infty}^{\infty} p_2^{s'}(\mathbf{y}) p_1^{1-s'}(\mathbf{y})\, d\mathbf{y} \tag{9.42}$$

By a sequence of steps identical to those that led to Eq. 9.40, one can establish that

$$\varepsilon_1 < e^{\mu'(s')+s'\tau} \tag{9.43}$$

Then by putting $s' = 1 - s$ and noticing that $\mu'(1-s) = \mu(s)$, we can write

$$\varepsilon_1 < e^{\mu(s)+(1+s)\tau} \tag{9.44}$$

The bounds given by Eqs. 9.40 and 9.44 are also referred to as Chernoff bounds. The tightest form of these bounds can be obtained by selecting a value of s so that the terms in the exponents are minimized. By taking the derivative of the exponent and setting the result to zero, one can see that the tightest bounds for both ε_1 and ε_2 are obtained when a value s_o is chosen such that

$$\left.\frac{d\mu(s)}{ds}\right|_{s=s_o} = \tau \tag{9.45}$$

The bound of Eq. 9.29 on the total probability of error can be established in an alternate way from the results of this subsection. The procedure is outlined in Problem 9.6. It can then be seen that the value s_o satisfying Eq. 9.45 also gives the tightest bound on the total probability of error (i.e., the Bayes error). In many cases, however, the bound has a rather broad flat character near the optimum value s_o. As a result it is often sufficient to choose $s = \frac{1}{2}$ as in the Bhattacharyya and thus to avoid the optimization problem.

9.3 BOUNDS ON THE PERFORMANCE OF THE NEAREST NEIGHBOR ALGORITHM

In the previous section, bounds were derived on the error resulting when known density functions were used in a likelihood ratio test. This section is somewhat different from the previous in that we are not deriving bounds on the Bayes error. Instead, the Bayes error is used to give bounds for the performance of the nearest neighbor decision algorithm. The results show that asymptotically, as the number of samples get large, the error probability for the nearest neighbor algorithm is very close to the Bayes error probability [6]. This is a rather astounding fact for this seemingly simple algorithm.

9.3.1 Bounds for the 1-Nearest Neighbor Algorithm

Bounds for the performance of the nearest neighbor algorithm are relatively straightforward to derive. Let $\mathbf{y}_o$ be a point to be classified and let $\mathbf{y}^k$ represent the sample that is its nearest neighbor. Also, assume that the class of $\mathbf{y}^k$ is ω_{s_k} and the true class of $\mathbf{y}_o$ is ω_p. Then, given $\mathbf{y}_o$ and $\mathbf{y}^k$, an error occurs with probability

$$\Pr[\omega_p \neq \omega_{s_k} | \mathbf{y}_o, \mathbf{y}^k] \tag{9.46}$$

Now if we use the fact that "$\mathbf{y}_o$ is of class ω_p" and "$\mathbf{y}^k$ is of class ω_{s_k}" are independent events and sum over all classes N_c, we obtain the conditional error probability for the nearest neighbor algorithm:

$$e_{NN}(\mathbf{y}_o) = \sum_{i=1}^{N_c} \Pr[\omega_p = \omega_i | \mathbf{y}_o](1 - \Pr[\omega_{s_k} = \omega_i | \mathbf{y}^k]) \tag{9.47}$$

Finally, if the density functions are continuous and the number of sample points is very large then the nearest neighbor $\mathbf{y}^k$ will be very close to $\mathbf{y}_o$ and it is reasonable to assume that

$$\Pr[\omega_{s_k} = \omega_i | \mathbf{y}^k] \approx \Pr[\omega_p = \omega_i | \mathbf{y}_o] \stackrel{\Delta}{=} \Pr[\omega_i | \mathbf{y}_o] \tag{9.48}$$

Therefore, from Eqs. 9.47 and 9.48

$$
\begin{aligned}
e_{NN}(\mathbf{y}_o) &= \sum_{i=1}^{N_c} \Pr[\omega_i|\mathbf{y}_o](1 - \Pr[\omega_i|\mathbf{y}_o]) \\
&= 1 - \sum_{i=1}^{N_c} (\Pr[\omega_i|\mathbf{y}_o])^2 \qquad (9.49)
\end{aligned}
$$

The next step is to relate $e_{NN}(\mathbf{y}_o)$ to the Bayes error. Let ω_B be the class chosen by the Bayes decision rule, that is,

$$\Pr[\omega_B|\mathbf{y}_o] = \max_j \Pr[\omega_j|\mathbf{y}_o]$$

Then the conditional error probability (see Eq. 3.6) for the Bayes decision rule is

$$e_B(\mathbf{y}_o) = \Pr[\text{error}|\mathbf{y}_o] = \sum_{i \neq B} \Pr[\omega_i|\mathbf{y}_o] = 1 - \Pr[\omega_B|\mathbf{y}_o] \qquad (9.50)$$

or

$$\Pr[\omega_B|\mathbf{y}_o] = 1 - e_B(\mathbf{y}_o) \qquad (9.51)$$

Now, to derive a bound on Eq. 9.49, write

$$\sum_{i=1}^{N_c} (\Pr[\omega_i|\mathbf{y}_o])^2 = (\Pr[\omega_B|\mathbf{y}_o])^2 + \sum_{i \neq B} (\Pr[\omega_i|\mathbf{y}_o])^2 \qquad (9.52)$$

Observe that for a fixed value of $\Pr[\omega_B|\mathbf{y}_o]$ this expression is minimized when all of the remaining probabilities are equal. Since, from Eq. 9.50 the remaining probabilities sum to $e_B(\mathbf{y}_o)$, it follows that the minimizing values are

$$\Pr[\omega_i|\mathbf{y}_o] = \frac{e_B(\mathbf{y}_o)}{N_c - 1} \qquad i \neq B \qquad (9.53)$$

Substituting Eqs. 9.51 and 9.53 into Eq. 9.52 then gives the bound

$$\sum_{i=1}^{N_c} (\Pr[\omega_i|\mathbf{y}_o])^2 \geq [1 - e_B(\mathbf{y}_o)]^2 + \frac{e_B^2(\mathbf{y}_o)}{N_c - 1} \qquad (9.54)$$

Finally, applying Eq. 9.54 to Eq. 9.49 and simplifying gives the relation

$$
\begin{aligned}
e_{NN}(\mathbf{y}_o) &\leq 1 - [1 - e_B(\mathbf{y}_o)]^2 - \frac{e_B^2(\mathbf{y}_o)}{N_c - 1} \\
&= 2e_B(\mathbf{y}_o) - \frac{N_c}{N_c - 1} e_B^2(\mathbf{y}_o) \qquad (9.55)
\end{aligned}
$$

Now observe that the nearest neighbor and the Bayes error probabilities are defined by

$$\varepsilon_{NN} = E[e_{NN}(\mathbf{y})] = \int_{-\infty}^{\infty} (1 - \sum_{i=1}^{N_c} (\Pr[\omega_i|\mathbf{y}])^2) p_{\mathbf{y}}(\mathbf{y})\, d\mathbf{y} \tag{9.56}$$

and

$$\varepsilon_B = E[e_B(\mathbf{y})] = \int_{-\infty}^{\infty} e_B(\mathbf{y}) p_{\mathbf{y}}(\mathbf{y})\, d\mathbf{y} \tag{9.57}$$

and that since the variance of $e_B(\mathbf{y})$ must be nonnegative

$$E[e_B^2(\mathbf{y})] \geq \varepsilon_B^2 \tag{9.58}$$

Then taking expectations of Eq. 9.55 and using Eqs. 9.56 to 9.58 yields the desired upper bound. Since any error, including the nearest neighbor, must be greater than or equal to the Bayes error, one has the complete set of bounds

$$\varepsilon_B \leq \varepsilon_{NN} \leq 2\varepsilon_B - \frac{N_c}{N_c - 1} \varepsilon_B^2 \tag{9.59}$$

This shows that when the number of samples is very large, the nearest neighbor error probability lies between the Bayes error and a number something less than twice the Bayes error probability.

9.3.2 Bounds for the *k*-Nearest Neighbor Algorithm

Bounds on the error probability for the k-nearest neighbor algorithm are not so easy to establish. However, when the number of classes N_c is equal to 2 it can be shown that ε_{NN} is upper-bounded by a certain concave function $\varphi_k(\varepsilon_B)$ belonging to a family of functions with the property

$$\varphi_k(\xi) \leq \varphi_{k-1}(\xi) \qquad \text{for } 0 \leq \xi \leq 1 \tag{9.60}$$

and with

$$\varphi_1(\xi) = 2\xi(1 - \xi) \tag{9.61}$$

These functions are plotted in Fig. 9.4, where it can be seen that for any two-class problem characterized by a Bayes error probability ε_B, the k-nearest neighbor error lies between the upper curve and the line $\varepsilon_{NN} = \varepsilon_B$.

9.3.3 Bounding the Bayes Error

The upper bounds on the nearest neighbor error probability can be inverted to yield lower bounds on the Bayes error. For example, the upper bound of Eq. 9.59 can be inverted to obtain

$$\varepsilon_B \geq \tfrac{1}{2}(1 - \sqrt{1 - \alpha\varepsilon_{NN}}) \tag{9.62}$$

where

$$\alpha = \frac{N_c - 1}{N_c} \tag{9.63}$$

Although it is possible, inverting the functions φ_k introduced in the previous section can be difficult and the best procedure may be a graphical one.

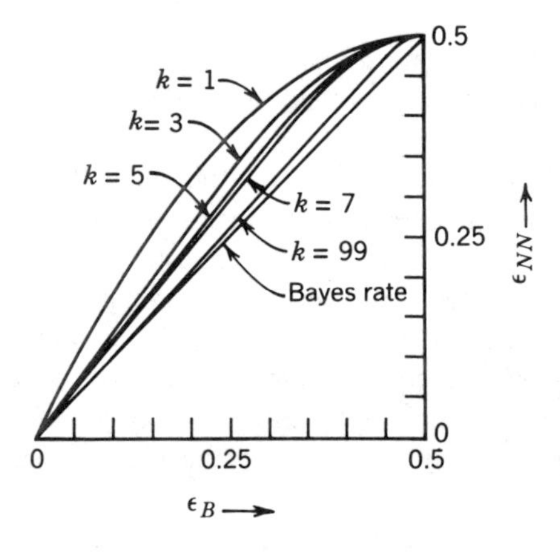

FIGURE 9.4 Bounds on the k-nearest neighbor error probability for two-class problems. (From R. O. Duda and P. E. Hart, *Pattern Classification and Scene Analysis*, John Wiley & Sons, Inc., New York, 1973. Reprinted by permission.)

9.4 METHODS OF TESTING

In most practical situations the error probability for a given pattern recognition problem is estimated by designing a classifier and testing it. The testing is illustrated in Fig. 9.5. A set of samples $\{\mathbf{y}^{(\ell)}\}$ with known classes is applied to the classifier, and a decision is made. Suppose that there are N_i independent samples of class i and let ε_i be the actual probability of error that characterizes this classifier's performance on samples of class i. Then the probability that any given sample will be misclassified is ε_i and the probability that any k_i samples will be misclassified is given by the binomial distribution

$$\Pr[k_i \text{ misclassified}] = \binom{N_i}{k_i} (\varepsilon_i)^{k_i} (1 - \varepsilon_i)^{N_i - k_i} \tag{9.64}$$

A maximum likelihood estimate for the error ε_i can be obtained by choosing ε_i to maximize Eq. 9.64. This value is given by

$$\tilde{\varepsilon}_i = \frac{k_i}{N_i} \tag{9.65}$$

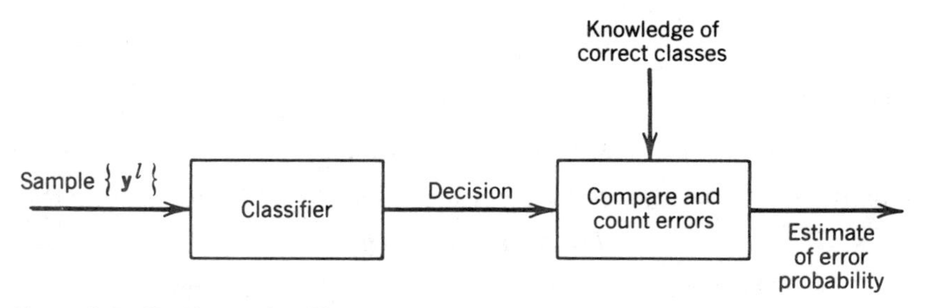

FIGURE 9.5 Testing a classifier.

(see Section 8.1.2.). Thus, in testing a classifier, an estimate of the probability of error can be obtained by dividing the number of misclassified samples by the total number of samples tested (see Fig. 9.5).

A very real problem that arises in almost any application is the following. There is available only a limited number of samples and one must decide how to use these samples to both design and test the classifier. If all of the samples are used to design the classifier, the classifier will have to be tested on the very same samples. This will tend to give an overly optimistic estimate of the performance. On the other hand, if only a small number of the samples is used to design the classifier, poor estimates of the classifier parameters may result and so the classifier may perform inadequately. Alternatively, if one uses only a small number of samples for testing, the estimated error performance may not be reliable.

In this section we shall try to deal with these issues of classifier design and performance estimation in a more analytical manner. Three basic procedures known as the *L, C,* and the *U* methods will be examined.

To carry out the analysis, assume that the data are from some distribution that is characterized by a set of parameters represented by the vector $\boldsymbol{\rho}$. In particular, assume that the samples used for design (i.e., the training samples) are characterized by the parameter vector $\boldsymbol{\rho}_D$ and that a Bayes optimal classifier is designed for these samples [7]. If the test samples are characterized by some other parameter vector $\boldsymbol{\rho}_T$, then the theoretical error is a function of the two parameter vectors

$$\varepsilon = \varepsilon(\boldsymbol{\rho}_D, \boldsymbol{\rho}_T) \tag{9.66}$$

Then for any set of test samples, $\varepsilon(\boldsymbol{\rho}_T, \boldsymbol{\rho}_T)$ represents the Bayes error probability for these samples, which we denote by $\varepsilon_B(\boldsymbol{\rho}_T)$. It follows that

$$\varepsilon_B(\boldsymbol{\rho}_T) = \varepsilon(\boldsymbol{\rho}_T, \boldsymbol{\rho}_T) \leq \varepsilon(\boldsymbol{\rho}_D, \boldsymbol{\rho}_T) \tag{9.67}$$

Now consider a problem where the data (both training and test data) are characterized by a true but unknown parameter $\boldsymbol{\rho}_o$. Furthermore, let $\tilde{\boldsymbol{\rho}}_N$ be an estimate of this parameter obtained from a training set of size N. Then, by the same reasoning that let to Eq. 9.67 we have

$$\varepsilon_B(\boldsymbol{\rho}_o) \leq \varepsilon(\tilde{\boldsymbol{\rho}}_N, \boldsymbol{\rho}_o) \tag{9.68}$$

and since $\tilde{\boldsymbol{\rho}}_N$ is a random variable

$$\varepsilon_B(\boldsymbol{\rho}_o) \leq E[\varepsilon(\tilde{\boldsymbol{\rho}}_N, \boldsymbol{\rho}_o)] \tag{9.69}$$

It also follows from Eq. 9.67 that

$$\varepsilon(\tilde{\boldsymbol{\rho}}_N, \tilde{\boldsymbol{\rho}}_N) \leq \varepsilon(\boldsymbol{\rho}_o, \tilde{\boldsymbol{\rho}}_N) \tag{9.70}$$

and thus that

$$E[\varepsilon(\tilde{\boldsymbol{\rho}}_N, \tilde{\boldsymbol{\rho}}_N)] \leq E[\varepsilon(\boldsymbol{\rho}_o, \tilde{\boldsymbol{\rho}}_N)] \tag{9.71}$$

Finally, if the estimate $\varepsilon(\boldsymbol{\rho}_o, \tilde{\boldsymbol{\rho}}_N)$ is an unbiased estimate of the true error, then

$$E[\varepsilon(\boldsymbol{\rho}_o, \tilde{\boldsymbol{\rho}}_N)] = \varepsilon_B(\boldsymbol{\rho}_o) \tag{9.72}$$

Eq. 9.72 would be difficult to prove in general, since the exact form of the function ε is usually not known. Nevertheless, it is entirely reasonable, since it states that

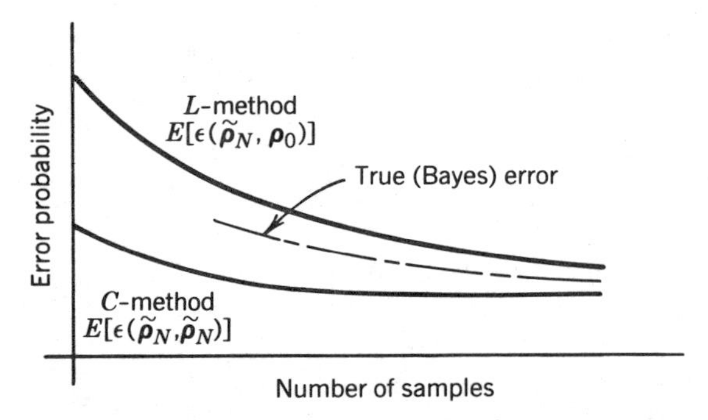

FIGURE 9.6 Bounding the probability of error with the *L* and *C* methods.

the error of the optimal classifier when averaged over all possible sets of N samples is equal to the Bayes error. A combination of Eqs. 9.69, 9.71, and 9.72 then yields

$$E[\varepsilon(\tilde{\boldsymbol{\rho}}_N, \tilde{\boldsymbol{\rho}}_N)] \leq \varepsilon_B(\boldsymbol{\rho}_o) \leq E[\varepsilon(\tilde{\boldsymbol{\rho}}_N, \boldsymbol{\rho}_o)] \tag{9.73}$$

Equation 9.73 gives upper and lower bounds on the Bayes error in terms of certain methods of classifier design and testing. The error $\varepsilon(\tilde{\boldsymbol{\rho}}_N, \tilde{\boldsymbol{\rho}}_N)$ results when the N training samples are used to both design and test the classifier. This procedure is known as the C method and yields performance that is a *lower* bound on the Bayes error. The error $\varepsilon(\hat{\boldsymbol{\rho}}_N, \boldsymbol{\rho}_o)$ results when N training samples are used to design the classifier and (other) samples from the true distribution are used to test it. This is known as a U (for unbiased) method. As discussed in the beginning of this section, one may not have a large number of samples from the true distribution available to test the classifier. If such samples were available, one might want to consider increasing the size of the training set. Fortunately, an alternative procedure is available for use with a limited total number of samples that yields independent training and test sets and provides the upper bound. This procedure is known as the L (for "leave-one-out") method. In this method a classifier is designed using all of the available samples except one. Then that remaining sample is used to test the classifier. This procedure is then repeated each time leaving out a different sample. The L method is easy to carry out for the nearest neighbor rule, since it merely involves classifying each of the available samples on the basis of their nearest neighbors. For parametric classifiers such as the Gaussian quadratic classifier, perturbation methods are available that make the parameters for the successive classifiers easy to compute. Figure 9.6 shows typical performance of the L and C methods as a function of the total number of available samples. For increasing numbers of samples, the error probabilities are found to draw close together and provide tight bounds on the true (Bayes) error.

9.5 SUMMARY

This chapter deals with bounds and estimates for the probability of error. The divergence and Bhattacharyya distance are introduced as measures of separability for two distributions and explicit closed form expressions for these quantities are given in the Gaussian case. The Bhattacharyya distance is used to derive a bound on the Bayes error. More general bounds on the class error probabilities and the total probability of error are given as Chernoff bounds; corresponding Bhattacharyya bounds are shown to be a special case. Bounds on the performance of the nearest neighbor classifier are then discussed. It is shown that asymptotically, as the number of samples increases, the nearest neighbor error is less than twice the Bayes error. Finally, practical methods for the design and testing of classifiers are discussed. It is argued that appropriate use of the L and C methods can provide converging upper and lower bounds on the true probability of error.

REFERENCES

1. S. KULLBACK. *Information Theory and Statistics*. New York: John Wiley & Sons Inc., 1959.
2. R. G. GALLAGHER. *Information Theory and Reliable Communication*. New York: John Wiley & Sons, Inc., 1968.
3. S. KULLBACK, and R. A. LEIBLER. "On Information and Sufficiency." *Ann. Math. Stat.*, Vol. 22, pp. 79–86 (1951).
4. A. BHATTACHARYYA. "On a Measure of Divergence Between Two Statistical Populations Defined by Their Probability Distributions." *Bull. Calcutta Math. Soc.*, Vol. 35, No. 3, pp. 99–110 (1943).
5. H. CHERNOFF. "A Measure of Asymptotic Efficiency for Tests of a Hypothesis Based on the Sum of Observations." *Annals Math. Stat.*, Vol. 23, pp. 493–507 (1962).
6. T. M. COVER, and P. E. HART. "Nearest Neighbor Pattern Classification." *IEEE Trans. Info. Theory,* Vol. IT-13, No. 1, pp. 21–27 (January 1967).
7. M. HILLS. "Allocation Rules and their Error Rates." *J. Roy. Stat. Soc. Series B,* Vol. 28, pp. 1–31 (1966).

PROBLEMS

9.1 **(a)** Let $\mathbf{y}'$ be a one-to-one linear transformation of $\mathbf{y}$. That is, $\mathbf{y}' = \mathbf{A}\mathbf{y}$, where $\mathbf{A}$ is a nonsingular square matrix. Show that the divergence and the Bhattacharyya distance for $\mathbf{y}'$ are the same as those for $\mathbf{y}$. That is, the divergence and the Bhattacharyya distance are *invariant* under a nonsingular linear transformation.

(b) Now let $\mathbf{y}'$ be derived as a general nonlinear but one-to-one transformation of $\mathbf{y}$. Show that the divergence and the Bhattacharyya distance are invariant under any such one-to-one transformation.

9.2 Prove the properties expressed by Eq. 9.8 for the divergence and the Bhattacharyya distance.

9.3 Show that the constant C defined by Eq. 9.18c can be expressed by Eq. 9.20. Show also that Eq. 9.21 is correct

Hint: Define the quantity $\mathbf{K}_A = \frac{1}{2}(\mathbf{K}_1 + \mathbf{K}_2)$. Show that

$$\mathbf{K}_2^{-1}\,\mathbf{K}_A\mathbf{K}_1^{-1} = \mathbf{K}_1^{-1}\,\mathbf{K}_A\mathbf{K}_2^{-1} = \mathbf{K}_p^{-1}$$

From this show that

$$\mathbf{K}_A^{-1} = \mathbf{K}_1^{-1}\,\mathbf{K}_p\mathbf{K}_2^{-1} = \mathbf{K}_2^{-1}\,\mathbf{K}_p\mathbf{K}_1^{-1}$$

and

$$\mathbf{K}_A^{-1} - 2\mathbf{K}_i^{-1} = -\mathbf{K}_i^{-1}\,\mathbf{K}_p\mathbf{K}_i^{-1} \qquad \text{for } i = 1, 2$$

Use these various relations to help simplify the expressions.

9.4 Show that the inequality (9.28) is true for all numbers a, b, and s in the range [0, 1].

9.5 By generalizing the development in Section 9.1.2 and Problem 9.3, show that the expression of Eq. 9.31 is correct. For purposes of this problem you may want to define the matrices $\mathbf{K}_p$ and $\mathbf{K}_A$ used in Problem 9.3 as

$$\mathbf{K}_p = (s\mathbf{K}_1^{-1} + (1 - s)\mathbf{K}_2^{-1})^{-1}$$

$$\mathbf{K}_A = s\mathbf{K}_2 + (1 - s)\mathbf{K}_1$$

9.6 **(a)** Beginning with the definition (3.5) show that

$$\varepsilon_1 = \int_{R_2} e^{\Lambda(\mathbf{y})} p_2(\mathbf{y})\, d\mathbf{y} = \int_{-\infty}^{\tau} e^{\Lambda} p_{\Lambda|\omega_2}(\Lambda|\omega_2)\, d\Lambda$$

Use this to establish the bound

$$\varepsilon_1 \leq \exp[^{\mu(s) + (1-s)\tau}] \int_{-\infty}^{\tau} p_\xi(\xi)\, d\xi \qquad (9.39')$$

Note that this implies the bound of Eq. 9.44.

(b) Now using Eqs. 9.39 and 9.39′ and the relation

$$\Pr[\text{error}] = \Pr[\omega_1]\varepsilon_1 + \Pr[\omega_2]\varepsilon_2$$

and using $\tau = \ln \dfrac{\Pr[\omega_2]}{\Pr[\omega_1]}$, derive the bound given by Eq. 9.29. Indicate why the value s_o satisfying Eq. 9.45 gives the tightest bound.

CHAPTER 10

Classification of Stationary Time Series

In many problems of practical interest, measurements are made that take the form of electrical signals that are a function of time. The signals can then be used to classify the underlying phenomenon. Since the observations are samples of the signal taken sequentially in time, the observations may have particular statistical structure that would not otherwise be present. This structure permits the development of classifiers that have advantages over the more general forms discussed earlier in this book [1]. These special forms of classifiers are the topic of the present chapter.

10.1 ORIGIN OF TIME SERIES

Sampled electrical signals or time series arise in a large number of areas. For example, in medicine, the EKG or EEG characterize the cardiovascular system and the central nervous system and allow doctors to draw inferences about the functioning of those systems. In industrial applications, certain acoustic or electrical signals relate to the proper operation of a machine or electronic equipment and permit fault detection and diagnosis. In military applications the energy reflected from a target to a radar or sonar produces a "signature" by which the target can be identified. Figure 10.1 shows the observation vector arising from uniform sampling of an electrical signal. The observation vector takes the specific form

$$\mathbf{x}_n = \begin{bmatrix} x_1 \\ x_2 \\ x_3 \\ \vdots \\ x_n \end{bmatrix} = \begin{bmatrix} x(t_1) \\ x(t_2) \\ x(t_3) \\ \vdots \\ x(t_n) \end{bmatrix} \tag{10.1}$$

Time series may also arise in applications that do not specifically involve the

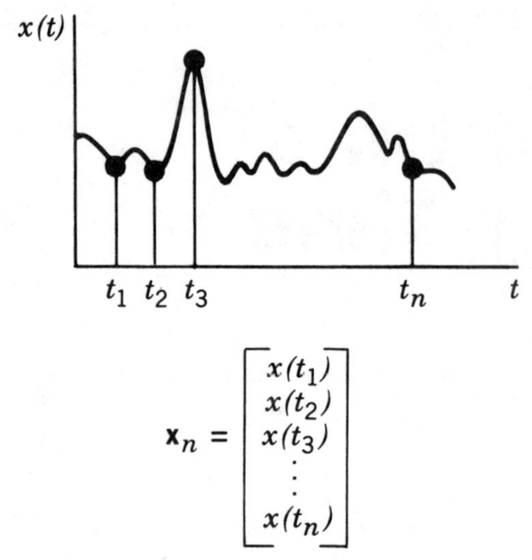

FIGURE 10.1 The formation of an observation vector for time series.

sampling of electrical signals. For example, the closing price of a stock is recorded daily and forms a time series. Various geological or meteorological data may be taken and recorded at specific intervals of time. In both of these examples, electrical signals play no fundamental role in the definition of the time series.

Regardless of its origin, a time series may possess a certain kind of statistical regularity that can result in simplifications in the classifier. At the very least, the time evolving nature of the measurements suggests that a recursive form of the classifier may be possible and desirable. This point is considered next.

10.2 A RECURSIVE FORM FOR THE QUADRATIC CLASSIFIER

Assume that there are two classes of time series to be dealt with and that for each class, the samples $x(t_j)$ are jointly Gaussian. Then the likelihood ratio test for these time series reduces to the quadratic classifier (see Chapter 6). It will be shown here that the quadratic classifier can be expressed as a sum of terms, corresponding to the order in which the observations are acquired in time. That is, we shall develop a classifier based on k observations $x(t_1), x(t_2), \ldots, x(t_k)$ and show how to update it when the next observation $x(t_{k+1})$ is available. The procedure can be continued until all observations $x(t_1), x(t_2), \ldots, x(t_n)$ are accounted for.

Let the vector of k observations be represented by $\mathbf{x}_k$ and let its corresponding mean vector and covariance matrix be denoted by $\mathbf{m}_k$ and $\mathbf{K}_k$. Thus the density function for k observations is given by

$$p_{\mathbf{x}_k}(\hat{\mathbf{x}}_k) = \frac{1}{(2\pi)^{k/2}|\mathbf{K}_k|^{1/2}} \exp - \tfrac{1}{2}(\hat{\mathbf{x}}_k - \mathbf{m}_k)^T \mathbf{K}_k^{-1} (\hat{\mathbf{x}}_k - \mathbf{m}_k) \qquad (10.2)$$

The vector of $k + 1$ observations and its mean and covariance will be represented by

$$\mathbf{x}_{k+1} = \left[\begin{array}{c} \mathbf{x}_k \\ \hline x_{k+1} \end{array}\right] \tag{10.3a}$$

$$\mathbf{m}_{k+1} = \left[\begin{array}{c} \mathbf{m}_k \\ \hline m_{k+1} \end{array}\right] \tag{10.3b}$$

$$\mathbf{K}_{k+1} = \left[\begin{array}{c|c} \mathbf{K}_k & \mathbf{r}_{k+1} \\ \hline \mathbf{r}_{k+1}^T & \sigma_{k+1}^2 \end{array}\right] \tag{10.3c}$$

The goal is to develop an expression for the density function for $k + 1$ observations in terms of the parameters appearing in Eqs. 10.2 and 10.3.

By performing a Gauss–Jordan reduction (see Problem 10.2), it can be shown that the inverse covariance matrix for $k + 1$ observations is given by

$$\mathbf{K}_{k+1}^{-1} = \left[\begin{array}{c|c} \mathbf{I} & -\mathbf{g}_{k+1} \\ \hline \mathbf{0}^T & 1 \end{array}\right] \left[\begin{array}{c|c} \mathbf{K}_k^{-1} & \mathbf{0} \\ \hline \mathbf{0}^T & 1/e_{k+1} \end{array}\right] \left[\begin{array}{c|c} \mathbf{I} & \mathbf{0} \\ \hline -\mathbf{g}_{k+1}^T & 1 \end{array}\right] \tag{10.4}$$

or the equivalent form

$$\mathbf{K}_{k+1}^{-1} = \left[\begin{array}{c|c} \mathbf{K}_k^{-1} & \mathbf{0} \\ \hline \mathbf{0}^T & 0 \end{array}\right] + \left[\begin{array}{c} -\mathbf{g}_{k+1} \\ \hline 1 \end{array}\right] \frac{1}{e_{k+1}} [-\mathbf{g}_{k+1}^T \mid 1] \tag{10.5}$$

where the terms $\mathbf{g}_{k+1}$ and e_{k+1} are defined by

$$\mathbf{g}_{k+1} = \mathbf{K}_k^{-1}\mathbf{r}_{k+1} \tag{10.6a}$$

$$e_{k+1} = \sigma_{k+1}^2 - \mathbf{r}_{k+1}^T \mathbf{K}_k^{-1}\mathbf{r}_{k+1} \tag{10.6b}$$

Observe that the first and last matrices on the right-hand side of Eq. 10.4 are upper and lower triangular with ones on the diagonal. Since the determinant of each of these triangular matrices is unity, the determinant of $\mathbf{K}_{k+1}^{-1}$ is equal to the determinant of the central matrix. Therefore,

$$|\mathbf{K}_{k+1}^{-1}| = |\mathbf{K}_k^{-1}| \frac{1}{e_{k+1}}$$

and thus

$$|\mathbf{K}_{k+1}| = |\mathbf{K}_k|\, e_{k+1} \tag{10.7}$$

Now consider the quadratic product (the Mahalanobis distance) appearing in the exponent in Eq. 10.2. For $k + 1$ observations we can use Eq. 10.5 to write

$$(\mathbf{x}_{k+1} - \mathbf{m}_{k+1})^T \mathbf{K}_{k+1}^{-1} (\mathbf{x}_{k+1} - \mathbf{m}_{k+1})$$

$$= \left[(\mathbf{x}_k - \mathbf{m}_k)^T,\ x_{k+1} - m_{k+1} \right] \left[\left[\begin{array}{c|c} \mathbf{K}_k^1 & \mathbf{0} \\ \hline \mathbf{0}^T & 0 \end{array} \right] + \left[\begin{array}{c} -\mathbf{g}_{k+1} \\ \hline 1 \end{array} \right] \frac{1}{e_{k+1}} [-\mathbf{g}_{k+1}^T, 1] \right] \left[\begin{array}{c} \mathbf{x}_k - \mathbf{m}_k \\ \hline x_{k+1} - m_{k+1} \end{array} \right] \tag{10.8}$$

$$= (\mathbf{x}_k - \mathbf{m}_k)^T \mathbf{K}_k^{-1} (\mathbf{x}_k - \mathbf{m}_k) + \frac{(x_{k+1} - m_{k+1} - \mathbf{g}_{k+1}^T (\mathbf{x}_k - \mathbf{m}_k))^2}{e_{k+1}}$$

Some simplification in notation can now be realized if $\mathbf{m}_k^{(i)}$ and $\mathbf{K}_k^{(i)}$ are used to represent the mean vector and covariance matrix of class i, and if $\mathbf{x}_{k+1}^{(i)}$ is defined as

$$\mathbf{x}_{k+1}^{(i)} = \mathbf{x}_{k+1} - \mathbf{m}_{k+1}^{(i)} = \left[\begin{array}{c} \mathbf{x}_k^{(i)} \\ \hline x_{k+1}^{(i)} \end{array} \right] = \left[\begin{array}{c} \mathbf{x}_k - \mathbf{m}_k^{(i)} \\ \hline x_{k+1} - m_{k+1}^{(i)} \end{array} \right] \qquad i = 1, 2 \tag{10.9}$$

Then by virtue of Eqs. 10.7 and 10.8 the density function for $k + 1$ observations from class i is given by

$$p_{\mathbf{x}_{k+1}|\omega_i} (\mathbf{x}_{k+1}|\omega_i)$$

$$= \frac{1}{(2\pi)^{(k+1)/2} |\mathbf{K}_{k+1}^{(i)}|^{1/2}} \exp \left[-\tfrac{1}{2} (\mathbf{x}_{k+1} - \mathbf{m}_{k+1}^{(i)})^T \mathbf{K}_{k+1}^{(i)^{-1}} (\mathbf{x}_{k+1} - \mathbf{m}_{k+1}^{(i)}) \right]$$

$$= \frac{1}{(2\pi)^{k/2} |\mathbf{K}_k|^{1/2}} \exp \left[-\frac{1}{2} \mathbf{x}_k^{(i)T} \mathbf{K}_k^{(i)^{-1}} \mathbf{x}_k^{(i)} \right] \times \frac{1}{\sqrt{2\pi} e_{k+1}^{1/2}} \exp \left[-\frac{1}{2} \frac{(x_{k+1}^{(i)} - \mathbf{g}_{k+1}^T \mathbf{x}_k^{(i)})^2}{e_{k+1}} \right] \tag{10.10}$$

Since $p_{\mathbf{x}_{k+1}|\omega_i} = p_{\mathbf{x}_k|\omega_i} p_{x_{k+1}|\mathbf{x}_k\omega_i}$ and since the first term on the right-hand side of Eq. 10.10 is $p_{\mathbf{x}_k|\omega_i}$, the last term on the right-hand side of Eq. 10.10 is evidently $p_{x_{k+1}|\mathbf{x}_k\omega_i}$. Note that this density function is also Gaussian.

Recall from Chapter 6 that the quadratic classifier was obtained by taking minus twice the logarithm of the likelihood ratio. Since the density functions are given by Eq. 10.10, it follows that the classifier can be expressed in a recursive form as

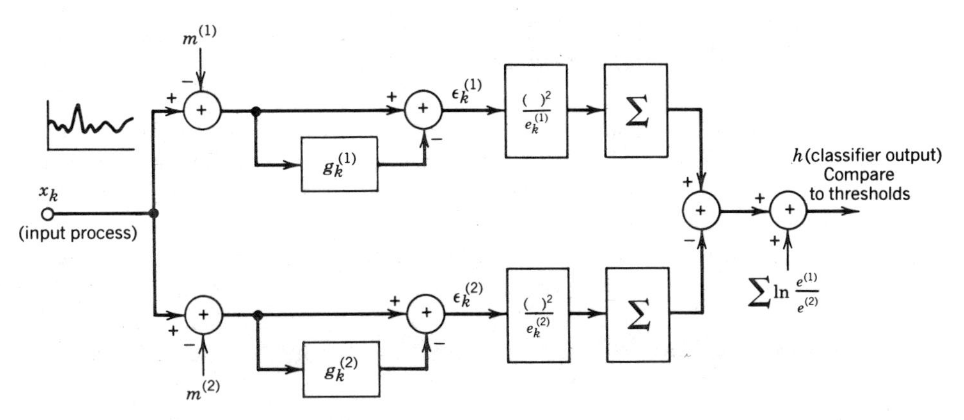

FIGURE 10.2 Classifier block diagram.

$$h_{k+1}(\mathbf{x}_{k+1}) = h_k(\mathbf{x}_k) + \Delta h_{k+1}(x_{k+1}|\mathbf{x}_k) \quad \underset{\omega_2}{\overset{\omega_1}{\lessgtr}} \quad T \tag{10.11}$$

where

$$h_k(\mathbf{x}_k) = \mathbf{x}_k^{(1)\mathrm{T}}\mathbf{K}_k^{(1)^{-1}}\mathbf{x}_k^{(1)} - \mathbf{x}_k^{(2)\mathrm{T}}\mathbf{K}_k^{(2)^{-1}}\mathbf{x}_k^{(2)} + \ln \frac{|\mathbf{K}_k^{(1)}|}{|\mathbf{K}_k^{(2)}|} \tag{10.12}$$

is the classifier for k observations and

$$\Delta h_{k+1}(x_{k+1}|\mathbf{x}_k) = \frac{(x_{k+1}^{(1)'} - \mathbf{g}_{k+1}^{(1)\mathrm{T}}\,\mathbf{x}_k^{(1)})^2}{e_{k+1}^{(1)}} - \frac{(x_{k+1}^{(2)} - \mathbf{g}_{k+1}^{(2)T}\,\mathbf{x}_k^{(2)})^2}{e_{k+1}^{(2)}} + \ln \frac{e_{k+1}^{(1)}}{e_{k+1}^{(2)}} \tag{10.13}$$

is a classifier derived from the conditional density functions $p_{x_{k+1}|\mathbf{x}_k\omega_i}$ Further interpretation of this expression will be given in the following sections. For now, it will only be pointed out that the conditional mean of the variable $x_{k+1}^{(i)}$ is $\mathbf{g}_{k+1}^{(i)T}\mathbf{x}_k^{(i)}$ and the conditional variance is $e_{k+1}^{(i)}$. A block diagram of the classifier is shown in Fig. 10.2. Observe that

$$h_n(\mathbf{x}_n) = \sum_{k=1}^{n} \Delta h_k(x_k|\mathbf{x}_{k-1}) \tag{10.14}$$

where for convenience of notation in Eq. 10.14, $\Delta h_1(x_1|\mathbf{x}_0)$ is taken to be

$$\Delta h_1(x_1|\mathbf{x}_0) = \frac{(x_1^{(1)})^2}{\sigma_{x_1}^{(1)^2}} - \frac{(x_1^{(2)})^2}{\sigma_{x_1}^{(2)^2}} + \ln \frac{\sigma_{x_1}^{(1)^2}}{\sigma_{x_1}^{(2)^2}} \tag{10.15}$$

(At the first sample it is not possible to define $\mathbf{g}_1^{(i)}$ and the variance of the measurement is the variance of the first sample $\sigma_{x_1}^{(i)^2}$.) Thus, as was stated in the first paragraph of this section, the classifier is comprised of a sum of terms corresponding to each individual observation.

10.3 INTERPRETATION OF THE RECURSIVE QUADRATIC CLASSIFIER

The alert reader may have noticed that there was nothing about the previous derivation that was dependent on the fact that the observation data were derived from a time series. The same algebraic operation can be applied to *any* data and the quadratic classifier can always be expressed in the recursive form. However, it is for time series data in particular that the recursive form of the classifier is most meaningful. This is particularly true for stationary time series data as discussed in Section 10.6. The reader may at this point wish to review Example 7.5 in Chapter 7, from which we can deduce for the present problem that since the quantity $\mathbf{g}_{k+1}^{(i)T}\,\mathbf{x}^i$ is the mean of the conditional density, it is both a mean-square and a maximum a posteriori estimate of $x_{k+1}^{(i)}$ given the measurements $\mathbf{x}_k^{(i)}$. The quantity

$$\varepsilon_{k+1}^{(i)} = x_{k+1}^{(i)} - \mathbf{g}_{k+1}^{(i)T}\mathbf{x}^{(i)} \tag{10.16}$$

which has a mean value of zero, represents the *error* in the estimate and $e_{k+1}^{(i)}$ represents the error variance. Equation (10.16) can be used to express Eq. 10.13 more concisely as

$$\Delta h_{k+1}(x_{k+1}|\mathbf{x}_k) = \frac{(\varepsilon_{k+1}^{(1)})^2}{e_{k+1}^{(1)}} - \frac{(\varepsilon_{k+1}^{(2)})^2}{e_{k+1}^{(2)}} + \ln\frac{e_{k+1}^{(1)}}{e_{k+1}^{(2)}} \tag{10.17}$$

The combination of Eqs. 10.14 and 10.17 then yields

$$h_n(\mathbf{x}_n) = \sum_{k=1}^{n}\frac{\varepsilon_k^{(1)2}}{e_k^{(1)}} - \sum_{k=1}^{n}\frac{\varepsilon_k^{(2)2}}{e_k^{(2)}} + \sum_{k=1}^{n}\ln\frac{e_k^{(1)}}{e_k^{(2)}} \tag{10.18}$$

where it is understood that $\varepsilon_1^{(i)} = x_1^{(i)}$ and $e_1^{(i)} = \sigma_{x_1}^{(i)}$. This form shows that the quadratic classifier compares the errors in estimating the data, assuming they are from class 1, to similar errors in estimation assuming the data are from class 2. When the normalized estimation errors for class 1 are lower than those for class 2, class 1 will be favored in the decision and vice versa.

Since only the errors in the estimation of the time series are used in the decision, a further interpretation is possible. The sequence of error terms $\varepsilon_1, \varepsilon_2, \varepsilon_3, \ldots$ is referred to in the literature of random processes as an *innovations process* [2]. The term ε_k represents only the *new* information inherent in the measurements x_k, that is, the information that cannot be predicted from the previous observations. In the next section it is shown that the successive error terms are *uncorrelated*. Thus the information that results from observing each new error term is indeed additive.

10.4 VIEWING THE RECURSIVE FORM OF THE CLASSIFIER AS A CAUSAL WHITENING PROCESS

Recall from Section 4.7.2 that the covariance matrix $\mathbf{K}_n$ for n observations can be written as

$$\mathbf{K}_n = \mathbf{L}_n\mathbf{D}_n\mathbf{L}_n^T \tag{10.19}$$

where $\mathbf{L}_n$ is a lower triangular matrix with ones on its diagonal and $\mathbf{D}_n$ is a diagonal matrix. Furthermore, if the vector variable $\mathbf{d}_n$ is defined as

$$\mathbf{d}_n = \mathbf{L}_n^{-1}(\mathbf{x}_n - \mathbf{m}_n) \tag{10.20}$$

then the covariance matrix for this vector is given by

$$\mathbf{L}_n^{-1}\mathbf{K}_n (\mathbf{L}_n^{-1})^T = \mathbf{D}_n \tag{10.21}$$

Recall that since $\mathbf{L}_n$ is a unit lower triangular matrix, $\mathbf{L}_n^{-1}$ has the same properties and thus Eq. 10.20 represents a *causal* transformation of the time series data. That is, the kth component of $\mathbf{d}_n$ depends only on samples $x(t_\ell)$ for $\ell \leqslant k$.

Since $\mathbf{D}_n$ is a diagonal matrix, the components of $\mathbf{d}_n$ are *uncorrelated*. Since $\mathbf{x}_n$ is Gaussian, the components of $\mathbf{d}_n$ are also *independent*. It will now be shown that these components are, in fact, the estimation errors defined by Eq. 10.16.

Observe that since $\mathbf{L}_n^{-1}$ is a unit lower triangular matrix, the determinant of the transformation in Eq. 10.20 is one. Therefore (see Eq. 4.11 and 4.66), the density function for $\mathbf{x}_n$ can be expressed as

$$p_{\mathbf{x}_n}(\mathbf{x}_n) = p_{\mathbf{d}_n}(\mathbf{d}_n) = \frac{1}{(2\pi)^{n/2}|\mathbf{D}_n|^{1/2}} \exp\left(-\frac{1}{2}\mathbf{d}_n^T\mathbf{D}_n^{-1}\mathbf{d}_n\right) \tag{10.22}$$

and the quadratic classifier for class 1 and class 2 takes the form

$$\mathbf{d}_n^{(1)T}\,\mathbf{D}_n^{(1)-1}\,\mathbf{d}_n^{(1)} - \mathbf{d}_n^{(2)T}\,\mathbf{D}_n^{(2)-1}\,\mathbf{d}_n^{(2)} + \ln\frac{|\mathbf{D}_n^{(1)}|}{|\mathbf{D}_n^{(2)}|} \underset{\omega_2}{\overset{\omega_1}{\gtrless}} T \tag{10.23}$$

Since the $\mathbf{D}_n^{(i)}$ are diagonal matrices, Eq. 10.23 can be expressed in the form of Eq. 10.18. Because both equations represent the same classifier, the error terms $\varepsilon_k^{(i)}$ must be the components of $\mathbf{d}_n^{(i)}$ and the error variances $e_k^{(i)}$ must be the diagonal elements of $\mathbf{D}_n^{(i)}$. Also, since the error terms are defined by both Eq. 10.16 and 10.20, the inverse transformation $\mathbf{L}_n^{-1}$ must have the form

$$\mathbf{L}_n^{(i)-1} = \begin{bmatrix} 1 & & & \\ -g_1^{(i)} & 1 & & 0 \\ -\mathbf{g}_2^{(i)T} & \rightarrow & 1 & \\ \vdots & & & \\ \leftarrow & -\mathbf{g}_n^{(i)T} & \rightarrow & 1 \end{bmatrix} \tag{10.24}$$

The foregoing derivation shows that the recursive form of the classifier can be derived from a purely algebraic approach and that the estimation errors are, in fact, independent random variables. A time series that consists of independent or uncorrelated random variables is referred to as "white noise," and a transformation that produces such a time series is called a whitening transformation. This derivation also shows the explicit relation between the causal whitening transformation and the parameters of the quadratic classifier.

10.5 RELATIONS TO LINEAR PREDICTION

The operations arising in the recursive form of the quadratic classifier have so far been interpreted in terms of estimation of a Gaussian time series. These operations have also been studied quite independently of any classification problems under the general topic of linear prediction [3]. Linear prediction has found application in speech and image modeling and analysis, in spectral analysis, in coding, and in many other areas [4]. For purposes of this chapter, it provides further interpretation of the classifier and gives some insight to its operation when the classifier is applied to non-Gaussian data.

Suppose that it is desired to estimate the value of the sample x_{k+1} from the set of previous samples $\mathbf{x}_k$ as before. However, in this case the samples are *not* assumed to be jointly Gaussian, but the estimation procedure must be *linear* and must minimize the mean-square error. That is, it is desired to find a weighting vector $\mathbf{b}$ such that

$$\tilde{x}_{k+1} = \mathbf{b}^T\mathbf{x}_k \tag{10.25}$$

and the quantity

$$\mathscr{E} = E[(x_{k+1} - \tilde{x}_{k+1})^2] \tag{10.26}$$

is minimized. This problem is known as the *linear prediction* problem; a theorem, which will be stated here without proof, provides the key to its solution.

THEOREM

> Let $\mathbf{x}_k$ be a set of observations taken from a zero-mean time series and let $\tilde{x}_{k+1} = \mathbf{b}^T\mathbf{x}_k$ be a linear prediction of x_{k+1}. Also, let $\varepsilon_{k+1} = x_{k+1} - \tilde{x}_{k+1}$ be the prediction error. Then $\mathbf{b}$ minimizes the mean-square error $\mathscr{E}$ if $\mathbf{b}$ is chosen such that $E[\varepsilon_{k+1}\mathbf{x}_k] = \mathbf{0}$; that is, if the error is *orthogonal* to the previous observations. Furthermore, the minimum mean-square error is given by $\mathscr{E}_{\min} = E[\varepsilon_{k+1}x_{k+1}]$.[1]

A proof of this theorem, known as the *orthogonality theorem,* is outlined in Problem 10.4. Here we consider only its implications.

The theorem requires that

$$\begin{aligned} E[\varepsilon_{k+1}\mathbf{x}_k] &= E[\mathbf{x}_k\varepsilon_{k+1}] = E[\mathbf{x}_k(x_{k+1} - \mathbf{b}^T\mathbf{x}_k)] \\ &= E[\mathbf{x}_k x_{k+1}] - E[\mathbf{x}_k\mathbf{x}_k^T]\mathbf{b} \\ &= \mathbf{r}_{k+1} - \mathbf{K}_k\mathbf{b} = \mathbf{0} \end{aligned} \tag{10.27}$$

and thus that

$$\mathbf{K}_k\mathbf{b} = \mathbf{r}_{k+1} \tag{10.28}$$

[1]Note that stating that two random variables are orthogonal in this context is equivalent to stating that they are *uncorrelated*. The use of the word *orthogonal* comes from a particular vector space interpretation of the problem and allows a geometric interpretation of the results (see Ref. 4).

The scalar equations represented by Eq. 10.28 are known as the *Normal equations*. The solution $\mathbf{b}$ is given by

$$\mathbf{b} = \mathbf{K}_k^{-1}\,\mathbf{r}_{k+1} = \mathbf{g}_{k+1} \tag{10.29}$$

where the last equality follows from Eq. 10.6a. Again, from the theorem, and Eq. 10.29, the minimum mean-square error is given by

$$\begin{aligned}\mathscr{E}_{\min} &= E[\varepsilon_{k+1}x_{k+1}] = E[(x_{k+1} - \mathbf{g}_{k+1}^T\mathbf{x}_k)x_{k+1}] \\ &= E[x_{k+1}^2] - \mathbf{g}_{k+1}^T\, E[\mathbf{x}_k x_{k+1}] \\ &= \sigma_{k+1}^2 - \mathbf{g}_{k+1}^T\mathbf{r}_{k+1} = \sigma_{k+1}^2 - \mathbf{r}_{k+1}^T\mathbf{K}_k^{-1}\mathbf{r}_{k+1} = e_{k+1}\end{aligned} \tag{10.30}$$

(see Eq. 10.6b). Thus the variables $\mathbf{g}_{k+1}$ and e_{k+1} introduced in Section 10.2 represent the optimal linear mean-square estimation vector and the estimation error variance *regardless* of the statistical distribution of the time series.

An important result can now be obtained about the performance of the quadratic classifier for non-Gaussian data. Assume that the criterion for classification is to minimize the probability of error and that the class prior probabilities $\Pr[\omega_1]$ and $\Pr[\omega_2]$ are equal. Then the threshold in the quadratic classifier is equal to zero and from Eq. 10.14 the decision rule is

$$h_n(\mathbf{x}_n) = \sum_{k=1}^{n} \Delta h_k(x_k|\mathbf{x}_{k+1}) \quad \underset{\omega_2}{\overset{\omega_1}{\lesseqgtr}} \quad 0 \tag{10.31}$$

Now, regardless of the statistical distribution of $\mathbf{x}_n$ it is possible to show that $E[\Delta h_k|\omega_1] < 0$ and $E[\Delta h_k|\omega_2] > 0$. Thus it also follows that

$$E[h_n(\mathbf{x}_n)|\omega_1] < 0 \tag{10.32a}$$

$$E[h_n(\mathbf{x}_n)|\omega_2] > 0 \tag{10.32b}$$

This says that *regardless of the distribution, application of Eq. 10.31 will on the average result in the correct decision.* The proof of this important result follows directly from the ideas of linear prediction.

Suppose, at first, that the observations are from class 1. Then it follows from Eq. 10.17 that

$$E[\Delta h_k|\omega_1] = \frac{1}{e_k^{(1)}}\,E[(\varepsilon_k^{(1)})^2|\omega_1] - \frac{1}{e_k^{(2)}}\,E[(\varepsilon_k^{(2)})^2|\omega_1] + \ln\frac{e_k^{(1)}}{e_k^{(2)}} \tag{10.33}$$

Since the observations are from class 1, one has by definition

$$E[(\varepsilon_k^{(1)})^2|\omega_1] = e_k^{(1)} \tag{10.34}$$

In addition, since $\varepsilon_k^{(2)}$ is the error resulting from predicting the class 1 data with a predictor that is not optimal for class 1, it follows that

$$E[(\varepsilon_k^{(2)})^2|\omega_1] > e_k^{(1)} \tag{10.35}$$

Substituting Eqs. 10.34 and 10.35 in Eq. 10.33 leads to

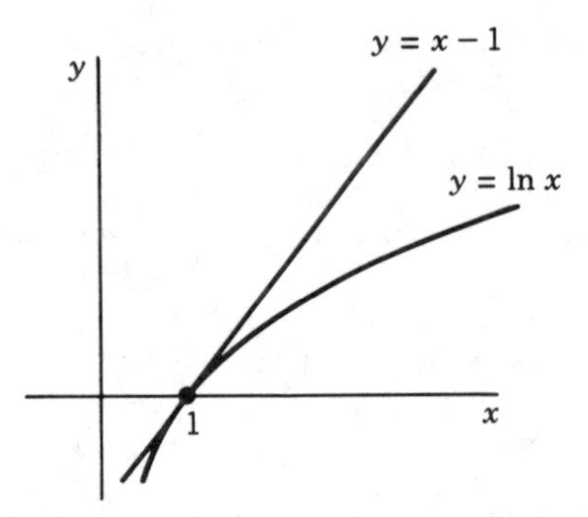

FIGURE 10.3 The graph of identity $\ln x \leq x - 1$.

$$E[\Delta h_k|\omega_1] < 1 - \frac{e_k^{(1)}}{e_k^{(2)}} + \ln \frac{e_k^{(1)}}{e_k^{(2)}} \tag{10.36}$$

However, since it is true that $\ln x \leq x - 1$ for any positive x (see Fig. 10.3), and the variances $e_k^{(i)}$ are always positive, the right-hand side of Eq. 10.36 is less than or equal to zero. Thus Eq. 10.32a follows. A completely symmetric argument establishes Eq. (10.32b).

10.6 APPLICATION TO STATIONARY TIME SERIES

Briefly stated, a time series is *stationary* if the joint density function for n samples is independent of the absolute time at which the samples are taken. This implies that the mean of a stationary time series is independent of time, and that the correlation between any two samples is a function only of their spacing and not of the actual time at which they occur. A time series that has only the latter two properties is said to be *wide-sense stationary*. The recursive quadratic classifier has a special advantage for (wide-sense) stationary time series because the parameters $\mathbf{g}_k$ and e_k of the classifier tend to converge to limiting values as the number of time samples increases. Thus very long lengths of time series data can be classified without explicitly inverting very large covariance matrices.

To better understand this property, it is helpful to describe the operations performed by the classifier as linear filtering operations. In the next subsection we describe the filtering operations that are performed in the classifier. Following that we discuss an efficient method for computation of the classifier parameters that derives from the stationary property of the time series and the filtering operations that are performed by the classifier.

10.6.1 Filtering of the Time Series

The process of linear prediction, represented by Eq. 10.25 can be described by what is known in signal processing as a discrete time *filtering* operation. In essence, the weighting coefficients represented by the components of $\mathbf{b}$ are lined up with

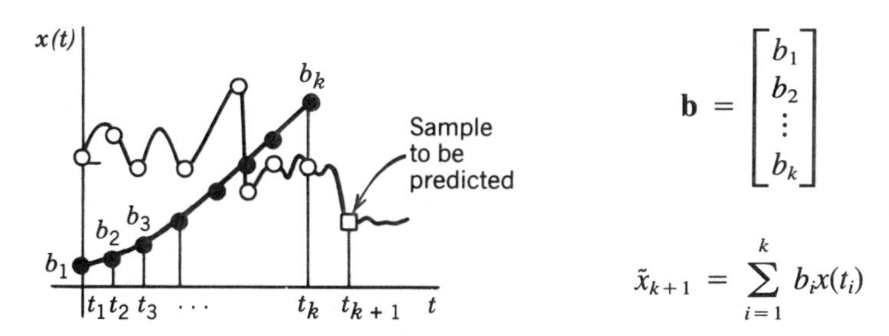

FIGURE 10.4 Linear predictive filtering of time series $\mathbf{x}(t)$.

the time series data and a sum of products operation is performed (see Fig. 10.4). Since the data are stationary it is reasonable to perform this same prediction operation anywhere in the time series using the same weighting coefficients. Thus the value of the sample at t_{k+2} could be predicted using the data from t_2 through t_{k+1}, and so on. When applied to the entire time series in this way, the operation is said to have filtered the time series.

In a signal processing context, one can think of applying the signal $x(t)$ to a box whose output is the signal $\tilde{x}(t)$. The box is called a filter. Filters are characterized by a data sequence known as their *impulse response,* which corresponds to the weighting coefficients reversed in time (see Fig. 10.5). This data sequence is called the impulse response because it is the result of applying the filter to a time series consisting of a single unit amplitude time sample or "impulse." Filters of the type described here are known as finite impulse response (FIR) filters because the impulse response is of finite duration.

The quadratic classifier can be thought of as implemented by a series of filters $\mathbf{g}_k^{(i)}$ whose impulse responses are of increasing length. However, when the time series data are stationary, the impulse responses of the filters in this series tend to converge to common values as depicted in Fig. 10.6(a) and the extended points in the impulse responses tend to approach zero. In addition, the prediction error variances tend to converge to a finite positive value as shown in Fig. 10.6(b). As

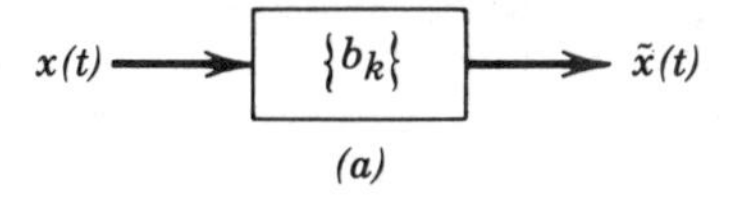

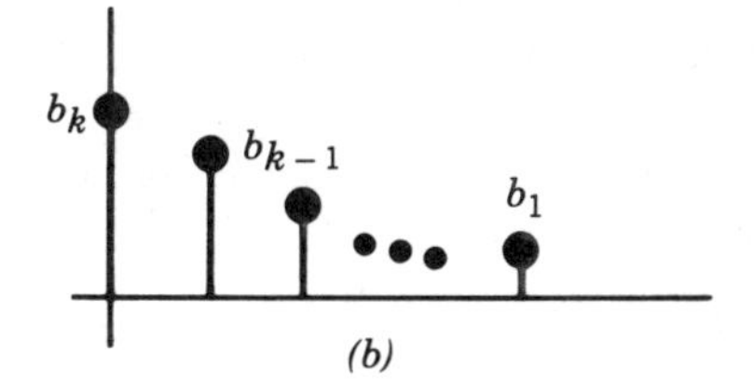

FIGURE 10.5 Linear predictive filter and its impulse response. (*a*) Filter representation. (*b*) Impulse response sequence.

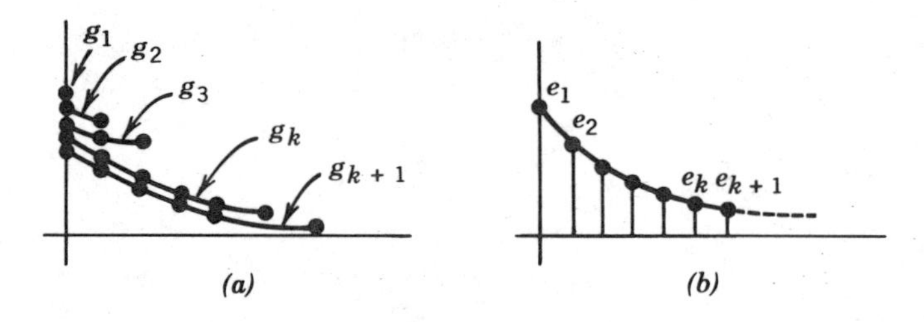

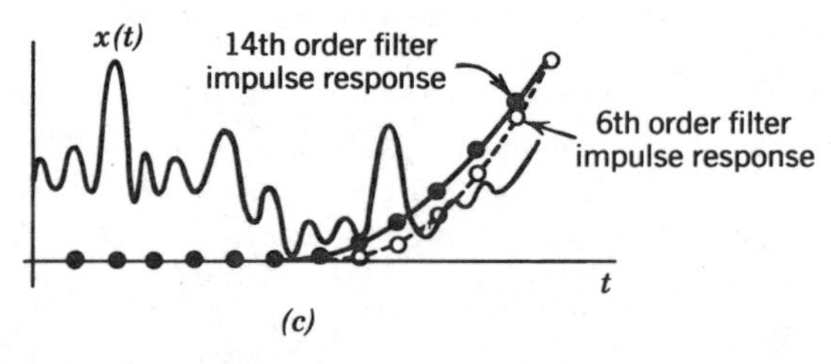

FIGURE 10.6 Comparison of various order classifier parameters for stationary time series. (*a*) Impulse responses. (*b*) Prediction error variance. (*c*) Comparison of typical high and low order prediction filters.

a result, the higher-order filter terms that would appear to be needed for classifying long time series (anywhere from say 20 to several hundred time points) can be replaced by lower-order terms (say of order 5 to 10) without any real degradation in the classifier performance (see Fig. 10.6c). The procedure is particularly useful in sequential classification of time series where the number of observations needed is not known a priori and the classification process may need to continue for an unspecified length of time.

The substantiation of the foregoing claims is related to the study of autoregressive processes and spectral analysis of time series and is beyond the scope of our treatment here. However, the topic can be pursued a bit further here by examining the special form of the Normal equations for stationary time series and developing a solution method known as the Levinson recursion [5]. The form of this recursion for the classifier parameters gives further evidence that the claims for convergence are correct.

10.6.2 Levinson Recursive Solution for the Classifier Parameters

Since the mean of a stationary time series is constant and the covariance between any two samples of a stationary time series is dependent only on the spacing between them, the covariance properties of the entire time series can be expressed as a function

$$\kappa(\ell) = E[(x_k - m_x)(x_{k-\ell} - m_x)] \tag{10.37}$$

where m_x is the constant mean ($m_x = E[x_k]$). Note that $\kappa(0)$ is equal to the variance of x_k. This function is called the *covariance function*. The covariance matrix for a set of $k + 1$ samples of a stationary time series thus has the form

$$\mathbf{K}_{k+1} = E[(\mathbf{x}_{k+1} - \mathbf{m}_{k+1})(\mathbf{x}_{k+1} - \mathbf{m}_{k+1})^T]$$

$$= \begin{bmatrix} \kappa(0) & \kappa(1) & \cdots & & \kappa(k) \\ \kappa(1) & \kappa(0) & & & \vdots \\ \vdots & & \ddots & \kappa(0) & \kappa(1) \\ \kappa(k) & \kappa(k-1) & & \kappa(1) & \kappa(0) \end{bmatrix} \tag{10.38}$$

and has the property that all elements along any diagonal are equal. A matrix having this property is known as a Toeplitz matrix. For the Toeplitz matrix of Eq. 10.38 the parameters $\mathbf{r}_{k+1}$ and σ_{k+1}^2 defined in Eq. 10.3c have the special form

$$\mathbf{r}_{k+1} = \begin{bmatrix} \kappa(k) \\ \vdots \\ \kappa(1) \end{bmatrix} \tag{10.39}$$

and

$$\sigma_{k+1}^2 = \kappa(0) \tag{10.40}$$

It will be necessary for the following discussion to define the *reversal* of a vector as another vector whose components are the components of the original vector in reverse order and denote the reversal by a bar over the vector. The reversal of the vector $\mathbf{r}_{k+1}$, is given by

$$\bar{\mathbf{r}}_{k+1} = \begin{bmatrix} \kappa(1) \\ \kappa(2) \\ \vdots \\ \kappa(k) \end{bmatrix} \tag{10.41}$$

from which it follows that

$$\bar{\mathbf{r}}_{k+1} = \begin{bmatrix} \bar{\mathbf{r}}_k \\ \text{------} \\ \kappa(k) \end{bmatrix} \tag{10.42}$$

In order to derive a simplified set of recursion relations for the classifier parameters, Eq. 10.6a will now be written in a form involving the reversals of $\mathbf{g}_{k+1}$ and $\mathbf{r}_{k+1}$. Equation 10.6a is first written in the form of the Normal equations

$$\mathbf{K}_k\mathbf{g}_{k+1} = \mathbf{r}_{k+1} \tag{10.43}$$

If both vectors in Eq. 10.43 are replaced by their reversals, then in order to maintain a true relation, the matrix $\mathbf{K}_k$ must be replaced by one obtained from itself by reflecting it first about the main diagonal and then about the reverse diagonal. However, because $\mathbf{K}_k$ is symmetric and Toeplitz, these two operations leave it unchanged. Therefore, it follows that

$$\mathbf{K}_k\,\bar{\mathbf{g}}_{k+1} = \bar{\mathbf{r}}_{k+1} \tag{10.44}$$

and thus

$$\bar{\mathbf{g}}_{k+1} = \mathbf{K}_k^{-1}\,\bar{r}_{k+1} \tag{10.45}$$

The desired simplified recursion now follows directly, because from Eqs. 10.45, 10.5, and 10.42 one can write

$$\begin{aligned}\bar{\mathbf{g}}_{k+1} &= \left[\left[\begin{array}{c|c}\mathbf{K}_{k-1}^{-1} & \mathbf{0}\\ \hline \mathbf{0}^T & 0\end{array}\right] + \frac{1}{e_k}\left[\begin{array}{c}-\mathbf{g}_k\\ \hline 1\end{array}\right]\left[\begin{array}{c|c}-\mathbf{g}_k^T & 1\end{array}\right]\right]\left[\begin{array}{c}\bar{\mathbf{r}}_k\\ \hline \kappa(k)\end{array}\right]\\ &= \left[\begin{array}{c|c}\mathbf{K}_{k-1}^{-1} & \mathbf{0}\\ \hline \mathbf{0}^T & 0\end{array}\right]\left[\begin{array}{c}\bar{\mathbf{r}}_k\\ \hline \kappa(k)\end{array}\right] + \left[\begin{array}{c}-\mathbf{g}_k\\ \hline 1\end{array}\right]\frac{[\kappa(k) - \mathbf{g}_k^T\,\bar{\mathbf{r}}_k]}{e_k}\end{aligned} \tag{10.46}$$

By employing Eq. 10.45 once again and taking the reversal of the result, we obtain

$$\mathbf{g}_{k+1} = \left[\begin{array}{c}0\\ \hline \mathbf{g}_k\end{array}\right] + \left[\begin{array}{c}1\\ \hline -\bar{\mathbf{g}}_k\end{array}\right]\rho_k \tag{10.47}$$

where

$$\rho_k = [\kappa(k) - \mathbf{g}_k^T\,\bar{\mathbf{r}}_k]/e_k \tag{10.48}$$

and where from Eqs. 10.6a, 10.6b, and 10.40

$$e_k = \kappa(0) - \mathbf{g}_k^T\,\mathbf{r}_k \tag{10.49}$$

Equations 10.47 through 10.49 comprise the Levinson recursion algorithm. The algorithm is usually expressed as a recursion on the impulse response of the filters. This can be done by defining a vector $\mathbf{a}_k$ whose components are the terms in the impulse response of the kth order filter. This vector is simply the reversal of the vector $\mathbf{g}_k$. The result of making this substitution in Eqs. 10.47 through 10.49 and rearranging terms is then

$$e_k = \kappa(0) - \mathbf{a}_k^T\,\bar{\mathbf{r}}_k \tag{10.50a}$$

$$\rho_k = [\kappa(k) - \mathbf{a}_k^T\mathbf{r}_k]/e_k \tag{10.50b}$$

$$\mathbf{a}_{k+1} = \left[\begin{array}{c}\mathbf{a}_k\\ \hline 0\end{array}\right] + \rho_k\left[\begin{array}{c}-\bar{\mathbf{a}}_k\\ \hline 1\end{array}\right] \tag{10.50c}$$

where the equations have been written in the order that they are used in the recursion. The variable ρ_k is called the "reflection coefficient" in linear prediction theory and the "partial correlation coefficient" in statistics. An engineering interpretation of the reflection coefficient is given in [Refs. 3 and 4]. By substituting Eq. 10.4 in Eq. 10.6b and using Eq. 10.40, one can show that

$$e_{k+1} = e_k(1 - \rho_k^2) \tag{10.51}$$

which can be used as an alternative to Eq. 10.49 or Eq. 10.50a in the recursion. Since the variance e_{k+1} is non-negative, the reflection coefficient ρ_k must always have a magnitude less than or equal to one. Thus the error variance is seen to decrease with k.

10.7 CASE STUDY—SEQUENTIAL CLASSIFIER

One of the applications for which the recursive form of the quadratic classifier is most useful is in sequential classification (see Section 3.3). For time series the recursive classifier can be updated as the observations $x(t_1)$ evolve in time. With each new observation the classifier output is compared to an upper and a lower threshold to determine if the observed time series will be classified as class 1 or class 2. If the classifier output falls between the two thresholds, another observation is taken and the process continues. The recursive form of the classifier is ideally suited to this sequential type of decision process.

Table 10.1 lists the results of an experiment to classify 500 time series from each of two classes using a sequential decision rule. These data were radar signatures on some objects of interest and thus represent a realistic application. Although each signature consisted of 16 time samples, the sequential classifier would use as few samples as possible to classify it. If after 16 samples, the classifier output had not crossed the upper or lower threshold, the signature was classified according to a single intermediate threshold. The classifier used reduced length filters that predicted the time series based on only the last 3 time samples. These filters were found to perform comparably to filters using up to the full 15 samples to predict the time series.

Table 10.1 shows that the signatures were classified with error rates of 6 percent for class 1 and 20 percent for class 2 using an average of about 9 time samples for class 1 and 8 samples for class 2. The classification performance was virtually identical to that for a fixed (nonsequential) quadratic classifier that achieved error rates of 5.8 and 20.4 percent and required 16 time samples to classify the signatures. Thus the recursive sequential classifier would have a significant advantage in a real-time application. In addition, storage and computational requirements for the recursive sequential classifier are about $\frac{1}{16}$ of those for the fixed quadratic classifier.

10.8 RELATED METHODS AND EXTENSIONS

The recursive classifier discussed in this chapter employs linear prediction to perform the classification of the input time series. Linear prediction is a special

TABLE 10.1
Classification Results for Sequential Classifier

Number of Time Samples	Total Number of Waveforms Classified		Error Rate (percent)		Average Number of Time Samples Used	
	Class 1	Class 2	Class 1	Class 2	Class 1	Class 1
1	1	76	100.0	0.0	1.0	1.0
2	11	115	9.1	0.0	1.9	1.3
3	24	149	12.5	0.0	2.5	1.7
4	63	179	6.3	0.6	3.4	2.1
5	106	214	5.7	0.5	4.1	2.6
6	166	243	5.4	0.4	4.8	3.0
7	218	263	4.1	0.8	5.3	3.3
8	257	289	3.5	1.4	5.7	3.7
9	294	305	3.4	2.3	6.1	4.0
10	329	318	3.0	2.8	6.5	4.2
11	369	327	2.7	4.0	7.0	4.4
12	401	336	2.7	4.2	7.4	4.6
13	418	349	3.1	5.2	7.6	4.9
14	431	353	3.2	5.1	7.8	5.0
15	448	363	3.3	5.5	8.1	5.3
16	454	368	3.3	5.7	8.2	5.5
16[a]	500	500	6.0	20.0	8.9	8.2

[a]Remaining waveforms classified according to a single default threshold.

form of mean-square estimation and linear mean-square estimation and classification are closely related for Gaussian random processes. Linear mean-square estimation when applied to time series is known as Wiener filtering, and the quintessential recursive form of the Wiener filter is the Kalman filter [6]. A procedure for the classification of Gaussian time series similar to that described here can be developed using the Kalman filter [7]. The procedure is considerably more complex, but is particularly suitable if one has a physical description for the observations.

Estimation also plays a central role in detection and classification for both continuous and discrete time Gaussian random signals. The extension of the correlation receiver discussed in Chapter 6 to the case of a *random* signal in noise is known as an estimator-correlation detector [8, 9]. This structure, which is used primarily in communications problems, is closely related to the recursive form of classifier discussed here.

Finally, the recursive methods of this chapter have been used as the basis for classification of a set of compound nonstationary random processes consisting of certain random signals in noise [10]. The signal here has a known form $s(\cdot)$ which is modulated by an imbedded random time-varying delay. The observations have the form

$$x(t_k) = s(t_k + \tau(t_k)) + w(t_k) \qquad k = 1, 2, \ldots$$

where both $\tau(t_k)$ (the "delay") and $w(t_k)$ (the "noise") are random sequences in time. Again estimation plays a key role in the classifier, which involves a special "loop" to track the delay. The structure is analogous to the phase-locked loop prevalent in communications problems.

10.9 SUMMARY

This chapter considers the classification of time series data and develops a recursive form of the quadratic classifier that has some major advantages. It is shown that the classifier for $k + 1$ time samples is obtained from the classifier for k samples by adding terms involving the prediction errors of the new data. Specifically, the waveform to be classified is predicted with a filter matched to each class of data. The classifier can be interpreted as choosing the class for which the sum of the normalized prediction errors is least.

The prediction filters are shown to perform a causal whitening of the data to which they are matched. It is also shown that the filter provides the best linear mean-square estimate of the time series data even if the data are not Gaussian, and that the classifier can be expected to make the correct decision on the average.

For stationary time series, it is argued that the waveforms can be adequately predicted with filters having a short impulse response and constant coefficients. Thus considerable computational savings can result. Moreover, waveforms containing hundreds of time samples can be classified by the recursive classifier. This would not be feasible with the standard form of the quadratic classifier.

A case study is described involving the classification of several hundred radar signatures. The example illustrates the advantages of a sequential decision algorithm when combined with a recursive quadratic classifier.

Finally, some related methods of classification are cited that highlight the role of estimation in the classification of certain types of random time series.

REFERENCES

1. C. W. Therrien. "A Sequential Approach to Target Discrimination." *IEEE Trans. Aerospace and Electronic Systems*. Vol. AES-14, No. 3, May 1978.
2. T. Kailath. "The Innovations Approach to Detection and Estimation Theory." *Proc. IEEE*, Vol. 58, pp. 680–695 (1970).
3. J. Makhoul. "Linear Prediction: A Tutorial Review." *Proc. IEEE*, Vol. 63, pp. 561–580 (1975).
4. S. J. Orfanidis. *Optimal Signal Processing*, 2nd ed. New York: Macmillan Publishing Company, 1988.
5. N. Levinson. "The Wiener RMS (Root Means Square) Error Criterion in Filter Design and Prediction." *J. Math Physics*, Vol. 25, No. 4, pp. 261–278 (1947). Also Appendix

B in N. Wiener, *Extrapolation: Interpolation and Smoothing of Stationary Time Series,* New York: Technology Press and John Wiley & Sons, Inc., 1957.

6. R. E. Kalman, and R. S. Bucy. "New Results in Linear Filtering and Prediction Theory." *Trans. ASME* Ser. D, *J. Basic Engineering,* Vol. 83, pp. 95–107 (March 1961).
7. A. E. Bryson, and Y. Ho. *Applied Optimal Control*. Waltham, MA: Ginn, 1969, Chapter 12.
8. H. L. Van Trees. *Detection, Estimation, and Modulation Theory,* Part III. New York: John Wiley and Sons, Inc., 1971.
9. S. C. Schwartz. "The Estimator-Correlator for Discrete Time Problems." *IEEE Trans. Inform. Theory,* Vol. II–23, No. 1, pp. 93–100 (January 1977).
10. C. W. Therrien. "Discrimination of a Set of Delay-Modulated Signals with Application to Radar Target Identification." Proc. 16th Asilomar Conference on Circuits, Systems, and Computers, Pacific Grove, CA (November 1982).

PROBLEMS

10.1 (a) The four waveforms shown are from the same class. Let the observation vector be defined as in Eq. 10.1 and compute the mean vector and covariance matrix for the class.

(b) If the waveforms are to be modeled as a stationary time series, then the mean vector should consist of constant components and the covariance matrix should have the form of Eq. 10.38. One way to insure the constant mean is to average the time samples in each waveform and then average the results for the four

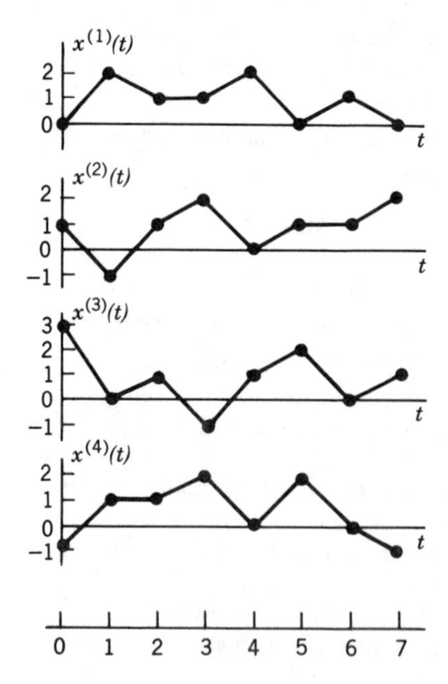

Waveforms For Problem 10.1.

waveforms. A way to compute the covariance is to compute the covariance function (10.37) for each waveform by summing over products of time samples and then averaging the four functions. Do these things and show that the results are equivalent to averaging the components of the mean vector computed in part (a) and averaging the diagonal elements of the covariance matrix computed in part (a).

10.2 One way to compute the inverse of a matrix is by the Gauss–Jordan reduction method. Simple linear operations are applied to the given matrix to reduce it to the identity. At the same time these operations are performed on a matrix that is originally the identity matrix. The result is the matrix inverse. In the following table the operations on the partitioned covariance matrix are shown as steps I through V.

Table 10.2 (Problem 10.2)

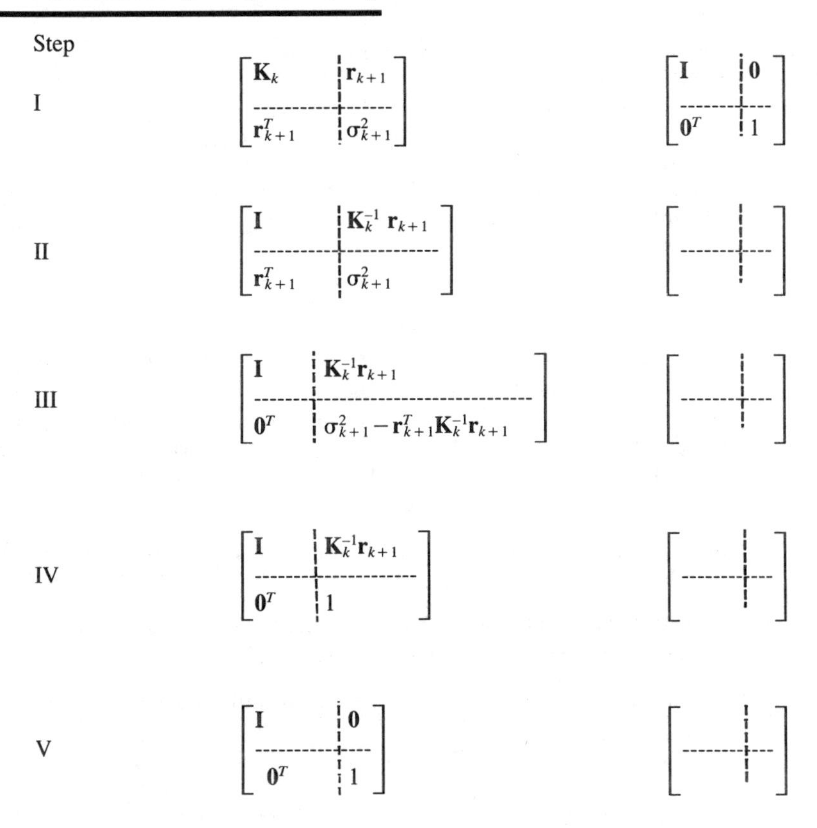

Step		
I	$\begin{bmatrix} \mathbf{K}_k & \mathbf{r}_{k+1} \\ \mathbf{r}_{k+1}^T & \sigma_{k+1}^2 \end{bmatrix}$	$\begin{bmatrix} \mathbf{I} & \mathbf{0} \\ \mathbf{0}^T & 1 \end{bmatrix}$
II	$\begin{bmatrix} \mathbf{I} & \mathbf{K}_k^{-1}\,\mathbf{r}_{k+1} \\ \mathbf{r}_{k+1}^T & \sigma_{k+1}^2 \end{bmatrix}$	$\begin{bmatrix} & \\ & \end{bmatrix}$
III	$\begin{bmatrix} \mathbf{I} & \mathbf{K}_k^{-1}\mathbf{r}_{k+1} \\ \mathbf{0}^T & \sigma_{k+1}^2 - \mathbf{r}_{k+1}^T\mathbf{K}_k^{-1}\mathbf{r}_{k+1} \end{bmatrix}$	$\begin{bmatrix} & \\ & \end{bmatrix}$
IV	$\begin{bmatrix} \mathbf{I} & \mathbf{K}_k^{-1}\mathbf{r}_{k+1} \\ \mathbf{0}^T & 1 \end{bmatrix}$	$\begin{bmatrix} & \\ & \end{bmatrix}$
V	$\begin{bmatrix} \mathbf{I} & \mathbf{0} \\ \mathbf{0}^T & 1 \end{bmatrix}$	$\begin{bmatrix} & \\ & \end{bmatrix}$

Complete the same operations on the identity matrix to show that the result is

$$\mathbf{K}_{k+1}^{-1} = \begin{bmatrix} \mathbf{K}_k^{-1} + \mathbf{g}_{k+1}e_{k+1}^{-1}\mathbf{g}_{k+1}^T & -\mathbf{g}_{k+1}e_{k+1}^{-1} \\ -e_{k+1}^{-1}\mathbf{g}_{k+1}^T & e_{k+1}^{-1} \end{bmatrix}$$

where $\mathbf{g}_{k+1}$ and e_{k+1} are defined by Eqs. 10.6. Use this to show that the matrix inverse has the product and sum forms given by Eqs. 10.4 and 10.5.

10.3 By computing the product with Eq. 10.3c and showing that the result is the identity matrix, verify that each of Eqs. 10.4 and 10.5 is a valid expression for the inverse covariance matrix.

10.4 Prove the orthogonality theorem by the following steps:

(1) Assume ε_n is orthogonal to $\mathbf{x}_{n+1}$. Show that if $\mathbf{A}$ is any linear transformation (matrix), and $\mathbf{y} = \mathbf{A}\mathbf{x}_{n-1}$, then ε_n is also orthogonal to $\mathbf{y}$ ($E[\varepsilon_n \mathbf{y}] = \mathbf{0}$).

(2) Now let $\mathbf{c}$ be any prediction weighting vector and let $\mathbf{b}$ be the one for which $E[\varepsilon_n \mathbf{x}_{n-1}] = \mathbf{0}$. Show that we can write the prediction error when $\mathbf{c}$ is used, as:

$$\varepsilon_n' = \varepsilon_n + (\mathbf{b} - \mathbf{c})^T \mathbf{x}_{n-1}$$

where ε_n is the error that results when $\mathbf{b}$ is used.

(3) Show now that

$$E[(\varepsilon_n')^2] = E[\varepsilon_n^2] + E[((\mathbf{b} - \mathbf{c})^T \mathbf{x}_{n-1})^2]$$

and thus it is clearly minimized for $\mathbf{c} = \mathbf{b}$. (*Hint:* Use the result of step 1).

(4) By writing one of the factors in ε_n^2 as $x_n - \mathbf{b}^T \mathbf{x}_{n-1}$, and using the result of step (1), show that

$$\mathscr{E}_{\min} = E[\varepsilon_n^2] = E[\varepsilon_n x_n]$$

10.5 (a) Let the matrix $\mathbf{A}$ in Problem 4.10 correspond to the covariance matrix for a time series. Partition this matrix appropriately and by direct solution of the Normal equations (10.43) find the parameters $\mathbf{g}_2$ and $\mathbf{g}_3$. Check that the quantities $(1, \mathbf{g}_i^T)$ do indeed comprise the rows of the lower triangular matrix $\mathbf{L}_3^{-1}$ found in Problem 4.10. Use Eq. 10.6b to solve for e_2 and e_3 and check that these are elements of the diagonal matrix $\mathbf{D}_3$.

(b) Solve for $\mathbf{g}_2$, e_2 and $\mathbf{g}_3$, e_3 *recursively* using Eq. 10.4 or 10.5 and 10.6. Start with $\mathbf{K}_1 = \sigma_1^2$.

(c) Show that the quantities $\mathbf{g}_i$, e_i that you computed in parts (a) and (b) satisfy the Levinson recursion relations (10.47) through (10.49) and (10.51).

10.6 A first-order autoregressive process is defined by the difference equation

$$x(t_k) = ax(t_{k-1}) + w(t_k)$$

where $w(t)$ is a zero mean white noise random process with covariance function

$$\kappa_w(\ell) = \begin{cases} \sigma_w^2 & \ell = 0 \\ 0 & \ell \neq 0 \end{cases}$$

It can be shown that the covariance function of the first-order autoregressive process is given by

$$\kappa_x(\ell) = \frac{\sigma_w^2}{1 - a^2} a^{|\ell|}$$

and thus the covariance matrix for any order k is Toeplitz and has the form

$$\mathbf{K}_k = \frac{\sigma_w^2}{1 - a^2} \begin{bmatrix} 1 & a & a^2 & \cdots & a^{k-1} \\ a & 1 & a & \cdots & a^{k-2} \\ \cdot & & & & \\ \cdot & & & & \\ \cdot & & & & \\ a^{k-1} & & \cdots & & 1 \end{bmatrix}$$

Show that the $\mathbf{g}$ and e parameters for such a time series are given by

$$\mathbf{g}_k = \begin{bmatrix} 0 \\ \vdots \\ 0 \\ a \end{bmatrix} \qquad e_k = \sigma_w^2$$

for any order $k > 1$.

10.7 **(a)** The following numbers are eight time points of a zero-mean white Gaussian noise process $w(t)$ with variance $\sigma_w^2 = 1$.

0.226 0.403 0.559 0.266 −0.724 −0.526

0.176 −0.169

Compute the first eight points of a first-order autoregressive process (see Problem 10.6) with parameter $a = 0.95$. Use the given values of the white noise and the initial condition $x(t_1) = w(t_1)$. Plot the result.

(b) Repeat part (a) for $a = -0.95$.

(c) Use the recursive form of the quadratic classifier to classify the waveform generated in part (a). Observe that according to the results of Problem 10.6 the classifier parameters are

$$m^{(1)} = m^{(2)} = 0; \qquad e_1^{(i)} = e_2^{(i)} = \sigma_w^2 = 1 \qquad i = 1, 2;$$

$$g_2^{(1)} = [0.95] \qquad g_2^{(2)} = [-0.95]$$

Plot $\varepsilon_k^{(1)}$, $\varepsilon_k^{(2)}$ and $h_k(\mathbf{x}_k)$ as a function of time.

CHAPTER 11

Context-Dependent Methods

Thus far the classification of objects was assumed to consist of the following steps. First observations were made on the object to be classified and (possibly) features were derived from the observations. Then the measurements (observations or features) were presented to a classifier that, based on the value of some discriminant function, would decide on a class for the object.

This chapter considers methods of classification for multiple objects when the classes of these objects are in some way interrelated. This type of problem occurs in image processing, for example, where the objects are image pixels and the classes of neighboring pixels are usually not independent. It also occurs in a number of other applications, where the classes of objects may be dependent on geometric proximity of the objects and/or prior knowledge of the numbers of objects in each class. In all of these cases the classifier should not make a decision about each object independently, that is, based only on the object's measurements. Rather, the classifier should form a decision that somehow takes into account decisions made about the classes of other related objects. This chapter deals with methods that permit this more general type of classification.

11.1 RELAXATION LABELING

11.1.1 Basic Method

A set of iterative classification methods has been described by Rosenfeld et al. [1, 2]. These methods are known as relaxation methods because of their resemblance to a set of iterative numerical techniques for solving simultaneous nonlinear equations.

Suppose that there exists a set of objects $A_1, A_2, \ldots, A_N$ each of which can belong to one of the classes $\omega_1, \omega_2, \ldots, \omega_{N_c}$. On the basis of some initial measurements, a set of discriminant functions is computed for each object that can be used to classify the object. For purposes of the following discussion, it is useful to think of the discriminant functions as producing a set of decision variables or "probabilities" $P_i(k)$ that object A_k belongs to class ω_i. These decision variables need not represent posterior probabilities in the usual sense of Chapter 3. However, their values are assumed to lie between 0 and 1 and for a fixed k the sum of the $P_i(k)$, $i = 1, 2, \ldots, N_c$ is equal to 1.[1]

The probabilities can be made to evolve in an iterative manner as follows. Assume that there exists a nonnegative function $c_{ij}(k, \ell)$ whose value is large when the hypothesis "A_k belongs to ω_i" is compatible with the hypothesis "A_ℓ belongs to ω_j" and small otherwise. Such a function will be referred to as a "compatibility function" and does not need to be symmetric [i.e., $c_{ij}(k, \ell) \neq c_{ji}(\ell, k)$, in general]. Assume further that a set of probabilities $P_i^{(r)}(k)$ has been computed at the rth iteration. Then for each object A_ℓ that is related to A_k one can define a credibility factor due to object A_ℓ as

$$\lambda_i^{(r)}(k; \ell) = \sum_{j=1}^{N_c} c_{ij}(k, \ell) P_j^{(r)}(\ell) \tag{11.1}$$

which will be used to update the probability $P_i^{(r)}(k)$. Note that $\lambda_i^{(r)}(k; \ell)$ will be large if the compatibilities $c_{ij}(k, \ell)$ are large and the probabilities $P_j^{(r)}(\ell)$ are high. Otherwise, $\lambda_i^{(r)}(k; \ell)$ will be small.

One way to iteratively update the probabilities is to multiply $P_i^{(r)}(k)$ by the factor

$$\frac{\lambda_i^{(r)}(k; \ell)}{\sum_{j=1}^{N_c} \lambda_j^{(r)}(k; \ell)\, P_j^{(r)}(k)} \tag{11.2}$$

where the denominator insures that the new values of $P_i(k)$ for $i = 1, 2, \ldots, N_c$ will sum to 1. If the results are averaged over all objects A_ℓ related to A_k, one obtains the relaxation formula

$$P_i^{(r+1)}(k) = \operatorname*{avg}_{\ell \neq k} \left[\frac{\lambda_i^{(r)}(k; \ell)\, P_i^{(r)}(k)}{\sum_{j=1}^{N_c} \lambda_j^{(r)}(k; \ell) P_j^{(r)}(k)} \right] \tag{11.3}$$

Each term in brackets resembles the computation of a posterior probability from a prior probability $P_i^{(r)}(k)$ (see Eq. 2.38), although the $\lambda_i^{(r)}(k; \ell)$ need not have the properties of a set of conditional probabilities. Furthermore, the updated estimate $P_i^{(r+1)}(k)$ is obtained by averaging all of the terms in brackets.

An alternative method of updating the probabilities is to multiply $P_i^{(r)}(k)$ by all factors $\lambda_i^{(r)}(k; \ell)$ and normalize. This results in the formula

[1]The explanations in this section are more intuitive if we refer to the $P_i(k)$ as probabilities. Later it will be appropriate to use the more general term "decision variable."

$$P_i^{(r+1)}(k) = \frac{P_i^{(r)}(k) \prod_{\ell=1}^{N} \lambda_i^{(r)}(k; \ell)}{\sum_{j=1}^{N_c} P_j^{(r)}(k) \prod_{\ell=1}^{N} \lambda_j^{(r)}(k; \ell)} \tag{11.4}$$

Both Eq. 11.3 and Eq. 11.4 have been found to work well in practical applications.

Relaxation is justified on intuitive grounds in that Eq. 11.3 or Eq. 11.4 adjusts the decision variables in a "reasonable" way. If an object A_ℓ has high probability of belonging to class ω_j and the compatibility $c_{ij}(k, \ell)$ is high, then the probability $P_i(k)$ that A_k belongs to ω_i will tend to increase. If, on the other hand, the probability $P_j(\ell)$ or the compatibility $c_{ij}(k, \ell)$ is small, then the probability $P_i(k)$ will tend to decrease. Note also that if $P_i^{(r+1)}(k)$ ever becomes equal to 0, further iterations will not make it nonzero. Similarly, if $P_i^{(r+1)}(k)$ is equal to 1, it will hold that value through any further iterations. Other than this, there is no guarantee that the iteration will converge, and true convergence may not even be necessary. In practical applications a few iterations may be all that is required to arrive at a reasonably consistent set of class decisions.

Thus far the form of the compatibility function has not been discussed. One way to define the compatibility function is to compute

$$c_{ij}(k, \ell) = \frac{\Pr[A_k \sim \omega_i \mid A_\ell \sim \omega_j]}{\Pr[A_k \sim \omega_i]} = \frac{\Pr[A_k \sim \omega_i, A_\ell \sim \omega_j]}{\Pr[A_k \sim \omega_i] \cdot \Pr[A_\ell \sim \omega_j]} \tag{11.5}$$

where the symbol $\sim$ should be read "belongs to" and the probabilities are estimated from training data. Although the function so defined has the stated properties of a compatibility function, it tends to weigh compatibility more heavily than incompatibility. A better choice involves the logarithm of Eq. 11.5. In particular, one can define

$$c'_{ij}(k, \ell) = 1 + \bar{c}_{ij}(k, \ell) \tag{11.6}$$

where $\bar{c}_{ij}(k, \ell)$ is a normalized or truncated version of $\log c_{ij}(k, \ell)$ so that $\bar{c}_{ij}$ has values in the interval $[-1, 1]$. Here positive values represent incompatibility, and values near zero represent indifference.

Another form of the relaxation method uses the functions $\bar{c}_{ij}$ with values in the interval $[-1, 1]$ directly. In this case, one can define

$$\lambda_i^{(r)}(k) = 1 + \operatorname*{avg}_{\ell \neq k} \left[\sum_{j=1}^{N_c} \bar{c}_{ij}(k, \ell) P_j^{(r)}(\ell) \right] \tag{11.7}$$

and use the relaxation formula

$$P_i^{(r+1)}(k) = \frac{\lambda_i^{(r)}(k)\, P_i^{(r)}(k)}{\sum_{j=1}^{N_c} \lambda_j^{(r)}(k) P_j^{(r)}(k)} \tag{11.8}$$

In this case, the iteration does indeed resemble Eq. 2.38 and since the $\lambda_i^{(r)}(k)$ are positive quantities, one is tempted to interpret a normalized set of $\lambda_i^{(r)}(k)$ as class conditional probabilities.[2] That is, if $P_i^{(r)}(k)$ represents the prior probability of the hypothesis $A_k \sim \omega_i$ and $P_i^{(r+1)}(k)$ represents the posterior probability of $A_k \sim \omega_i$ given the "external evidence," then $\lambda_i^{(r)}(k)$ would be the probability of the external evidence given that $A_k \sim \omega_i$. Interpretations such as this attempt to place relaxation on a more firm theoretical basis. There have been several other related interpretations of relaxation, one of which is discussed in Section 11.3.

11.1.2 Variations and Generalizations

The basic relaxation method described in the last section is sometimes called "probabilistic relaxation." This term is used because the decision variables have the general properties of probabilities. Other forms of relaxation are possible where the decision variables do not resemble probabilities. These other forms of relaxation are described briefly here.

Fuzzy Relaxation A first generalization of the relaxation method is based on fuzzy set theory [3] and is known as "fuzzy relaxation." In this case the decision variables $P_i(k)$ represent degrees of "fuzzy set membership." Although fuzzy set theory is an extensive discipline in itself, a detailed description of the theory is not necessary for the present discussion.

Fuzzy relaxation can be used, for example, when one is interested in deciding that "object A_k has property α_i," where α_i is a member of a set of properties α_1, $\alpha_2, \ldots, \alpha_{N_c}$. Although this problem includes the object classification problem, it is clearly more general. A given object could have *many* properties and thus correspond to several of the α_i or it could have *none* of the properties and so correspond to none of the α_i.

Another context for fuzzy relaxation is in pattern matching, where it is desired to match each object A_k with one or more of the possibly corresponding entities α_i. In both of these cases, a relaxation procedure is possible because correspondences such as $A_k \sim \alpha_i$ and $A_\ell \sim \alpha_j$ may be interrelated.

In fuzzy relaxation the decision variable $P_i(k)$ represents a degree of plausibility for the correspondence $A_k \sim \alpha_i$. The value of $P_i(k)$ is high if the correspondence $A_k \sim \alpha_i$ is likely and small otherwise. The compatibility functions $c_{ij}(k, \ell)$ are similar to those used in probabilistic relaxation and can be assumed to have positive values.

Since the $P_i(k)$ do not have to bear the constraints of probabilities, the update formula can be somewhat simpler. Consider a typical product

$$c_{ij}(k, \ell)P_j^{(r)}(\ell)$$

[2] If the $\lambda_i^{(r)}(k)$ are replaced $\lambda_i^{(r)}(k) \Big/ \sum_{j=1}^{N_c} \lambda_i^{(r)}(k)$, then the new variables have values in the interval [0, 1] and sum to 1. The iteration of Eq. 11.8 is, of course, not changed by this normalization.

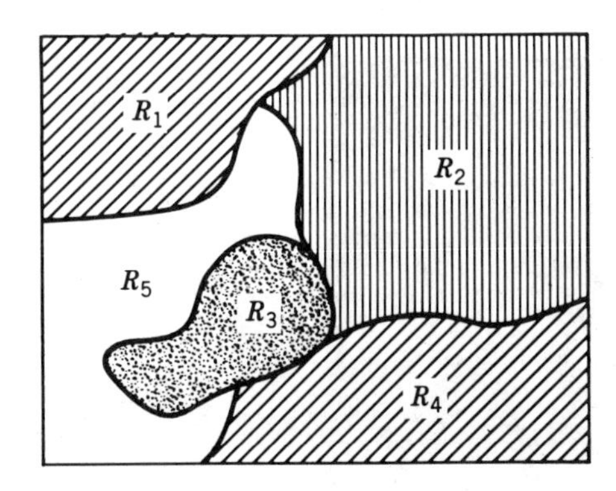

FIGURE 11.1 Regions of an image to be found by segmentation.

used in the update formula. Because of the one-to-many correspondence of the A_k and the α_i, a small value for this product does not necessarily imply that the correspondence $A_k \sim \alpha_i$ is unlikely. However, a large value for the product gives strong support to the premise $A_k \sim \alpha_i$. Therefore, an update method based on the maximum (over j) of the product terms rather than the average seems appropriate. Rosenfeld et al. suggest a relaxation formula of the form

$$P_i^{(r+1)}(k) = \frac{1}{N} \sum_{\ell=1}^{N} \max_j c_{ij}(k, \ell) P_j^{(r)}(\ell) \tag{11.9}$$

where the sum yields the average contribution for all objects considered. Other formulas are also possible.

Discrete Relaxation Discrete relaxation is in some sense the simplest form of relaxation, since it is concerned with only if the premises $A_k \sim \alpha_i$ are *possible*. The method may be used for *classification* of the A_k as in Section 11.1.1 or simply for matching the A_k to the α_i.

In discrete relaxation the values of the decision variables are either 1 or 0 corresponding to the possibility or impossibility of the premise $A_k \sim \alpha_i$. In a similar manner the compatibility functions have values of 1 or 0 corresponding to the compatibility or incompatibility of the premises. The update formula

$$P_i^{(r+1)}(k) = \min_\ell \{\max_j c_{ij}(k, \ell) P_j^{(r)}(\ell)\} \tag{11.10}$$

is similar to Eq. 11.9 except that the averaging operation is replaced by a minimum over the objects. The minimum operator ensures that the result will be 1 or 0 and will be equal to 1 only if all of the possible other premises are compatible with the given premise $A_k \sim \alpha_i$.

11.1.3 Image-Processing Example

A simple example of the application of the probabilistic relaxation will be given from the field of image processing. One is given an image consisting of multiple regions of data as shown in Fig. 11.1. Within each region, the image is homoge-

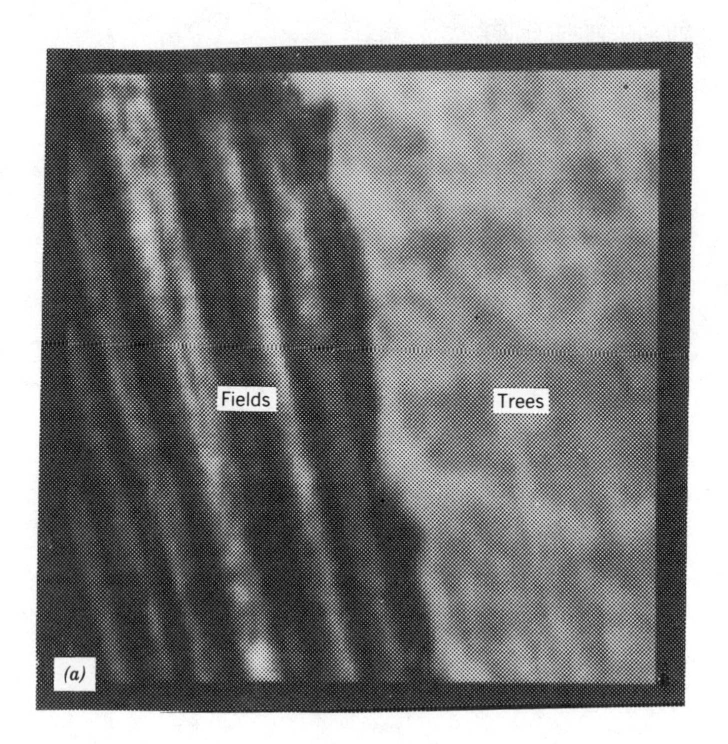

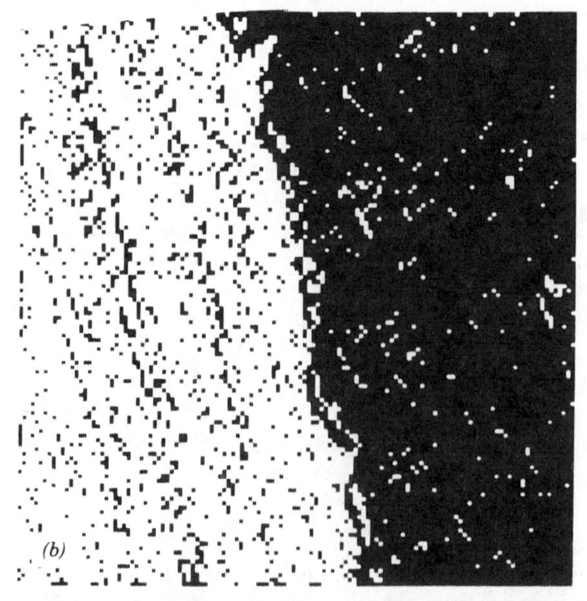

FIGURE 11.2 The segmentation of an image by relaxation. (*a*) An image of fields and trees. (*b*) Initial pixel classification. (*c*) Pixel classification using relaxation, $\beta = 0.75$. (*d*) Pixel classification using relaxation, $\beta = 0.90$.

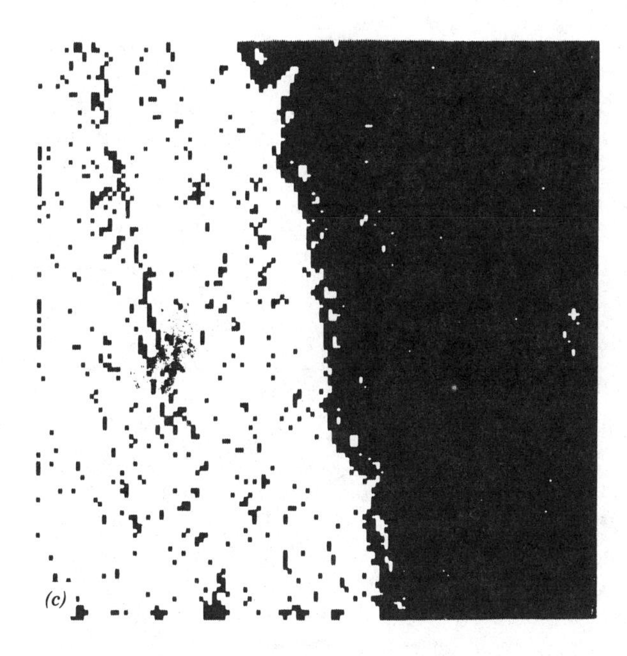

FIGURE 11.2 Continued

neous. For example, within a region, the image could be all one shade of gray or could contain a texture of a single type. The image is corrupted by noise or otherwise made random so that the ability to identify regions requires a statistical decision process. The procedure of identifying the regions is known as *image segmentation*.

The observation data consist of the image intensity or gray level measured at each of the discrete points or *pixels* comprising the image. A typical digital image consists of a very large number of pixels such as $256 \times 256 = 65{,}536$. Although the intensity values of pixels in the image are clearly related, it is impractical to develop a joint probability density function for this many variables. However, a combination of pattern recognition and relaxation provides a way to perform the image segmentation.

To be specific, assume that each region may contain only one of two *types* of data (e.g., two different textures representing "objects" and "background"). However, there may be any *number* of regions. In this case one can view the segmentation problem as one of assigning classes (ω_1 or ω_2) to the pixels corresponding to the type of region in which they are located. If the probability density function for the intensity of pixels is known for each class (this can be done by training the segmentation algorithm on data that is similar to that appearing in the images), then a class decision can first be made for each pixel as if the pixels were independent. Relaxation can then be used to achieve an improved classification that is more consistent between neighboring pixels.

It may occur to the reader that where texture is concerned, independent classification of neighboring pixels (even initially) seems foolish since texture is a local area phenomenon and cannot be judged by examining a single pixel. However, it *is* possible to make independent decisions after first processing the texture with a two-dimensional linear predictive filter [4] analogous to the filters described in Chapter 10. The processed image then consists of pixel data that is approximately independent and summarizes the statistical properties of the texture in a small area.

Figure 11.2(a) shows an aerial photograph of an area of fields and trees and the results of segmenting the image by this method. In this case, the relaxation was performed using Eq. 11.3. A neighborhood of related pixels was defined as in Fig. 11.3. For these pixels a simple compatibility function was defined according to Table 11.1 Hence A_k represents the pixel to be classified and A_ℓ represents one of

TABLE 11.1 Compatibility Function for Image Processing

$c_{11}(k,\ell)$	β
$c_{12}(k,\ell)$	$1-\beta$
$c_{21}(k,\ell)$	$1-\beta$
$c_{22}(k,\ell)$	β

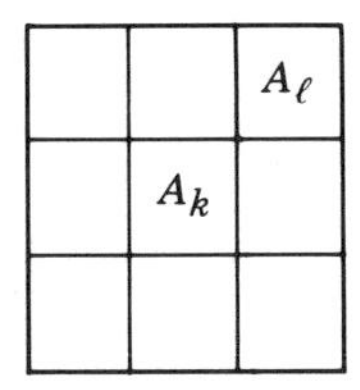

FIGURE 11.3 An image pixel and neighbors.

its eight neighbors (see Fig. 11.3). The parameter β is a number between zero and one. A high value of β (near 1) represents a strong dependence of the class of pixel A_k on the class of its neighbor A_ℓ. Figure 11.2(b) shows the initial classification of the pixels before relaxation. Figure 11.2(c) and (d) shows the results after relaxation using values of $\beta = 0.75$ and $\beta = 0.90$.

11.2 MARKOV METHODS

In probabilistic relaxation the dependence of the class of one object on that of another is brought to bear in a heuristic manner. Some types of object class dependence can be represented in a formal statistical way through Markov models.

11.2.1 Markov Chains

The simplest form of Markov model is a Markov chain and is appropriate where there exists a natural sequence or ordering of the objects to be classified. For example, consider a communication problem, where the observed signals represent binary digits 1 and 0. If the signals are corrupted by noise, then statistical methods must be used to decide if a given received signal is a 1 or a 0. Now if the joint probability of *sequences* of ones and zeros is known, then this information can be used to make better decisions about blocks of received data than if each digit were classified separately. In such a problem, it may be sufficient to assume that the conditional probability that a received signal is a 1 or a 0 depends on only the previous digit that was sent. In other words suppose that $A_1, A_2, \ldots, A_N$ represents the set of signals in the order in which they are observed, and ω_{s_k} is the class associated with signal A_k. (Assume that $s_k = 1$ represents binary 1 and $s_k = 2$ represents binary 0.) Then, for $1 < k \leq N$,

$$\begin{aligned}&\Pr[A_k \sim \omega_{s_k} \mid A_{k-1} \sim \omega_{s_{k-1}}, A_{k-2} \sim \omega_{s_{k-2}} \cdots A_1 \sim \omega_{s_1}] \\ &= \Pr[A_k \sim \omega_{s_k} \mid A_{k-1} \sim \omega_{s_{k-1}}]\end{aligned} \tag{11.11}$$

This dependence is known as Markov dependence among the objects and permits the joint probability for the objects to be written in a very simple way. In particular, Eq. 11.11 implies that

$$\Pr[A_N \sim \omega_{s_N}, A_{N-1} \sim \omega_{s_{N-1}}, \ldots, A_1 \sim \omega_{s_1}]$$

$$= \left[\prod_{k=2}^{N} \Pr[A_k \sim \omega_{s_k} \mid A_{k-1} \sim \omega_{s_{k-1}}, \ldots, A_1 \sim \omega_{s_1}]\right] \Pr[A_1 \sim \omega_{s_1}]$$

$$= \left[\prod_{k=2}^{N} \Pr[A_k \sim \omega_{s_k} \mid A_{k-1} \sim \omega_{s_{k-1}}]\right] \Pr[A_1 \sim \omega_{s_1}] \tag{11.12}$$

Note that since in this case there are only two possible classes ω_1 and ω_2 for each signal, each of the ω_{s_j} in Eq. 11.12 is equal to either ω_1 or ω_2. Note also that the only parameters needed to compute the probability of any sequence are the four conditional probabilities $P_{i|j} = \Pr[A_k \sim \omega_i \mid A_{k-1} \sim \omega_j]$ for $i = 1, 2$ and $j = 1, 2$. The quantities $P_{i|j}$ are known as Markov *transition probabilities* and can usually be estimated from training data.

In general, the elements A_k of a Markov chain can correspond to any number N_c of classes. In this case the parameters of the model are most conveniently represented as the $N_c \times N_c$ transition probability matrix $\mathbf{P}^T$ whose ijth element is $P_{i|j}$. Markov chains represent suitable models for a variety of problems in communications, queuing theory, and many other areas. Their behavior can be studied formally in terms of state models (discussed briefly in the next section) and properties of the transition matrix. A good introductory treatment of the topic can be found in Chapter 5 of Ref. 5.

Markov models can also be generalized so that the class probability for A_k depends on the classes of any finite number L of previous objects. The generalized dependence is called Lth order Markov. The principles of analysis are similar to those for the first-order Markov model, but the analysis is more complex. These more general higher-order Markov models will not be considered here.

Although the concept of a Markov chain seems fairly simple, the decision procedures for problems involving Markov chains require some rather complex algorithms. Some of these algorithms are given in Section 11.4.

11.2.2 Hidden Markov Models

Definition and State Estimation An interesting use of the Markov chain appears in what has come to be known as a hidden Markov model [6]. In a hidden Markov model a number of different stochastic processes are combined with a Markov chain to produce observations that are dependent on both the statistical properties of the various stochastic processes and the statistical properties of the Markov chain. Usually, one can think of the stochastic process as a set of observations evolving in time and indexed by an integer variable k.

The procedure is illustrated in Fig. 11.4. A random time series is observed that consists of several adjoining data segments of various lengths [see Fig. 11.4(a)]. Assume for simplicity that each segment can correspond to only one of two distinct types of random processes $x_1(k)$ and $x_2(k)$. The observed time series $y(k)$ can be

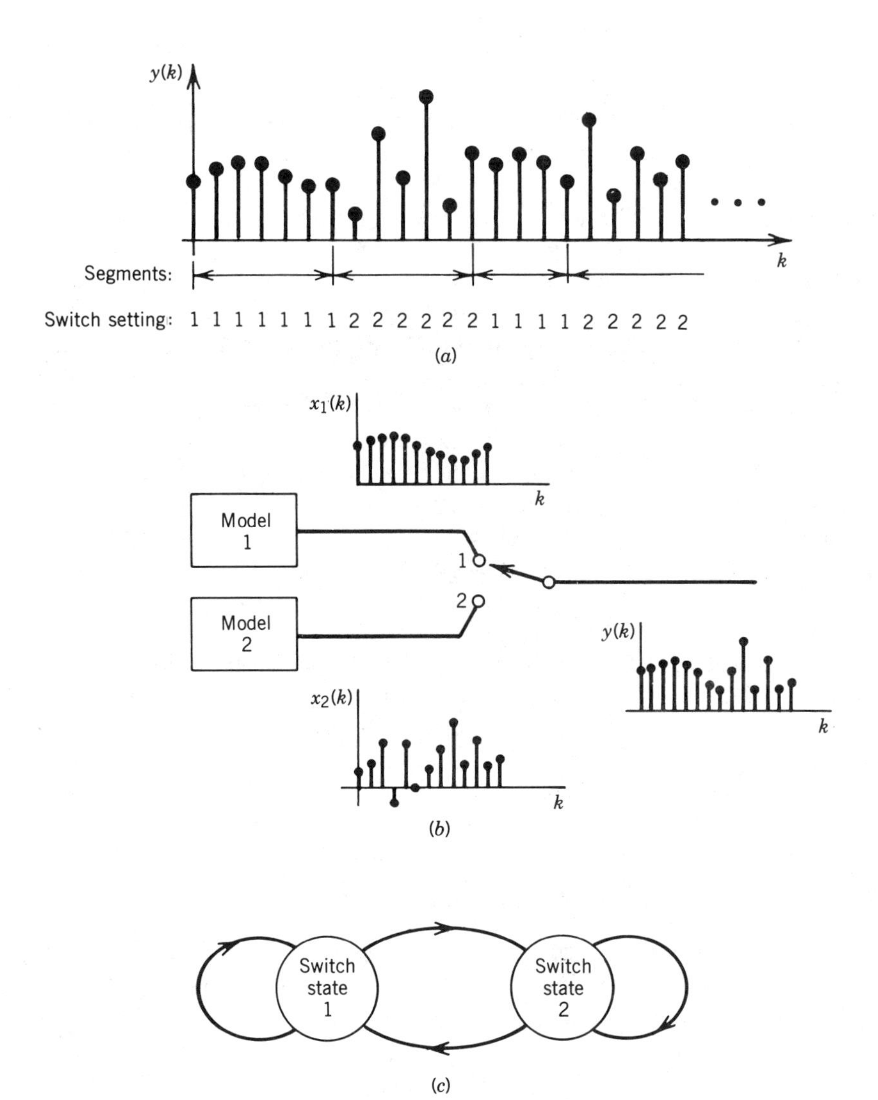

FIGURE 11.4 A hidden Markov model. (*a*) Time series of observations. (*b*) The formation of observation sequence. (*c*) A state transition diagram.

thought of as formed by randomly setting a switch to select one of the time series $x_1(k)$ or $x_2(k)$ produced by two distinct models [see Fig. 11.4(*b*)]. For each value of k, the switch can either remain in its current position or change to select the other model. The switch position corresponding to the time series illustrated in Fig. 11.4(a) is shown beneath the time series.

The position of the switch is described by a Markov chain whose properties are conveniently represented by the state transition diagram of Fig. 11.4(*c*). Each circle represents a "state" or position of the switch and the branches with arrows represent transitions that occur according to the transition probabilities of the Markov chain. Usually, the transition probabilities are such that the state does not change erratically but tends to stay fixed for some reasonable length of time.

The name hidden Markov model comes from the consideration that the Markov state cannot be observed directly. The state can only be inferred from observation of the time series. Thus the underlying Markov model is "hidden."

Hidden Markov models are useful for a variety of problems where the time series of observations may go through distinct transitions and change character. Examples occur in communications, geophysics, medical monitoring and diagnosis, electronic surveillance, and in many other areas. An area of recent interest has been that of speech recognition [7]. The speech waveform can be represented by a catenation of several distinct random processes that are stationary over only a very short time interval. Portions of a single word corresponding to voiced sounds (such as vowels), and unvoiced sounds (consonants, and fricatives such as "th" or "sh" sounds) have different statistical characteristics. The observed waveform corresponding to even a single isolated word is therefore rather complex. Hidden Markov models have been used effectively to characterize speech and as a basis to perform word recognition.

Consider now the following problem. A sequence of N values of the time series $Y = \{y(1), y(2), \ldots, y(N)\}$ is observed, and it is desired to determine the underlying state sequence $S = \{s_1, s_2, \ldots, s_N\}$. It is assumed that the states of the model are numbered consecutively and so each of the variables s_k is an integer between 1 and the maximum number of states N_s. Observe that determining the state associated with each observation can be posed as an equivalent classification problem. Since s_k is the state associated with observation $y(k)$, one can think of associating $y(k)$ with a class ω_{s_k}. The set of states $S = \{s_0, s_1, \ldots, s_N\}$ is thus isomorphic to the set of classes $\Omega = \{\omega_{s_1}, \omega_{s_2}, \ldots, \omega_{s_N}\}$.

Since infering the states is equivalent to a classification problem, we know that the state sequence that minimizes the probability of error is the state sequence that maximizes the posterior probability[3]

$$\Pr[S \mid Y] = \frac{p_{Y|S}(Y \mid S) \Pr[S]}{p_Y(Y)} \tag{11.13}$$

From an estimation theory point of view, the set of values S that maximizes Eq. 11.13 is an MAP estimate for the states.

Since the states form a Markov chain, one can write by analogy with Eq. 11.12

$$\Pr[S] = \Pr[s_1, s_2, \ldots, s_N] = \left[\prod_{k=2}^{N} P_{s_k|s_{k-1}} \right] P_{s_1} \tag{11.14}$$

where $P_{i|j}$ are the Markov transition probabilities and P_{s_1} is the probability that the

[3]Although S is not an event, for simplicity we here use the abusive notation $\Pr[S]$ and $\Pr[S \mid Y]$ to mean the probability and the conditional probability that states take on a particular set of values.

first state takes on a particular value s_1. Now, let us initially assume that the sequence of observations arising from any state is independent, and for convenience, let us denote the probability density function for the observation $y(k)$ given state s_k as $p_{s_k}(y(k))$. Since the observation $y(k)$ depends only on the state at time k and not on the states at any other time or the previous observations, it follows that

$$p_{Y|S}(Y|S) = p_{Y|S}(y(1), \ldots, y(N) \mid s_1, \ldots, s_N) = \prod_{k=1}^{N} p_{s_k}(y(k)) \tag{11.15}$$

By substitution of these last two equations in Eq. 11.13, the numerator can be written as

$$p_{Y|S}(Y \mid S) \Pr[S] = \prod_{k=1}^{N} p_{s_k}(y(k))\, P_{s_k|s_{k-1}} \tag{11.16}$$

where for convenience we take $P_{s_1|s_0}$ to mean the unconditional probability P_{s_1}. Since the denominator of Eq. 11.13 is not a function of the states, maximizing Eq. 11.13 is equivalent to maximizing Eq. 11.16. The sequence of states that maximizes Eq. 11.16 can be found by the dynamic programming algorithm known as the Viterbi algorithm [8]. The algorithm is described in Section 11.4.

The current problem can be generalized somewhat to the case where the observed sequence does not consist of independent random variables, but the values of the sequence are interrelated. To obtain a tractible solution, assume that the sequence of observation values produced in any state is itself a (first-order) Markov sequence. This means that for any state s_k and subsequence of M observations $y(k)$, $y(k+1), \ldots, y(k+M-1)$, where the system remains in state s_k, the joint density for the observations has the form

$$\left[\prod_{\ell=k+1}^{k+M-1} p_{s_k}(y(\ell) \mid y(\ell-1))\right] p_{s_k}(y(k))$$

In this case, the quantity to be maximized has the form

$$p_{Y|S}(Y \mid S) \Pr[S] = \prod_{k=1}^{N} p_{s_k}(y(k) \mid y(k-1)) P_{s_k|s_{k-1}} \tag{11.17}$$

where we have taken $P_{s_1|s_0} = P_{s_1}$ as before and $p_{s_k}(y(k) \mid y(k-1))$ is simply equal to the unconditional density $p_{s_k}(y(k))$ when state s_{k-1} is not the same as state s_k. The state sequence to maximize Eq. 11.17 can again be found by the Viterbi algorithm.

An example of a first-order Markov sequence is a first-order Gaussian autoregressive process. The observation sequence satisfies the difference equation

$$y(k) = a_s y(k-1) + w(k) \tag{11.18}$$

where a_s is a parameter with $| a_s | < 1$ and $w(k)$ are independent identically distributed zero mean Gaussian random variables with variance σ_s^2 (white noise samples). In this case, the conditional density function is given by

$$p_{s_k}(y(k) \mid y(k-1)) = \frac{1}{\sqrt{2\pi}\,\sigma_{s_k}} \exp\left[-\frac{(y(k) - a_{s_k}y(k-1))^2}{2\sigma_{s_k}^2} \right] \tag{11.19}$$

Autogressive models are closely related to the linear prediction models discussed in Chapter 10. If the autocorrelation function of the model is known, the autoregressive model parameters can be found by solving a set of Normal equations identical to those used in linear prediction.

Classification Using a Set of Hidden Markov Models Another problem involving hidden Markov models is the following. We have an entire *set* of different hidden Markov models. Each is characterized by known Markov transition probabilities and statistical parameters characterizing the observation sequence in each state. A sequence $\boldsymbol{Y}$ is observed and it is desired to determine which model is the most likely model for the sequence. The word recognition problem described earlier is a problem of this type. For this, it is necessary to compute the likelihood $p_{\boldsymbol{Y}}(\boldsymbol{Y})$ of the observed output sequence using each of the models and to select the model with the highest likelihood. Since the given sequence $\boldsymbol{Y} = \{y(1), y(2), \ldots, y(N)\}$ could arise from many different underlying state transitions, evaluation of the likelihood for each model could be a large combinatorial problem. Straightforward enumeration of all possible state transitions requires a number of calculations proportional to N_s^N, where N_s is the number of states. Since the growth is exponential in N, the computation quickly gets out of hand. Fortunately, a more efficient procedure exists that requires only on the order of N_s^2N calculations. (This growth is only linear in N.) Since the algorithm can be readily understood as a modification of the Viterbi algorithm, its description will also be deferred to Section 11.4.

Estimation of Hidden Markov Model Parameters A final issue with respect to hidden Markov models is the estimation of the model parameters from training data. For this let us first assume that the observations $y(k)$ at each point in time are independent and further that the observations produced in any state i take on only a discrete set of values $y_1, y_2, \ldots, y_Q$. These values have probabilities $\pi_i(1), \pi_i(2), \ldots, \pi_i(Q)$. The assumption of a discrete set of values is equivalent to approximating the density functions $p_{s_k}(y)$ with histograms as discussed in Chapter 8. The distribution for the observation sequence $\boldsymbol{Y}$ is then characterized by a set of matrix parameters $\mathbf{P}^T$ and $\mathbf{\Pi}$, where $\mathbf{P}^T$ is the transition probability matrix and the elements of $\mathbf{\Pi}$ are the probabilities $\pi_i(q)$. A maximum likelihood estimate for the parameters would be obtained by choosing $\mathbf{P}^T$ and $\mathbf{\Pi}$ to maximize the likelihood function defined by

$$\Pr[\boldsymbol{Y}; \mathbf{P}^T, \mathbf{\Pi}] \tag{11.20}$$

where $\boldsymbol{Y}$ is the given observation sequence. Although there is, in general, no analytic method for obtaining this estimate, the following algorithm known as the Baum–Welch reestimation procedure converges to a solution.

Define the quantities $P_{ji|\boldsymbol{Y}}(k)$ and $P_{i|\boldsymbol{Y}}(k)$ as

$$P_{ji|\boldsymbol{Y}}(k) = \Pr[s_{k-1} = j, s_k = i \mid \boldsymbol{Y}] \tag{11.21a}$$

$$P_{i|\boldsymbol{Y}}(k) = \Pr[s_k = i \mid \boldsymbol{Y}] \tag{11.21b}$$

Then since events $\{s_{k-1} = j\}$ conditioned on the observations are mutually exclusive and collectively exhaustive, it follows that

$$P_{i|\boldsymbol{Y}}(k) = \sum_{j=1}^{N_S} P_{ji|\boldsymbol{Y}}(k) \tag{11.22}$$

The Markov transition probabilities and the probabilities of the observations can then be estimated from the formulas

$$\tilde{P}_{i|j} = \frac{\sum_{k=2}^{N} P_{ji|\boldsymbol{Y}}(k)}{\sum_{k=2}^{N} P_{j|\boldsymbol{Y}}(k)} \tag{11.23}$$

and

$$\tilde{\pi}_i(q) = \frac{\sum_{\substack{k=1 \\ y(k)=y_q}}^{N} P_{i|\boldsymbol{Y}}(k)}{\sum_{k=1}^{N} P_{i|\boldsymbol{Y}}(k)} \tag{11.24}$$

Equation 11.23 develops an estimate for the transition probability by dividing the average joint probability of two consecutive states j and i given the observations by the average probability of being in state j given the observations. Equation 11.24 is a measure of the relative frequency of occurrence of the value y_q for the state i given the observations. The formulas of Eqs. 11.22 through 11.24 are applied iteratively to compute estimated values for $P_{i|j}$ and $\pi_i(q)$. With each iteration, the previous values of $\tilde{P}_{i|j}$ and $\tilde{\pi}_i(q)$ are taken as the model parameters and used to compute a new value for $P_{ji|\boldsymbol{Y}}(k)$. The method of computation is discussed in Section 11.4. The new value of $P_{i|\boldsymbol{Y}}(k)$ is computed from Eq. 11.22 and new estimates $\tilde{P}_{i|j}$ and $\tilde{\pi}_i(q)$ are then computed from Eqs. 11.23 and 11.24. The iteration ends when the values of $\tilde{P}_{i|j}$ and $\tilde{\pi}_k(q)$ no longer change by any significant amount.

When the observations are characterized by a continuous density function $p_{s_k}(y)$, the following modifications to the Baum–Welch algorithm can be suggested. First, if a parametric form for the density function exists, the observation values produced in state i can be used to develop a sample statistic for the parameter. For example, if the parameter needed to determine the density for state i is the mean, an estimate for that parameter can be developed from

$$\tilde{m}_i = \frac{\sum_{k=1}^{N} y(k) P_{i|Y}(k)}{\sum_{k=1}^{N} P_{i|Y}(k)} \tag{11.25}$$

(see Problem 11.3). This formula replaces Eq. 11.24 in the iteration. The density function thus specified can be used to compute the probabilities $p_{ji|Y}(k)$ and so continue the iteration.

If a nonparametric form for the density function is used, Eq. 11.24 can be replaced by a Parzen-type of estimate for the density. In particular, if $\gamma(y)$ is a suitable Parzen kernel, then a reasonable estimate (see Problem 11.4) for the density of state i is

$$p_i(y) = \frac{\sum_{k=1}^{N} \gamma(y - y(k))\, P_{i|Y}(k)}{\sum_{k=1}^{N} P_{i|Y}(k)} \tag{11.26}$$

This computation replaces Eq. 11.24 in the iteration.

When the observations produced by the model are not independent, but characterized by the conditional density $p_{s_k}(y(k) \mid y(k - 1))$, a similar procedure could be used to estimate the model parameters. In this case, however, Eqs. 11.24 through 11.26 need to be modified to show the conditioning on the value of the previous observations (see Problem 11.5).

11.2.3 Markov Random Fields and Image Processing

Markov chains are one-dimensional in the sense that the objects comprising the chain are fully ordered with respect to one another and so can be organized along a line. It is also possible to have two-dimensional Markov dependence among objects whose interrelationships would have to be represented in a plane. These more general Markov models are known as Markov random fields. The use of Markov random fields will be described in terms of an image-processing example.

Consider the image segmentation problem described in Section 11.1.3. Assume again that there are only two *types* of regions in the image although there may be multiple regions. Here it will be useful to identify the class to which a pixel has been assigned as a "state" $s_{k,\ell}$ (k and ℓ represent pixel coordinates). For the problem to be considered here, the state $s_{k,\ell}$ will take on only values 1 and 2 corresponding to the two region types. Thus the pixel classification $\omega_{s_{k,\ell}}$ can only be ω_1 or ω_2. The objective of image segmentation will be to determine a set of states for all of the pixels that has largest probability, given the observed image. That is, if $\boldsymbol{Y}$ represents the entire set of observed pixel intensity values and S represents the entire set of states, one seeks to find the set S that maximizes $\Pr[S \mid \boldsymbol{Y}]$. By using Bayes's rule and dropping the term $p_{\boldsymbol{Y}}(\boldsymbol{Y})$, we see that this is equivalent to maximizing

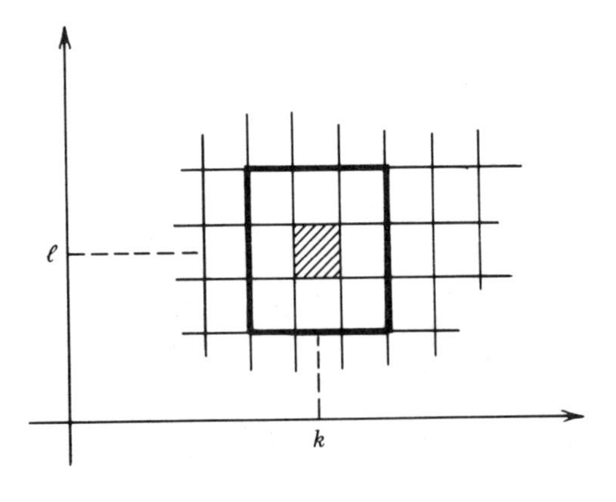

Figure 11.5 An image pixel at coordinates (k, ℓ) and neighborhood.

$$p_{Y|S}(Y \mid S) \cdot \Pr[S] \tag{11.27}$$

This is an MAP estimate for the states.

The set of states S for the image represents what is known as a binary valued random field. It would be extremely convenient if the term $\Pr[S]$ could be decomposed using some relation analogous to Eq. 11.14 so that the computation of this probability could be represented as a composite of simpler terms. A Markov chain representation is not possible because of the two-dimensional nature of the problem and the lack of a full ordering relation for the pixels. However, a generalization does exist in the form of a Markov random field [9].

The basic idea of a Markov random field is that the conditional probability for a state $s_{k,\ell}$ for a pixel at coordinates (k, ℓ), given all of the other states in the image, is the same as the conditional probability of $s_{k,\ell}$, given the states in only some local neighborhood. A neighborhood could be defined for example as in Fig. 11.5.[4] Let $S_{k,\ell}$ denote the *set* of states for the pixels in the neighborhood and let S' denote the set of all states in the image except $s_{k,l}$. Then

$$\Pr[s_{k,\ell} \mid S'] = \Pr[s_{k,\ell} \mid S_{k,\ell}] \tag{11.28}$$

This is the Markov condition.

Figure 11.6(a) shows a pixel and two possible choices of a "neighborhood" of pixels related to the pixel. For each neighborhood, it is possible to define *cliques* as groups of pixels such that all pixels in a clique are neighbors of each other according to the choice of neighborhood structure. The cliques for each of the neighborhood structures shown in Fig. 11.6(a) are given in Fig. 11.6(b).

Now, denote one of the cliques of the pixel at (k, ℓ) by $\mathcal{C}_j(k, \ell)$. A class of

[4]*Note:* Here k and ℓ are used to denote coordinate locations and do not have the same meaning as the indices k and ℓ used in the discussion of relaxation and Fig. 11.3.

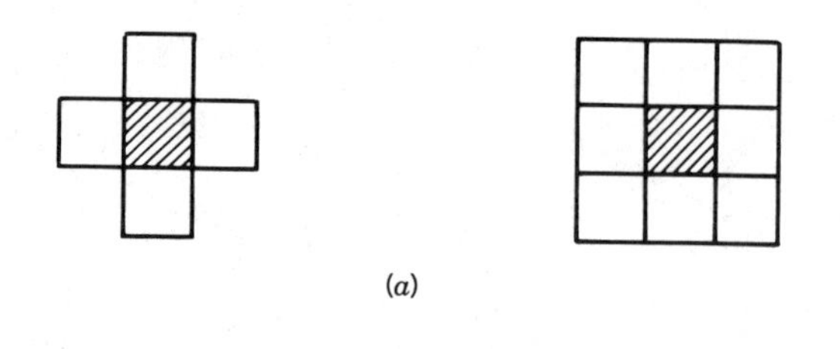

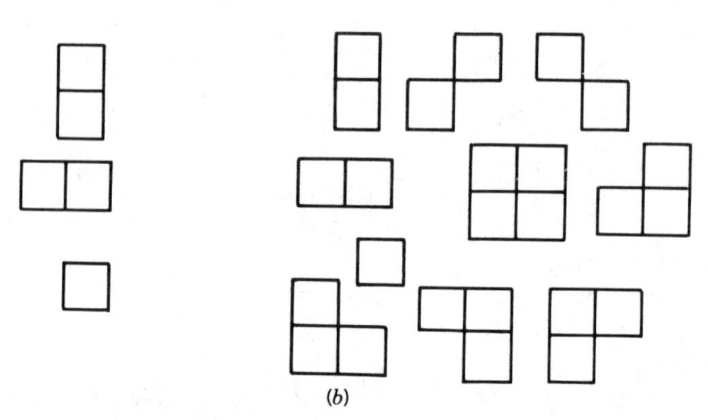

FIGURE 11.6 Neighborhood structures for states in a Markov model. (*a*) Two neighborhood structures for a pixel. (*b*) Corresponding sets of cliques.

Markov random fields known as Gibbsian random fields exists for which the conditional probabilities have the form

$$\Pr[s_{k,\ell} \mid S_{k,\ell}] = \frac{1}{Z_s} \exp\left[-\frac{1}{T} \sum_j F_j(\mathscr{C}_j(k, \ell)) \right] \tag{11.29}$$

where Z_s is a normalizing constant determined so the probabilities sum to 1 and T is a parameter whose role will be discussed shortly. The terms $F_j(\mathscr{C}_j)$ are functions of the states of the pixels in the cliques $\mathscr{C}_j$ and the sum is over all cliques involving the pixel at (k, ℓ). Typically, for image processing, simple functions are used in Eq. 11.29 such as linear functions of products of elements in the cliques. For the four-neighbor structure of Fig. 11.6 the exponent in Eq. 11.29 would thus be of the form

$$-\frac{1}{T} s_{k,\ell} [\alpha + \beta_1(s_{k-1,\ell} + s_{k+1,\ell}) + \beta_2(s_{k,\ell-1} + s_{k,\ell+1})] \tag{11.30}$$

where α, β_1, and β_2 are parameters of the distribution. For the eight-neighbor structure the exponent would be of the form

$$
\begin{aligned}
-\frac{1}{T} s_{k,\ell}[\alpha &+ \beta_1(s_{k-1,\ell} + s_{k+1,\ell}) + \beta_2(s_{k,\ell-1} + s_{k,\ell+1}) \\
&+ \gamma_1(s_{k-1,\ell-1} + s_{k+1,\ell+1}) + \gamma_2(s_{k-1,\ell+1} + s_{k+1,\ell-1}) \\
&+ \xi_1(s_{k-1,\ell}s_{k,\ell-1} + s_{k,\ell+1}s_{k-1,\ell+1} + s_{k+1,\ell-1}s_{k-1,\ell}) \\
&+ \xi_2(s_{k-1,\ell}s_{k-1,\ell-1} + s_{k+1,\ell+1}s_{k,\ell+1} + s_{k,\ell-1}s_{k+1,\ell}) \qquad (11.31) \\
&+ \xi_3(s_{k-1,\ell}s_{k-1,\ell+1} + s_{k+1,\ell-1}s_{k,\ell-1} + s_{k,\ell+1}\, s_{k+1,\ell}) \\
&+ \xi_4(s_{k-1,\ell}s_{k,\ell+1} + s_{k,\ell-1}s_{k-1,\ell-1} + s_{k+1,\ell+1}s_{k+1,\ell}) \\
&+ \eta(s_{k-1,\ell}s_{k,\ell-1}s_{k-1,\ell-1} + s_{k+1,\ell}s_{k,\ell+1}s_{k+1,\ell+1} \\
&\qquad + s_{k-1,\ell}s_{k,\ell+1}\, s_{k-1,\ell+1} + s_{k+1,\ell}s_{k,\ell-1}s_{k+1,\ell-1})\,]
\end{aligned}
$$

where the α, β_i, γ_i, ξ_i, and η are parameters. We see that the function gets considerably more complicated with larger neighborhood structures.

The probability for the entire set of states S for the Gibbsian model has the form

$$
\Pr[S] = \exp - \left(\frac{U(S)}{T}\right) \qquad (11.32)
$$

where

$$
U(S) = \sum_{k,\ell} \sum_{j} F_j\,(\mathscr{C}_j(k, \ell)) \qquad (11.33)
$$

is the sum of the functions over all possible cliques.

The Gibbsian random field models are analogous to some well-known statistical mechanical models for certain crystaline structures. For these structures the quantity U can be identified as an energy function and T represents the temperature. The problem of maximizing Eq. 11.27 can be compared to that of finding a minimum energy state for the physical model. More will be said about this later in this section.

Let us now return to the problem of image segmentation. Finding a maximum of Eq. 11.27 is evidently a very difficult problem. In fact, given the state $s_{k,\ell}$ (or equivalently the class $\omega_{s_{k,\ell}}$) the observation $y(k, \ell)$ representing the intensity of the pixel is, in general, randomly distributed according to the density function for class $\omega_{s_{k,\ell}}$. In fact, the model for the image is the two-dimensional analog of a hidden Markov model and the segmentation problem corresponds to estimating the states from the observations. Recall from the discussion of hidden Markov models that this problem requires a form of dynamic programming. Because of the two-dimensional Markov random field dependence, however, such an algorithm would be very complex.

A suboptimal solution to the problem that has been found to yield good results in practice focuses on the conditional probabilities. Specifically, let the conditional density for the observation $y(k,\ell)$ given the state $s_{k,\ell}$ be denoted by $p_{s_{k,\ell}}(y(k, \ell))$. Then given an initial assignment of the states for all pixels, the states can be iteratively updated by applying the decision rule

$$p_1(y(k,\ell))\ \Pr[1 \mid S_{k,\ell}] \underset{\omega_2}{\overset{\omega_1}{\gtrless}} p_2\,(y(k,\ \ell))\Pr[2 \mid S_{k,\ell}] \qquad (11.34)$$

where the terms $\Pr[s_{k,\ell} \mid S_{k,\ell}]$ are in the form of Eq. 11.29 (recall that according to our assumption $s_{k,\ell}$ can only take on the values 1 and 2).

The iteration proceeds as follows. At the first step a set of classes is chosen for the pixels according to

$$p_1(y(k,\ \ell)) \underset{\omega_2}{\overset{\omega_1}{\gtrless}} p_2(y(k,\ \ell)) \qquad (11.35)$$

Thereafter the states of the previous iteration are used to determine $s_{k,\ell}$ and the corresponding values $\Pr[s_{k,\ell} \mid S_{k,\ell}]$. These values are used in Eq. 11.34 to determine a new set of class assignments. The procedure ends when class assignments no longer change or oscillate back and forth.

The iterative algorithm implied by Eq. 11.34 is grossly similar to probabilistic relaxation but is based on a definite probabilistic model. Figure 11.7 shows the results of segmenting the field-tree image by this procedure.

The application of Markov random fields to image processing has been further advanced by some results due to Geman and Geman [10]. Their results apply when the distribution of states, conditioned on the observations, is a Gibbsian Markov random field. Such a model is possible, for example, when the underlying image consists of regions of constant gray level subjected to blurring and noise. This form of model is also appropriate when the regions contain a pattern or texture that is itself generated by a Markov process such as a two-dimensional autoregressive model or another Gibbs random field [4, 11, 12]. In these cases a combination of procedures known as stochastic relaxation (not to be confused with probabilistic relaxation) and simulated annealing can be used to find an MAP estimate for the states. The term *simulated annealing* derives from an analogy with the annealing of materials where, as we mentioned, the variable T in Eqs. 11.29 and 11.32 represents temperature. The process now to be described corresponds to a procedure in which the material is slowly driven from a high temperature to a lower temperature and a stable low-energy configuration. For purposes of image processing, the variable T intuitively serves to raise or lower the coupling of the states through their conditional probabilities. By starting with a high value of T (loose coupling) and iteratively relaxing to a lower value (tight coupling) there is less danger of becoming trapped at a local maximum. The algorithm is as follows:

1. Start with some arbitrary initial setting of the states and set T to the highest value.
2. For each pixel, choose $s_{k,\ell}$ randomly according to the distribution of Eq. 11.29. In so doing, use the current values of the states for $S_{k,\ell}$.
3. Lower the temperature T by a prescribed amount and go to step 2.

Note that in step 2, the new state is chosen *randomly* according to the specified

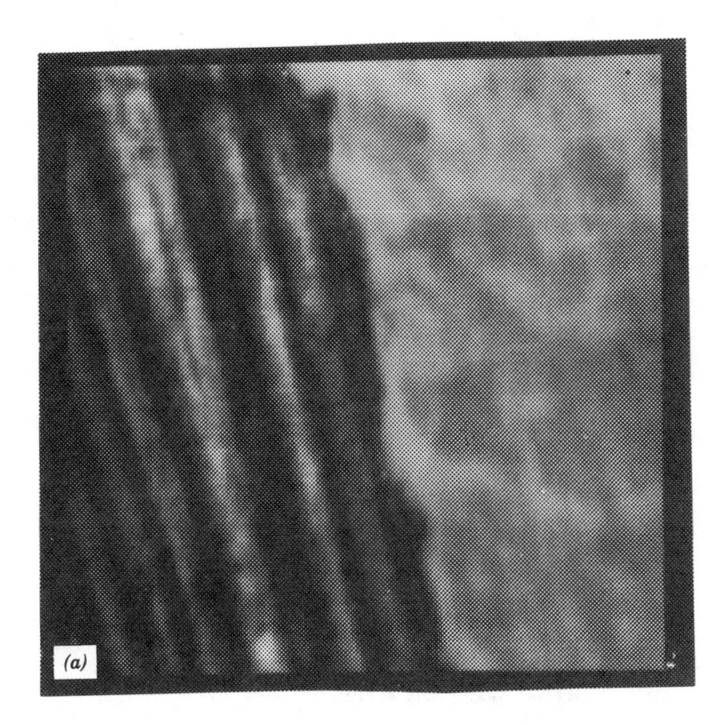

FIGURE 11.7 The segmentation of an image using Markov dependency model. (*a*) An image of fields and trees. (*b*) Segmentation.

distribution. This randomness accounts for the name *stochastic relaxation* and is crucial in avoiding a local maximum. In fact, since this step may actually *increase* the posterior probability, convergence of the algorithm is not monotonic. Geman and Geman show that convergence to the maximum is theoretically assured as long as the temperature is maintained above some lower bound that decreases with time. This lower bound or "schedule" decreases after updating the state of each pixel but results in only a gradual decrease in the temperature. In image processing applications the theoretical schedule for reducing the temperature is much too slow to be practical. The authors thus suggest a more realistic schedule of the form

$$T(r) \propto \frac{1}{\log(1 + r)} \tag{11.36}$$

where $T(r)$ is the temperature after r iterations and an iteration represents an updating of the complete set of states S for all the pixels in the image. Although the dependence of Eq. 11.36 is not known to guarantee convergence to the global maximum, it has provided good results in practical applications.

11.3 A GENERAL THEORY FOR CLASSIFICATION IN CONTEXT

Haralick [13] and others sought to develop a general theory for classification in context. Some of this work will be cited next.

One can imagine that for a set of N related objects there is a joint conditional probability density function

$$p_{Y|\Omega,\mathcal{P}}(Y \mid \Omega, \mathcal{P}) \tag{11.37}$$

where Y represents the joint set of measurements $\{\mathbf{y}_1, \mathbf{y}_2, \ldots, \mathbf{y}_N\}$, Ω is an ordered set of class assignments $\{\omega_{s_1}, \omega_{s_2}, \ldots, \omega_{s_N}\}$ and $\mathcal{P}$ represents the "prior knowledge" about the compatibility of decisions. Thus

$$p_{Y|\Omega,\mathcal{P}}(Y \mid \Omega, \mathcal{P})\, \Delta\mathbf{y}_1\, \Delta\mathbf{y}_2 \ldots \Delta\mathbf{y}_N \tag{11.38}$$

represents the joint probability of the measurements $\mathbf{y}_k$ given that they came from class ω_{s_k} for $k = 1, 2, \ldots, N$ and given the prior knowledge. The joint prior probability of the classes will be denoted by

$$\Pr[\Omega] = \Pr[A_1 \sim \omega_{s_1}, \ldots, A_N \sim \omega_{s_N}] \tag{11.39}$$

and is also assumed to be available.

Now let $\Omega_t = \{\omega_{t_1}, \omega_{t_2}, \ldots, \omega_{t_N}\}$ represent the set of *true* classes for the objects. Note that both ω_{s_k} and ω_{t_k} take on values in the set $\{\omega_1, \omega_2, \ldots, \omega_{N_c}\}$ of possible classes. For example, if this is a two-class problem, each of the ω_{s_k} and ω_{t_ℓ} can only be equal to ω_1 or ω_2. There is in general no relation between the number of classes N_c, and the number of objects N.

A cost function C can now be defined as

$$C(\Omega, \Omega_t) = \text{cost of deciding } \{\omega_{s_1}, \omega_{s_2}, \ldots, \omega_{s_N}\}$$
$$\text{when the true classes are } \{\omega_{t_1}, \omega_{t_2}, \ldots \omega_{t_N}\} \tag{11.40}$$

A Bayesian approach to classification is then defined as one that minimizes the expected value of the cost. That is, the Bayesian approach results in a *rule* for mapping all of the observations $\boldsymbol{Y}$ into classes $\Omega = \Omega(\boldsymbol{Y})$ such that

$$E[C(\Omega, \Omega_t) \mid \mathcal{P}] = \sum_{\Omega} \sum_{\Omega_t} C(\Omega, \Omega_t)\Pr[\Omega, \Omega_t \mid \mathcal{P}] \tag{11.41}$$

is minimized. Observe that since $\boldsymbol{Y}$ is random, Ω is also random, and therefore the expectation in Eq. 11.41 involves a sum over Ω. The term $\Pr[\Omega, \Omega_t \mid \mathcal{P}]$ should be interpreted as the probability of a particular joint configuration $\{\omega_{s_1}, \ldots, \omega_{s_N}\}, \{\omega_{t_1}, \ldots, \omega_{t_N}\}$ using the given rule $\Omega = \Omega(\boldsymbol{Y})$ and conditioned on the prior knowledge. Equation 11.41 is, in fact, a generalization of the Bayes risk discussed in Chapter 3 (see Eq. 3.8).

11.3.1 Relation to Classification Without Context

To see how the general form of the decision problem relates to decision problems *without* context, consider the case where the classes of the objects are independent and there is no prior knowledge $\mathcal{P}$. Observe that in this case

$$\Pr[\Omega, \Omega_t \mid \mathcal{P}] = \Pr[\Omega, \Omega_t] = \Pr[\Omega \mid \Omega_t] \cdot \Pr[\Omega_t] \tag{11.42}$$

and since there is no interrelation among the objects

$$\Pr[\Omega_t] = \prod_{k=1}^{N} \Pr[\omega_{t_k}] \tag{11.43}$$

Also, since an *independent* decision is made about each object,

$$\begin{aligned}\Pr[\Omega \mid \Omega_t] &= \Pr[\omega_{s_1}, \ldots, \omega_{s_N} \mid \omega_{t_1}, \ldots, \omega_{t_N}] \\ &= \prod_{k=1}^{N} \Pr[\omega_{s_k} \mid \omega_{t_1}, \ldots, \omega_{t_N}] = \prod_{k=1}^{N} \Pr[\omega_{s_k} \mid \omega_{t_k}]\end{aligned} \tag{11.44}$$

The joint probability $\Pr[\Omega, \Omega_t]$ is therefore

$$\begin{aligned}\Pr[\Omega, \Omega_t] &= \left[\prod_{k=1}^{N} \Pr[\omega_{s_k} \mid \omega_{t_k}]\right]\left[\prod_{k=1}^{N} \Pr[\omega_{t_k}]\right] \\ &= \prod_{k=1}^{N} \Pr[\omega_{s_k} \mid \omega_{t_k}] \Pr[\omega_{t_k}] = \prod_{k=1}^{N} \Pr[\omega_{s_k}, \omega_{t_k}]\end{aligned} \tag{11.45}$$

Finally, since there is no context, a separate individual cost $C_k(\omega_{s_k}, \omega_{t_k})$ is assigned to each object. If the individual cost is a nonnegative function of its arguments, then it is reasonable to define the global cost as a sum or product of the separate costs. That is,

$$C(\Omega, \Omega_t) = C_1(\omega_{s_1}, \omega_{t_1}) + \cdots + C_N(\omega_{s_N}, \omega_{t_N}) \tag{11.46a}$$

or

$$C(\Omega, \Omega_t) = C_1(\omega_{s_1}, \omega_{t_1}) \cdot \ldots \cdot C_N(\omega_{s_N}\ \omega_{t_N}) \tag{11.46b}$$

Then, in view of Eq. 11.45, the expected value of C is minimized when the expected value of each of the individual costs is minimized. In either case this leads to individual decision rules for each object such as Eq. 3.14 (where $N_c = 2$).

If the individual cost functions are all identical, then a global cost defined as

$$C(\Omega, \Omega_t) = \max_k C_k(\omega_{s_k}, \omega_{t_k}) \tag{11.46c}$$

also leads to the same decision rule. A particular special case arises when

$$C_k(\omega_{s_k}, \omega_{t_k}) = \begin{cases} 0 & \omega_{s_k} = \omega_{t_k} \\ 1 & \omega_{s_k} \neq \omega_{t_k} \end{cases} \tag{11.47}$$

In this case, Eq. 11.46a counts the total number of objects misclassified, Eq. 11.46b is zero if *any* object is correct and one otherwise, while Eq. 11.46c is zero only if *all* objects are correct (and one otherwise). In all three of these cases the optimal decision rule is the one that chooses the largest posterior probability of the class, that is,

$$\Pr[\omega_{s_k} \mid \mathbf{y}_k] = \max_i \Pr[\omega_i \mid \mathbf{y}_k] \tag{11.48}$$

11.3.2 Analysis of Typical Problems Involving Context

The foregoing discussion serves to illustrate how the general case of classification with context relates to the special case when context is not present or is ignored. When context is taken into account, the probabilities $\Pr[\Omega, \Omega_t]$ and the cost $C[\Omega, \Omega_t]$ will be more general functions of all the variables.

The criterion for the Bayes decision (Eq. 11.41) can be written in a slightly different form, namely

$$E[C(\Omega\ \Omega_t) \mid \mathcal{P}]\ ] = \Sigma_{\Omega_t} \left(\sum_{\Omega} C(\Omega, \Omega_t)\Pr[\Omega \mid \Omega_t, \mathcal{P}] \right) \Pr[\Omega_t \mid \mathcal{P}] \tag{11.49}$$

Notice that the inner sum is a conditional expectation of the cost $C(\Omega, \Omega_t)$ with respect to Ω. Since the set of classes chosen is a function of the measurements $\boldsymbol{Y}$, the expectation can be taken with respect to $\boldsymbol{Y}$. If the integration and summation are then interchanged, this yields

$$E[C(\Omega, \Omega_t \mid \mathcal{P}]$$
$$= \int_{-\infty}^{\infty} \cdots \int_{-\infty}^{\infty} \sum_{\Omega_t} C(\Omega, \Omega_t) \Pr[\Omega_t \mid \mathcal{P}]\, p_{Y|\Omega_t,\mathcal{P}}(Y \mid \Omega_t, \mathcal{P})\, d\mathbf{y}_1 \cdots d\mathbf{y}_N \tag{11.50}$$

Since the cost and all other quantities in Eq. 11.50 are nonnegative, Eq. 11.50 will be minimized if the integrand is minimized for all values of $\boldsymbol{Y}$. Thus a decision rule that minimizes Eq. 11.41 is equivalent to one that minimizes

$$\sum_{\Omega_t} C(\Omega, \Omega_t) \Pr[\Omega_t \mid \mathcal{P}]\, p_{Y|\Omega_t,\mathcal{P}}(Y \mid \Omega_t, \mathcal{P}) \tag{11.51}$$

A common condition in decision problems with context is that the measurements for a particular object, conditioned on the object classes and the prior knowledge, are independent. Furthermore, the measurements made on a particular object depend only on its own class and not on the classes of the other objects and the prior knowledge. These conditions imply that

$$p_{\mathbf{Y}|\Omega_t,\mathcal{P}}(Y \mid \Omega_t, \mathcal{P}) = \prod_{k=1}^{N} p_{\mathbf{y}_k|\Omega_t,\mathcal{P}}(\mathbf{y}_k \mid \Omega_t, \mathcal{P}) = \prod_{k=1}^{N} p_{\mathbf{y}_k|\omega_{t_k}}(\mathbf{y}_k \mid \omega_{t_k}) \tag{11.52}$$

and so Eq. 11.51 becomes

$$\sum_{\Omega_t} C(\Omega, \Omega_t) \Pr[\Omega_t|\mathcal{P}] \prod_{k=1}^{N} p_{\mathbf{y}_k|\omega_{t_k}}(\mathbf{y}_k \mid \omega_{t_k}) \tag{11.53}$$

If there is no context so that $\Pr[\Omega_t, \mathcal{P}]$ is given by Eq. 11.43, then cost functions such as Eqs. 11.46a to 11.46c with C_k given by Eq. 11.47 are easily shown to lead to Eq. 11.48. Other cases are not so trivial. One of the simpler cases is discussed next.

11.3.3 Markov Chain Dependence

A reasonably neat solution to the problem of classification in context results when the classes of the objects form a Markov chain, that is,

$$\Pr[\omega_{t_k} \mid \omega_{t_{k-1}}, \ldots, \omega_{t_1}, \mathcal{P}] = \Pr[\omega_{t_k} \mid \omega_{t_{k-1}}] \tag{11.54}$$

In this case the probability $\Pr[\Omega_t, \mathcal{P}]$ can be written as the product

$$\Pr[\Omega_t, \mathcal{P}] = \prod_{k=1}^{N} \Pr[\omega_{t_k} \mid \omega_{t_{k-1}}] \tag{11.55}$$

where it is understood in Eq. 11.55 that the first term in the product is actually $\Pr[\omega_{t_1}]$. (This slight abuse of notation simplifies the equations that follow.) With the cost function defined by Eqs. 11.46c and 11.47, Eq. 11.53 becomes

$$\sum_{\Omega_t} (\max_{\ell} C_\ell (\omega_{s_\ell}, \omega_{t_\ell})) \prod_{k=1}^{N} \Pr[\omega_{t_k} \mid \omega_{t_{k-1}}]\, p_{\mathbf{y}_k|\omega_{t_k}}(\mathbf{y}_k \mid \omega_{t_k}) \tag{11.56}$$

Observe that the sum of Eq. 11.56 is over all possible choices of the set $\{\omega_{t_1}, \omega_{t_2}, \ldots, \omega_{t_N}\}$ and that the cost function appearing in Eq. 11.56 is equal to 1 for every term except when $\{\omega_{t_1}, \ldots, \omega_{t_N}\}$ is equal to $\{\omega_{s_1}, \ldots, \omega_{s_N}\}$. For this term the cost function is zero. Thus Eq. 11.56 can be written as

$$\sum_{\Omega_t} \prod_{k=1}^{N} \Pr[\omega_{t_k} \mid \omega_{t_{k-1}}]\, p_{\mathbf{y}_k|\omega_{t_k}}(\mathbf{y}_k \mid \omega_{t_k}) - \prod_{k=1}^{N} \Pr[\omega_{s_k} \mid \omega_{s_{k-1}}]\, p_{\mathbf{y}_k|\omega_{s_k}}(\mathbf{y}_k \mid \omega_{s_k}) \qquad (11.57)$$

Since the first term is a sum over all possible choices of Ω_t it is not a function of the particular sequence $\{\omega_{s_1}, \ldots, \omega_{s_N}\}$ Equation 11.57 is therefore minimized by maximizing

$$\prod_{k=1}^{N} \Pr[\omega_{s_k} \mid \omega_{s_{k-1}}]\, p_{\mathbf{y}_k|\omega_{s_k}}(\mathbf{y}_k \mid \omega_{s_k}) \qquad (11.58)$$

Choosing the classes (or states of the Markov chain) to maximize Eq. 11.58 is a problem already encountered in Sections 11.2.1 and 11.2.2. The procedure for the solution is the Viterbi algorithm (see Section 11.4).

11.3.4 Relation to Relaxation Labeling

This section cites a particular interpretation of relaxation that places it within the general theory of classification in context. The treatment here is brief, since the proofs are long and complicated and the results do not lead to any further practical applications.

For this interpretation, one defines the *neighbors* for each object A_k as those objects that are directly related to A_k. The compatibility functions are then defined by Eq. 11.5 when A_ℓ is a neighbor of A_k and set equal to zero when A_ℓ is not a neighbor of A_k. Furthermore, one defines the "rth level context" for A_k as the set of measurements on A_k, its neighbors, the neighbors' neighbors, and so on up to r levels of neighbors of neighbors.

If one allows the interpretation that $P_i^{(r)}(k)$ is the probability that object A_k has class ω_i given the rth level context, then the relaxation formula (Eq. 11.4) serves to update the probabilities until the largest possible context for object A_k is taken into account. The interested reader is referred to the paper by Haralick [13] for more details on this particular interpretation.

11.4 THE VITERBI AND RELATED ALGORITHMS

11.4.1 The Viterbi Algorithm

Several different related problems were discussed earlier in this chapter whose solution involved the Viterbi algorithm. To treat a specific case, consider the quantity on the right-hand side of Eq. 11.16. Given the sequence of observations $\{y(1), y(2), \ldots, y(N)\}$, it is desired to choose values for the states s_n to maximize

$$\prod_{k=1}^{N} p_{s_k}(y(k))\, P_{s_k|s_{k-1}} \tag{11.59}$$

In order to describe the algorithm initially, let us take the logarithm of the above quantity and focus on the equivalent problem of maximizing

$$\sum_{k=1}^{N} A_i(k) + B_{ji}(k) \tag{11.60}$$

where we have let $s_k = i$ and $s_{k-1} = j$ and have defined

$$A_i(k) = \log p_i(y(k)) \tag{11.61a}$$

$$B_{ji}(k) = \log P_{i|j} \tag{11.61b}$$

with $B_{0i}(1) = \log P_i$, where the P_i are the initial (unconditional) probabilities of the states.[5]

The maximization of Eq. 11.60 can be thought of in terms of a graph known as a "trellis" (see Fig. 11.8). The graph consists of N columns of nodes with each column corresponding to a value of the time index k. Within each column the nodes correspond to the N_s possible states. A particular sequence of states corresponds to a path through the trellis such as the one shown. Corresponding to each node, we associate the weight $A_i(k)$; corresponding to each branch in a path we associate the weight $B_{ji}(k)$. The *weight of the path* is defined as the sum of the weights of the nodes and branches in the path. The path weight is thus equal to the value of Eq. 11.60 for the chosen set of states.

The Viterbi algorithm is seen to interpret the maximization of Eq. (11.60) as a problem of choosing a path in the trellis from column 1 to column N that has highest weight. The search for the optimal path proceeds as follows. Suppose that an optimal path has been determined from column 1 to each node j in some column $k - 1$. Denote the weight of each of these optimal paths by $W_j(k - 1)$. Then an optimal path to any particular node i in column k can be constructed by choosing the path from some node j', in column $k - 1$ to our node i in column k that maximizes the quantity

$$W_{j'}(k - 1) + B_{j'i}(k) + A_i(k) \tag{11.62}$$

The maximizing node j' can be easily found by considering each node in column

[5]The solution to the other Markov chain problems can also be viewed as a maximization of Eq. 11.60 with A_i and B_{ji} defined appropriately. For example, to maximize Eq. 11.58 of Section 11.3.3, we can define

$$A_i(k) = \log p_{\mathbf{y}_k|\omega_i}(\mathbf{y}_k|\omega_i)$$

$$B_{ji}(k) = \log \Pr[\omega_i \mid \omega_j]$$

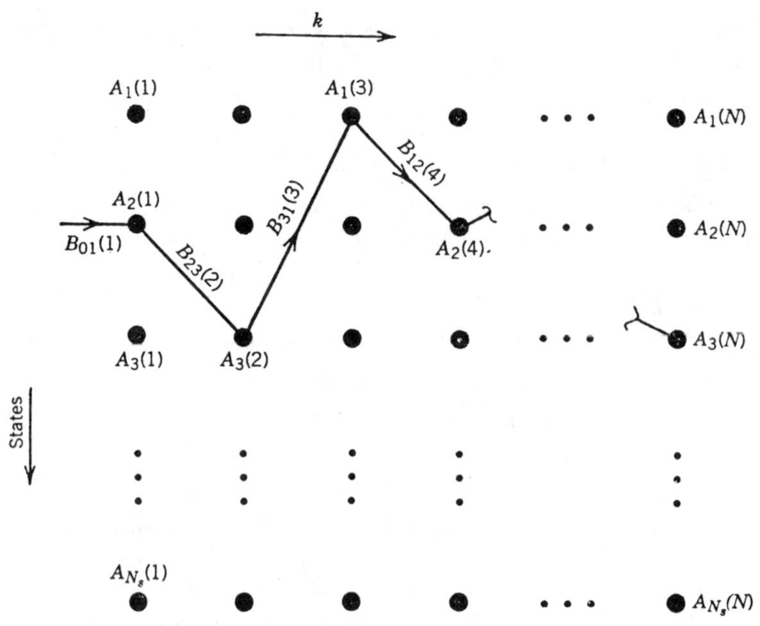

FIGURE 11.8 Trellis for the Viterbi algorithm.

$k - 1$ and evaluating Eq. 11.62. By this procedure, one determines the optimal path and its weight $W_i(k)$ for each node i in the column k, that is,

$$W_i(k) = \max_{j'} \left[W_{j'}(k - 1) + B_{j'i}(k) \right] + A_i(k) \qquad (11.63)$$

The weight of the optimal path so computed and the node j' in the previous column from which the path extends is stored with the node i. Thus, at any stage of the algorithm, one only needs to consider the nodes in two adjacent columns.

After optimum path weights $W_i(k)$ have been computed for all nodes in the array, then the optimum path from column 1 to column N can be determined easily. To do so, one simply chooses the node in column N that has the largest optimal path weight and traces its path backward through the array. This backtracing is possible, since the optimal path from each node back to the previous column has been saved.

Simplifications arise when all of the optimal paths to the nodes in column k pass through a small subset of the nodes in column $k - 1$. Then optimal paths to the other nodes in column $k - 1$ can be removed from consideration. For example, suppose that in Fig. 11.8 all optimal paths to the nodes in column 4 pass through the single node in column 3 with weight $A_1(3)$. Then it is clear that the optimal path to column N must have the initial segment $A_2(1)$, $A_3(2)$, $A_1(3)$ [assuming this is the optimal path to $A_1(3)$]. Thus the optimal path to column N has been partly determined after consideration of just the first three columns without the need for any backtracing. This kind of reasoning is helpful when N is very large and it is necessary to do "block processing" of the data. That is, because of storage availability it may be necessary to consider only a subset $M < N$ of the columns at a time. In our example, the determination of the initial path $A_2(1), A_3(2), A_1(3)$ allows columns 1 to 3 to be shifted out of computer memory and three more columns $M + 1, M + 2, M + 3$ to be shifted in.

11.4.2 Forward–Backward Analysis

Observe that in describing the Viterbi algorithm it was convenient, but not necessary, to take logarithms and transform Eq. 11.59 to Eq. 11.60. The algorithm could also be described by associating weights $p_i(y(k))$ with the nodes in column k of the trellis and associating weights $P_{i|j}$ with the branches. In this case the path weights would be defined as *products* of the node and branch weights, and the algorithm for finding the optimal path would be the same. A set of procedures based on the Viterbi trellis, known as the forward and backward procedures, can be developed that permit efficient solution of the other problems described in Section 11.2.2.

Recall that one problem cited in Section 11.2.2 was to find the likelihood of a *given* observation sequence $\{y(1), y(2), \ldots, y(N)\}$ for a hidden Markov model whose parameters were known. To attack this problem, let us define the "forward" variable $f_i(k)$ as the joint density of the partial sequence of observations $y(1)$, $y(2), \ldots, y(k)$ and the event "$s_k = i$." Dropping the subscript on the density function to simplify notation, we can write

$$f_i(k) = p(y(1), y(2), \ldots, y(k), s_k = i) \tag{11.64}$$

This density function can now be expressed as

$$p(y(1), \ldots, y(k), s_k = i) \tag{11.65}$$

$$= \left[\sum_{j=1}^{N_s} p(y(1), \ldots, y(k-1), s_{k-1} = j) \Pr[s_k = i \mid s_{k-1} = j] \right] p_i(y(k))$$

The term in brackets merely computes the joint density of $y(1), \ldots, y(k-1)$ and the event "$s_k = i$." Multiplication by the density function for state i then gives the desired result. Equation 11.65 can be written as a recursion on the forward variables

$$f_i(k) = \left[\sum_{j=1}^{N_s} f_j(k-1) P_{i|j} \right] p_i(y(k)) \qquad \begin{matrix} i = 1, 2, \ldots, N \\ k = 2, 3, \ldots, N_s \end{matrix} \tag{11.66}$$

The recursion is initialized by taking

$$f_i(1) = P_i \, p_i(y(k)) \qquad i = 1, 2, \ldots, N_s \tag{11.67}$$

Figure 11.9 shows a Viterbi trellis where the nodes have associated forward variables $f_i(k)$ and density functions $p_i(y(k))$ and the branches have weights $P_{i|j}$. In the Viterbi algorithm the path weight for a node of the new column is formed by selecting the

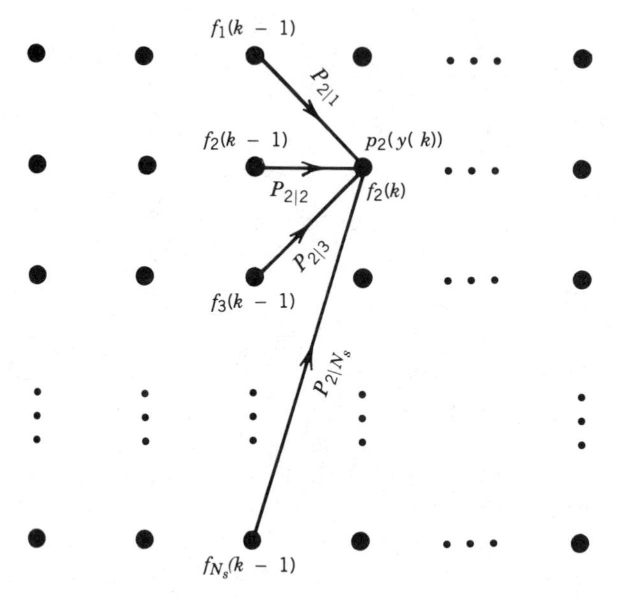

FIGURE 11.9 The use of Viterbi trellis in forward procedure.

maximum of the path weights from the nodes of the previous column. Here the forward variable in the new column is formed by *summing* the contributions from the nodes in the previous column. In fact, the Viterbi algorithm can be obtained from Eq. 11.66 if the forward variables are replaced by the path weights (defined as a *product*) and the summation is replaced by a maximization.

Once the forward variables are computed for all nodes in the last column, the likelihood of the given observation sequence can be computed from

$$\begin{aligned} p_Y(Y) &= \sum_{i=1}^{N_s} p(y(1), y(2), \ldots, y(N), s_N = i) \\ &= \sum_{i=1}^{N_s} f_i(N) \end{aligned} \tag{11.66}$$

A similar recursive procedure can be developed by defining the "backward" variables $b_i(k)$ as the probability density of the partial sequence $y(k+1), \ldots, y(N)$, given the state $s_k = i$,

$$b_i(k) = p(y(k+1), \ldots, y(N) \mid s_k = i) \tag{11.67}$$

Using conditional probability and summing over the states, one can write

$$\begin{aligned} & p(y(k+1), \ldots, y(N) \mid s_k = i) \\ &= \sum_{j=1}^{N_s} \Big[p(y(k+1) \mid s_{k+1} = j) p(y(k+2), \ldots, y(N) \mid s_{k+1} = j) \\ &\qquad \times \Pr[s_{k+1} = j \mid s_k = i] \Big] \end{aligned} \tag{11.68}$$

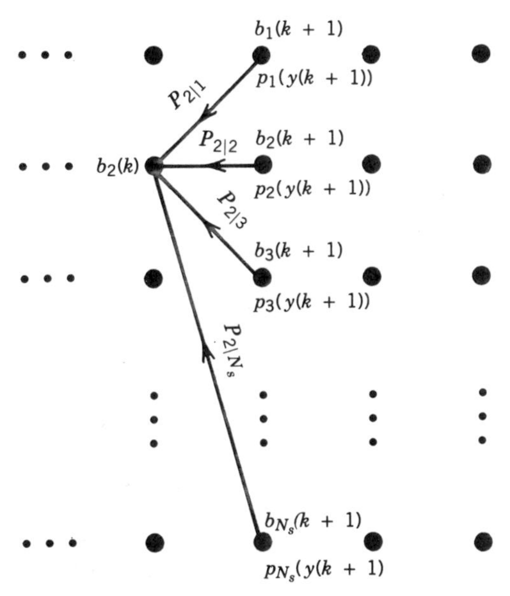

FIGURE 11.10 The use of Viterbi trellis in backward procedure.

Then by identifying terms with Eq. 11.67 and noting that $p(y(k+1) \mid s_{k+1} = j)$ is just the density $p_j(y(k+1))$, we have the backward recursion

$$b_i(k) = \sum_{j=1}^{N_s} p_j(y(k+1) b_j(k+1) P_{j|i} \qquad \begin{matrix} i = 1, 2, \ldots, N_s \\ k = N-1, N-2, \ldots, 1 \end{matrix} \tag{11.69}$$

The recursion is initialized by taking

$$b_i(N) = 1 \qquad i = 1, 2, \ldots, N_s \tag{11.70}$$

Figure 11.10 depicts the operations carried out in the backward recursion. The likelihood of the observation sequence is given by

$$\begin{aligned} p_Y(Y) &= \sum_{i=1}^{N_s} p(y(1) \mid s_1 = i) p(y(2), \ldots, y(N) \mid s_l = i) \Pr[s_1 = i] \\ &= \sum_{i=1}^{N_s} p_i(y(1))\, b_i(1)\, P_i \end{aligned} \tag{11.71}$$

Thus it is seen that the likelihood of the observation sequence can be computed by using either the forward *or* the backward procedure.

The final result that will be described here is the computation of the variables $P_{ji|Y}(k)$ needed in the Baum–Welch reestimation procedure. For this we need both the forward and the backward variables.

From Eq. 11.21a we have

$$P_{ji|Y}(k) = \Pr[s_{k-1} = j,\ s_k = i \mid Y] \qquad (11.72)$$
$$= \frac{p(y(1), y(2), \ldots, y(N), s_{k-1} = j, s_k = i)}{p_Y(Y)}$$

Then, by a straightforward use of conditional probability, we can write the numerator as

$$p(y(1), y(2), \ldots, y(N), s_{k-1} = j, s_k = i)$$
$$= p(y(k+1), \ldots, y(N) \mid s_k = i, s_{k-1} = j, y(1), \ldots, y(k))$$
$$\cdot\, p(y(k) \mid s_k = i, s_{k-1} = j, y(1), \ldots y(k-1))$$
$$\cdot\, \Pr[s_k = i \mid s_{k-1} = j, y(1), \ldots y(k-1)] \qquad (11.73)$$
$$\cdot\, p(y(1), \ldots, y(k-1), s_{k-1} = j)$$

Now look at the first term on the right-hand side of Eq. 11.73. Since the observations $y(k + 1), \ldots, y(N)$ conditioned on $s_k = i$ do not further depend on the event $s_{k-1} = j$ or on the observations $y(1), \ldots, y(k)$, we have

$$p(y(k+1), \ldots, y(N) \mid s_k = i, s_{k-1} = j, y(1), \ldots, y(k))$$
$$= p(y(k+1), \ldots, y(N) \mid s_k = i) = b_i(k) \qquad (11.74)$$

By similar reasoning we find that the second term is

$$p(y(k) \mid s_k = i, s_{k-1} = j, y(1), \ldots, y(k-1))$$
$$= p(y(k) \mid s_k = i) = p_i(y(k)) \qquad (11.75)$$

and that the third term is

$$\Pr[s_k = i \mid s_{k-1} = j, y(1), \ldots, y(k-1)]$$
$$= \Pr[s_k = i \mid s_{k-1} = j] = P_{i|j} \qquad (11.76)$$

Finally, from Eq. 11.64 we recognize the last term on the right-hand of Eq. 11.73 as $f_j(k - 1)$. Then, combining Eq. 11.64 and Eqs. 11.72 through 11.76, we have finally

$$P_{ji|Y}(k) = \frac{f_j(k-1)\, P_{i|j}\, p_i(y(k))\, b_i(k)}{p_Y(Y)} \qquad (11.77)$$

This is the remaining formula needed in the Baum–Welch restimation procedure. Since the numbers in the procedure can become very small, direct application of Eq. 11.77 is often not possible without some kind of scaling procedure. One such procedure is discussed in Ref. 7.

11.5 SUMMARY

This chapter discusses classification for sets of objects that are in some way related. In such cases, it is not appropriate to classify an individual object without taking into account the classes of other objects.

Probabilistic relaxation is described as a heuristic but practical method for classifying objects. Here is an initial classification of the objects based on independent consideration of each object is iteratively updated to arrive at a revised set of classifications that are more consistent with each other. Variations on the basic method allow one to address more general problems such as to assign certain properties to objects or to find a set of statements about the objects that are mutually consistent.

Markov models are then introduced as a formal way to specify some kinds of interrelations among objects. The chapter goes on to describe some decision and estimation problems associated with hidden Markov models and Markov random fields. Hidden Markov models find applications in the analysis of random processes such as speech that undergo random distinct changes in character. Markov random fields have been applied in digital image processing.

Next, a more general theory of classification in context is presented. This work generalizes Bayes theory for classification of individual objects and succeeds in representing certain types of Markov processes and relaxation procedures as special cases of the general theory.

Finally, a class of iterative procedures for the solution of certain problems related to Markov models is presented. The Viterbi algorithm is developed as a method of optimizing the class or state assignments in a Markov chain. Then some algorithms known as the forward and backward procedures are described that are a key ingredient to the theory and application of hidden Markov models.

REFERENCES

1. A. Rosenfeld, R. A. Hummel, and S. W. Zucker. "Scene Labeling by Relaxation Operations. *IEEE Trans. Systems. Man. and Cybernetics,* Vol. SMC-6, No. 6 (June 1976).
2. A. Rosenfeld, and A. Kak. *Digital Picture Processing,* 2nd ed., Vol. 2. New York: Academic Press, 1982.
3. L. Zadeh, K. S. Fu, K. Tanaka, and M. Shimura. *Fuzzy Sets and Their Applications to Cognitive and Decision Processes.* New York: Academic Press, 1975.
4. C. W. Therrien. "An Estimation-Theoretic Approach to Terrain Image Segmentation." *Computer Vision, Graphics, and Image Processing,* Vol. 22, pp. 313–326 (1983).
5. A. W. Drake. *Fundamentals of Applied Probability Theory.* New York: McGraw Hill Book Company, 1967.
6. L. R. Rabiner, and B. H. Juang. "An Introduction to Hidden Markov Models." *IEEE ASSP Magazine,* Vol. 3, No. 1, pp. 4–16 (January 1986).
7. S. E. Levinson, L. R. Rabiner, and M. M. Sondhi. "An Introduction to the Application of the Theory of Probabilistic Functions of a Markov Process to Automatic Speech Recognition." *Bell System Technical Journal,* Vol. 62, No. 4, pp. 1035–1075 (April 1983).
8. G. D. Forney. "The Viterbi Algorithm." *Proc. IEEE,* Vol. 6, pp. 268–278 (1973).
9. J. Besag. "Spatial Interaction and the Statistical Analysis of Lattice Systems." *J. Royal Stat. Soc.* Ser. B, Vol. 36, pp. 192–236 (1974).

10. S. GEMAN, and D. GEMAN. "Stochastic Relaxation, Gibbs Distributions, and the Bayesian Restoration of Images." *IEEE Trans. Pattern Analysis and Machine Intelligence,* Vol. PAMI-6, No. 6 (July 1984).
11. R. CHELLAPA, and R. L. KASHYAP. "Texture Synthesis Using 2-D Noncausal Autoregressive Models," *IEEE Trans. Acoustics, Speech, and Sig. Proc.,* Vol. ASSP-33, No. 1 pp. 194–203 (February 1985).
12. H. DERIN. "Segmentation of Textured Images Using Gibbs Random Fields." *Computer Vision, Graphics, and Image Processing,* Vol. 35, pp. 72–98 (1986).
13. R. M. HARALICK. "Decision Making in Context." *IEEE Trans. Pattern Analysis and Machine Intelligence,* Vol. PAMI-5, No. 4 (July 1983).

PROBLEMS

11.1 Write the outline of a program that would apply the relaxation method of Eq. 11.3 to the segmentation of an image. Assume that the image consists of an M by M array of pixels and that there are two types of regions in the image corresponding to "dark" areas and "light" areas. Assume that an initial set of probabilities $P_1^{(0)}(k)$ and $P_2^{(0)}(k)$ are obtained by evaluating a Gaussian probability density function for each class with known mean and variance. Draw a flowchart for the program, dimension all required arrays, and write the main loop of the program in a high-level language such as FORTRAN, PASCAL, or C.

11.2 Show any differences that arise in the program of Problem 11.1 if the relaxation formulas (11.4) and (11.8) are used in place of Eq. 11.3.

11.3 Show that if the parameter needed to determine the density function for state i of a hidden Markov model is the mean, then Eq. 11.25 is a reasonable estimate.
Hint: Let the values of $y(k)$ be quantized so that each $y(k) \approx y_q$ for some value of q. Then begin with the estimate

$$\sum_{q=1}^{Q} y_q \bar{\pi}_i(q)$$

and substitute Eq. 11.24.

11.4 Show that Eq. 11.26 is a reasonable nonparametric estimate for the density function for state i of a hidden Markov model.
Hint: Use the ideas of Parzen estimation similar to those in Section 8.1.1 and Eq. 11.24.

11.5 Suggest how the procedures for estimating the hidden Markov model parameters discussed on page 193 might be generalized to the case of dependent observations. Assume that the observations for any state themselves form a Markov process.

11.6 Cars bound for town A enter a highway at rush hour with arrival rate α_A. Those bound for towns B and C enter with arrival rates of α_B and α_C. The interarrival times of cars bound for a particular town are described by an exponential probability density function. For example, if the next car to appear is bound for town A, its arrival time occurs T seconds after the last car with probability density

$$p_T(T) = \begin{cases} \alpha_A e^{-\alpha_A T} & T \geq 0 \\ 0 & T < 0 \end{cases}$$

Given that a car just entered the highway bound for town A, the probability that the next car entering will be bound for town B is denoted by Pr[B |A]. Assume that the highway has a single outbound lane and that cars do not pass each other. A hitchhiker at some point down the highway observes a set of interarrival times $T_1, T_2, \ldots, T_M$ for $M + 1$ successive cars. On the basis of this observation, he would like to guess the destination of the last M cars. Assume that (even partially) incorrect decisions are equally costly and that the cost of a correct decision (i.e., all M destinations correct) is zero.

(a) Write the simplest form of the equation that the hitchhiker must maximize to minimize the expected value of the cost.

(b) Suppose that the arrival rates are

$$\alpha_A = 10 \text{ cars/minute}$$

$$\alpha_B = 60 \text{ cars/minute}$$

$$\alpha_C = 30 \text{ cars/minute}$$

and the conditional probabilities for the class of the next car are described by the Markov transition matrix

$$\begin{array}{c} \\ A \\ B \\ C \end{array} \begin{bmatrix} A & B & C \\ 0.2 & 0.4 & 0.4 \\ 0.35 & 0.3 & 0.35 \\ 0.15 & 0.15 & 0.7 \end{bmatrix}$$

That is, an entry in the ith row and the jth column is $\Pr[\omega_i \mid \omega_j]$. The hitchhiker observes the interarrival times $T_1 = 2, T_2 = 0.5, T_3 = 4, T_4 = 0.5$, and $T_5 = 1$ second. Draw the trellis for the Viterbi algorithm and find the hitchhiker's best guess for the classes of the last four cars.

11.7 Beginning with Eq. 11.53 and assuming no context so that $\Pr[\Omega_t \mid \mathcal{P}]$ is given by Eq. 11.43, show that a form for the cost function given by Eq. 11.47 and any of equations 11.46 leads to the decision rule of Eq. 11.48. What can you say about the resulting decision rule if Eq. 11.43 does not hold but there is no prior knowledge and $\Pr[\Omega_t \mid \mathcal{P}]$ is a more general distribution $\Pr[\Omega_t]$? Give your answer for each of the cases represented by Eqs. 11.46a to 11.46c.

11.8 Tell if the forward–backward procedures of Section 11.4.2 can be generalized to the case of dependent Markov observations. If so, state what the modifications to the existing algorithm would be.

CHAPTER 12

Other Methods of Classification

Several different methods of classification were developed in the earlier chapters. In most cases the classes were specified rather completely and the problem reduced to evaluating some known form of discriminant function to make a decision.

In this chapter, three problem areas are described that differ from the previous chapters in one way or another. The first area is that of unsupervised learning or clustering. This type of problem was introduced in Chapter 1 and some basic methods that pertain to it are discussed here. A well-known algorithm called ISODATA is outlined and discussed and a signal coding method known as vector quantization is shown to involve a clustering problem. The second area is that of classification by significance testing. Most supervised problems are based on hypothesis testing, which is appropriate when the statistical properties of all classes are known. Significance testing can be used when statistical properties of only a single class are known. The final area is that of distributed classification. In this problem, various statistical information may be known about the classes, but for reasons of efficiency and practicality, the decision making must be carried on at geographically distributed sites. Each site has access to only a portion of the total observations and the sites must act cooperatively under the constraint of limited communication to make decisions. Research in the area of distributed classification is still in a relatively embryonic stage and we consider the topic only briefly.

12.1 UNSUPERVISED CLASSIFICATION

It was mentioned in Chapter 1 that there exist problems in pattern recognition where a definition of the classes and perhaps even the *number* of classes of objects is unknown. The problem is not only to classify the given data, but also in so doing to *define* the classes.

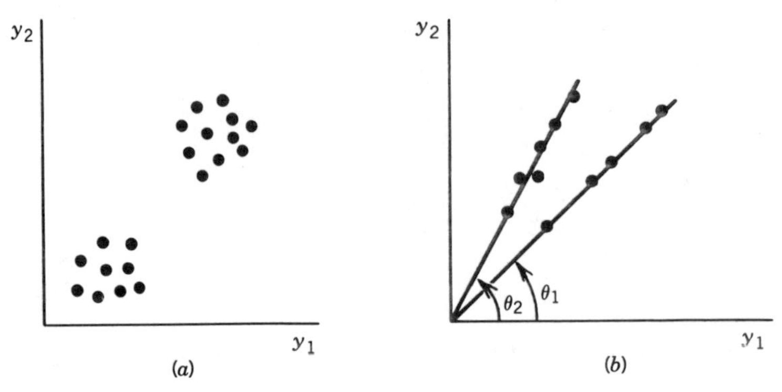

FIGURE 12.1 The identification of clusters. (a) Clusters defined by distance. (b) Clusters defined by subspaces.

There are a number of valid approaches to this problem. One approach is to represent the density function for all the data by a mixture density

$$p_{\mathbf{y}}(\mathbf{y}) = \sum_{i=1}^{N_c} w_i p_{\mathbf{y}|\omega_i}(\mathbf{y}|\omega_i) \tag{12.1}$$

and to fit a set of weights w_i and component densities $p_{\mathbf{y}|\omega_i}$ to the given data. The classes are then identified as the "modes" of the distribution, which in turn are represented by the component densities. The methods for this approximation may or may not assume parametric forms for the component densities and thus lead to either parametric or nonparametric algorithms. Rather thorough discussion of these methods is given in Ref. [1] and also in Refs. [2] and [3].

An alternative, and in some sense equivalent, method for defining the classes is to seek clusters of the points in the measurement space. The procedure is known as *clustering*. In the most general case, the *clusters* are defined as groups of points that are "similar" according to some measure of similarity. Usually, "similarity" is defined as proximity of the points according to a distance function [see Fig. 12.1(a)], but measures of similarity could be based on other properties such as the direction of the vectors in the measurement space. This would be appropriate, for example, when the samples lie in lower dimensional subspaces [see Fig. 12.1(b)]. The method for finding the clusters may have a heuristic basis or may be more rigorously dependent on minimization of a mathematical clustering criterion. In either case, iterative procedures are generally used to find the clusters.

In the subsections that follow, an algorithm to minimize a simple clustering criterion is examined and it is shown that with some simplifying assumptions, an intuitively reasonable procedure known as the K-means algorithm results. The latter is the basis for a well-developed clustering procedure called ISODATA [4], which is described in the succeeding section. An example is then given of the use of clustering in an image segmentation problem. Finally, vector quantization is discussed as a technique involving clustering that is used in signal coding.

12.1.1 A Simple Clustering Algorithm

This section begins with a procedure for clustering in its most essential form and shows that in a specific case this procedure reduces to a simple and intuitively reasonable algorithm. For the present, it will be assumed that the number of clusters N_c is known at the outset.

Denote by $\boldsymbol{Y}$ the set of samples $\{\mathbf{y}^{(i)}\}$ to be classified and by Ω an ordered set of class labels assigned to the samples. If there are N samples in $\boldsymbol{Y}$, then there will be N corresponding labels in Ω each of which could be ω_1 or ω_2 or $\cdots$ or ω_{N_c}. Since the procedure to be described is iterative, let $\Omega^{(r)}$ be the set of class labels at the rth iteration.

Next, assume that there is a criterion function $J(Y,\Omega)$ that measures the optimality of the classification; in particular, assume that the classification of the samples is optimal when J is minimized. Then the following general procedure can be used in an attempt to minimize J.

1. Choose an initial classification $\Omega^{(0)}$ and evaluate J.
2. Change the classification in a way that tends to decrease J.
3. If the new classification is the same as the old (i.e., if it is not possible to decrease J in step 2) then stop; else go to step 2.

These steps form the essence of all classical optimization procedures. Whether or not the algorithm achieves its objective of minimizing J depends on the form of the criterion function and on the specific procedure used to change the classification in step 2. In general, one can only hope to find a *local* minimum and even that may not be guaranteed.

In many optimization problems the variables on which the criterion is based are continuous, so methods involving gradients can be used. In clustering the variables are the class labels, which are discrete. A reasonable procedure, therefore, is to determine the change in the class label for each sample that would result in the greatest decrease in J and apply these changes in step 2. Specifically assume that at the rth iteration the classification is $\Omega^{(r)} = \{\omega_{s_1}, \omega_{s_2}, \ldots, \omega_{s_N}\}$. Then, if ΔJ_i is the largest *negative* change in J that can be made by reclassifying sample $\mathbf{y}^{(i)}$, and $\omega_{s_i'}$, is the corresponding new label for $\mathbf{y}^{(i)}$, then the new set of labels would be chosen as $\Omega^{(r+1)} = \{\omega_{s_1'}, \omega_{s_2'}, \ldots, \omega_{s_N'},\}$.

Note that since Δ_i is evaluated by making one change at a time and $\Omega^{(r+1)}$ has all changes occurring simultaneously, the new value of the criterion will *not*, in general, be given by

$$J + \sum_{i=1}^{N} \Delta J_i \tag{12.2}$$

It is hoped that the new value will be less than the old value, however.

An alternative is to find

$$|\Delta J_\ell| = \max_i |\Delta J_i| \tag{12.3}$$

at each iteration and to make a change in the class of only the ℓth sample. This guarantees that J will decrease monotonically, but the procedure is relatively inefficient.

An algorithm known as K-means (N_c-means in our case) can be developed by choosing a similarity measure that is the Euclidean distance of the samples and a criterion J defined by

$$J = \sum_{k=1}^{N_c} \sum_{\mathbf{y}^{(i)} \sim \omega_k} |\mathbf{y}^{(i)} - \boldsymbol{\mu}_k|^2 \tag{12.4}$$

where the second sum is over all samples in the kth cluster and $\boldsymbol{\mu}_k$ is the "center" of the cluster.[1] It is easy to show (see Problem 12.1) that for a fixed set of samples and class assignments J is minimized by choosing $\boldsymbol{\mu}_k$ to be the *sample mean* of the kth cluster. Furthermore, when $\boldsymbol{\mu}_k$ is thus fixed, J is minimized by choosing the class of $\mathbf{y}^{(i)}$ as the class of the cluster with the nearest mean. An algorithm for minimization of the criterion can thus be written in the following specific form:

K-MEANS ALGORITHM

1. Begin with an arbitrary assignment of samples to clusters or begin with an arbitrary set of cluster centers and assign samples to nearest centers.
2. Compute the sample mean of each cluster.
3. Reassign each sample to the cluster with the nearest mean.
4. If the classification of all samples has not changed, stop; else go to step 2.

12.1.2 The ISODATA Method

The clustering algorithm described in the previous subsection forms the basis for a well-known algorithm known as ISODATA [4]. However, ISODATA also provides a means for determining the number of clusters N_c. In particular, it includes heuristic provisions for splitting an existing cluster into two and for merging two existing clusters into a single cluster.

The main procedure for ISODATA is outlined in the following box. Note that there are three subprocedures that form the algorithm. Although the logic in step 2 seems complicated, the effect is to always try to split if the number of clusters is less than half the desired number, to always try to merge if the number of clusters is more than twice the desired number, and otherwise to try to merge or to split

[1] A number of other criteria are given in [5].

on every other iteration. Note that N_c, the number of clusters, can be changed by each subprocedure.

ISODATA ALGORITHM

T = threshold on number of samples in a cluster

N_D = approximate (desired) number of clusters

σ_S^2 = maximum spread parameter for splitting

D_m = maximum distance separation for merging

N_{max} = maximum number of clusters that can be merged

1. Cluster the existing data into N_c classes but eliminate any data and classes with fewer than T members and decrease N_c accordingly (Procedure I). *Exit* when classification of the samples has not changed.
2. If $N_c \leq \frac{N_D}{2}$ or $N_c < 2N_D$ and iteration odd, then
   a. Split any clusters whose samples form sufficiently disjoint groups and increase N_c accordingly (Procedure II).
   b. If any clusters have been split, go to step 1.
3. Merge any pair of clusters whose samples are sufficiently close and/or overlapping and decrease N_c accordingly (Procedure III).
4. Go to step 1.

Procedure I is a simple variant of the K-means procedure (without the loop). A flowchart is given in Fig. 12.2.

The procedure for splitting is heuristic and rather lengthy to explain. ISODATA assumes that the user enters with an estimated or desired number of clusters. Call this number N_D. Then the following quantities are computed for each of the existing clusters

$$d_k = \frac{1}{N_k} \sum_{\mathbf{y}^{(i)} \sim \omega_k} |\mathbf{y}^{(i)} - \boldsymbol{\mu}_k|; \qquad k = 1, 2, \ldots, N_c \tag{12.5}$$

$$\sigma_k^2 = \max_j \frac{1}{N_k} \sum_{\mathbf{y}^{(i)} \sim \omega_k} (y_j^{(i)} - \mu_{k_j})^2; \qquad k = 1, 2, \ldots, N_c \tag{12.6}$$

where N_k is the number of samples in cluster k, the sum is over all samples in the

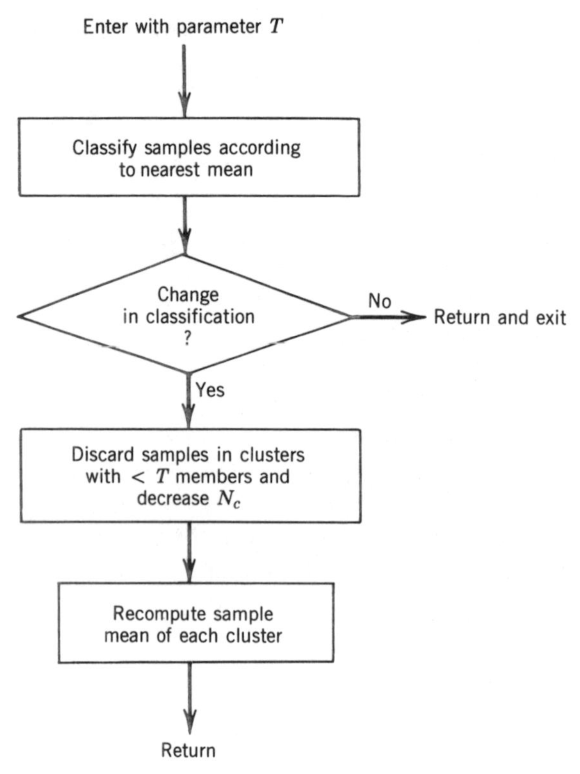

FIGURE 12.2 A flowchart for Procedure I (K−means).

cluster, and the subscript j in Eq. 12.6 refers to the jth component of the vector. The quantity d_k is the average distance of samples from the mean for the kth cluster and the σ_k^2 is the largest variance along the coordinate axes. The overall average distance of samples d is defined by

$$d = \frac{1}{N} \sum_{k=1}^{N_c} N_k d_k \tag{12.7}$$

A maximum spread parameter σ_S^2 is also assumed to have been input by the user. Now, if for any k, σ_k^2 is greater than σ_S^2, then the cluster is split provided that either

$$d_k > d \qquad \text{and} \qquad N_k > 2(T + 1) \tag{12.8}$$

or the number of clusters N_c is less than $N_D/2$.

The ISODATA method for splitting is to replace the original cluster center by two centers displaced slightly in opposite directions along the axis k of largest variance. Usually, an amount of displacement equal to a small fraction of σ_k is satisfactory. A flowchart for the splitting algorithm is given in Fig. 12.3. Depending on the exact implementation, a reindexing step may have to be included at the end of the procedure to account for the additional clusters.

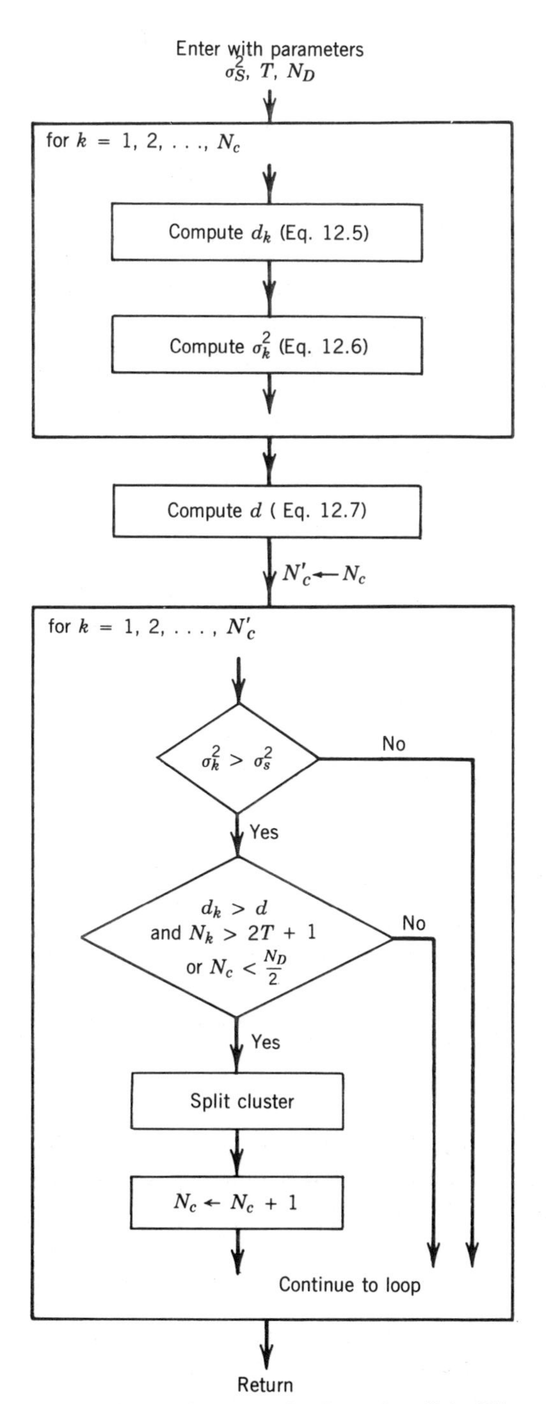

FIGURE 12.3 A flowchart for Procedure II (split).

The algorithm for merging is as follows. All of the pairwise distances $|\boldsymbol{\mu}_i - \boldsymbol{\mu}_j|$ between cluster centers are computed and compared to a threshold D_m. Those pairs of clusters corresponding to distances that are less than the threshold are arranged in a list according to increasing distance. As the first step, the pair of clusters corresponding to the first item on the list (i.e., those clusters with smallest distance) is merged. Then the pair of clusters corresponding to the next item on the list is merged if neither cluster is one of the clusters merged in the first step. The clusters corresponding to the third item on the list are then merged only if neither cluster has been merged in the previous two steps, and so on. This continues as long as the total number of merged clusters does not exceed the input parameter $N_{\max}$. Since the new cluster center for each merger is the mean of both sets of samples, it is not necessary to compute the new centers from scratch. For any two clusters i and j that have been merged, the new mean $\boldsymbol{\mu}'$ can be computed from

$$\boldsymbol{\mu}' = \frac{1}{N_i + N_j}(N_i\boldsymbol{\mu}_i + N_j\boldsymbol{\mu}_j) \tag{12.9}$$

This saves computation. The merging algorithm is shown as a flowchart in Fig. 12.4.

12.1.3 An Image-Processing Example

To demonstrate the application of clustering in a practical example, we consider an image segmentation problem similar to the one in Chapter 11, Section 11.1.3. The image shown in Fig. 12.5(a) is to be segmented into two regions corresponding to fields and trees. Recall that in Chapter 11, the algorithm for performing the segmentation had to be trained on sample images of fields and trees in order to perform the statistical filtering operation that would lead to the segmentation. In this section, clustering is used as a means of automatically identifying the data within the image on which the segmentation algorithm will be trained. As a result, the overall algorithm is unsupervised.

The unsupervised segmentation algorithm proceeds as follows. The image is divided arbitrarily into very small sections as shown by the grid overlayed in Fig. 12.5(b). In this case the larger image of 128×128 pixels is divided into 256 small sections of 8×8 pixels. For each of the small sections, a suitable set of features is estimated and the data are clustered in the feature space. In this example the features used are two coefficients of a two-dimensional linear predictive filter for each small section. The result of clustering the sections is shown in Fig. 12.5(c) and (d). For each set of clustered data, a rectangular region of the largest possible size is formed by combining sections in the corresponding portion of the image. This is shown by the white boxes in Fig. 12.5(c) and 12.5(d). The segmentation algorithm is then trained on these data and applied to the overall image. This produces the segmented image shown in Fig. 12.5(e). A final spatial filtering of the segmented image to remove isolated points and lines then leads to the result shown in Fig. 12.5(f).

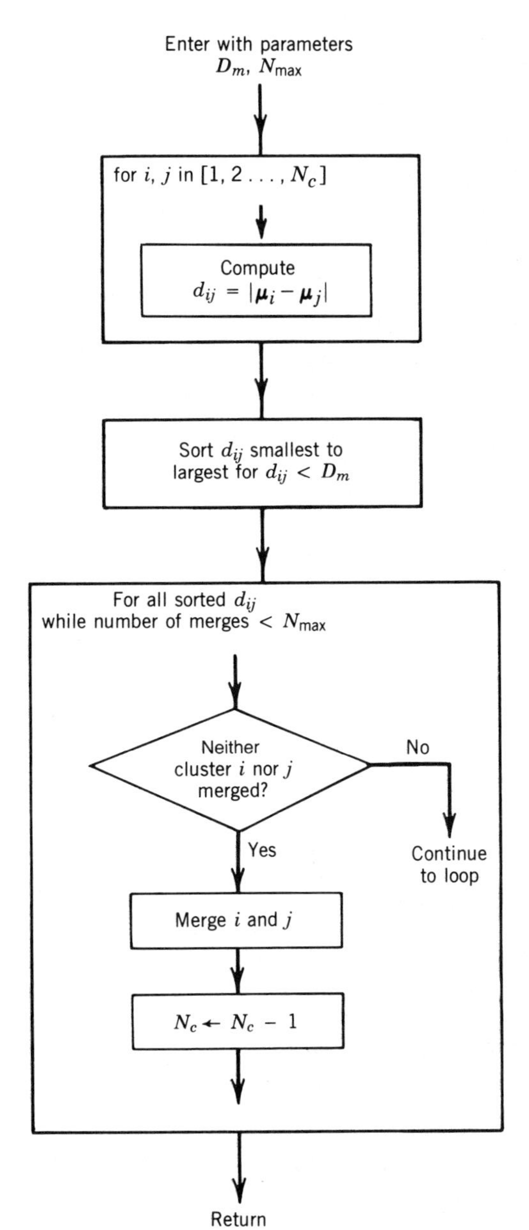

FIGURE 12.4 A flowchart for Procedure III (merge).

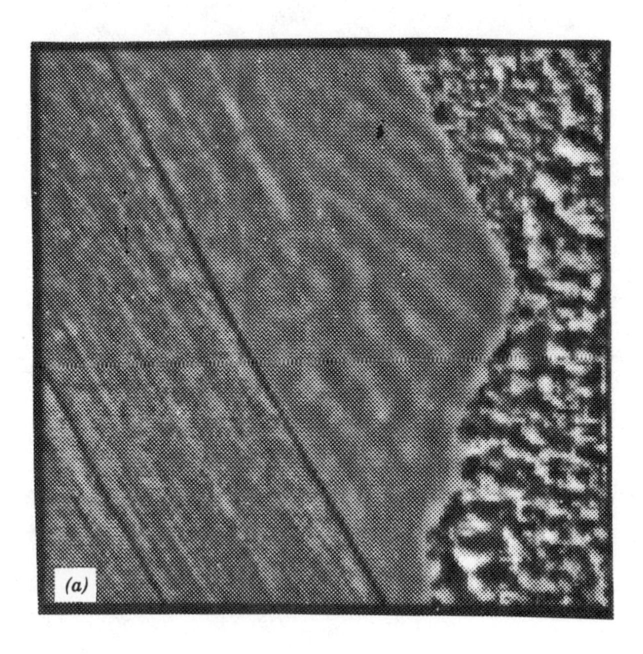

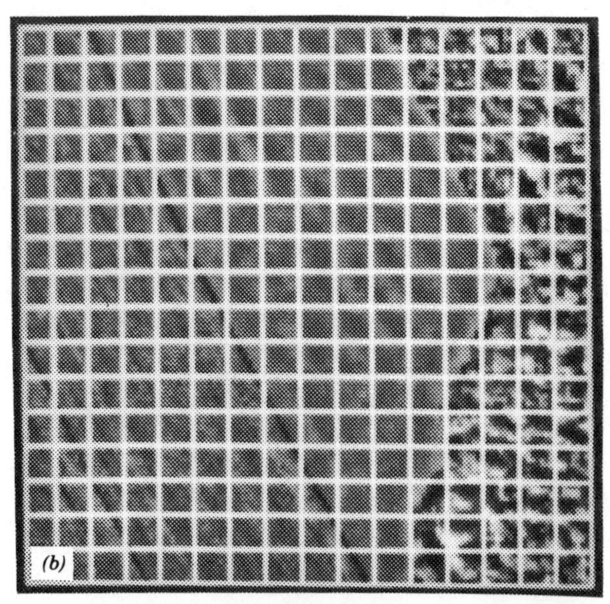

FIGURE 12.5 The unsupervised segmentation of an image. (*a*) The original image. (*b*) Small sections. (*c*) Class 1 sections. (*d*) Class 2 sections. (*e*) The segmented image. (*f*) The filtered result.

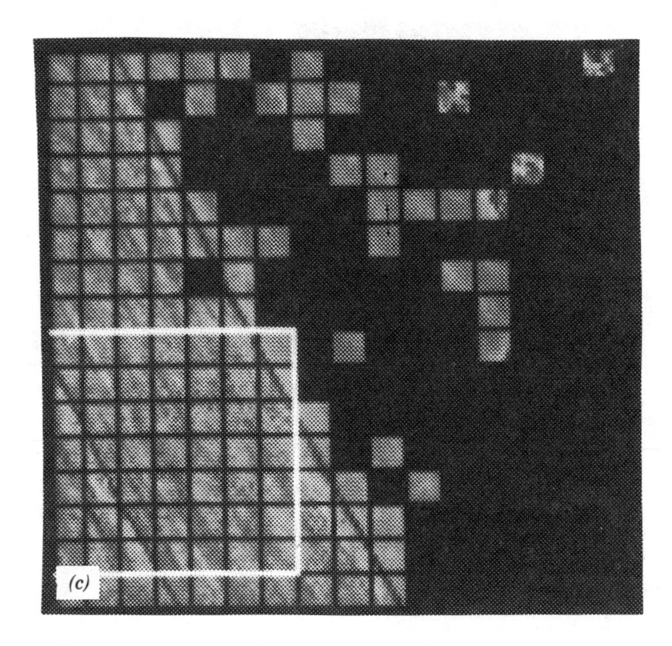

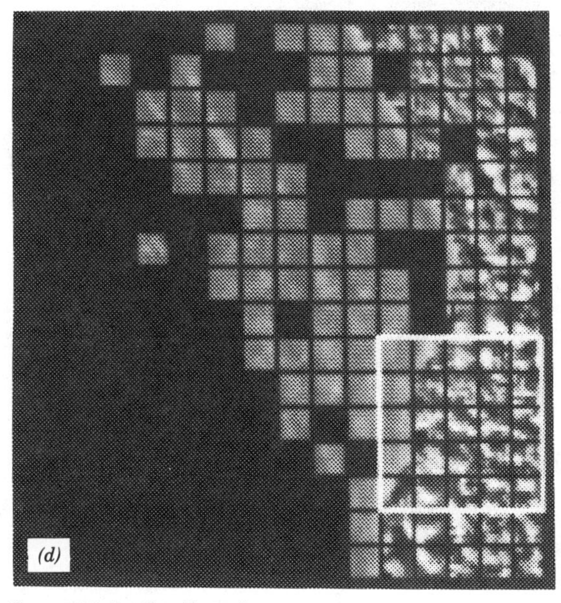

FIGURE 12.5 Continued

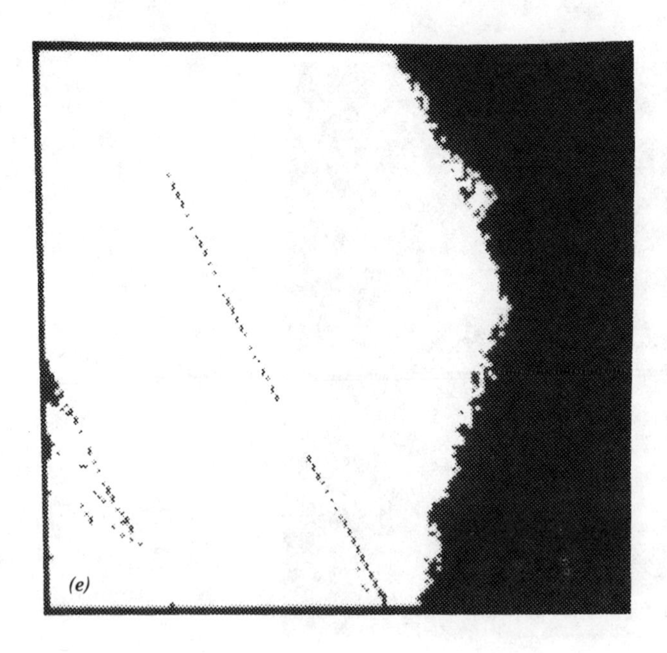

FIGURE 12.5 Continued

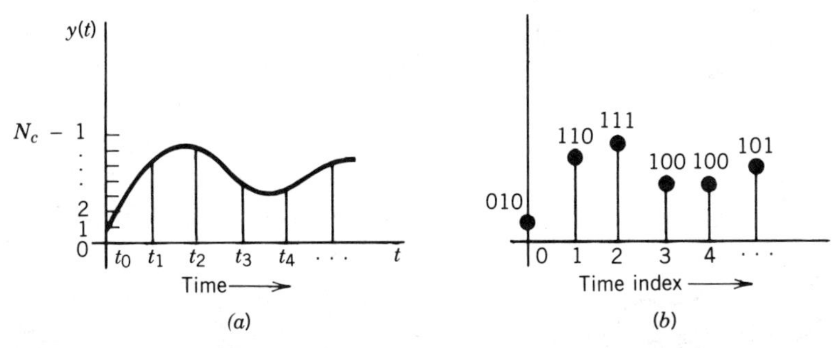

Figure 12.6 The sampling and quantization of a signal. (*a*) The original continuous signal. (*b*) The corresponding digital signal.

12.1.4 Vector Quantization

An important application related to clustering comes from the fields of digital signal processing and communication. As a part of the coding of signals for transmission or storage, the signal values are usually quantized. Figure 12.6(a) depicts a sampled electrical signal that could represent a speech or music waveform, the intensity level in a scanned image, or any number of other phenomena. The range of possible values of the signal is divided into N_c levels; if the sampled signal value $y(t_k)$ falls between two adjacent levels, the signal is represented by a fixed discrete value, perhaps midway between the levels.

Usually, the number of levels N_c is taken to be a power of two, so that the quantized value can be represented by a binary number with $\log_2 N_c$ bits. This results in the digital signal shown in Fig. 12.6(*b*), which is represented by a sequence of binary numbers. In image processing, for example, it is common to use 256 levels of intensity and so to represent an image as a sequence of 8-bit binary numbers (bytes).

Quantization can be thought of as shown in Fig. 12.7(*a*). The value y of the original signal is represented along a line, which is a one-dimensional space. Bins are defined by two adjacent levels. If the value of the original signal falls within the jth bin, then it is mapped to the discrete value μ_j, which represents that bin. When this idea is generalized to m dimensions, the procedure is referred to as *vector quantization*. A block of m adjacent samples of the signal are used to form a vector $\mathbf{y}$. The components of $\mathbf{y}$, which are the signal values, thus represent coordinates of a point in an m-dimensional space. The space is divided into cells with centers $\boldsymbol{\mu}_j$. If a point falls within the jth cell, it is mapped to (i.e., represented by) the center $\boldsymbol{\mu}_j$. The idea is shown in Fig. 12.7(*b*) for $m = 2$.

Vector quantization can be significantly more efficient for signal coding than ordinary scalar quantization. That is, fewer bits are generally required if a block of data is coded as a vector than if the samples are quantized and coded individually. The issue of how to choose the center is a problem in clustering.

Vector quantization coding uses many ideas that are familiar to pattern recognition but with different terminology. As in pattern recognition a distance function

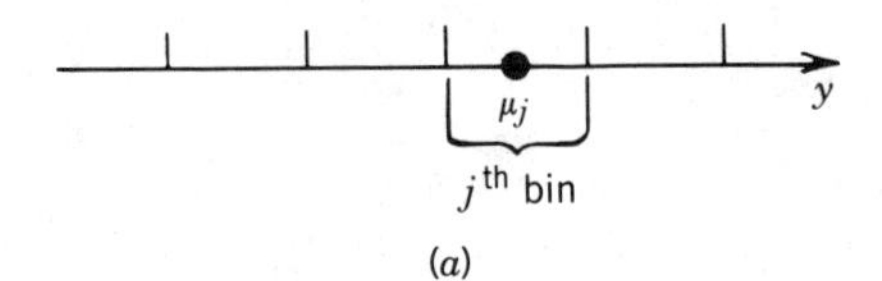

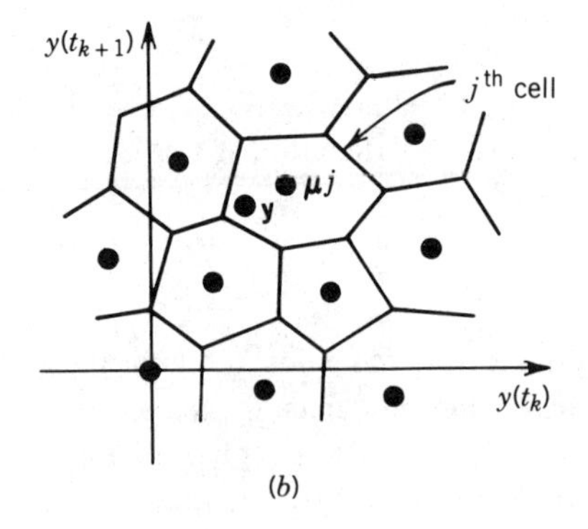

FIGURE 12.7 Scalar and vector quantization. (a) Scalar quantization. (b) Vector quantization.

d must be chosen. The cells are defined implicitly by assigning a vector to the center to which it is nearest. That is, vector quantization consists of the mapping

$$\mathbf{y} \rightarrow \boldsymbol{\mu}_k \tag{12.10a}$$

where

$$d(\mathbf{y}, \boldsymbol{\mu}_k) = \min_j d(\mathbf{y}, \boldsymbol{\mu}_j) \tag{12.10b}$$

The centers are selected to minimize a criterion similar to Eq. 12.4, which is called the *average distortion*. The general form is

$$D = \frac{1}{N} \sum_{k=1}^{N_c} \sum\nolimits_{\mathbf{y}(i) \rightarrow \boldsymbol{\mu}_k} d(\mathbf{y}^{(i)}, \boldsymbol{\mu}_k) \tag{12.11}$$

where N is the total number of vectors $\mathbf{y}^{(i)}$. The set of centers is called the "codebook" and the problem of choosing the centers is called "codebook design." When the distance function (also called the distortion function) is taken to be the Euclidean distance, then a suitable codebook design algorithm is the K-means algorithm. In a classic paper on vector quantization [6] Linde, Buzo, and Gray showed that the algorithm works with a large choice of distortion functions, including some that are not true distance functions as defined in Chapter 4 (see Eq. 4.8). As a result, the K-means algorithm, which is the one most used in practice, is usually referred to in the literature of vector quantization as the Linde–Buzo–Gray (LBG) algorithm.

An excellent review article on vector quantization is the paper by Makhoul et al. [7]. The reader is referred to that paper for further treatment of the subject.

12.2 CLASSIFICATION BY SIGNIFICANCE TESTING

12.2.1 Theory and Methods of Classification

In some problems in pattern recognition, one is faced with recognizing a single class of objects among two or more classes of objects when the statistical properties of the other class or classes is unknown. Examples of this type of problem include recognition of a particular key such as a written signature or code word for access purposes, detection of certain warning signals or fault conditions in diagnostic monitoring, and detection of objects in images against a variety of backgrounds. In all of these cases, one may have an adequate statistical characterization of the class of object to be recognized, but one may not be able to (or may not want to) characterize the other classes. The statistical theory of significance testing is appropriate for dealing with such problems.

In significance testing, a *single* hypothesis is tested against all possible alternatives. The ideas are illustrated in Fig. 12.8. The figure shows a typical probability density function for the class of interest. On the basis of the density function and perhaps other a priori information, one defines a so-called *critical region* corresponding to an "unlikely event." That is, one decides on some basis that certain values of the measurement are unlikely and identifies the corresponding region in the measurement space. The integral of the density function over the critical region is the probability of the unlikely event and is referred to as the *significance level* of the test. One could, for example, define the critical region so that the unlikely event has probability 0.05. In this case, it would be said that the test is being carried out "at the 5 percent significance level."

The procedure for classification is as follows. One begins with the density function for the class of interest and sets a significance level and chooses the critical region. The hypothesis that the measurements come from the given distribution is called the *null hypothesis*. A set of measurements is then taken. If the measurements fall within the critical region, the null hypothesis is rejected. Otherwise, the null hypothesis is accepted.

In significance testing, one is only concerned with the significance level of the test. This is what could be considered to be the class 1 error probability ε_1. One

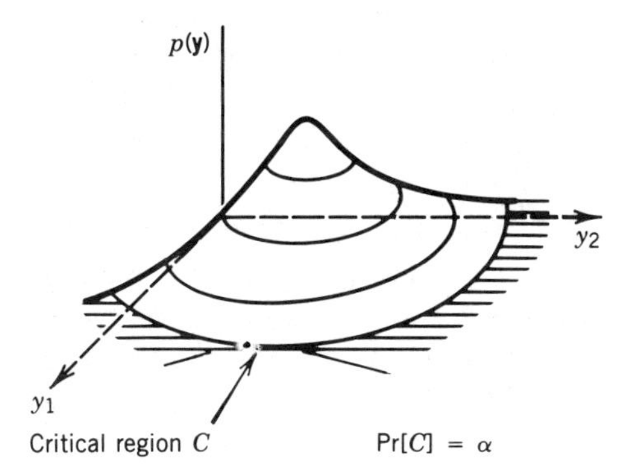

FIGURE 12.8 The probability density with critical region C.

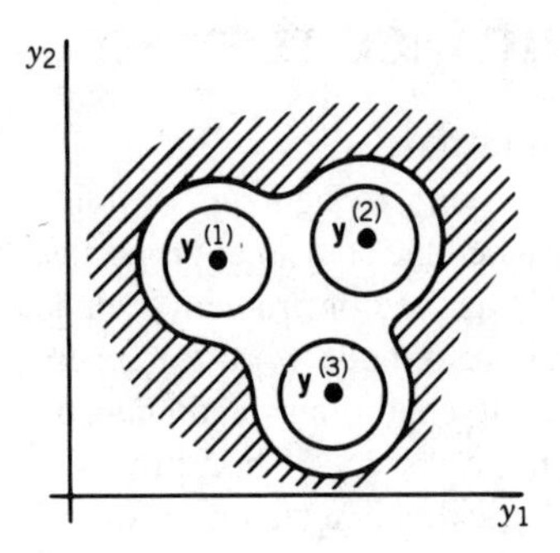

FIGURE 12.9 A critical region for the Parzen density estimate.

is not concerned with the error probabilities for other classes (i.e., the false alarms). These would depend on the distribution of the other classes, which are considered to be unknown.

For multivariate Gaussian observations, a significance test can be written in the form

$$p_{\mathbf{y}}(\hat{\mathbf{y}}) = \frac{1}{(2\pi)^{m/2} |\mathbf{K}|^{1/2}} \exp\left[-\frac{1}{2} (\hat{\mathbf{y}} - \mathbf{m})^T \mathbf{K}^{-1} (\hat{\mathbf{y}} - \mathbf{m}) \right] \geq T_s \qquad (12.12)$$

where the sense of the inequality is written such that the known class is chosen when Eq. 12.12 is satisfied. The threshold T_s corresponding to a given desired level of significance can be found from tables. The test (12.12) can be written in the equivalent form

$$(\hat{\mathbf{y}} - \mathbf{m})^T \mathbf{K}^{-1} (\hat{\mathbf{y}} - \mathbf{m}) \leq (m \ln 2\pi + \ln |\mathbf{K}| - 2 \ln T_s) \qquad (12.13)$$

This shows that the critical region consists of the points outside of a hyperellipse that are beyond a given Mahalanobis distance from the mean. Other forms for the critical region could also be selected such as bounds on specific components of the measurement vector. However, for these other forms, it may be more difficult to establish the significance level of the test.

For nonparametric density estimates, the ideas of significance testing can still be applied, but it is difficult to relate the parameters of the test to the actual significance level. Consider, for example, the Parzen estimate, Eq. 8.4. If the kernel function γ is Gaussian, then a critical region could be defined by the condition

$$\bigcap_{i=1}^{N} [\gamma(\mathbf{y} - \mathbf{y}^{(i)}) < T_s'] \qquad (12.14)$$

where $\mathbf{y}^{(i)}$ are given training samples and T_s' is a chosen threshold parameter. The form of this region is illustrated in Figure 12.9. It consists of an intersection of regions in the measurement space, where points are greater than some specified distance from each of the training samples. A similar kind of decision rule could be derived from the nearest-neighbor estimation procedure. The difficulty of relating the parameter T_s' to the significance level in a high-dimensional measurement space

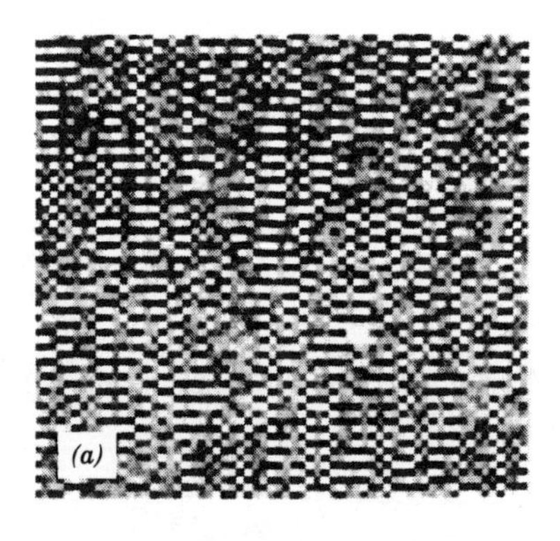

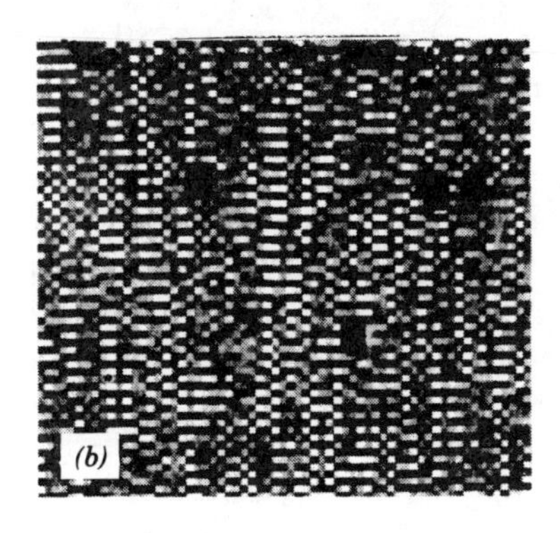

FIGURE 12.10 The application of significance testing to small-object detection in images. (*a*) A texture image. (*b*) Detected objects solid black.

is obvious. However, it is possible to set the threshold experimentally by testing the classifier with data.

12.2.2 Application to Object Detection in Images

An interesting application of significance testing can be found in an image-processing application considered in [8]. The application will be described without too much detail, but it illustrates the range of possible approaches to decision problems.

It was desired to detect objects only a few pixels in size in images with unknown backgrounds. Figure 12.10(a) shows an image of synthetically generated texture, where a few small areas of the image have been replaced by areas whose spatial correlation properties do not match those of the background. To the human observer these areas are difficult to detect. In this problem neither the statistical distribution of the background nor that of the small objects is known. However, since the background probability density function could be estimated, it was decided to make the background correspond to the null hypothesis.

The procedure was as follows. An area a few pixels wide and centered at image coordinates (k_0, ℓ_o) was to be examined to see if it contained any part of an object. This is shown in Fig. 12.11, where the area to be tested is shaded and labeled "decision window." Since the null hypothesis was that all pixels in the decision

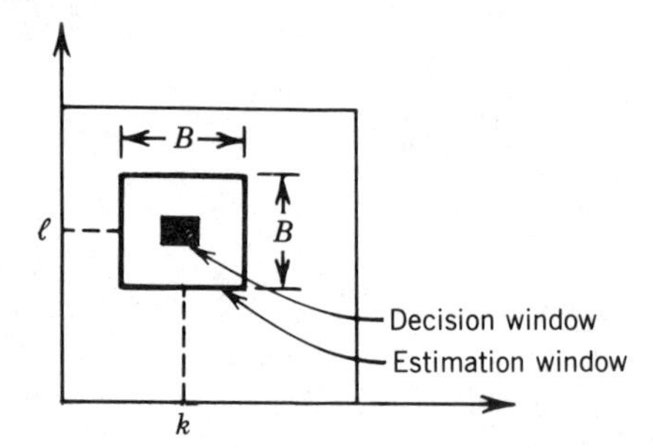

FIGURE 12.11 The processing of an image for object detection.

window belong to the background, a critical region was chosen in the measurement space for the background. The region was chosen such that if parts of *objects* appear in the decision window, the resulting measurements will be unlikely and thus fall in the critical region. Data in a larger window called the estimation window were used to estimate the probability density function for the background. The latter window was chosen large enough so that even if objects were present, the estimation of the background density function would still be accurate. The process was repeated at every point in the image and those points corresponding to decision windows with objects present were highlighted. To make the processing efficient, the algorithm was formulated in terms of two-dimensional linear predictive filtering applied to the image. The results of this processing is shown in Fig. 12.10(b). As seen there, most of the pixels corresponding to "objects" (i.e., pixels not belonging to the background) were detected. The procedure was further applied to aerial photographic images with some success [8]. However, since the only criterion was to find pixels that did not match the local background, a typically large number of objects were detected.

12.3 DISTRIBUTED CLASSIFICATION

12.3.1 Problems in Distributed Classification

In certain types of decision problems, one has to deal with situations where the data being collected are geographically or otherwise distributed. Examples may occur in the sensing of the atmosphere or the ocean in some types of geological or oceanographic studies and in military applications where two or more spatially separated sensors observe a common set of targets for purposes of identification and classification.

The problem in distributed classification is that the data acquired by the sensors are too voluminous to simply transmit to some centralized location, where it can be input to a classifier. The design of classifiers based on hundreds of dimensions is impractical and the communication bandwidth for transmission of large amounts of data may not be available. On the other hand, it is not unreasonable to assume that each sensor can be provided with some processing capability and that each

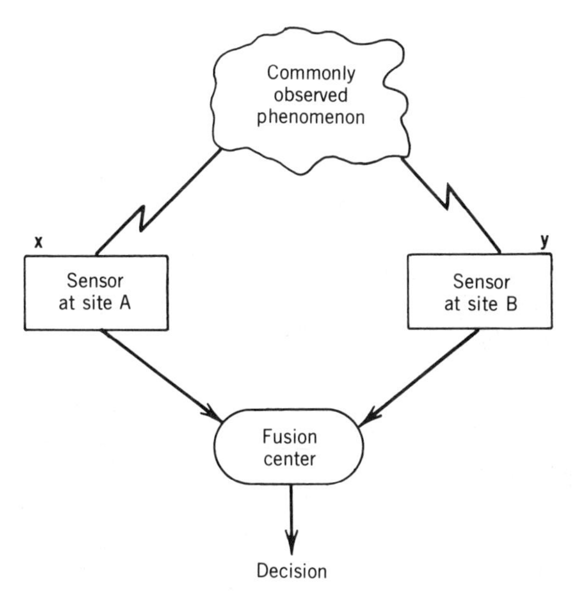

FIGURE 12.12 The sensors at geographically distributed sites observing a common phenomenon.

sensor can perform a portion of the overall task of classification. The sensors can then exchange more limited information with each other in order to arrive at a final decision.

Given a set of communicating sensors, several specific scenarios can be envisioned. At one extreme all sensors could send reduced data to a central fusion node that would combine results to make an overall decision. At the other extreme, one can conceive of completely distributed operation where there is no central node, but through local processing and limited intercommunication, the sites arrive at a decision. (The latter is called a Distributed Sensor Network.)

To focus on a specific case, consider two geographically distributed sensors observing the same phenomenon and communicating with a central node or fusion center that will make the final decision. The situation is depicted in Fig. 12.12. Assume that this is a two-class decision problem so that the ultimate decision will be either ω_1 or ω_2. Also assume that the prior probabilities $\Pr[\omega_i]$ are known, that a Bayes cost function in the form of Eq. 3.7 is specified, and that given the class ω_1 or ω_2, the observations $\mathbf{x}$ and $\mathbf{y}$ made by each sensor are conditionally *independent*.

Now consider what will be called the *centralized* decision rule. This is the decision rule that would be used if both sets of observations $\mathbf{x}$ and $\mathbf{y}$ were available in one place. Since the observations are conditionally independent, the decision rule to minimize the risk globally is given by

$$\Lambda_{\mathbf{xy}}(\hat{\mathbf{x}},\hat{\mathbf{y}}) = \ln \frac{p_{\mathbf{x}|\omega_1}(\hat{\mathbf{x}}|\omega_1)\, p_{\mathbf{y}|\omega_1}(\hat{\mathbf{y}}|\omega_1)}{p_{\mathbf{x}|\omega_2}(\hat{\mathbf{x}}|\omega_2)\, p_{\mathbf{y}|\omega_2}(\hat{\mathbf{y}}|\omega_2)} \quad \mathop{\gtrless}_{\omega_2}^{\omega_1} \quad \ln \lambda_B \tag{12.15}$$

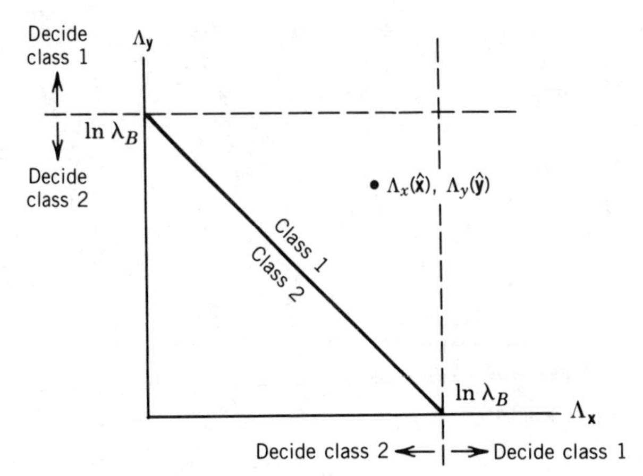

FIGURE 12.13 The optimal decision rules for joint and individual observations.

where λ_B is the Bayes decision threshold given by Eq. 3.14b. The last equation can thus be written in the form

$$\Lambda_{\mathbf{x}}(\hat{\mathbf{x}}) + \Lambda_{\mathbf{y}}(\hat{\mathbf{y}}) \underset{\omega_2}{\overset{\omega_1}{\gtrless}} \ln \lambda_B \tag{12.16}$$

where

$$\Lambda_{\mathbf{x}}(\hat{\mathbf{x}}) = \ln \frac{p_{\mathbf{x}|\omega_1}(\hat{\mathbf{x}}|\omega_1)}{p_{\mathbf{x}|\omega_2}(\hat{\mathbf{x}}|\omega_2)} \tag{12.17a}$$

and

$$\Lambda_{\mathbf{y}}(\hat{\mathbf{y}}) = \ln \frac{p_{\mathbf{y}|\omega_1}(\hat{\mathbf{y}}|\omega_1)}{p_{\mathbf{y}|\omega_2}(\hat{\mathbf{y}}|\omega_2)} \tag{12.17b}$$

Equation (12.16) corresponds to the decision regions shown in Fig. 12.13. If the point represented by the value of the log likelihood ratios falls above the diagonal line, the decision is ω_1; if it falls below the line, the decision is ω_2.

Consider now the case where each sensor separately makes a decision to minimize the Bayes risk based on its own observations and sends that decision to the fusion center. The local decision rules are of the form

$$\Lambda_{\mathbf{x}}(\hat{\mathbf{x}}) = \underset{\omega_2}{\overset{\omega_1}{\gtrless}} \ln \lambda_B \tag{12.18a}$$

and

$$\Lambda_{\mathbf{y}}(\hat{\mathbf{y}}) = \underset{\omega_2}{\overset{\omega_1}{\gtrless}} \ln \lambda_B \tag{12.18b}$$

and the decision boundaries (shown in Fig. 12.13) correspond to the vertical and horizontal dashed lines passing through the points ln λ_B on the $\Lambda_\mathbf{x}$ and $\Lambda_\mathbf{y}$ axes. In this situation it is easy to find points corresponding to observations $\hat{\mathbf{x}}$ and $\hat{\mathbf{y}}$ (such as that shown) where *both* sites using Eq. 12.18 would decide ω_2 while the globally optimal (i.e., lower risk) decision according to Eq. 12.16 is actually ω_1. Thus, even if the fusion center opts to choose ω_2 if and only if both sensors report ω_2 (and thus be conservative with respect to choosing class 2), there will be many cases when it makes a globally suboptimal decision by choosing ω_2.

It is clear from this example that allowing the sensors to make locally optimal decisions does not, in general, result in a globally optimal decision. This is really not surprising, because in so doing, the log likelihood ratios $\Lambda_\mathbf{x}$ and $\Lambda_\mathbf{y}$, which are the sufficient statistics, are effectively quantized to one bit of information each. This has to result in a loss of optimality.

If $\Lambda_\mathbf{x}$ and $\Lambda_\mathbf{y}$ were sent to the fusion center without quantization, then the centralized test of Eq. 12.16 could be carried out in a distributed manner and there would be no loss of global optimality. However, since $\Lambda_\mathbf{x}$ and $\Lambda_\mathbf{y}$ are real numbers, their transmission to the fusion center in a finite time would in theory require infinite communication bandwidth. Tenney and Sandell [9] considered the case of minimizing the risk under the constraint of single-bit quantization and showed that optimization required a local likelihood ratio test at each sensor with threshold dependent on that of the other sensor. Al Bassiouni [10] examined the more general case of quantization of the statistics with a finite number of bits and showed how to select the quantization levels. These problems are discussed in the next subsections.

12.3.2 Fusion of Local Decisions

Here we consider the distributed decision problem depicted in Fig. 12.12 again under the assumption that the phenomenon belongs to either class 1 (ω_1) or class 2 (ω_2). Each sensor is to make its own preliminary decision and report that as a single bit of information to the fusion center. The fusion center will output a single combined decision (ω_1 or ω_2).

There are four combinations of decisions that can be reported to the fusion center. With these four combinations, there are 16 possible fusion rules that the center could implement.[2] Of these, only two do not represent special cases or are not otherwise unreasonable. The two are the AND and the OR rules given in Table 12.1. The corresponding decision boundaries are shown in Fig. 12.14. Although the two decision rules are distinct, their analysis is mathematically equivalent, since one rule can be converted to the other by relabeling the classes. Tenney and Sandell showed that the globally optimal distributed decision rule under AND fusion is two local likelihood ratio tests with coupled thresholds. Thus the globally optimal procedure can be thought of as quantizing the local log likelihood ratio to 1 bit using

[2]It is easy to show that there are 2^{2^N} possible binary functions of N bits.

TABLE 12.1
AND and OR Fusion Rules

Sensor A decision	Sensor B decision	AND output	OR output
ω_1	ω_1	ω_1	ω_1
ω_1	ω_2	ω_2	ω_1
ω_2	ω_1	ω_2	ω_1
ω_2	ω_2	ω_2	ω_2

an appropriate threshold and transmitting the 1-bit quantized value to the fusion center.

The thresholds τ_x and τ_y selected for the local log likelihood ratios are not equal to ln λ_B as in our earlier example but can be derived from the following considerations. For the AND fusion rule the class error probabilities are given by

$$\varepsilon_1 = \Pr[\text{error}|\omega_1] = 1 - \int_{\tau_x}^{\infty}\int_{\tau_y}^{\infty} p_{\Lambda_x\Lambda_y|\omega_1}(\Lambda_x, \Lambda_y|\omega_1)\, d\Lambda_y\, d\Lambda_x \tag{12.19a}$$

and

$$\varepsilon_2 = \Pr[\text{error}|\omega_2] = \int_{\tau_x}^{\infty}\int_{\tau_y}^{\infty} p_{\Lambda_x\Lambda_y|\omega_2}(\Lambda_x, \Lambda_y|\omega_2)\, d\Lambda_y\, d\Lambda_x \tag{12.19b}$$

The risk is given in terms of ε_1 and ε_2 by Eq. 3.15. For convenience one can write Eq. 3.15 as

$$\mathcal{R} = \Pr[\omega_1]\, C_{11} + \Pr[\omega_2]\, C_{22} + \Pr[\omega_1](C_{21} - C_{11})\, \mathcal{R}' \tag{12.20}$$

where

$$\mathcal{R}' = \varepsilon_1 + \lambda_B \varepsilon_2 \tag{12.21}$$

and λ_B is the Bayes decision threshold given by Eq. 3.14b. Clearly, since the other

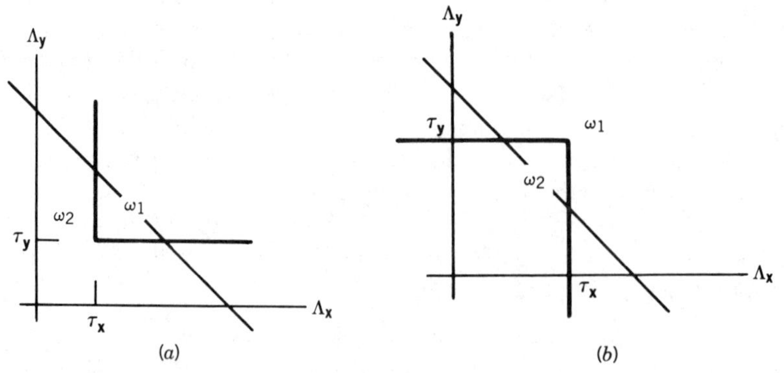

FIGURE 12.14 The decision boundaries for AND and OR fusion. (*a*) AND. (*b*) OR.

terms in Eq. 12.20 are constant, and $C_{21} > C_{11}$, minimizing the risk is equivalent to minimizing $\mathcal{R}'$.

The necessary conditions for minimizing the risk can be obtained by requiring

$$\frac{\partial \mathcal{R}'}{\partial \tau_{\mathbf{x}}} = \frac{\partial \mathcal{R}'}{\partial \tau_{\mathbf{y}}} = 0$$

Thus from Eqs. 12.21 and 12.19 it follows that

$$\frac{\partial \mathcal{R}'}{\partial \tau_{\mathbf{x}}} = -\int_{\tau_{\mathbf{y}}}^{\infty} p_{\Lambda_{\mathbf{x}}\Lambda_{\mathbf{y}}|\omega_1}(\tau_{\mathbf{x}}, \Lambda_{\mathbf{y}}|\omega_1)\, d\Lambda_{\mathbf{y}} + \lambda_B \int_{\tau_{\mathbf{y}}}^{\infty} p_{\Lambda_{\mathbf{x}}\Lambda_{\mathbf{y}}|\omega_2}(\tau_{\mathbf{x}}, \Lambda_{\mathbf{y}}|\omega_2)\, d\Lambda_{\mathbf{y}} = 0$$

or

$$\lambda_B \int_{\tau_{\mathbf{y}}}^{\infty} p_{\Lambda_{\mathbf{x}}\Lambda_{\mathbf{y}}|\omega_2}(\tau_{\mathbf{x}}, \Lambda_{\mathbf{y}}|\omega_2)\, d\Lambda_{\mathbf{y}} = \int_{\tau_{\mathbf{y}}}^{\infty} p_{\Lambda_{\mathbf{x}}\Lambda_{\mathbf{y}}|\omega_1}(\tau_{\mathbf{x}}, \Lambda_{\mathbf{y}}|\omega_1)\, d\Lambda_{\mathbf{y}} \quad (12.22a)$$

and similarly that

$$\frac{\partial \mathcal{R}'}{\partial \tau_{\mathbf{y}}} = -\int_{\tau_{\mathbf{x}}}^{\infty} p_{\Lambda_{\mathbf{x}}\Lambda_{\mathbf{y}}|\omega_1}(\Lambda_{\mathbf{x}}, \tau_{\mathbf{y}}|\omega_1)\, d\Lambda_{\mathbf{x}} + \lambda_B \int_{\tau_{\mathbf{x}}}^{\infty} p_{\Lambda_{\mathbf{x}}\Lambda_{\mathbf{y}}|\omega_2}(\Lambda_{\mathbf{x}}, \tau_{\mathbf{y}}|\omega_2)\, d\Lambda_{\mathbf{x}} = 0$$

or

$$\lambda_B \int_{\tau_{\mathbf{x}}}^{\infty} p_{\Lambda_{\mathbf{x}}\Lambda_{\mathbf{y}}|\omega_2}(\Lambda_{\mathbf{x}}, \tau_{\mathbf{y}}|\omega_2)\, d\Lambda_{\mathbf{x}} = \int_{\tau_{\mathbf{x}}}^{\infty} p_{\Lambda_{\mathbf{x}}\Lambda_{\mathbf{y}}|\omega_1}(\Lambda_{\mathbf{x}}, \tau_{\mathbf{y}}|\omega_1)\, d\Lambda_{\mathbf{x}} \quad (12.22b)$$

Equations 12.22 are a pair of integral equation whose simultaneous solution yields the desired thresholds. However, multiple solutions may exist and so each must be checked for optimality. Equations 12.22 apply even if the observations are not conditionally independent, but they are optimal only if we insist on fixed data-independent thresholds [9, 11].

When the observations *are* conditionally independent, the probability densities in Eq. 12.22 factor into a product of conditional densities for $\Lambda_{\mathbf{x}}$ and $\Lambda_{\mathbf{y}}$. For this case, the equations can be written as

$$\frac{p_{\Lambda_{\mathbf{x}}|\omega_1}(\tau_{\mathbf{x}}|\omega_1)}{p_{\Lambda_{\mathbf{x}}|\omega_2}(\tau_{\mathbf{x}}|\omega_2)} = \lambda_B \frac{\int_{\tau_{\mathbf{y}}}^{\infty} p_{\Lambda_{\mathbf{y}}|\omega_2}(\Lambda_{\mathbf{y}}|\omega_2)\, d\Lambda_{\mathbf{y}}}{\int_{\tau_{\mathbf{y}}}^{\infty} p_{\Lambda_{\mathbf{y}}|\omega_1}(\Lambda_{\mathbf{y}}|\omega_1)\, d\Lambda_{\mathbf{y}}} \quad (12.23a)$$

and

$$\frac{p_{\Lambda_y|\omega_1}(\tau_y|\omega_1)}{p_{\Lambda_y|\omega_2}(\tau_y|\omega_2)} = \lambda_B \frac{\int_{\tau_x}^{\infty} p_{\Lambda_x|\omega_2}(\Lambda_x|\omega_2)\, d\Lambda_x}{\int_{\tau_x}^{\infty} p_{\Lambda_x|\omega_1}(\Lambda_x|\omega_1)\, d\Lambda_x} \tag{12.23b}$$

Finally, if the following quantities, which are related to the local decision procedures, are defined

$$\ell_{\Lambda_x}(\Lambda_x) = \frac{p_{\Lambda_x|\omega_1}(\Lambda_x|\omega_1)}{p_{\Lambda_x|\omega_2}(\Lambda_x|\omega_2)} \tag{12.24a}$$

$$\ell_{\Lambda_y}(\Lambda_y) = \frac{p_{\Lambda_y|\omega_1}(\Lambda_y|\omega_1)}{p_{\Lambda_y|\omega_2}(\Lambda_y|\omega_2)} \tag{12.24b}$$

$$\varepsilon_{x1} = \int_{-\infty}^{\tau_x} p_{\Lambda_x|\omega_1}(\Lambda_x|\omega_1)\, d\Lambda_x \tag{12.25a}$$

$$\varepsilon_{x2} = \int_{\tau_x}^{\infty} p_{\Lambda_x|\omega_2}(\Lambda_x|\omega_2)\, d\Lambda_x \tag{12.25b}$$

$$\varepsilon_{y1} = \int_{-\infty}^{\tau_y} p_{\Lambda_y|\omega_1}(\Lambda_y|\omega_1)\, d\Lambda_y \tag{12.25c}$$

$$\varepsilon_{y2} = \int_{\tau_y}^{\infty} p_{\Lambda_y|\omega_2}(\Lambda_y|\omega_2)\, d\Lambda_y \tag{12.25d}$$

then Eq. 12.23, which expresses the coupling between the thresholds, can be written as

$$\ell_{\Lambda_x}(\tau_x) = \lambda_B \frac{\varepsilon_{y2}}{1 - \varepsilon_{y1}} \tag{12.26a}$$

$$\ell_{\Lambda_y}(\tau_y) = \lambda_B \frac{\varepsilon_{x2}}{1 - \varepsilon_{x1}} \tag{12.26b}$$

This gives a concise description of the coupling between the decision thresholds demonstrated by Tenney and Sandell.

12.3.3 Classification Using Quantized Statistics

In section 12.3.1, it was observed that when the observations of two sensors viewing a common phenomenon were conditionally independent, the optimal centralized classification algorithm could be implemented in a distributed manner. Each sensor can compute a log likelihood ratio based on its own observations and transmit that statistic to the fusion center. The fusion center can then arrive at an optimal decision by adding the two statistics and comparing the result to a fixed threshold ($\ln \lambda_B$). It was further observed however, that in principle, the transmission of the local log likelihood ratio statistics would require infinite communication bandwidth.

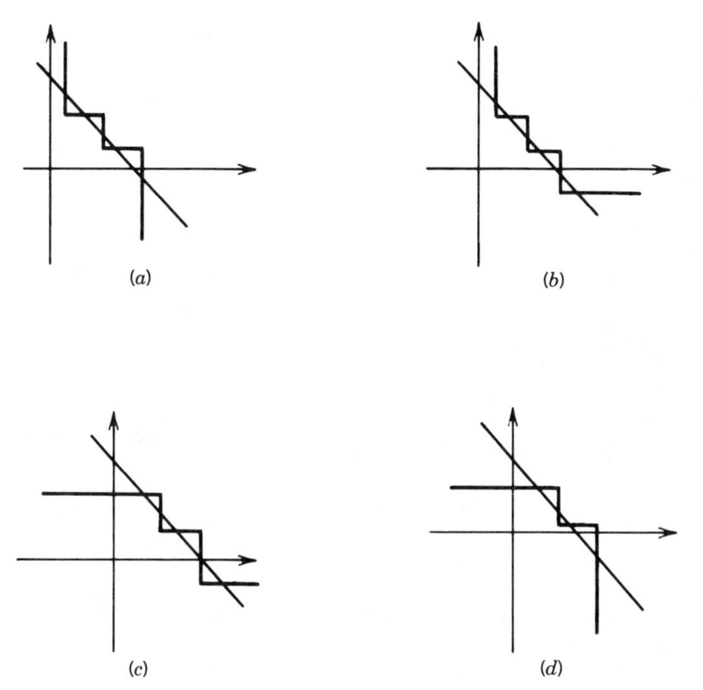

FIGURE 12.15 Various approximations of the centralized decision boundary.

In Section 12.3.2, we considered the problem where each sensor makes its own decision based on the local observations and sends the result to the fusion center. The fusion center then makes a combined decision using AND or OR logic. This problem can be thought of as a quantization of the local log likelihood ratios to 1 bit. It was shown in this case that special thresholds are required in the local likelihood ratio tests that are different from the Bayes threshold and that the thresholds for the two sensors are coupled through a pair of integral equations.

Al Bassiouni [10] filled in the gap between these two extreme cases by considering the problem when the log likelihood ratios are quantized to an arbitrary, finite number of bits and showed how to perform the quantization optimally.

The analysis proceeds as follows. The Tenney–Sandell procedure results in the decision boundary shown in Fig. 12.14(a). This can be considered to be a very rough approximation to the decision boundary for the centralized test based on 1-bit quantization of the local log likelihood ratios. If the log likelihood ratios Λ_x and Λ_y are instead quantized to Q discrete values, this results in a staircaselike decision boundary that can be made to yield a better approximation to the centralized test. Four examples of staircaselike decision boundaries approximating a centralized decision boundary are shown in Fig. 12.15. In the approach to be considered, one of these approximation forms is selected and the threshold values, which correspond to break points on the boundary, are chosen to minimize the Bayes risk.

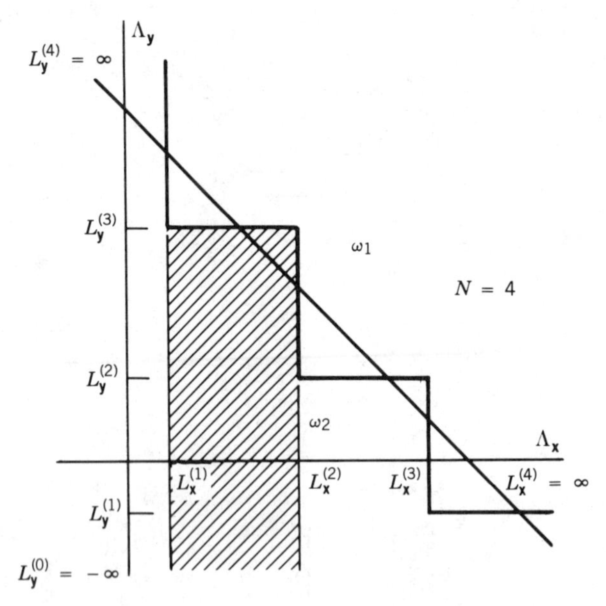

FIGURE 12.16 A selection of levels on a staircase approximation to the centralized decision boundary.

To see how this is done, the decision boundary of Fig. 12.15(b) is redrawn in Fig. 12.16. The break points are identified by thresholds $L_{\mathbf{x}}^{(i)}$ along the $\Lambda_{\mathbf{x}}$ axis and $L_{\mathbf{y}}^{(i)}$ along the $\Lambda_{\mathbf{y}}$ axis as shown in the figure. Since class 1 is not chosen when the values of $\Lambda_{\mathbf{x}}$ and $\Lambda_{\mathbf{y}}$ lie below the boundary, the class 1 error can be obtained by integrating along vertical strips in this region, as illustrated in Fig. 12.16. If the break points are indexed from 0 to Q, the class 1 error probability can thus be written as

$$\varepsilon_1 = \sum_{i=0}^{Q-1} \int_{-\infty}^{L_{\mathbf{y}}^{(Q-i)}} \int_{L_{\mathbf{x}}^{(i)}}^{L_{\mathbf{x}}^{(i+1)}} p_{\Lambda_{\mathbf{x}}\Lambda_{\mathbf{y}}|\omega_1}(\Lambda_{\mathbf{x}}, \Lambda_{\mathbf{y}}|\omega_1)\, d\Lambda_{\mathbf{x}}\, d\Lambda_{\mathbf{y}} \tag{12.27}$$

where for the boundary shown here $L_{\mathbf{x}}^{(Q)} = L_{\mathbf{y}}^{(Q)} = \infty$ and $L_{\mathbf{x}}^{(0)} = -\infty$. The class 2 error probability can be obtained in a similar manner by integrating along horizontal strips in the region above the boundary. The result is

$$\varepsilon_2 = \sum_{i=1}^{Q-1} \int_{L_{\mathbf{y}}^{(i)}}^{L_{\mathbf{y}}^{(i+1)}} \int_{L_{\mathbf{x}}^{(Q-i)}}^{\infty} p_{\Lambda_{\mathbf{x}}\Lambda_{\mathbf{y}}|\omega_2}(\Lambda_{\mathbf{x}}, \Lambda_{\mathbf{y}}|\omega_2)\, d\Lambda_{\mathbf{x}}\, d\Lambda_{\mathbf{y}} \tag{12.28}$$

To select the thresholds $L_{\mathbf{x}}^{(i)}$ and $L_{\mathbf{y}}^{(i)}$ to minimize the risk, we require

$$\frac{\partial \mathcal{R}'}{\partial L_{\mathbf{x}}^{(k)}} = \frac{\partial \varepsilon_1}{\partial L_{\mathbf{x}}^{(k)}} + \lambda_B \frac{\partial \varepsilon_2}{\partial L_{\mathbf{x}}^{(k)}} = 0 \qquad k = 1, 2, \ldots, Q-1 \tag{12.29a}$$

and

$$\frac{\partial \mathcal{R}'}{\partial L_{\mathbf{y}}^{(k)}} = \frac{\partial \varepsilon_1}{\partial L_{\mathbf{y}}^{(k)}} + \lambda_B \frac{\partial \varepsilon_2}{\partial L_{\mathbf{y}}^{(k)}} = 0 \qquad k = 1, 2, \ldots, Q-1 \quad (12.29b)$$

This leads to as many equations as there are unknowns.

Now observe from Eq. 12.27 that

$$\frac{\partial \varepsilon_1}{\partial L_{\mathbf{x}}^{(k)}} = \int_{-\infty}^{L_{\mathbf{y}}^{(Q-k+1)}} p_{\Lambda_{\mathbf{x}}\Lambda_{\mathbf{y}}|\omega_1}(L_{\mathbf{x}}^{(k)}, \Lambda_{\mathbf{y}}|\omega_1)\, d\Lambda_{\mathbf{y}} - \int_{-\infty}^{L_{\mathbf{y}}^{(Q-k)}} p_{\Lambda_{\mathbf{x}}\Lambda_{\mathbf{y}}|\omega_1}(L_{\mathbf{x}}^{(k)}, \Lambda_{\mathbf{y}}|\omega_1)\, d\Lambda_{\mathbf{y}}$$

$$= \int_{L_{\mathbf{y}}^{(Q-k)}}^{L_{\mathbf{y}}^{(Q-k+1)}} p_{\Lambda_{\mathbf{x}}\Lambda_{\mathbf{y}}|\omega_1}(L_{\mathbf{x}}^{(k)}, \Lambda_{\mathbf{y}}|\omega_1)\, d\Lambda_{\mathbf{y}} \quad (12.30a)$$

and

$$\frac{\partial \varepsilon_1}{\partial L_{\mathbf{y}}^{(k)}} = \int_{L_{\mathbf{x}}^{(Q-k)}}^{L_{\mathbf{x}}^{(Q-k+1)}} p_{\Lambda_{\mathbf{x}}\Lambda_{\mathbf{y}}|\omega_1}(\Lambda_{\mathbf{x}}, L_{\mathbf{y}}^{(k)}|\omega_1)\, d\Lambda_{\mathbf{x}} \quad (12.30b)$$

Also, from Eq. 12.28 we have

$$\frac{\partial \varepsilon_2}{\partial L_{\mathbf{x}}^{(k)}} = -\int_{L_{\mathbf{y}}^{(Q-k)}}^{L_{\mathbf{y}}^{(Q-k+1)}} p_{\Lambda_{\mathbf{x}}\Lambda_{\mathbf{y}}|\omega_2}(L_{\mathbf{x}}^{(k)}, \Lambda_{\mathbf{y}}|\omega_2)\, d\Lambda_{\mathbf{y}} \quad (12.31a)$$

and

$$\frac{\partial \varepsilon_2}{\partial L_{\mathbf{y}}^{(k)}} = -\int_{L_{\mathbf{x}}^{(Q-k)}}^{L_{\mathbf{x}}^{(Q-k+1)}} p_{\Lambda_{\mathbf{x}}\Lambda_{\mathbf{y}}|\omega_2}(\Lambda_{\mathbf{x}}, L_{\mathbf{y}}^{(k)}|\omega_2)\, d\Lambda_{\mathbf{x}} \quad (12.31b)$$

If Eqs. 12.30 and 12.31 are substituted into Eq. 12.29, the result is

$$\int_{L_{\mathbf{y}}^{(Q-k)}}^{L_{\mathbf{y}}^{(Q-k+1)}} p_{\Lambda_{\mathbf{x}}\Lambda_{\mathbf{y}}|\omega_1}(L_{\mathbf{x}}^{(k)}, \Lambda_{\mathbf{y}}|\omega_1)\, d\Lambda_{\mathbf{y}} = \lambda_B \int_{L_{\mathbf{y}}^{(Q-k)}}^{L_{\mathbf{y}}^{(Q-k+1)}} p_{\Lambda_{\mathbf{x}}\Lambda_{\mathbf{y}}|\omega_2}(L_{\mathbf{x}}^{(k)}, \Lambda_{\mathbf{y}}|\omega_2)\, d\Lambda_{\mathbf{y}} \quad (12.32a)$$

and

$$\int_{L_{\mathbf{x}}^{(Q-k)}}^{L_{\mathbf{x}}^{(Q-k+1)}} p_{\Lambda_{\mathbf{x}}\Lambda_{\mathbf{y}}|\omega_1}(\Lambda_{\mathbf{x}}, L_{\mathbf{y}}^{(k)}|\omega_1)\, d\Lambda_{\mathbf{x}} = \lambda_B \int_{L_{\mathbf{x}}^{(Q-k)}}^{L_{\mathbf{x}}^{(Q-k+1)}} p_{\Lambda_{\mathbf{x}}\Lambda_{\mathbf{y}}|\omega_2}(\Lambda_{\mathbf{x}}, L_{\mathbf{y}}^{(k)}|\omega_2)\, d\Lambda_{\mathbf{x}} \quad (12.32b)$$

Finally, since the observations are conditionally independent, the class conditional density functions for $\Lambda_{\mathbf{x}}$ and $\Lambda_{\mathbf{y}}$ factor and these last questions can be written as

$$\ell_{\Lambda_{\mathbf{x}}}(L_{\mathbf{x}}^{(k)}) = \lambda_B \frac{\displaystyle\int_{L_{\mathbf{y}}^{(Q-k)}}^{L_{\mathbf{y}}^{(Q-k+1)}} p_{\Lambda_{\mathbf{y}}|\omega_2}(\Lambda_{\mathbf{y}}|\omega_2)\, d\Lambda_{\mathbf{y}}}{\displaystyle\int_{L_{\mathbf{y}}^{(Q-k)}}^{L_{\mathbf{y}}^{(Q-k+1)}} p_{\Lambda_{\mathbf{y}}|\omega_1}(\Lambda_{\mathbf{y}}|\omega_1)\, d\Lambda_{\mathbf{y}}} \qquad k = 1, 2, \ldots, Q-1 \tag{12.33a}$$

$$\ell_{\Lambda_{\mathbf{y}}}(L_{\mathbf{y}}^{(k)}) = \lambda_B \frac{\displaystyle\int_{L_{\mathbf{x}}^{(Q-k)}}^{L_{\mathbf{x}}^{(Q-k+1)}} p_{\Lambda_{\mathbf{x}}|\omega_2}(\Lambda_{\mathbf{x}}|\omega_2)\, d\Lambda_{\mathbf{x}}}{\displaystyle\int_{L_{\mathbf{x}}^{(Q-k)}}^{L_{\mathbf{x}}^{(Q-k+1)}} p_{\Lambda_{\mathbf{x}}|\omega_1}(\Lambda_{\mathbf{x}}|\omega_1)\, d\Lambda_{\mathbf{x}}} \qquad k = 1, 2, \ldots, Q-1 \tag{12.33b}$$

The simultaneous solution of Eq. 12.33 (which must be performed numerically, and checked for optimality) yields the optimal quantization levels.

12.3.4 The Problem of Correlated Observations

A fundamental problem arises when the observations $\mathbf{x}$ and $\mathbf{y}$ taken by two sensors are not conditionally independent. Let us ignore the quantization problem for the moment. It was seen that when the observations are independent the log likelihood ratio of Eq. 12.15 could be written as the sum of two parts as in Eq. 12.16. In principle, the first sensor could compute the portion depending only on $\mathbf{x}$ and the second sensor could compute the portion depending only on $\mathbf{y}$ and the results could be sent to the fusion center. Thus the additive separability of the log likelihood ratio permits the distributed computation.

Special cases exist for correlated observations when a distributed computation is still possible. The detection of a deterministic signal in additive Gaussian noise is one such case. If we form the combined observation vector

$$\begin{bmatrix} \mathbf{x} \\ \mathbf{y} \end{bmatrix}$$

for this problem, the class conditional density functions for the combined observations will have equal covariance matrices, whether or not $\mathbf{x}$ is correlated with $\mathbf{y}$. Thus the Bayes optimal classifier is a linear classifier (see Chapter 6), which can be written in the general form

$$\mathbf{b}^T \begin{bmatrix} \mathbf{x} \\ \mathbf{y} \end{bmatrix} = \mathbf{b}_1^T\mathbf{x} + \mathbf{b}_2^T\mathbf{y} \quad \underset{\omega_2}{\overset{\omega_1}{\lessgtr}} \quad T' \tag{12.34}$$

where T' is a function of λ_B. Therefore, the computation can be distributed between the two sensors and the fusion center.

In general, the log likelihood ratio for correlated observations is not separable. Tenney and Sandell observed that for their problem this leads to thresholds on the local decisions that *depend on the other sensor's observations.* This contradicts the principle of distributed computation. Lauer and Sandell [11], and Al Bassiouni considered suboptimal problems involving fixed thresholds. In these cases the solutions are similar to those developed for conditionally independent observations. Specifically, the densities $p_{\Lambda_\mathbf{x}|\omega_i}(\Lambda_\mathbf{x}|\omega_i)$ and $p_{\Lambda_\mathbf{y}|\omega_i}(\Lambda_\mathbf{y}|\omega_i)$ appearing in the integrals in Eq. 12.23 are replaced by the densities $p_{\Lambda_\mathbf{x}|\Lambda_\mathbf{y}\omega_i}(\Lambda_\mathbf{x}|\tau_\mathbf{y}, \omega_i)$ and $p_{\Lambda_\mathbf{y}|\Lambda_\mathbf{x}\omega_i}(\Lambda_\mathbf{y}|\tau_\mathbf{x}, \omega_i)$. In Eq. 12.33 these terms are replaced by $p_{\Lambda_\mathbf{x}|\Lambda_\mathbf{y}\omega_i}(\Lambda_\mathbf{x}|L_\mathbf{y}^{(k)}, \omega_i)$ and $p_{\Lambda_\mathbf{y}|\Lambda_\mathbf{x}\omega_i}(\Lambda_\mathbf{y}|L_\mathbf{x}^{(k)}, \omega_i)$.

Another approach that seems reasonable is to write the log likelihood ratio for the observations in the form

$$\Lambda_{\mathbf{xy}}(\hat{\mathbf{x}}, \hat{\mathbf{y}}) = \Lambda_{\mathbf{x}|\mathbf{y}}(\hat{\mathbf{x}}|\hat{\mathbf{y}}) + \Lambda_\mathbf{y}(\hat{\mathbf{y}}) \tag{12.35}$$

where $\Lambda_{\mathbf{x}|\mathbf{y}}(\hat{\mathbf{x}}|\hat{\mathbf{y}})$ is defined by

$$\Lambda_{\mathbf{x}|\mathbf{y}}(\hat{\mathbf{x}}|\hat{\mathbf{y}}) = \ln \frac{p_{\mathbf{x}|\mathbf{y}\omega_1}(\hat{\mathbf{x}}|\hat{\mathbf{y}}, \omega_1)}{p_{\mathbf{x}|\mathbf{y}\omega_2}(\hat{\mathbf{x}}|\hat{\mathbf{y}}, \omega_2)} \tag{12.36}$$

and $\Lambda_\mathbf{y}(\hat{\mathbf{y}})$ is given by Eq. 12.17b. Then the sensor with observations $\mathbf{x}$ could make some estimate for the other observations $\mathbf{y}$ based on its own observations and use Eq. 12.36 for its likelihood ratio test. Hahn [12] tried this approach for jointly Gaussian observations using maximum likelihood estimation. Experimentally, the results were quite good and compared well with the centralized test. However, the procedure is largely heuristic and nothing has been claimed about its optimality.

12.4 SUMMARY

This chapter discusses some approaches to classification that differ in various respects from the methods discussed in other chapters. The chapter begins with a treatment of unsupervised classification. A basic framework for clustering is considered and a particular algorithm known as ISODATA is described. An example is given of clustering applied to an image segmentation problem, and the role of clustering in a signal coding procedure known as vector quantization is described.

The statistical procedure of significance testing is then presented. Significance testing provides an appropriate theoretical basis for classification when the density function for only a single class is known. Finally, the new area of distributed classification is introduced. In distributed problems, observations on objects or phenomena to be classified are collected by geographically dispersed sensors. The sensors must work autonomously but cooperatively to reduce the observations to appropriate statistics that can then be used to make a final decision. In the version of the problem described, the reduced statistics are sent to a central fusion center. The system is optimized to globally minimize the Bayes risk.

REFERENCES

1. R. O. DUDA and P. E. HART. *Pattern Recognition and Scene Analysis*, New York: John Wiley & Sons Inc., 1973.
2. P. A. DEVIJVER, and J. KITTLER. *Pattern Recognition: A Statistical Approach*. Englewood Cliffs, NJ: Prentice-Hall, Inc., 1962.
3. W. S. MEISEL. *Computer-Oriented Approaches to Pattern Recognition*. New York: Academic Press, 1972.
4. G. H. BALL, and D. J. HALL. "Isodata, A Novel Method of Data Analysis and Pattern Classification." Stanford Research Institute Technical Report, (NTIS AD699616) Stanford, CA, 1965.
5. K. FUKUNAGA. *Introduction to Statistical Pattern Recognition*, New York: Academic Press, 1972.
6. Y. LINDE, A. BUZO, and R. M. GRAY. "An Algorithm for Vector Quantizer Design." *IEEE Trans. Communications*, Vol. COM-28, No. 1, pp. 84–95 (January 1980).
7. J. MAKHOUL, S. ROUCAS, and H. GISH. "Vector Quantization in Speech Coding." *Proc. IEEE*, Vol. 73, No. 11, pp. 1551–1588 (November 1985).
8. C. W. THERRIEN, T. F. QUATIERI, and D. E. DUDGEON. "Statistical Model-Based Algorithms for Image Analysis." *Proc. IEEE*, Vol. 74, No. 4 (April 1986).
9. R. R. TENNEY, and N. R. SANDELL. "Detection with Distributed Sensors." *IEEE Trans. Aerospace and Electronic Systems*, Vol. AES-22, No. 2 (March 1986).
10. A. M. AL-BASSIOUNI. "Optimal Signal Processing in Distributed Sensor Systems." PhD Dissertation, Naval Postgraduate School, Monterey, CA, December 1987.
11. G. LAUER, and N. R. SANDELL. "Distributed Detection of Known Signal in Noise." Report 160, ALPHATECH, Burlington, MA, March 1982.
12. S. C. HAHN. "Analysis of a Distributed Decision Algorithm." M. S. Thesis, Department of Electrical and Computer Engineering, Naval Postgraduate School, December 1985.

PROBLEMS

12.1 Show that for a fixed set of samples $\boldsymbol{Y} = \{\mathbf{y}^{(i)}\}$ and a fixed set of class assignments $\Omega = \{\omega_{s_i}\}$ Eq. 12.4 is minimized by choosing

$$\boldsymbol{\mu}_k = \frac{1}{N_k} \sum_{\mathbf{y}^{(i)} \sim \omega_k} \mathbf{y}^{(i)}$$

where N_k is the number of samples with label ω_k. Show also that when the $\boldsymbol{\mu}_k$ are fixed, the class ω_{s_i} for sample $\mathbf{y}^{(i)}$ that maximizes $|\Delta J_i|$ is given by

$$\omega_{s_i} = \omega_\ell \qquad \text{where } |\mathbf{y}^{(i)} - \boldsymbol{\mu}_\ell| = \min_k |\mathbf{y}^{(i)} - \boldsymbol{\mu}_k|$$

that is, $|\Delta J_i|$ is maximized by assigning $\mathbf{y}^{(i)}$ to the cluster with the nearest mean.

12.2 When the Crumble-Little Cookie Company closes, the traffic on route I99 increases to an average of 30 cars per minute. Interarrival times T between two successive cars are independent and described by the exponential density function

$$p_T(\hat{T}) = \begin{cases} 30\, e^{-30\hat{T}} & \hat{T} \geq 0 \\ 0 & \hat{T} < 0 \end{cases}$$

A set of four interarrival times T_1, T_2, T_3, and T_4 between five consecutive cars on the road is observed. It is desired to decide on the basis of these observations if the cookie company has closed.

(a) The decision is to be made at the 5 percent significance level by choosing a critical region in the T space of the form

$$T_i > T' \qquad i = 1, 2, 3, 4$$

What is the required value of the threshold parameter T'?

(b) A particular set of values $\hat{T}_1 = 0.03$, $\hat{T}_2 = 0.004$, $\hat{T}_3 = 0.01$, $\hat{T}_4 = 0.001$ is observed. What can you conclude about the status of the Cookie Company?

12.3 Suppose that in a distributed decision problem, the observations x and y each consist of a single scalar Gaussian random variable. Assume that these observations are uncorrelated and that for class 1, x and y have means m_x and m_y and variances σ_x^2 and σ_y^2 and for class 2, x and y have means equal to zero and the same variances σ_x^2 and σ_y^2. In terms of the parameters given, show the explicit form of the densities $p_{\Lambda_x|\omega_i}$ and $p_{\Lambda_y|\omega_i}$ and the explicit form of the equations (12.23) that must be solved in order to determine the thresholds τ_x and τ_y in the distributed decision problem. Generalize the results to the case of vectors of n independent observations x_i, y_i, $i = 1, 2, \ldots, n$.

12.4 Consider a distributed decision problem where the observation vectors $\mathbf{x}$ and $\mathbf{y}$ are jointly Gaussian with a covariance matrix

$$\mathbf{K} = \begin{bmatrix} \mathbf{K_{xx}} & \mathbf{K_{xy}} \\ \mathbf{K_{xy}^{\mathit{T}}} & \mathbf{K_{yy}} \end{bmatrix}$$

which is the same for both ω_1 and ω_2. Assume that the mean vectors for the class 1 observations are $\mathbf{m_x}$ and $\mathbf{m_y}$ and the mean vectors for the class 2 observations are both $\mathbf{0}$. Develop expressions for a pair of sufficient statistics $S_\mathbf{x}$ and $S_\mathbf{y}$ that if computed by each sensor and sent to the fusion center would allow the fusion center to perform the optimal centralized decision rule. What would be the equations to determine the optimum Q-level quantization thresholds for these statistics if quantized values of the statistics were to be sent to the fusion center? Write these equations in terms of the joint class conditional density functions for $S_\mathbf{x}$ and $S_\mathbf{y}$. What are the values of the parameters that describe the joint class conditional density functions for $S_\mathbf{x}$ and $S_\mathbf{y}$?

INDEX